HEBRIDEAN SONG-MAKER
IAIN MACNEACAIL OF THE ISLE OF SKYE

HEBRIDEAN SONG-MAKER
IAIN MACNEACAIL OF THE ISLE OF SKYE

Thomas A. McKean

Polygon
Edinburgh

© Thomas A. McKean
Songs © Iain MacNeacail
Òran a' Veto © Aonghas Fleidsear

Published by
Polygon
22 George Square
Edinburgh

Set in Joanna
by Nene Phototypesetters, Northampton
Printed and bound in Great Britain

ISBN 0 7486 6214 6

A CIP record for this title is available

The Publisher gratefully acknowledges subsidy
from the Scotland Inheritance Fund

The Publisher acknowledges subsidy from

THE SCOTTISH ARTS COUNCIL

towards the publication of this volume.

CONTENTS

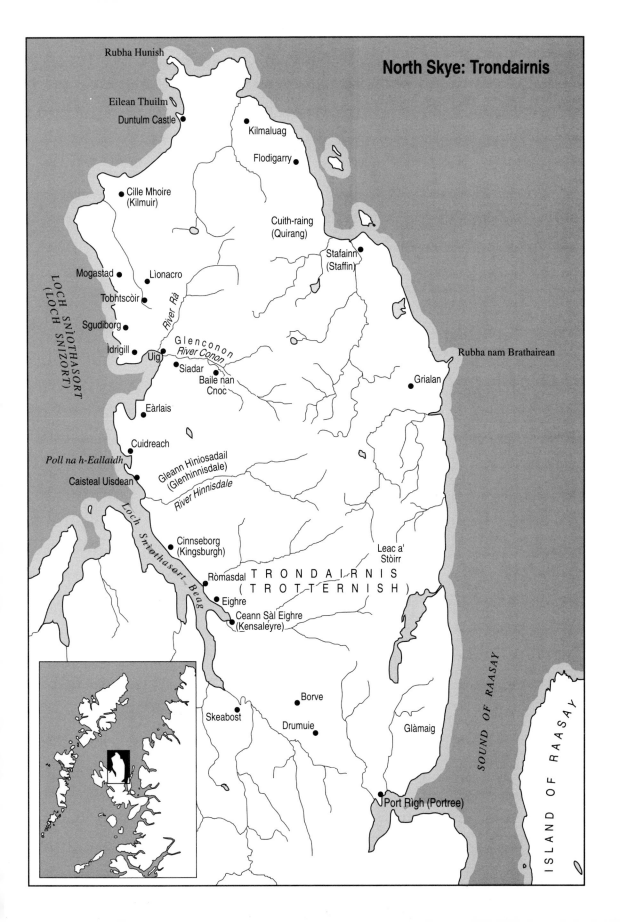

North Skye: Trondairnis

Rubha Hunish

Eilean Thuilm

Duntulm Castle

Kilmaluag

Flodigarry

Cille Mhoire
(Kilmuir)

Cuith-raing
(Quirang)

Stafainn
(Staffin)

Mogastad   Lìonacro

LOCH SNÌOTHASORT
(LOCH SNIZORT)

Tobhtscòir

River Rà

Sgudiborg

Glenconon

Rubha nam Brathairean

Ìdrigill

Uig

River Conon

Siadar

Baile nan
Cnoc

Grialan

Eàrlais

Cuidreach

Gleann Hìniosadail
(Glenhinnisdale)

Poll na h-Eallaidh

River Hinnisdale

Caisteal Uisdean

Loch Sniothasort Beag

Cinnseborg
(Kingsburgh)

Leac a'
Stòirr

Ròmasdal   T R O N D A I R N I S

Eighre   (T R O T T E R N I S H)

Ceann Sàl Eighre
(Kensaleyre)

Borve

Skeabost

Drumuie

Glàmaig

SOUND OF RAASAY

ISLAND OF RAASAY

Port Rìgh (Portree)

LIST OF PLATES

INTRODUCTION

"Historians do not trouble themselves much about skippers."
Francis James Child, writing about the ballad *Sir Patrick Spens*
(1965, Vol. 2:19)

This study of Iain MacNeacail, 'an Sgiobair' [John Nicolson, 'the Skipper'], will change all that.

I first visited Scotland from America in 1980, on a trip inspired by an interest in its dance music and (Lowland) songs, and by the most tenuous of family connections. On that trip, I came in contact with the Gaelic language for the first time and was fascinated by the intriguing place names of the Hebrides, names such as Rubha Ardvule, Sgurr Dearg and Beinn Mhór, the pronunciation of which defeated me. Upon my return home, I located a tutor, Catrìona NicIomhair Parsons, a native of Lewis and a fine singer, who introduced me to the basics of Gaelic. My university was less than encouraging, saying that I would not be allowed to take Gaelic as part of my course: "It's not a very pretty language, is it?" said the registrar.

Several years after graduating, during which time my interest had not diminished, I decided to return to Scotland and in 1987 enrolled in the Department of Celtic at the University of Edinburgh, for a post-graduate degree. My initial aims were to learn Gaelic and to work with a singer, though I suspect that these goals were quite unclear to both of my patient supervisors. By the end of my first year, I was torn between wanting to explore the world of a singer in detail, who (I expected at that time) would be Lowland, and a project involving Gaelic song-poetry.

These two seemingly irreconcilable interests were united by Margaret Bennett's inspired suggestion that I work with Iain MacNeacail, a *bàrd baile* [Gaelic township poet] then in his mid-eighties. I was intrigued both by the possibility of uniting my enthusiasms and, as I thought further about the project, by the opportunity of making a unique contribution to Gaelic culture and folklore studies.

In recent decades, there has been a strong movement in the field of folklore towards documentation of the context, background and practical social function of items of lore. As Alan Lomax has said, "the study of musical style should embrace the total human situation which produces the music." (Nash 1961:188) The point of departure is therefore information gathered from within the tradition, rather than external theories of function and meaning. Many important studies of folk and 'primitive' music have been preoccupied with African, Amer-Indian, or Southern Pacific musical cultures, in other words, with radically 'foreign' societies. Merriam's comprehensive *The Anthropology of Music* purports to cover the field of folk-song thoroughly and yet there is a lack of first-hand testimony from participants in European song-culture. This is, perhaps, because song-making is no longer seen as a standard form of expression in mainstream, literate European culture, while it continues to be seen as such in 'primitive' cultures around the world. Community song traditions closer to home have therefore, in large measure, been overlooked.

Even studies that do take in Western European song traditions are generally based on written or printed sources and observation, rather than first-hand testimony.[1] They do not ask song-makers them-selves how and why they make their songs. Studies of Gaelic song are no exception; they have almost exclusively focused on the study of texts and, occasionally, musicology. I have seen numerous collections of Gaelic songs in the libraries, and indeed in the sound archives of the School of Scottish Studies, and yet have been struck by the isolation of text and music from background and contextual information.[2] The majority of printed collections were made posthumously, but even when they were not, they fall short of the standards of context rightly recommended by Van Gennep and the interwar folklorists (e.g. Halpert, Herzog, the Warners, the Lomaxes).

In contrast, this book looks at songs in the context of a song-maker's life and at his own reflections on their place and function therein. I am concerned, broadly speaking, with why someone makes songs, how they make them and the role the songs and the composer play in the community. Though my approach is neither literary nor textual, I have endeavoured to provide accurate, annotated texts, should anyone choose to examine the language and imagery of MacNeacail's song-making at a future date. On the musical side, this book includes a compact disc of nearly all the songs that I have recovered, as it is not within the scope of this study to transcribe or analyse the melodies musicologically. Listen-ing is really the only way to gain an accurate impression of Iain's rhythms, melodies, timing, the timbre of his voice and his vocal expression. It would be futile to try to describe, even with complex musical notation, what is easily experienced by listening. I have cross-referenced the numerous renditions of some of the songs in the textual notes in Appendix Two to facilitate future work.

Despite her slightly dated emphasis on the 'non-literate peasantry', Countess Martinengo-Cesaresco describes my point of departure well:

> [The collector] should approach popular songs and traditions from some other standpoint than that of mere criticism; and divesting himself of preconcerted ideas, he should try to live the life and think the thoughts of people whose only literature is that which they carry in their heads.[3] (1886:xii)

Such an internal approach means that in writing about someone's life, one elicits the subject's own point of view before taking in any other perspectives. As Lauri Honko says, "A modern folklore docu-ment permits the voice of the people to be heard exactly as it was uttered." (1992:5) This is perhaps the opposite of a more anthropological or sociological point of view, where theoretical conclusions are based more on external observations.

The approach, as Lynwood Montell points out, also draws attention to the "critical distinction between folk history and history written by orthodox methods of research," which usually relies heavily on documentary evidence. The folklorist's approach considers "the people as a living force," so that their oral history and tradition "can serve as a historical record in those areas where written accounts have not been preserved."[4] (1970:xx, vii) There is no reason not to extend this use of oral sources to an informant's ruminations on the hows and whys of his own behaviour; indeed it is essential to get the participant's own perspective clear first, before building any sort of theoretical construct.

In recording MacNeacail, I have had the chance of which many folklorists only dream: to interview and write about a person who is not only a great tradition-bearer, but who also creates from within a strong tradition. I hope that the resulting picture of a song-maker from his own perspective answers some of the questions, outlined above, that have been concerning folklorists studying other cultures.

My interviews with MacNeacail have taken place periodically since December of 1988, when I was first introduced to him by Margaret Bennett. That first occasion was greatly eased by her presence, as she belongs to the same glen. She was treated almost as family, and was therefore an excellent passport for an acculturating outsider.

I have occasionally, especially at the beginning, felt out of my depth in this culture. My fieldwork notebook was invaluable in these circumstances; it allowed me to note down any point obscure to me, which I could then discuss with my advisers, Skye natives and other Gaels of my acquaintance. There is also something to be said for being an outside observer. According to Mantle Hood, there may be instinctive things about a culture the outsider can never fully understand, but because of his training and perspective, the outsider "is capable of insights and evaluations which no [native], even with training abroad…could ever duplicate" (1971:374).

Most of my interviews for this book have been tape-recorded. Inevitably, after I finish recording for the evening, thinking 'He must be getting tired,' Iain will talk animatedly long into the night, seated in his little armchair close to the fire and his bookshelf. I then make frequent use of my notebook, jotting down visual impressions and capturing observations after the tape machine has been turned off. This leads, of course, to another recording session the next day to follow up things hastily scribbled down the night before.

There is much to be said, too, for visiting without taping in building up trust and a rapport, free of the formality of an interview and the obtrusive equipment. Both Iain and his wife Màiri also have fairly clear (though differing) ideas about what kinds of information are worth my while recording. Indeed, Màiri refuses to speak at all while the machine is on, though she sometimes maintains a quiet running commentary on the alleged worthlessness of some of the things he is relating to me (sometimes she or he will say the next day, something like, "Cha d'fhuair thu ach rubbish a-raoir." ["You just got rubbish last night."])[5] Simply visiting, then, without taping, can sometimes yield information that one or both had thought would not interest me. I can then ask about it on my next visit. This raises the question of whether such material may be freely used, without the consent that a formal tape-recorded interview implies. My feeling is that the use of all such information must be cleared with those concerned.

Naturally I would like to have interviewed Iain entirely in Gaelic, as his thoughts on his life and work would have come all the more naturally. I was not, however, sufficiently fluent at the start, and, in those early days, MacNeacail would either translate for me, or speak his distinctive Highland English. As my fluency has improved, so has the proportion of fieldwork done in Gaelic, until the present when my visits are entirely in his native language. The tape extracts used in this book, therefore, will be a mixture of Gaelic and English.

Iain has always been more than willing to record and is keen to give me the songs or history about which I ask. He is quite pleased that someone has taken an interest in his songs and is delighted to think that his lore will be preserved as a memorial to his proud ancestors and to himself. Keeping up with this ninety-three year old when he is 'on a roll' has been a challenge, and I have collected far more wonderful anecdotes and traditional stories than I could possibly include in this book.

I have, therefore, been forced to make innumerable choices, in the interests both of space and of keeping the focus relatively narrow. And it is relatively narrow in the broad canvas of MacNeacail's fascinating life.[6] Some of the history and facts covered may not, at times, seem obviously germane, but

I believe that they all illuminate the man and the image of the song-maker. A large part of my task, then, has been to weave interview material into a coherent and convincing whole, rather like assembling a complex jigsaw puzzle whose final dimensions and appearance are not known.

Writing someone's biography can never be an easy undertaking, for one is also, inevitably, forced to divide his life in various ways, for example, chronologically (birth, youth, adulthood, etc.), or functionally (song-maker, father, crofter, soldier, etc.). These divisions are necessary to allow analysis, for language is very good at discussing limited and clearly defined areas, but is less than ideal at representing the totality of a person. The book is therefore in two main sections: Part I looks at Iain's songs where they naturally belong, woven into the fabric of his life and also at the community setting of the song-maker; Part II looks at the process of song-making, the function of song in a Skye community and MacNeacail's place in bardic tradition. In some ways, the sections run parallel and may be thought of as layers, the aggregate of which makes up a picture of the individual.

Keeping in mind Bruno Nettl's caution that scholars often "come as students, but quickly pretend to become masters" (1983:260) and Herbert Halpert's dictum that there is nothing as dead as the jargon of an outdated theory,[7] I have tried to tell MacNeacail's story, examine his song-making techniques and look at the function of his songs largely through his own words. I hope the resulting portrait does justice to this talented and fascinating man.

(A note on methodology: Most quotes are taken from my tape-recorded interviews with Iain Mac-Neacail, or from my fieldwork notebook; sources for these can be found after the endnotes. Other quotes are taken from books, which are cited in the text (and listed in the bibliography). The endnotes expand upon certain points and provide supplementary information.

The informant, unless stated otherwise, is Iain MacNeacail. Tape extracts are verbatim (unless marked with an asterisk) and are indented, with translations from the Gaelic in italics next to them, or following in square brackets.

The songs are numbered in the order in which I believe they were made (though one appears out of order in the first chapter). This allows us to follow Iain's development as a song-maker, from his early beginnings, through his most productive and fluent periods, and into the latter years.

Each song has its own line numbers; choral refrains are numbered only the first time they appear. All translations are fairly literal and are indented and numbered like the Gaelic originals to make line-by-line reference easier. For details on individual versions of songs, see Appendix Two.

The book contains all but one of the songs that I have recorded, the exception being a satire on a local character of his youth. Due to the song's humorously scathing nature, Iain prefers that it should not see the light of day.

See Appendix One for full details of methodology, including transcription, citation and editing conventions.)

Summary of abbreviations

AM   Aonghas MacNeacail, 'Aonghas Dubh'
FW   Fieldwork notebook
IM   Iain MacNeacail, 'an Sgiobair'
IP   Iain Peutan

IR	Isabel Ross, née Gillies, 'Beileag'
JAM	John Angus MacNeacail, one of Iain's sons
l., ll.	line, lines
lit.	literary
MB	Margaret Bennett
MM	Murchadh MacCoinnich, 'Murchadh Sgudiborg'
MN	Màiri NicNeacail, Iain's wife
MS	Murchadh Stiùbhart, Murdo Stewart
NG	Norman Gillies, 'Tarmad Ruairidh'
PS	Peter Stewart
SA	School of Scottish Studies Sound Archive
TM	Thomas McKean
UM	Uilleam MacNeacail
USR	Uig School Register

About the author

Thomas A. McKean was born in Cambridge, Massachusetts in 1961. He came to Scotland in 1987 to complete a Ph.D. in Folklore at the School of Scottish Studies, and Celtic Department, Edinburgh. While Traditional Music resident at Banff and Buchan District Council he set up the North East Folklore Archive. He is currently Research Fellow at the Elphinstone Institute, University of Aberdeen.

PART I

1. Iain MacNeacail in the doorway of his house, March 14, 1993. (T. A. McKean)

PRELUDE

No song, no performance, no act of creation can be properly understood apart from the culture or sub-culture in which it is found and of which it is a part; nor should any "work of art" be looked on as a thing in itself apart from the continuum of creation-consumption. (Ives 1978:434)

When I first met Iain, I was surprised by his small stature. I had perhaps been imagining a slightly dangerous-looking poet of stereotypical commanding presence. He answered the door dressed in trousers, shirt and waistcoat with a pair of worn burgundy slippers, which I was to come to know as his customary house wear. He had just passed his eighty-fifth birthday and looked every year of it.

I realised gradually, however, that his *was* a commanding presence and the years fell away as he animatedly discussed the old days, song-poetry, his favourite song-makers, local history, local characters and his ancestors; with such vivacity he quickly becomes the focus of any gathering.[8] And as I have come to know him, he seems to have grown in stature, fixing his listener with penetrating blue eyes and reciting poetry in direct communication. There is an immediacy, an intensity about him when he speaks of poetry and poets, which has not abated with age. Though he walks slowly and sometimes very stiffly, his mind is always far ahead.

Sometimes in recent days, his memory lapses and he cannot remember a song that he has known for fifty years. At other times, such as on my most recent visit, I quote him two lines that someone said he made at the age of twenty-four, and he recites a whole song I had not previously heard. A few minutes later, he is unable to recall the last verse of it. On another occasion, I showed him a transcription of a song he said he did not remember. He sang the first line from the paper, lifted his eyes, sang the rest of the verse and the other five verses, all the while folding the paper rhythmically. The paper is forgotten, and his eyes gaze intently at his chosen audience. Memory, at the age of ninety-three, is a difficult and unquantifiable thing; as a person ages it performs more and more in its own time. But for MacNeacail, for whom it is practically life's blood, it usually responds to his taxing demands.

I have visited Iain mostly at his home in Cuidreach, just a few miles south of Uig. It lies close to the shore, just a few hundred yards away from Cuidreach House, at the end of a narrow track winding down nearly to sea level from the height of the main Uig–Portree road. The house had been the stables for 'the big house' before its complete conversion to a dwelling for Iain and his wife Màiri when they married in 1947. It is of white-washed stone with a slated roof, four bedrooms upstairs, and a hall, sitting-room, kitchen and bathroom on the ground floor. A large building attached at right angles to this houses supplies for the sheep and bits of machinery used round the croft by Iain's sons. Only two hundred yards away is the sea and across the loch, the Waternish peninsula.

2. The MacNeacail home on the shores of Poll na h-Ealaidh on Loch Snìothasort. Across the bay is Aird nan Eireachd behind the island of Dùn Maraig. The road to the right leads to Cuidreach House about a hundred yards away. (T. A. McKean)

Chapter One

FROM SIADAR AND GLENCONON TO THE FIELDS OF FRANCE

FROM SIADAR TO GLENCONON

Iain MacNeacail was born on the 30th of October, 1903 in Siadar, Isle of Skye, the sixth of Mór and Uilleam MacNeacail's eight children.[9]

Iain MacNeacail: I never got baptised and neither has [my wife Màiri], because our parents weren't religious to extremes at all. But they were quite as good in their ways and practice as those people who were [there], you know, but...they weren't thinking they were good enough for it.

Uilleam crofted, but also worked part time on the Urquhart estate, "Aye, my father was working there with the factors, [he was] a coachman. He was keeping two cows and such like." His mother was well known for her songs and stories. "Oh aye, she would know the old times [that were] going.... She was from Siadar."

IM: They would seem to be quite popular anyhow, these [MacNeacails], mo sheanair, co-dhiù, Alasdair Chaluim [my grandfather, anyway, Alasdair son of Calum],[10] he was well noted for his honesty, he was terrible honest.... Och he would be going with anybody and working,...but my father was with the factors.

The house in which Iain was born, near Baile nan Cnoc at the eastern end of Siadar, was a typical Skye blackhouse.

IM: 'S e balla cloicheadh a bha muigh timcheall uile, 's e, o balla...cloicheadh. Och bha ceangail air a chur air, fhios agad, air mullach a' bhalla a-rithist mar sin, [demonstrates arched cruck shape with hands] 's dòcha ceithir na cóig dhiubh. 'S bha...na biorainean eile beaga dol suas air a' rud 's bha sgrath a' dol air muin sin. Bha thu buain sgrathan...le caibe-làir.

Tom McKean: ['S] dé bha air a' mhullach?

IM: O tughadh,...cha robh tughadh och luachair, rushes.... Sin a bhiodh agad...air na taighean dubh' uile aig an àm a bha sin.

Bha thu go math dìonach leis a' luachair; bha thu 'ga cur, fhios agaibh, air muin a chéile mar sin,...bad ri beul, mun fhaid sin bho chéile. [measures about half a foot with hands] 'S bha i air a cuir gu math tiugh air.... Och bha fiùrain, fhios agad, fèidhpe [foidhpe].... Bha thu cur sgrath air muin an fhiodh a bha sin, 's bha luachair an uair sin a' dol air muin na sgrath. Sin am mullach aige;...bha e math gu leòr, bha e dìonach gu leòr.

IM: It was stone walls all round, oh yes, stone walls. [And] then couples [poles running from the ridge-pole to the walls] were put on it, you know, on top of the wall, like this, [demonstrates arched cruck shape with hands] maybe four or five of them. And the other small sticks went atop that and turf was going above that. You cut turves with a flauchter spade.[11]]

TM: And what was on the roof?

IM: Oh thatch, [well] not thatch, but rushes. That's what you'd have on all the blackhouses at that time.

You were quite watertight with the rushes; you put them, you know, atop each other like that, top to bottom, about that far from each other. [measures about half a foot with hands] And they were put very close together. But there were saplings [or branches], you know, under them. You were putting turf atop the wood there, and then rushes were going on top of the turf. That [was] its roof; it was fine, it was plenty watertight.

5

TM: Agus an uair sin lìon os [a] cionn.

IM: ...Bhiodh ad a' dèanamh an lìon ad fhéin.... Dòcha ma bha lìon iasgaich aca, chuireadh ad air uachdar e cuideachd. 'S chuireadh ad clachan beaga orra, fhios agaibh, a chumadh sìos a' lìon 's a bha e fuireach mar sin.

Dhèanadh e bliadhnaichean math air sin.... Nam biodh e fàs steallach, bha thu falbh a bhuain tuilleadh luachrach 's ga chur air.

TM: Agus bha an teine aig meadhan an ùrlair...as an taigh agaibh fhéin?

IM: O bha, o bha, dìreach far a robh e. Uel gheibheadh tu h-uile duine a bh'ann timcheall...an teine a's a' meadhan an ùrlair. (TM: Gheibheadh.) Gheibheadh...dusan a's an taigh, bha rùm gu leòr ann...airson...bh'e 'm meadhan an ùrlair....

'S bha clach ann, cabhsair clach, far a robh an teine....

TM: 'S an e 'clach an teintean' a bh'oirre?

IM: 'S e, clach an teintean, sin far a robh an teine.... Bha clachan [beaga] air a chur ann...timcheall uile-gu-léir. 'S bha an teine air a thogail air meadhan a' chlach a bha siud.

Uel cha robh duine a' dol 'na chòir och gum biodh tu muigh aige 's tu 'na do shuidhe timcheall air an teine. Bha h-uile duine a bh'ann...faotainn an teine. O sin a bha dol.

TM: 'S bha toll ann airson an ceò.

IM: Bha toll am meadhan...an taighe, na ceann an taighe mas ann a bha e. Och...thàinig e sin gu robh ad a' cur suas 'similear chrochaidh', a chanadh ad ris.... Bha ad a' cur suas bòrd ann a sheo...is ga cheangail shuas agus fear eile agus bha ad ga dhùnadh a-null ann a sheo [*makes rectangle shape with hands*] agus bha an ceò dol suas a-nise mach air a' rud. Bha sin aca...airson an ceò a chur a-mach. Aig cuid, och cha robh e aig a h-uile duine.

Bha ad [na taighean dubha] blàth 's bha ad seasgair is cha chluinneadh tu taigh a' dol 'na theine.... Cha chluinneadh agus bha gu leòr a chuireadh 'na theine, fhios agad,...le tughadh 's le fraoch a bhith air agus...luachair.... Bha i fàs cho crìon 's cho tioram an déidh a bhith air mullach an taighe, ta, cha robh teine dol 'na còir,...bha e eagalach iongantach.

Och cha robh gual a' dol an uair sin ann ach mòine.... Bha an ceò aig a' mhòine...cumail caran àrd;...cha robh e tighinn a-nuas càil sam bith a' seo, oir a bha toll...mach air am mullach. Bha e dol suas, a-mach ron t-similear; bha cuid eile fuireach air, *halfway up*, bha. B'e sin a bh'as na taighean uile-gu-léir an uair sin gos na thòisich na taighean [ùra] air an togail.

TM: *And then a net on top of it?*

IM: *They'd make the net themselves. Perhaps if they had a fishing net, they would put it on top of it too. And they'd put little stones on them, you know, to keep the net down and it stayed like that.*

It'd last a good few years like that. If it grew leaky, you were away cutting more rushes and putting them on.

TM: *And the fire was in the middle of the floor in your own house?*

IM: *Oh yes, oh yes, [that's] just where it was. Well, you'd get everyone there around the fire in the middle of the floor. (TM: Yes.) A dozen could get in the house, there was plenty of room because it was [in] the middle of the floor.*

And there was stone, a flagstone, where the fire was.

TM: *And was it called the 'hearthstone'?*

IM: *Yes, the hearthstone, that's where the fire was. [Small] stones were put around about. And the fire was built in the middle of that [flag]stone. Well, no one went [too] near it, but you'd be at its edge, sitting round the fire. Everyone got the fire. That's how it was.*

TM: *And there was a hole for the smoke.*

IM: *There was a hole in the middle of the house, or the end of the house if that's where it was. But then they started putting up a 'hanging chimney' [or 'hingin lum'], they called it. They were putting up a board here, tying it up and another one and they were closing it over here [makes rectangle shape with hands] and then the smoke went out of it. They had that to put the smoke out. Some, but not everyone had it.*

They [the blackhouses] were warm and they were comfortable and dry and you didn't hear of any houses going on fire. No you didn't, and there was plenty to burn, you know, with thatch and heather on them and rushes. It got so dry and desiccated after being on the roof of the house, but anyway, the fire didn't get to it, it's very surprising.

There wasn't any coal then, just peat. The smoke of the peat stayed fairly high; it wasn't coming down here at all, since there was a hole out of the roof. It was going up, out through the chimney; another part stayed there, halfway up. That's how all the houses were then, until the new houses began to be built.

3. Mór Chaimbeul [Marion Campbell], Iain's mother, in 1893 at the age of twenty-seven, two years before her marriage. She was working as a house-servant in Glasgow at the time. (MacNeacail collection)

4. *A blackhouse in Baile nan Cnoc, ca. 1938. Clearly, the roof has not been renewed in some time. Number 15 Glenconon can be seen across the glen.* (George Bennett)

5. *"A Skye crofter's dwelling" in the late 19th century. A chimney has been added latterly.* (Reproduced with permission from the George Washington Wilson photographic archive, Aberdeen University Library, C7409x)

6. Iain inspects the last remaining wall of the house in which he was born on our visit to Siadar, May 16, 1992. All but one of Uilleam's and Mór's children were born there. After the move across the glen in 1910, Uilleam kept several cattle here and the children would cross the river twice a day to milk the cows. (T. A. McKean)

There were several small window openings in many blackhouses, but owing to the thickness of the walls, these let in very little light. The interior space of the house was divided by a stone partition into a living area and a byre area for the cows, which had its own door towards one end. There would have been little in the way of furnishings, perhaps a settle or two, a dresser and a few box beds.

IM: Och I remember there were the cows coming in [to the byre], but they had a door of their own, you know, on the other end.... They were under the same roof,...but you weren't sleeping with them.

TM: How big was the house?

IM: Och it would be quite big, about fifty feet long or more, you know, but half of it was for the cattle. [There] was another door for yourself and the cattle were coming in the side.

TM: Did the cattle keep you warm in the winter?

IM: Oh well, I don' know, but they were no harm to us at all; they were going out of their own door and coming in, and that's the way they were.

But still although it was like that, it wasn't the milk of the cow that our children was getting; they were from the breast, every one of them! We had eight of family and everyone of it was the mother's breast we got. But today it's the bottle, everywhere. I don't say it's anything better [than breastfeeding]. No, and [it] didn't do the mothers any harm either, eh? My mother was eighty-seven when she died and she was as strong as a bullock!

Sometimes a mother would be unable to breastfeed for one reason or another and "the next neighbour would come and breast feed for that baby till she could go home."

Both sides of the MacNeacail family had been on the island for generations.

IM: [My mother's people] were from Skye,...as far [back] as I can remember. And my father's people too, from Skye, as far as I can go back anyhow....

Oh yes, that was their origins, but quite a lot of my father's people (they were MacKinnons through my grandmother, you know) went to Canada. And New Zealand too, and Australia.... But they made quite good business down there, I think. One of them was the Governor of Prince Edward Island, mhm aye....[13]

Well, it was the people that went over there [that] had it very severe. But the generation coming after, they benefit[ted] quite a lot, better than being in Skye today. Oh yes, but it was hard times when they had to clear, aye.[14]

MacNeacails/Nicolsons are found throughout Skye: "Tha an *Clan* MacNeacail...còrr is mìle bliadhna a's an Eilean Sgitheanach...ach chan eil càil air an *Chief* an diugh!" [*"The MacNeacail Clan has been in Skye over a thousand years, but there's no sign of the Chief today!"*]

This concentration of surnames makes *far-ainmean* [nicknames] and family genealogy a necessity. Among the many Nicolsons not related to Iain's family was a curious character in Siadar who used to wear a sou'wester called An Sagart [the Priest], an unusual nickname for a man in an almost wholly Presbyterian island.

IM: Yes, I knew that man! He used to come up here, aye, since I came here [to Cuidreach], aye he used to be [there].

Margaret Bennett: What was his name, his right name?

IM: Murchadh, Mura' Chaluim [Murdo son of Calum], [a] Nicolson he was too.

MB: Was he related to you?

IM: No, but they came from the Braes at Portree. I think his uncle was a sea captain [whose] sister belonged to Siadar, and that was an auntie of Murchadh, and they came down with Murchadh, you know, in Siadar.

MB: Was he married, the Sagart?

IM: No no, himself and Mórag, the sister, got together. Well she died of cancer, oh forty years before that....

MB: Why did he get called Sagart?

IM: He was out there questioning you everything, [like] where you were.... Aye, because if I was going to [or] from Siadar...as a child, "Ca'il thu dol?" ["*Where are you going?*"]

"Tha mi a' falbh a dh'Uige." ["*I'm away to Uig.*"]

"Dé tha thu dol a dh'iarraidh?" ["*What are you going to get?*"] I had to tell him everything, you know....

MB: Confession.

IM: Aye, and he met me one time too and my father sent me down for a bottle of whisky because my niece was cutting [the umbilical] cord.[15] And he gave me three and six for the bottle, that's what I was paying for it, at Taylor's where the hotel is today, three and six for the bottle of whisky. I went to Neil MacKinnon there, Niall na Drochaid a chanadh ad ris. [*Neil of the Bridge, they called him.*][16] And "Where do you come from ghille? [*laddie?*] Oh, you can't get anything. Who are you, who [do] you belong to?"

"Ach," I says, "Willie Nicolson."

"William Nicolson, oh all right, a bhalaich. Eil còt' agad?" ["*...boy. Do you have a coat?*"]

"Aye."

"Have you got a coat?"

"Yes," I says, "I've got [one]"

"Dìreach feuch nach fhaic duine e. Na inns e do dhuine." ["*Make sure no one sees it. Don't tell any-one.*"]

"O chan inns," arsa mise. ["*Oh, I won't,*" said I.] But I got it, I gave [MacKinnon] the three and six, he gave me six of it back, so it was three shillings. That's [the cost of] a bottle of whisky then, that would be about 1914 or 13, that was the price of it. So I took the bottle, and who would I meet but the Sagart up the way, "Where were you?"

"I was down at the Hotel."

"What were you doing there?"

"Ach, bha mi ag iarraidh botal uisge-beatha." ["*Ach, I was getting a bottle of whisky.*"] The fool, [I] told it, which I wasn't supposed to! [*general laughter*] But I thought, when I met the like of him [an] old man, that I had to...tell it. I had that impression that I had to be so...honest to people and speak right and [tell the] truth to them [*laughs*]. Ohh well, I knew there where it was [i.e. I realised my mistake].

Uilleam (Iain's son): So you told him that you were [down] for a bottle of whisky, eh?

IM: Aye, I thought,...well I had to tell it, because I was told at home to tell the truth and not tell lies to anybody, so I didn't want to. That was fine, but [now] I would say to him [*laughs*] "Get out of here, what have you to do [with it]?" Well that's what they would tell him today, the children. Aye, they would! "Dé an gnothaich a th'agadsa gu dé tha mi dèanamh?" ["*What business is it of yours what I'm up to?*"] But that was him [i.e. the way he was] with me and my kind that were brought up then. They were all alike like me: you had to tell the truth. [Even] if you thought that [it] would hang you, you had to tell it. Oh but [it's] a different system today.

TM: You learned your lesson.

IM: Yes, but it's too late. But...that's what he [did] with me and to everybody, and that's how he was called the Sagart, aye. Oh yes.

At the time of Iain's birth, most of Uig was owned by John Urquhart, who bought the estates of Linicro, Mogastad and Kilmuir from the Nairnshire landowner Captain William Fraser. He, in turn, had purchased them from Lord MacDonald in 1855, and quickly made them "one of the few places where crofters could claim to suffer, like their Irish counterparts, from rack-renting.[17]... Crofting rental of the property had almost doubled, despite a substantial reduction in the amount of land available to crofters." (Hunter 1976:133)

IM: Well it was him that built this tower.[18] You've seen the tower...and there was *The Sea Horse* [Fraser's boat]. She would be coming in and they would be firing two shots from the tower, [as a] welcome, you know, or saluting him when he would come. That was the reason he built it....

I remember my father and all these people, they knew...when the tower was built there. They were young then at that time.... It's over a hundred years old anyhow, by now, I'm sure.

TM: So how much [of an estate] did...Fraser own?

IM: Oh the Kilmuir estate...and up to Gleann Hìonasdail. The rest belonged to Lord MacDonald, see. [Fraser's land] was going down to Kilmuir way, beyond Uig and to [the] Staffin side, aye. Oh he would have quite a big [estate].... Aye I think he was an army Captain.

As the Captain's policies impoverished his tenants, land clearance became a reality. Many families were driven from the more fertile north side of Glenconon to the meagre topsoil of the Siadar side, the rocky coastline of Cùil, and overseas as well.

IM: Well some of them went. Those that was capable of going at the time, they went.... They couldn't very well put them away all then, but those that was capable of going had to go. You got no liberty [i.e. no choice in the matter]. Oh it was a cruel law! But that was Gladstone you know, the Irish Prime Minister, [who allowed it to happen].[19]

In October 1877, Captain Fraser received what many islanders considered a divine retribution for his methods.

IM: [His house] was in the centre, down at the bay.... Well just at the edge,...maybe fifty yards out [i.e. inshore] from the sea anyhow, but that's where Captain Fraser had his house, down there, and the lodge when he had it.

TM: Is there anything left of it?...

IM: Well you see the foundations where it was, oh yes, 1877, that was [when] the flood came, in October.

TM: Were there heavy rains?

IM: No, definitely not. I heard my father and mother speak about it at times. [It was] coming down just, you know, gently, but it continued for twenty-four hours. And what was very strange, there was no estate in Skye that suffered but Fraser's estate. Whether there was judgement coming on the laird or not, people did believe that at that time. And...Màiri Mhór was saying too that it was [a] judgement that came on him some way, [because] the bodies were coming in[to] Talisker, on the shore.[20]

These bodies were from the cemetery in Uig, which was almost entirely washed away in the flood. Murdo Stewart of Glenconon heard tell of it in his youth as well: "*I heard it was the 14th of October many a time,...it was my birthday." The graveyard – there was no church there – was beside the

7 and 8. Two 19th century views of Uig Bay from the South and the North. Note the blackhouses, the narrow fields and Captain Fraser's tower overlooking the bay. The marines landed on the shore just below the tower in 1884. Glenconon can be seen above the white tower in the upper picture and in the centre of the lower one. (Reproduced with permission from the George Washington Wilson photographic archive, Aberdeen University Library, C1126 and C1680)

Conon, just above the bridge and was reached by a small path beyond today's cattle grid.

MS: *People thought it was a breitheanas [judgement] that came on them. I believe you'd see the foundations of the wall that was on the graveyard yet. Most of the bodies were reburied in Giùbaig, between Greshornish and Waternish, where they washed ashore. There's a green slope above the shoulder of the shore, they were just washed up there.[21]

The impressions of these new graves can still be seen in Giùbaig today, Murdo added.

Fraser's estate manager David Ferguson was drowned in the flood and The Highlander magazine featured an uncompromising editorial which ended saying that the tenants "do not hesitate to express their regret that the proprietor was not in the place of the manager when he was swept away."[22] The Captain promptly sued the editor, Iain MacMhuirich, for libel and demanded one thousand pounds in compensation. The great Màiri Mhór nan Oran [Great Mary of the Songs] made a song about the flood and the Captain: Duilleag bho Bhealach nan Cabar [A letter from Bealach nan Cabar].

IM: Ah, thuirt i,...thug e suas iad, fhios agad, agus dh'iarr e dà mhìle not [she said, he brought them up [on charges], you know, and he sought two thousand pounds] for defamation of character.... The sheriff said, in the court, when Fraser was suing:... "I'm not very certain," he says, "I haven't got the evidence strong enough to say that it wasn't, so I award you fifty pounds." Agus thuirt Màiri Mhór [And Màiri Mhór said], "Fhuair thu leth-cheud spìocach is rinn iad fiach de dh'fhanaid ort!" They made more mockery of you out of your fifty than what you have obtained![23]

"They said the captain wasn't the worst at all," MacNeacail maintains, "but those that was acting for him." Even so there are plenty of local stories about Fraser's miserliness.

IM: I heard the man that took Cuidreach House there at the time, a Stewart he was, [rented] the land from Captain Fraser. And Captain Fraser met him,...he had the gun under his arm, and had a...brace of grouse. "What are you doing with the brace?"

"Oh," he says, "I'm gone shooting."

"Oh no,...you didn't get the shooting [rights as part of the rent," Fraser] says.

"Oh, if that's the case, that's your land" and he threw it up to him [i.e. threw dirt in his face] and left him that way, because he wouldn't give away...the shooting. [Fraser] was going to have the shooting himself, although he was renting [out] the land.[24]

In 1884, largely due to requests from Fraser, a detachment of Royal Marines was sent to Skye to control crofters' unrest. Land raids and rent strikes had become commonplace throughout the Highlands and resistance had been increasingly violent, culminating in the deforcement[25] of several parties of Sheriff Officers. Landowners, in collusion with the government, rightly concluded that the crofters' attitude to the police had become contemptuous; the only way to display a credible threat was to bring in Government troops. Captain Fraser warned of continued and increasing violent unrest unless this course was followed.

IM: Well you see,...there was a thousand marines come to Skye [in 1884] against crofters, to keep them down.[26] If Mrs. Thatcher had done that today, where would she be? But Gladstone did that though, 'the Irish cut-throat,' that's him what he was.

MacNeacail and many other islanders hold Gladstone largely responsible for sending the Marines, but it was mostly through the depredations of the (often native) landlords that the situation reached such extremes at all. Gladstone must, however, bear some responsibility for the tardiness of the 1886 legislation which was to ease the crofters' plight.

Two hundred and fifty of the Marines were brought ashore in the first landing.

IM: Of course it's in Uig, I think, there were...more molestors...than anywhere else.

TM: So that's where the marines landed.

IM: Aye, aye, just underneath the tower...up there [in Uig]; there was a pier there....

TM: So your mother remembered?

IM: Oh yes, and my father too. Oh yes, yes....

TM: And they marched up around the North, right? Through to Staffin?

IM: Oh yes...and Kilmuir. They went out to Kilmuir, I heard my father speak about it, on a grand day....
They marched out [to] Kilmuir, and oh they seen a mass of people, you know, coming out [of a building]. They went in battle order there. But who was this but a communion service and the congregation was dispersing [*laughs*]. A lot of [the soldiers] at that time believed that they were coming against the army, but they weren't. Nobody lifted a finger against the army.

On the whole, and contrary to their own expectations, the soldiers encountered a population quite at peace. The residents had come to resent the police as agents of the landlord and therefore received the Marines with rather more cordiality. (Hunter 1976:150)

IM: Och they couldn't do much about it anyhow....

MB: Did people used to talk about that for years and years afterwards?

IM: Yes,...we would be here in the céilidhs, you know, when your grandfather and great-grandfather [Iain and Pàdraig Stiùbhart would] come there and...speak of this happening and this happening. I was only a kid then and I was hearing the talking between my father and them, you know, about what was happening then.

In a report at the time, *The Times* wrote that the crofters appeared "amazed rather than intimidated by the display".[27] There was little for the soldiers to do in Skye.

IM: Nothing at all! The soldiers was having the time of their lives here. They were in céilidhs at night and everywhere you know. They had no command on them at all but going here and there, and there was quite a lot of them got married in Skye, aye. Och yes, they were all the ordinary boys, you know and [they just] happened to be in the army. That's the only job you would get then.

TM: So it wasn't a difficult posting?

IM: N-o-o-o! It wasn't, that's it!

Soon after the Marines arrived, *The Graphic*, a London illustrated magazine, featured an article on the deployment, with several engravings of the soldiers in 'action': marching off the boat and playing cards while lounging in one of the rooms of Uig School where they were billeted. Below these engravings are others of the Hudson River, and elsewhere in the magazine, Egypt and India, showing just how foreign the Highlands and Islands of Scotland seemed to nineteenth-century London.[28]

MacNeacail has heard of only one incident during these manoeuvres in which an officer was harmed by a native of the island. "*There was a woman who threw a peat at Sheriff Hamilton in Kilmuir. Well it hit him in the back [and injured his lung] and he never rose again!" Iain says Hamilton died shortly thereafter and that the woman "got three months...not for murder, but for the injury."

The billeting of the troops in Staffin from November 1884 to the following June was too much for the laird:

IM: That's what finished Captain Fraser. He had to pay for the time the army was in Skye, so he died in the asylum in Inverness. He went off his nut [and] he had to meet the expense.

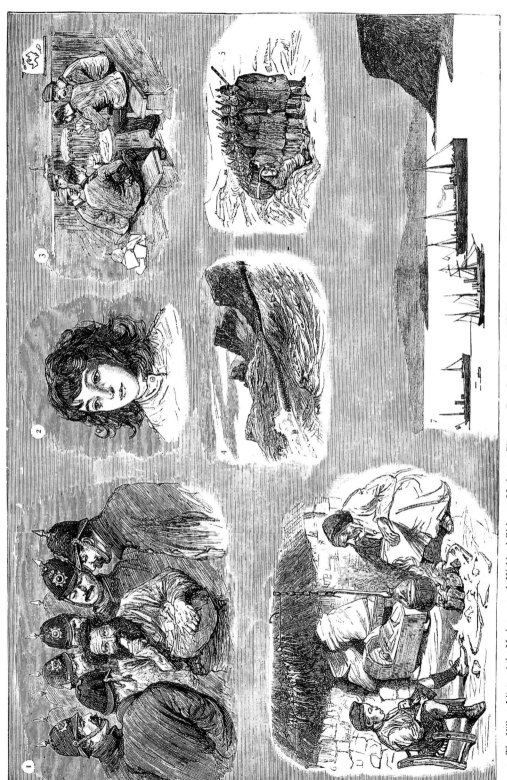

1. The Village Idiot and the Marines.—2. A Highland Girl.—3. Marines at Play.—4. Pass Leading to Staffin Bay.—5. One of the Enemy.—6. Interior of a Crofter's Hut.—7. H.M.S. "Assistance," Gunboat, and "Lochiel" in Uig Bay.

THE AGITATION AMONG THE SKYE CROFTERS

FROM SKETCHES BY AN ARTIST WHO IS VISITING THE DISTURBED DISTRICTS

THE SKYE CROFTERS

No such warlike demonstration probably has been witnessed in the bleak island of Skye since the stirring days of the "Forty-five" as that which took place on the 18th ult. A body of 250 fully armed men, forty of them constables, the remainder marines in brilliant scarlet tunics and glistening helmets, were landed at Uig from the Government vessels, and marched thence along the bleak hill-side road to Staffin, the display being witnessed by groups of natives. Rigorous military discipline was observed by the troops, and no greater caution could have been adopted if they had been marching in the Soudan or through an Afghan pass. As the expedition started from Uig, the gunboat *Forester* and the steamer *Lochiel* weighed anchor, and steamed out of the bay to Staffin, there to await the arrival of the troops overland. The crofters by the wayside paused in their work, and curiously contemplated the invaders. Fisher-girls made game of the soldiers, who were nothing loth to return their chaff; a withered crone danced a derisive break-down; a village idiot, barefooted and bare-breasted, joined the procession, and by his inane laughter provoked among the troops alternate sallies of mirth and expressions of pity. Some of the crofters' huts or shielings are very poor places, built of peat, and unprovided with chimneys, because chimneys let in the cold, so that the air within is thick with "peat-reek."—Our engravings are from sketches made on the spot by Mr. W. Lockhart Bogle.

9 and 10. The etchings and article from The Graphic, Dec. 6, 1884, shortly after the marines were sent to Skye. The third etching shows some of the marines playing cards in Uig School, where they were billeted.

But...about twenty years ago there was...a daughter of him, she was over eighty anyhow, coming to ask about her friends when Captain Fraser was here. Well there was nobody here but one or two that could give her information and they didn't give it! No! He was a tyrant he was. So she went back. She was in Uig there. Aye, I remember it well, [it was] since I came here [to Cuidreach].

30. A time will come, a time will go

Several years ago, in response to frequent questions about the Clearances from English speakers, Iain made a song on the subject (see Chapter Five for a detailed study).

1.   A time will come, a time will go,
       but ne'er forgotten be it:
       the Highland Clearance that deprived
       our land of stalwart heroes.

2.   They were men of great renown   5
       for liberty and freedom
       and all they gained as a reward
       was exile without reason.

3.   The land was wrenched out of their grasp,
       their homes were burnt to cinders;   10
       no more evil could befall our race,
       by devilish type of landlords.

4.   Prime Minister Gladstone was to blame
       with his evil clique around him,
       sent one thousand marines to Skye,   15
       the people there to hound them.

5.   The Skyemen gallantly did stand
       as always did to foe-men
       and didn't yield an inch to them,
       but routed all before them.   20

6.   Those that were able to survive
       were driven across the ocean,
       to find land by sweat and toil,
       to make their new aboding.

7.   The final end to the dispute   25
       was by Commission Royal,
       that the land be graced by gallant men
       that won such fame and glory.

8.   Though wounds may heal the scars remain
       and so it's with the Highlands;   30
       the men that made our nation great,
       gain nothing but remembrance.

11. Uilleam MacNeacail driving the Uig estate coach, just north of Flodigarry on the way from Staffin to Uig. He worked as a coachman on the estate and kept a croft in Siadar as well. The men seated in the coach are John Urquhart (Màiri NicNeacail's grandfather) and Seumas Ruadh MacCoinnich [Red-(haired) James MacKenzie]. The right-hand peak in the distance may be Sròn Bhaornaill, mentioned in Màiri Mhór nan Oran's Soraidh le Eilean a' Cheò. (Màiri and Iseabail NicNeacail collection)

In 1886, John Urquhart, the owner of the Uig Hotel, bought the estate from Fraser.[29] His factors, and the men with whom Iain's father worked as coachman, were

IM: a MacIntosh and...James MacKenzie that was in Earlish, [?]my grandfather and him, he was a factor too. But MacIntosh was the last one there and it was [at] that time that they split Glenconon. It was taken from the Urquharts when John Urquhart died,...the land was broken, and the same with Lìonacro and Mogastad.

Upon Urquhart's death in 1910, the Glen was bought by the Congested Districts Board, as the Kilmuir estate had been in 1904. This body, the forerunner of the Department of Agriculture and Fisheries and the Scottish Office, reapportioned the glen into sixteen crofts. According to Iain, "people were crying for the land and everybody that was wanting a croft, he got a croft then." In fact, many more applied for than received crofts, but Uilleam MacNeacail was one whose application was successful.

IM: Well, my parents...took a croft at Glenconon...opposite them [i.e. across from Siadar]. It was broken up, you know, at that time after 1910.... The Land League was going then, and the farmers [i.e. landowners] had to break it up. It was Mary's grandfather, [John Urquhart,] that had Glenconon then and a lot of Siadar too.

The croft has since passed to Iain's brother Alec and on to Alec's son William, who holds it today.

Many of those who were awarded crofts had to make do with temporary accommodation.

12. Uilleam and Mór NicNeacail at the end of their crofthouse, No. 15 Glenconon, in the 1930s. They were apportioned the croft in 1910 and moved across from Siadar. Their grandson, Willie, has the croft today. (MacNeacail collection)

IM: Cha robh taigh…idir idir air, och bha seann làraichean ann…. Bha cuid a rinn suas na seann làraichean temporar[il]y …agus dh'fhuirich ad ann gos an d'fhuair ad fhéin 'taigh geal' a thogail a-rithist – sin an dòigh a bh'aca.

IM: *There was no house on it* [i.e. the croft] *at all, but there were old foundations. There were some who did up the old foundations temporarily and they stayed there until they got a 'white-house' built after – that was their way.*[30]

While the old blackhouse in Siadar had accommodated the family and their stock under the same roof, the new croft-house at Number Fifteen Glenconon was quite different.

IM: Och, well what I remember about it [was that] I found it a bit strange, you know, the house…. The cattle wasn't in at all at that time, because in Siadar you had the cows [in] the other end of the house. But here the cows were out, in another byre of their own when I went to Glenconon, you know.

MB: You found that funny then, not living with the cows.

IM: That's it, you see it, because you were accustomed to them [in Siadar].

Though the new house was not strictly a blackhouse, it was not a new 'white-house' with a slated roof either.

IM: Och,…well it was a thatched cottage; rushes and things like that was the thatch on it. But at that time you know, they would have [had] plenty of good [improved] houses in Skye, but you weren't allowed to do it, because [the landlords] could come there [at any time and say,] "What are you doing? Ach you're away [evicted] next week!" You had no time at all, no fixture of tenure, nothing.

Iain refers to the era before the 1886 Crofters' Act when the landlords could evict their tenants virtually at will. As crofters had no inheritance rights over their homes, there was little incentive to improve the property in any permanent way. And under men like Captain Fraser, "arguably the worst landlord in the Highlands" (Hunter 1976:155), MacNeacail affirms that "the rent was terrible. That's how the revolt came, you know, that the clearances started."

The reapportionment of areas like Glenconon was a momentous step in crofting history, as land fought for in the agitations of the 1880s was finally delivered. The crofters at last had legal recourse in the face of rack-renting and evictions. No longer had they to resort to land raids and rent strikes which had been the only recourse for decades.

Along with the crofts themselves, the new tenants in Glenconon regained their common grazing rights. Pasture land was once again shared, the sheep were owned communally and the village kept a full-time shepherd.

IM: You would cut the wool, sell the lamb, sell the sheep, sell everything. Everybody got…a share of it. That has been broken away now and everybody has his own [sheep].

Murdo Stewart told an amusing story of a day at the fank when he was very young:

MS: *I remember one day the Sgiobair was up dipping. Dòmhnall Oighrig [Donald (son of) Effie (MacInnes)] was standing at the gate [of the fank] and letting the sheep out [one by one]. Well, the Sgiobair was coming to get a sheep and Dòmhnall Oighrig was letting each one go [a little before the Sgiobair would get there], and the Sgiobair had to catch every one! I don't think one escaped. Oh, the Sgiobair was fast right enough, and tough!

Iain's sons still take part in the semi-annual sheep dipping in Glenconon, in addition to that of their own flock in Cuidreach.

SCHOOL AND SCHOOLMASTERS

In 1909 at the age of six, shortly before the move across the glen, Iain had started to attend Uig School. It was here that he acquired the nickname by which he is still known, an Sgiobair [the Skipper], despite the fact that he never captained a boat.

IM: Ach well, I used to be about boats and things like that and I used to have a sailor suit on when I was going to school and everybody [who] was going to school had some name of some kind.... But people believed I was [a skipper]! They had the impression,...people that didn't know me, you know.... They thought I was, till they found out.

The poet Aonghas Dubh MacNeacail,[31] also from Uig, says Sgiobair got the name because he wore a skipped cap. Iain's own explanation may well be correct, but perhaps this far-ainm [nickname] was bestowed because he showed signs, even then, of an authoritarian manner. In any case, most of the children attending school would have been given a far-ainm, as the tradition is strong in Gaelic society.[32]

Schooling had become compulsory with the passing of the 1872 Education (Scotland) Act and both of Iain's parents could therefore read and write English to some extent. By 1909, the Act and the mechanisms for its enforcement were well established.

IM: Oh yes, yes.... When the Education Act came you were fined and [?]punished if you weren't regular in the school without a good excuse. No, you couldn't stay off. There was a Compulsory Officer going round. If you were off two days, he was at your home next day: "What's wrong with the boy that he wasn't there yesterday?" So you had to give some excuse and be back there next day. Oh they were quite tough on them then.[33]

MacNeacail often refers to the Act in conversation, reflecting his interest in learning and achievement. Before the Act, however, education was a more individual endeavour: "Aye, aye,...the church had classes where people could voluntarily go...before the Education Act came in force."

IM: You could learn from a minister [or] somebody. He would be conducting classes and learning people to read and write.[34]

They were in certain places, you know, and they were making seats...to sit on, of the earth...where you were going to sit.... How many hours I can't tell you, but they [i.e. the students] were there, just volunteering to go there. That's how some people had good English although they weren't going to school at that time, even before the Education Act.

Of course the English was universal some way or other [i.e. somehow] although it wasn't [then] taught by the Education Act.

TM: But did people use English at all?

IM: Oh no, at that time; they hadn't got the art of doing it, because if they were among themselves it was the Gàidhlig. But there were some people who would be working with farmers and things like that [who did], and ploughmen and all these people, and people that was going with gigs and horses, carrying gentry. So...they were learning the English from them, mouth to mouth.

Though Gaelic was undoubtedly still the prevalent language in the home and the community in MacNeacail's youth, the use of English was on the rise. Iain's father, Uilleam, was "very good at English, because he was at the coachman and driving people that had the English."

IM: Oh yes, because he would be going with all these big nobs. He was with the factor and the factor would be hav[ing] so many [visitors] coming to him and all that, and they had two horses and a gig maybe. [There were] so many...going around Quirang and all these places with him to see the sceneries and [the locals] were learning the language like that.

Many jobs in this economy, still in transition from a subsistence to a cash basis, required English. In addition, the nationalised educational system required scholars to learn through the medium of that language: "that's where I learned my English, what I have of it," says Iain. English quickly became the language of economic and social progress. Gaels themselves felt it essential to learn it, often in place of their own language.

At Uig school, assessment of the pupils' progress in English was a regular concern of the Inspector. According to regular entries in the register, the scholars' grammar was in "a most backward state." (1896)

> There is a general lack of life and smartness, and the children habitually speak – when they speak at all – in an inarticulate tone of voice. More practice in connected English speech is essential. (1902)

In all probability, and unsurprisingly, the children would have been greatly intimidated by the Inspector and not felt fluent enough to speak with confidence. In any case, many monoglot Gaelic speakers, as most children starting school at that time were, did not take to the immersion style of language acquisition. One such was John Beaton of Glenconon who retained a strong preference for Gaelic throughout his school days. Latterly, in his eighties, when his son and English-speaking daughter-in-law moved back to Glenconon, he quickly became fluent. He was a good scholar otherwise, but obviously made a deliberate choice to shun English in school.

Iain would have enjoyed the chance to study his native language at school, but "didn't get the advantage of that," indeed they were not supposed even to speak it.

IM: We had a Lewis schoolmaster and he was a very good man.... He wouldn't object to you, right enough, but he wasn't teaching us [Gàidhlig].

[When the Education Act came in,] you were punished if you were speaking Gàidhlig, in school, but that has been done away with, and a good job [it was]. I don't know why was that [i.e. why you were punished]. Of course it was all English-speaking schoolmasters they were sending up then, up here. And you had to go by [i.e. obey] him. But they [were] not allowed to be speaking Gàidhlig in the playground or anything, among the boys, or girls too.

TM: Were you ever punished for using Gàidhlig?

IM: Oh no. No, no, but ah, they would prefer me to speak the English, just the same, rather than Gàidhlig.[35]

So, although he was never punished for using his own language, Iain had to teach himself to read it.

IM: I just learned [taught] myself. Well there's not much words in the Gàidhlig that I can't understand by reading it. [I would read] songbooks and stories of old you know. You get a lot of these stories in books in Gàidhlig.

He also taught himself to write Gaelic through looking at books of poetry and prose.

IM: Ah, not perfect. Well I could [write], you know, but to have it grammatically put down I would [have to] have a book there to keep the spelling of it. But I know how to write, right enough.

When MacNeacail says "grammatically" here, he means spelt correctly. Naturally his spoken Gaelic is grammatical and even elegant, but transferring that to the page can be problematic, even to the scholar. Gaelic spelling is again in flux and there are many words for which several acceptable spellings exist, reflecting numerous regional pronunciations. MacNeacail, therefore, is being modest in his assessment of his self-taught writing skills.

Sometimes, Iain's father would help him with English schoolwork.

IM: Oh, my father would dictate to me how I would write, in his own language [i.e. in his own words] in [the] English language; he would tell me how to write down. Oh he could write himself too, but not to [the] extent I would.[36] But if he talked to me in English, he would tell me...what to say. He would put that in order right enough. Mhm.

TM: So he helped you with your schoolwork?

IM: Aye. So that's how it was, from one person to another.

Even today, Iain does a good deal of reading in his sizeable collection of Gaelic song and poetry books. These he gives pride of place on the shelf next to his small, comfortable armchair by the fire.

IM: Ach at times [I read a lot],...I have some over there too.... What's the good of reading with me now, I'm finished.... [But] it's nice to have time to read. Well, you know, it passes the time for you, right enough. It's good to have something to concentrate on.

It may come as a surprise to many people outside the Highlands that a boy growing up in a croft house in Skye should be so well-read, or that there would be a source of books in such a place. Even today, rural societies are often assumed to be illiterate and, indeed, are sometimes thought to hold a prejudice against 'book learning'. The very opposite applies to Gaelic society, which for centuries has placed a high premium on learning and intellectual pursuits. Education also may be measured on different scales; many Gaels, like MacNeacail, have a great store of traditional knowledge such as songs and local history. Such lore was not acquired in any formal school, nevertheless the village céilidh-house could provide a comprehensive training.[37]

MacNeacail is also quick to appreciate and point out intellectual achievements of his fellow Gaels who have won nation- and world-wide recognition for their academic, scientific or political achievements. As John Smith points out in his article about the effects of the 1872 Education Act, an English-centred educational system "has in fact...produced, or failed to prevent the production of, a number of fine Gaelic scholars." (1981:52)

The school in Iain's day featured a wide range of subjects, including Navigation and Algebra, in addition to Reading, Writing and Arithmetic.

IM: Oh yes, we had History and Geography and Maps, you know, and things like that. And we had books to write the arithmetic [and other work] we were doing.... They [were] giving us sums and these were [handed in] and they were corrected again, if they were right or wrong.... You were getting [assessed] according to your marks then. You were top of the class or somewhere like that, you know.

The pupils would do their homework in the long winter nights by paraffin lamp.

IM: [You] could write and read with it but I'm not sure that you could do it today because I think the electricity has ruined the whole thing [i.e. spoiled people's eyes], makes everything a blur to you.... No you wouldn't do anything with the paraffin lamp today.... You don't see at all...if you are putting it up.

You would if you had the Tilley [lamp]. It would be equal to the electric.... But oh, you know, the paraffin lamp was [a] thing of the past.... Basical[ly] you would see everybody in the house and know everybody by their face and all that, but it would be quite different for you today to read with it, what [i.e. like] we used to do when we were small. Aye.

Fuel for the lamps was obtained from a merchant's shop located on Uig pier.

IM: He would have a cask of [it] and you would be going for a gallon or a bottle or three bottles of it and you were putting it in a lamp.... A bottle of paraffin a night would do you in the lamp all right. She [the lamp] was hanging down from the, from the ceiling there. [points up to a rafter]

The scholars' schoolbooks themselves were supplied by the Education Authority, whose property they remained.

IM: Oh we hadn't got to pay for the books at all, oh no. But when you were leaving the class [i.e. school], these books were [given] to the juniors again.... You were taking the other man's as they were coming and leaving school. That's how the books were working.... Oh by gosh, you had it if you put any mark on them! Of course you could have your name on it, on the outside cover or something like that, but that's all. Oh aye, they were tough on them that way.

The first of MacNeacail's two schoolmasters was a minister from Uist, Mr. MacDonald, who was there only a year.

IM: His throat gave away, so he went in for the schoolmaster's job then. He couldn't preach you know, likely with his throat....

Well, [a] Lewisman came in his place and he, he wasn't a college man at all, but my word, he was making scholars better than those with the degrees! Whatever [i.e. however] hard he had to [work to] do it. They were passing every place, his scholars here from Uig. And those with the learning couldn't do them [i.e. make scholars] anything like him. Mhm. Angus MacDonald aye, that was his name.... He was about sixteen or seventeen years in Uig.

Angus MacDonald took over from the Uistman on the 3rd of October, 1913 and according to several of his students to whom I have spoken, he was an exceptional teacher.

IM: Oh, he was 18 years [old] I think anyway. And they said...he never went to university or college...and there wasn't a schoolmaster in Uig ever like him, that made such scholars.... Oh he was a clever schoolmaster.... And my word he would keep you in after hours too, to get the subject done and people were complaining about that. And he had a clock and he would turn it that way [to face the wall] when it got coming near four o'clock in case the people would be seeing it.

"*Every scholar had to bring a peat to the school" every day. In this way, each family provided its share of heating and there was no need to buy peats for the school.

IM: *You had to walk [to school]. If you got drenched, you stayed drenched all day. There were about a hundred children and I don't know how they survived. And the schoolmaster was hard on them too. Some had coaches [to get to school], otherwise you got drenched.

And like any good teacher, MacDonald knew how to get the best from his students in such conditions: according to the Register, "A cup of cocoa is served to each scholar at twelve noon. Consequently the attendance this week has been very steady."

There were two assistant teachers for the younger students, "There was one for infants, that was Aonghas Lamont's mother...and then there was a Jetta MacLeod from Portree." MacDonald, however, taught most of the classes.

IM: But how was he doing it? He was giving us all the subjects and he had...four classes himself to do and a subject of every kind. Oh, he was good. There was nothing like him anyhow here since he left.

Part of the Uig scholars' achievement can perhaps be attributed to environment.

IM: We were very fortunate here, you know, that way. There was a fairly good education...because there was nothing to draw [the pupils] attentions such as [motion] pictures, or anything like that that would put you off it.

The isolation from urban 'improvements' even attracted the attention of a mainland schoolmaster, a MacAskill from Harris who was master of Dalwhinnie school. On a visit to Uig he remarked on MacDonald's scholars:

IM: "I'm," he said, "so disgusted with this crowd up here [in Dalwhinnie]; I can't put nothing in their heads. And those that come from the islands here and there, they're coming out with their first degrees everywhere in the colleges and I can't do nothing with them here." Of course the attraction they had was the pictures and things like that. He was blaming that for it.

The Sgiobair has great admiration for students of rural background who achieve recognition in modern urban society (especially against the odds).

IM: There was a lot of Ministers and Doctors and even Professor…Magnus MacLean [who located the break in the trans-Atlantic cable when it broke down]. Aye, and he used to work in these quarries and go to the university [as well] and back and forward till he gained his merit.

His admiration for self-education is most enthusiastic, however, when he speaks of the traditionally educated Gaelic bards who serve as his own models. (See Chapter Six for MacNeacail's assessment of these bards and his view of his own place in the tradition.)

Other Uig schoolmasters whom MacNeacail remembers were of lesser ability than the outstanding Angus MacDonald. One used corporal punishment freely, to the objection of one of his students.

IM: Och, Dùghall Ruadh, that was in Earlish, knocked him in the fireplace and went to school no more. Oh he [the schoolmaster] started battering Dùghall…. Probably [Dùghall] wasn't picking up [i.e. learning] the thing right and he was hammering him over it. Well he got that! [Dùghall] got a hold of him and put his head in the fireplace and off he went home and never went to school any more….

Oh he would throttle them…. There was nobody to say anything about it…. Oh [Dùghall] would be about fourteen at that time or something nearly it anyhow, but he never went to school again. Dùghall Ruadh, aye…. [It's] some thirty years, I think, since he died now, aye.

On another occasion the master had beaten Uilleam Gillies of Siadar. The boy told his stepmother Anna Màiri Mhór, so called because she was a cousin of the famous song-maker.

IM: Anna came down and gave hell, "How [i.e. what] did you do?" to the schoolmaster, and said to him, "Ged a b'e Papanaich a bh'air ceann na sgoile cha bhiodh ad nas miosa na tha ad. Chan eil thu toirt leasan Bìobaille fhéin dhaibh!" [*"Even if there were Papists at the head of the school, they wouldn't be as bad as they are [with you]. You are not giving them a Biblical example!"*]. He started it then!

The next master, Barclay, had a short tenure; he suffered a heart attack one morning soon after his arrival and was found dead above the schoolhouse.

IM: Well, it was Iain Stiùbhart[, son of Glenconon crofter and fisherman Pàdraig Stiùbhart,] that took over the school then, till they got another teacher…. Aye, my sister used to belong in Siadar, she would have known him when he was there. And my other sister, of course she's dead now, she would tell me [about] "Iain Stiùbhart a bha 'na thidsear againn." [*"John Stewart who was our teacher."*]

Stiùbhart had been the 'pupil-teacher', the schoolmaster's teaching assistant, in the last two years of his own schooling, so he was well prepared to fill in until a permanent schoolmaster was found.

The pupil-teacher system allowed an older student to take on some of the master's teaching load. He was selected on the basis of his marks as recorded by the schools' inspector.

IM: You had the inspector coming three times a year maybe and that was the day, and we had to be smart.... And the inspector was a Lewisman too. There's only a couple of years since he died; he died in Ayrshire. I think it was…Morrison his name was, a hundred and four, I think, when he died. And he was the Director of Education…that got Angus MacDonald in Uig at the time. The Lewismen were very clannish that way you know, supporting one another very much.

Uig school record books of this period tell their own story of life in Skye at the turn of the century. In them, the schoolmaster records outstanding pupils, occurrences of note (such as the inspectors' entries mentioned above) and most often, before the First World War, the absence of a large percentage of the pupils at harvest time. Often the school would be closed for up two weeks due to insufficient attendance, which is matter-of-factly recorded each August and September in the register (for example, "School closed for harvest 7-22 September"). Another telling entry reveals that, while schoolmasters did not tolerate the use of Gaelic as a medium of communication, they at least encouraged retention of some of its cultural aspects by annually closing the school for a day to allow the choir to compete in the Portree Mòd.

John Urquhart, while he owned the Uig estates, would occasionally call at the school. His sense of proprietorial duty meant that he took an active interest in the education of his tenants' children. "All was well," reads a typical register entry in his own hand, "attendance good and registers correctly marked."

Religion was not taught as a separate subject, but the children studied Catechism and started each day with the Lord's Prayer in English.

IM: "Our father which art in heaven, hallowed be thy name" and all. Aye we had that on our tongue and everybody saying it.… We all stood, you know, and that was that. "Hallowed be thy name, thy kingdom come, will be done, on earth as in heaven. Give us this day our daily bread and forgive us our debtors, we forgive our debts [sic]. Lead us not in temptation, thine is the kingdom, the power and glory, amen." Aye, mhm. That was the day.

Though raised in the Free Church, "I never went to Sunday school.... No, I was too old before they... erected one here.... But I was going to church, oh usually..... Och aye [it was] all Gàidhlig." Sometimes, Iain can appear quite dismissive of organised religion, for instance in his gleeful stories of ministers outsmarted by bards or doctors.[38] To a great degree, his true faith is in Gaelic poetic tradition. The visitor who hears him say, however, that "We had to…go there anyhow," may think he only attended church when pressed, but in fact he was, and is, a faithful attender. In addition, a look at his song *Tha mealladh mór am measg an t-sluaigh* (24) will show that he does not appreciate 'amateur' attempts at God's work. Perhaps his attitude to religion seems rebellious only when compared with that of some other islanders of his generation.

Back in the schoolroom, the scholars' command of the Catechism was tested by visiting ministers. This yielded varying results, as noted by the sometimes wry examiner in the school register, "Catechism was very good, and though not much was attempted in the Senior Division, it is better to do this than profess much, and know it but indifferently."

The register also reveals some candid opinions on the native language of the scholars. "The infants were partly examined [on religious matters] in Gaelic," the Inspector wrote. "It is difficult to make other than slow progress, owing to the difficulty of the language."[39] The government's attitude to Gaelic did relax a little early in this century, and having a teacher who knew the language was seen to be of some use in disciplining and examining children who did not take to English. The Education (Scotland) Act of 1908, therefore, contained provisions which allowed the enrollment of a Gaelic-speaking teacher at Uig School; the salary was ten pounds per year.

STOCK-KEEPING AND FISHING BETWEEN THE WARS

When the First World War broke out in 1914, Iain was only eleven years of age, far too young to enlist. His father, at age thirty-two, was too old. "But my brother Donald, he was just called up [just as] the war was stopped and the calling up was cancelled."

IM: It was after that that Donald [Stiùbhart]...went in the Army...and Alec... – he was young at the time, maybe he would be twenty or something – ...he was called up and that's what he was killed over. Oh everyone was there. Your grand-uncles was there, two of them killed.

MB: Donald and Alec, did you know them?

IM: Oh-h isd! Aye, I knew them, knew them well too. Yes, I did that.

MB: I only ever saw pictures, good-looking men.

IM: Aye, they were that. Donald was a good-looking man too. He was very similar to your grandfather, [Iain Stiùbhart,] but he was taller and straighter. Mhm. Yes, but he volunteered for the army at the time, but Alec didn't. Of course he was conscript[ed]. He was...driving there with Alasdair Mór on a farm they had [at the] time and they took him and Angus Fletcher too, both of them they had. That was the First World War. But there was quite a lot...that was conscripted there [and] was killed there. Och yes, quite a lot in Portree. The First World War, oh aye.

Yes and down at Uig too. Oh yes. Calum Gorm and Angus Graham and all these Grahams, they were...school teachers and captains too and they were killed, aye, mhm. Oh quite a lot. And down Kilmuir too, yes. But in [the Second] World War, not so many; they didn't...put them all in bunches, but I think...they got a few branches from here and put them into the front firing line, and that's where they were got, aye.

Rural areas such as Skye did not undergo the same material hardships as urban locales during either of the World Wars. As far as food was concerned, "they didn't know there was a war on. There was no rations in the First World War.... [Here in Skye] you had your own meat, you had your own milk, you had your own everything."

Nevertheless, for MacNeacail, it was important not to be a burden on his family. During his last two and a half years at school he worked every day for a couple in Earlish, just a mile south of Uig.

IM: [I] went with Mary's [Iain's future wife's] grandmother up at Earlish...because when Johnny, her son, went to the [Navy] she was all alone, and Big Johnny, [her husband,] liked to be gallivanting. So [Johnny] was at me to go up, go up, go up. So he persuaded me. I went up, so I was handy [i.e. useful] there with them; I would take home water pails and buckets of water, put out the cows, clean the byre, go to school in the morning and home at night again.

He had to bicycle the two miles from Glenconon down to Earlish, before and after school to do the farmwork. Sometimes he would stay over, and though the house was only a thatched cottage, there was ample room for everyone.

IM: There was only himself [Big Johnny] and Mary's grandmother and me.... The other daughter was married down at Lìonacro to a Roddy Gillies.... Oh I was there 'til after 1917.

1. Ho-ró tha mi fo smalan dheth

Around this time, Iain made his first song and I asked him why.

IM: Uel, chan eil fhios am air thalamh, och...bha feadhainn ann bha dèanadh òran.... 'S bha mi fhìn a' smaoineachadh gun gabhadh òran dèanadh. Sin mar a thòisich mi air an toiseach....

'S e Oran 'n tombaca a rinneadh an toiseach. Bhithinn mu cheithir deug nuair a thòisich mi air òran.... Can an tombaca,...cha ghabhadh e faoist' an àite sam bith agus bhiodh a h-uile duine ag iarraidh an tombaca 's chan fhaigheadh ad e 's.[40]

IM: *Well, I have no idea at all, but there were some [people] around who were making song[s]. And I was thinking that making a song was possible. That's how I started at first.*

It's The Tobacco Song that was made first. I would have been about fourteen when I began [the] song. Like the tobacco, it couldn't be gotten anywhere at all and everybody was wanting the tobacco and they couldn't get it.[40]

Iain sang this song on my first visit to Cuidreach, though it had been many years (possibly as many as seventy) since he had last sung it.

MB: Were you smoking at fourteen?

IM: No I, well probably I would have to take the pipe so's I wouldn't tell on the others.... You know the others was older and...if I didn't get [i.e. smoke] it, I would tell on them.... If I took it,...I was ruined myself. So they had the way to work with that....

MB: If they made you smoke you couldn't tell on them?

IM: No I couldn't, that's it; that was the dodge.... Oh it'll be about fourteen or fifteen, I'm thinking. No more anyhow because it would leave me sick by then if I did take it. Then I got accustomed to it....

Uilleam MacNeacail: What was the song then?

IM: Oh [I] can't. [*hums to try to recall the song*]

13. *The Earlish Post Office.* (Joan MacKenzie)

14. *Peigi Beaton's shop at the foot of Glenconon brae, ca. 1915.* (John Rankin)

Ho-ró tha mi fo smalan dheth

1. Ho-ró tha mi fo smalan dheth
   's mi 'n còmhnaidh air an allaban,
   falbh airson tombac' a chàch
   's th'e toirt mo chiall is m' aithne bhuam.
   Ho-ró tha mi fo smalan dheth.

2. 'S gun d'ràinig mi bùth Rosaich thall
   's ann labhair e gu crosda rium,
   gun duirt e nach robh mìr san tìr dheth,
   's creidibh mi gun d'dh'osnaich mi.
   Ho-ró tha mi...

3. Sin mar thubhairt Màiri rium,
   "Fhuair thu, bhròinein, tàir gu leòr.
   Cha chuir faobhar air an arbhar-s'
   gos a' falbh gad shàrachadh."
   Ho-ró tha mi...

4. 'S gun deachaidh mi gu bùth Fhlòraidh suas
   gun dh'iarr mi pìos son ceò oirre,

Ho-ró it depresses me

1. Ho-ró it depresses me
   as I continually wander aimlessly
   going for tobacco for others
   and it is taking my reason and my recognition [i.e.
       senses] from me.
   Ho-ró it depresses me.   5

2. I reached [Angus] Ross' shop over there
   [and] he spoke crossly to me.
   He said that there wasn't a bit of it in the country,
   and you may believe me I sighed.
   Ho-ró it...

3. Then Mary said to me,   10
   "You, poor thing, got plenty of hassle.
   There'll be no blade put to this corn
   till your trouble departs."
   Ho-ró it...

4. And then I went up to Flora [MacKenzie]'s shop,
   I sought a piece [of tobacco] for smok[ing] from her; 15

gun duirt i rium gun d'theirig e dhìse
's dh'fhalbh mi fhìn 's bu bhrònach mi.
    Ho-ró tha mi...

she said to me that it [i.e. her supply] was exhausted
and I went away and I was sorrowful.
    Ho-ró it...

5. 'S gun d'ràinig mi bùth Phèutanaich,
   's gun d'labhair i gu beucach rium.
   Thùirt i rium nach fhaighinn mìr;
   cha b'àist mi bhith déiligeadh.
       Ho-ró tha mi...

5. And then I reached Beaton's shop
   and she spoke to me in a bellow.
   She said to me that I would not get a crumb;   20
   I was not a regular customer.
       Ho-ró it...

6. Sin nuair thubhairt Iain rium
   "Chuireadh bìdeag fhéin am pian-sa dhiom.
   Ach mur faigh mi e go màireach,
   gu bràth cha chumar ciall orm."
       Ho-ró tha mi...

6. That was when Iain said to me,
   "Even a little bit would relieve me of this pain.
   But if I don't get it till tomorrow,
   I'll never be kept sensible."   25
       Ho-ró it...

7. Shiubhail mi uile 'n dùthaich seo,
   feuch an tàrrainn unnsa dheth;
   leis na thug e a choiseachd 's mo shàilean,
   's cunnart gu fàg e crùbach mi.
       Ho-ró tha mi...

7. I searched all this country,
   trying to catch an ounce of it [still in stock];
   with the way it took the walking out of my heels,
   there's a danger it will leave me crippled.
       Ho-ró it...

TM: That's the first song you remember composing?

IM: Oh yes, I think so....

MB: Had you left school when you made it?...

IM: Oh aye, I would be going to school [still].

MB: Still going.

IM: ...'Airson tombac' a chàich', people were sending me for tobacco for them, you know.

TM: Mhm.

IM: 'Tombaca oir do chàch', not for myself.

TM: [Bùth Fhlòraidh] is in Earlish, is that where the post office is?

IM: Aye the [post office], aye. Bùth Fhlòraidh, she has a shop there too, Flòraidh [NicCoinnich], she was keeping tobacco. And she said that she had sold the last of it and had nothing when I went.... It was a shortage.

TM: Why was there a shortage?... Nobody had any tobacco?

IM: No, I think there was a strike with the boats at the time and all the provision was coming from Glasgow...by boat to Uig pier and everything was coming [in that way]....

TM: See [the song] comes back....

IM: Aye. It does....

TM: Now where was [Angus] Ross' shop again?...

IM: That's just, well the Co-operative was there once upon a time. It's...just a quarter of a mile from the road...Kilmuir way...by those bends in the road [just north of Uig], mhm. Now the Co-operative took it over from him, you know, and...the Co-operative's now in Portree and [the Rosses] left Uig, aye. Mhm.

The subject of tobacco forms a link with a lad Iain met just a few years earlier, who was to become one of his lifelong friends, the late Murchadh MacCoinnich. Murchadh Sgudiborg, as he was called, became an expert piper, composer and an authority on local tradition. His attitude to life was exemplary and his sense of humour shows through in his story of how he first met Iain.

Murchadh MacCoinnich: Bhithinn mu thrì bliadhna dh'aois. Agus bh'e fhéin is na balaich òga eile, bhiodh ad cruinneachadh 'n crodh...'s gan doirt dachaigh. Bh'e 'na sgalag... aig a[n] nàbaidhean. Agus a' dol a sgoil cuideachd.... [Chan] eil Sgiobair suas ri naodh bliadhn' nas sine na mis'. Och bha Sgiobair ag obair air [tombaca] – tha tombac' aig an aois a bha sin, sgian aige.... 'S chuir e cùl a' chùl aige. 'S bha dùil amasa[41] gu robh *sweeties* a bh'aige. 'S bha mi 'g amharc, fhios a'ad, agus bha mi 'g ràdh, "Dé eile *sweeties*, co-dhiù?" Aig an [?]aois a bha sin!

Agus "Uel," arsesan, "Eil thu airson gròbag air seo...dhen a' tombaca?"

'S, "O bha." O uel chagaich mi sin agus cha robh mi riamh cho tinn 'na mo bheatha agus...'s e sin a chuir mi an aghaidh tombaca. Cha do ghabh mi riamh tuilleadh ris.

TM: Cha do ghabh, 's cinnteach nach do ghabh.

MM: Siud [a' rud] nas fheàrr a thachair riamh...riumsa,...airson a' duine a chuir...bhàrr a' tombaca....

Murdo MacKenzie: *I was about three years old. And he and the other boys, they were gathering the cattle and taking them home. He was a [farm-]servant for their neighbours. And going to school too. Sgiobair is just under nine years older than me. But Sgiobair was taking some tobacco – he had tobacco at that age, and a knife. And he put [it] behind him. And I thought it was sweeties he had. And I was looking, you know, and I said, "D'you have any other sweeties?" At that age!*

And "Well," he said, "D'you want a bittie of this, of tobacco?"

And, "Oh yes!" Oh well, I chewed it and I was never so sick in my life and that's what turned me against tobacco. I have never tried it again.

TM: *No, definitely not.*

MM: *That's the best [thing] that ever happened to me, to put someone off tobacco.*

About this time, Iain kept stock for people in Earlish for a short while before finding work with the Idrigill blacksmith:

IM: Well I was in the blacksmith's shop down at Lìonacro a couple of years before [going to Gleann Hìonasdail], aye. I was about eighteen and I used to be in the blacksmith's shop working the big hammer,[42] you know, taking the hot iron out for the blacksmith on the anvil.

2. Ho ho-ró air gach cailleach (Oran a' cheàird)

Despite a lower wage with the smith, Iain seems to have had a good deal of fun in his employ. It was while working here that he made the next song we have.

IM: O [nu]air a bha mi 'na mo bhalach, dh'fhalbh mi a dhèanamh aithris air a' cheàird mar [tha] fhios agaibh fhéin.... Bhiodh na ceàirdean...a' ruith bho daras go daras, 's ag iarraidh siud 's ag iarraidh seo. 'S bha feodhainn ag ràdh rium gu robh ad a' toirt seachad móran dhaibhs'.... Agus dh'fhalbh mi fhìn a dhearbhadh co-dhiù a' robh siud ceart gos nach robh. Agus chaidh mi thall 's a-bhos agus tha mi dìreach ag innse dhuibh, am beagan thaighean a's an deachaidh mi, mar a dh'éirich ad rium. Agus tha mi cinnteach gur ann mar sin a bha 'n ceàird uile-gu-léir. Agus seo agaibh mar a thòisich mi orra [nu]air a bha mi 'na mo bhalach aig an àm a bh'ann.

IM: *Oh when I was a boy, I began referring to the tinker, as you know. The tinkers used to run from door to door, asking for this and asking for that. And some said they gave them lots. And I went to see whether that was right or not. And I went here and there and [in the song] I'm just explaining to you, the few houses I went into, how they responded to me. And I'm sure the tinker was exactly like that. And this is how I got started on them, when I was a boy at that time.*

IM: I was going out in [costume as] the tinker, you know, and with a bag and going and asking for a sheaf of corn and [*laughs*] things like that. They were refusing me! And asking for bag of peats...in the dark of night, myself and the blacksmith, he was with me, and...that's who was there. I was at my father, you know, he was supposed to be tricked at the old trick. Oh, when they heard that [the] next morning, you know, they were so vexed that they were deceived by the tinker. [*laughs*] And that's how I composed the song about that, you know.

Ho ho-ró air gach cailleach (Oran a' cheàird)

1. Ho ho-ró air gach cailleach
   's air gach bodach anns an àit'.
   Gu bheil iad an dràsd' fo smalan –
   chaidh am mealladh leis a' cheàrd.
       Ho ho-ró air gach cailleach.

2. Gur ann greis an déidh na Callainn
   chaidh mi dh'atharrais air a' cheàrd.
   Chaidh mi sìos far a' robh Calum,
   'n dùil ri ceannach na làir bhàin.
       Ho ho-ró...

3. 'S nuair a thòisich mi ri ceannach
   's ann a tharraing e gun dàil;
   thuirt e rium, "Na bi ri fanaid,
   's math as aithne domh thu, shàir!"
       Ho ho-ró...

4. Chaidh mi far robh Mórag thall ad
   's ann a labhair i gu h-àrd.
   Thuirt i rium, "Bi triall gu h-ealamh,
   no bidh Alasdair 'nad chràic."
       Ho ho-ró...

5. 'S ann thuirt mi rith', "Dèan air do shocair,
   's dòch' gu faigh mi ploc na fàd?"
   'S ann thuirt i rium, "Chan fhaigh na
       caoran;
   cha b'ann saor a bha i dha."
       Ho ho-ró...

6. 'S chaidh mi far robh Maor a' Bhaile
   's thùirt a' chailleach rium gun dàil,
   "Chan eil è an dràsd' aig baile,
   chaidh e rathad na Creig Aird."
       Ho ho-ró...

7. 'S ann dh'fhaighnich mi am biodh e fada.
   Thubhairt i, "Madainn, mar as àist.
   Dh'fhalbh e às a seo le cabhaig
   's thug e maide leis 'na làimh."
       Ho ho-ró...

Ho ho-ró on every old woman (The song of the tinker)

1. Ho ho-ró on every old woman
   and on every old man in the place.
   They are upset just now
   that they were deceived by the tinker.
       Ho ho-ró on every old woman.   5

2. It was a little after Hogmanay
   I imitated the tinker.
   I went down where Calum was,
   hoping to buy the white mare.
       Ho ho-ró...

3. And when I started to buy   10
   he went off without delay;
   he said to me, "Don't be mocking,
   it's well I know you, my good man!"
       Ho ho-ró...

4. I went yonder where Mórag was
   and she spoke loudly,   15
   she said to me, "Be on your way quickly,
   or Alasdair will be in your hair."
       Ho ho-ró...

5. Then I said to her, "Take it easy,
   perhaps I'll get [at least] a clod or a peat?"
   She said to me, "No [you] won't, [not even] a
       particle.   20
   it wasn't easily gotten for him."
       Ho ho-ró...

6. And I went where the Ground Officer was
   and the old wife immediately said to me,
   "He isn't home just now,
   he went [up] the Creag Ard road."   25
       Ho ho-ró...

7. I asked if he would be long.
   She said, "[He would be gone for the] morning, as usual.
   He went out of here in a hurry
   and he took a walking-stick with him, in his hand."
       Ho ho-ró...

8. 'S ann chaidh mi far a robh Tarmad
      Mhaoilis,
    dh'fhaighneachd e gu dé bha bhuam.
    Thuirt mi ris gu robh mi farraid,
    tighinn a cheannach an eich ruaidh.
        Ho ho-ró...

8. Then I went where Norman [son of] Myles was,   30
    [and] he asked me what I wanted.
    I said to him that I was enquiring,
    coming to buy the brown horse.
        Ho ho-ró...

9. 'S ann thuirt e rium, "Thig dha do gharadh,
    nì a' chailleach cupa tì.
    'S bheir mi dhuts' an t-each a-màireach,
    's fhad on bha e *guaranteed.*"
        Ho ho-ró...

9. Then he said to me, "Come warm yourself,
    the old woman will make a cup of tea.   35
    I will give you the horse tomorrow,
    it's guaranteed long since."
        Ho ho-ró...

10. 'S ann chaidh mi far 'n robh bean Iain
       Sheumais,
     's chuir mi i far ghleus a' sguab.
     'S ann a ghabh i staigh 's i 'g éigheach
     gu robh bhéist a' goid sa chruaich.
         Ho ho-ró...

10. Then I went where the wife of Iain [son of] James was,
     and I put her sweeping off kilter.
     She ran inside shouting   40
     that this monster was stealing in the stack.
         Ho ho-ró...

11. 'S ann a dh'fhalbh mi, chaidh mi dhachaigh,
     chuir mi 'n sac ad air mo cheann.
     Fhuair mi clòimh gu leòr is craicinn
     's nì iad plaideachan gun taing.
         Ho ho-ró...

11. Then I left, I went home,
     I put yon sack upon my head.
     I found enough wool and skins
     and they will make plenty of blankets.   45
         Ho ho-ró...

12. 'S ann a dh'fhalbh mi is mo mhaighstir,
     's gur e bha aighearach a's an àm.
     Bhiodh dùil aige gu faigheadh e spòrs oirnn
     nuair a thòisich sinn ri cainnt.
         Ho ho-ró...

12. Then I and my master went away
     and it's he who was light-hearted at the time.
     He hoped to have some fun with us
     when we began to speak.
         Ho ho-ró...

TM: Who was Calum?

IM: Calum Gillies,...he had a white mare; I wanted to buy the mare of him.... "Well I know you," he says, and he went away.

       [Mórag] she was a sister of the shoemaker that was there,..."bidh Alasdair 'nad chràic", because she was going to make out [that] her brother [was out].

TM: He was the shoemaker.

IM: Aye aye, but it was her that came to the door, and she told me to get off quick or Alasdair would be out, you know. Hm-hm. [*laughs under breath*]

TM: Or Alasdair will be beating you.

IM: Aye aye, he would be, just [to] get me out or something. She was trying to frighten me, you know. [Creag Ard] – that was a girl he [the old woman's son] was at [i.e. courting][43].... [He] went up to the High Rock where she was [and] his mother swore that he went [up] Rathad na Creig Àird to see the girl, you know.... He went away with a stick in his hand [to aid in a long walk], so he wasn't coming back in time, you see.

       [Tarmad Mhaoilis] – Oh, oh aye, I was going to buy his red horse.... "'S fhad o'n bha e *guaranteed*," ["*It's guaranteed long since,*"] I would get the horse....

15. *Iain at the fank in Gleann Hìonasdail, ca. 1920. The others are Ciorstaigh NicNeacail, Murchadh MacGilleain ('an Geàrr-loch'), ?, Iain and, with his back to the camera, Ruairidh MacNeacail.* (Dòmhnull MacNeacail)

[Bean Iain Sheumais] – She was an old lady too, you know. "'S chuir mi i air ghleus o sguab", to ask for a sheaf corn. Oh Dhia! [*Oh God!* She] would take the head off you....

Nothing of that happened though, but they were at me just the same, "get out!" aye!

Iain remained in school throughout his employment in Earlish and Linicro. School-leaving age was fourteen and since Iain was born in October, he was only thirteen at the beginning of the 1917 school year. After completing an extra term, he left school in the spring of 1918. The servicemen would soon be home from Europe and Iain was fortunate to find a new fee.

IM: Well, I left [the smith] and I went to Gleann Hìonasdail and I got treble the wage there, you know. They were eager to get somebody to keep the croft going.

I was twelve years in Gleann Hìonasdail.... It was the old soldier in [the] Glen that got me there and he says that Eilidh and Alasdair Og [Matheson]...was [wanting someone], and a nice gentleman he was too.... When I left school I was all out to do the crofting for them.... They could afford to give me a good wage;...I was getting equal to farm servants [on] the mainland...because she had a well-off brother there, over in Dunvegan and he was thirty years in Australia,...it was him that took the first train to Kyle. Well, I was on my own that way, you know, but I was doing just the ordinary work, about three cows, a horse and couple of sheep.

Both Glenconon and Glen Hinnisdale were ploughed and planted as croft lands between the wars, but this has changed dramatically in the late 'seventies and 'eighties: "That's finished now. They don't do any ploughing or any corn or anything. *Chan eil sgrìob idir sa ghleann an-diugh." [*"There's not a furrow in the glen today at all."*]

3. An t-each iarainn

Just at the end of the First World War, while Iain was working for the Mathesons, he was still living at home and used a bicycle to travel from Glenconon to Glen Hinnisdale.

IM: Mhm. Well we called that 'each iarainn' [the 'iron horse'].... That's what it was called here. When you'd see a man with a bicycle and regarding him [you'd remark], "mun each iarainn aige". ["*about his iron horse*".] Well, that's how it was known, as the 'iron horse'.

TM: Agus a robh 'each iarainn' agad? [*And did you have a bicycle?*]

IM: Bha [*Yes*], bicycle, aye, aye, yes, oh yes. What I had when I was in Gleann Hìonasdail, coming up and down [to school in Uig] here, aye.... Well, I had a motor-bicycle too, but not now. But I used to have a push-bike,...that was the 'each iarainn' same as you would call it: a modern bicycle, just the same.

TM: And that was when you were up working in Gleann Hìonasdail?

IM: Aye, aye.

TM: And you'd go down to school.

IM: Aye, aye, aye and going home to Glenconon and where I was [staying], you know, at our house.

TM: That must have been quite a bike ride up the hill.

IM: Oh well, it was...about six miles from Gleann Hìonasdail down to Uig when you were pedalling there. Well, I had a motor-bicycle after that, but it was to the bicycle, really, this [song] was, the bicycle aye. Mhm.

An t-each iarainn

1. Chuala sibh mu'n each iarainn,
   's mìorbhail e san t-saoghal seo:
   cha chuir e feum air deoch na biadh;
       chan iarr e srian na taod chur ann.
   Nì mi falbh leis nuair as miann liom,
   's luaith' na fiadh an aonaich e.
   Cha ghearain e air a dhroch dhìol
       's cha drùidh sian an aonaich air.

2. Seo an t-each dha bheil an t-ioghnadh,
   gur iomadh aon tha eòlach air:
   gun fheòil, gun ghaoiseid air a chnàmh,
       e lom gun àite-còmhnaidh aig'.
   Chan ionnan e is eich an t-sléibh',
   's ann dh'fheumas tu gach dòigh thoirt dhaibh;
   gur tric a bhios tu air do phianadh
       a' cur dìon mun phòr aca.

3. Ach seo am fear nach iarr aon nì
   de shlìobadh mar a' seòrsa sin.
   Chan eil mìothlachd air ri inns';
       's gura grinn an òrdugh e.
   Gu h-aotrom gluaisidh e a cheum;

The iron horse

1. You have heard about the iron horse [i.e. bicycle],
   it's a marvel in this world:
   it needs not food nor drink;
       it does not want [i.e. require] a bridle or a halter put
       on it.
   I can go off with it when I wish,   5
   it's faster than the moorland deer.
   It won't complain of bad treatment
       and no moorland storm will drench it.

2. Here's the horse which is wondrous,
   many a one knows about it: 10
   without flesh, without hair on its bone[s],
       it [is] bare without a dwelling-place.
   It isn't the same as the horses of the hill,
   you must give them their way in everything;
   how frequently you'll be tormented   15
       protecting the crop because of them.

3. But this is the one that will not seek any [sort]
   of stroking [i.e. care] of that kind.
   There's no unpleasantness to tell of [i.e. about] it;
       it is excellent and neat in array.   20
   It lightly moves its step;

cha toir e leum ron bhòcan às.
Chan fhaic thu e ri gearradh shìnteag;
    cha téid e aig *speed* mar 's deòin a chur.

4. Nuair a leumas mi 'na dhìollaid,
    's e nach iarr an t-sràc thoirt da.
    Nì e siubhal liom 'na dheann;
        cha chrom e cheann san làr orm.
    Cha tig braon air a dh'fhallas,
    anail cha dèan fàilneachadh.
    Chan eagal leis ro nì air thalamh,
        dh'aindeoin 's na bheir tàire dha.

it will not give a start before a spectre.
You will not see it cutting capers;
    it won't go at any speed it wants.

4. *When I jump in its saddle,*   25
    it does not need a blow given to it.
    It will travel with me full speed;
        it will not bend its head down to the ground on me.
    No drop of sweat will appear on it,
    its breath will not fail.   30
    It has no fear of anything on earth,
        despite whatever gives it trouble.

IM: Aye, they were Mathesons, but they're not there now. They died you know; they were old. I was keeping their croft going and things like that.... Alasdair Matheson he was, aye. Himself and his wife were there...and, of course, they'd rather have somebody to look after them and...keep the home just the same; they did want to have it....

TM: Earlier, you mentioned driving sheep up Gleann Hìonasdail. Was that their sheep?

IM: Oh yes, yes. That was their sheep, and I would go into Portree with them too and going to wintering too. You would put them up to the contractor up in Portree and he was taking them away south. And he was taking some for slaughtering too. That's what I was doing there and, well, we had three cows and a horse, and there would be a hundred and twenty sheep or something like that. Well, we [were] sending away so many sheep every year, cast ewes and so on. And that was my life until I went to the [forestry and then the] army.

In those days, the Glen was a lively community of many crofting families with an active céilidh scene. Iain still sings several songs he made during this period, one of his most productive in terms of composition. The songs that follow reflect Iain's life there and many of them serve as a kind of biography in themselves.

4. Tarbh Bhràigh Uige

Any event in a close-knit crofting community like Glenconon or Glen Hinnisdale was bound to create a stir and was a perfect subject for a song.

Murdo Stewart of Glenconon:

MS: *It was the year I left school, [1930]. It was a big, yellow Highland bull and it ended up at the bottom of Number Eight. My father, [Iain Stiùbhart,] kept thirty stirks there. And the Board of Agriculture inspector came and was chased up the hill. He was scared at first, it [?]rushed at him.

The bull belonged to the Board of Agriculture, which provides the animals to crofting townships in order that they may improve their bloodlines. The bull is exchanged periodically so that the gene pool does not become too limited, but this particular bull got out of hand. (See Chapters Five and Six for more information on local reaction to this song.)

An cuala sibh mu tharbh Bhràigh Uige | Did you hear about the bull of Uig Braes

1. An cuala sibh mu tharbh Bhràigh Uige?
    Gun do chaill e thùr, 's cha b' nàr dha –
theich a-mach e ris na gleanntan;
    cha do sheall e air crodh dàra.
Rinn e call air feadh na dùthcha,
    leagail is a' bùrach ghàrradh:
shaltair e gach pòr o chasan;
    thug e 'n gaiseadh às a' bhuntàta.

2. Gun do dh'éirich fir a' bhaile
    mach ri bealach air a shàillibh.
Chaidh ad oidhche mu seach ga chaithris,
    iad ga fhaire mar an nàmhaid.
Nuair a gheibheadh e air almsadh,
    dhèanadh e falbh far am b' àill leis;
dh'itheadh e a leòr 's gach arbhar –
    bha mìle marbhphaisg air a' mheàirleach.

3. 'S gu togarrach a dh'fhalbh na balaich,
    "Si' a bhalais" is Eàirdsidh Phàdraig;
bha ann Donnchadh Beag mo charaid,
    a' Sagart 's Murchadh Dhòmhnaill
        Mhàrtainn –
h-uile fear le cabar daraich,
    mach ri bealach air a shàillibh.
Bha ad a' bòide fo an anail
    gun tugte ri phrannadh air a chnàmhan.

4. Nuair a fhuair na seòid mu chùlaibh,
    chaidh a stiùireadh le mór [?]àmhghair.
Anns an fhaing gun deach a phunndadh,
    far nach b' chiùin e ri dhol dàn' air.

[conjectural order:]

E bùrach le cheann 's a chasan,
    's adhbhar seallaidh mar a bha e;
chluinneadh tu mac-talla chreagan
    a' toirt freagairt a chuid ràn aig'.

5. Theich an ear 's an iar na fearaibh
    gad bu smearail iad sa chòmhraig;
rinn gach fear dhiubh air a' bhaile
    man tugadh e an t-anam beò dhiubh.

6. Dh'fhalbh a' Sagart is e 'na chabhaig
    is chan fhanadh e 'na bhrògan.
Rinn e suas air na sparran,
    bha e tarsainn a's a' chlòsaid.
'S ann a chaidh e orr' am falach

1. Did you hear about the bull of Uig Braes?
    He lost his senses, and no shame on him –
he escaped up to the glens;
    he did not [even] notice cows in heat.
He caused damage throughout the countryside,   5
    laying low and uprooting garden dykes:
he trod every crop beneath his feet;
    he knocked the blight into the potatoes.

2. The men of the township arose
    out to the pass in pursuit of him.   10
They went night-about to watch for him;
    they looked out for him as an enemy.
When he got the chance,
    he would go wherever he liked;
he would eat his fill of every grain crop –   15
    a thousand curses were on the thief.

3. Lively went the boys,
    'Come on boy' and Archie [son of] Peter;
Wee Duncan, my friend, was there,
    The Priest and Murdo [son of] Donald [son of]
        Martin –   20
each one with an oak cudgel,
    out to the pass in pursuit of him.
They were swearing under their breath
    that his bones would be given a pounding.

4. When the heroes got behind him,   25
    he was guided with great difficulty.
In the fank he was pounded,
    where it wasn't easy to get near him.

[conjectural order:]

He [was] digging up [the earth] with his head and feet,
    he was a sight, the way he was;   30
you could hear the echo[es off the] rocks
    answering his bellows.

5   The men fled east and west
    though they were courageous in battle;
each one made for the village   35
    in case he'd snuff out their living souls.

6. The Priest ran off in a hurry
    and he didn't wait in his shoes.
He made off up to the rafters;
    he was lying cross-wise in the back room.   40
He hid on them,

air na sparran a's a' chlòsaid;
bh'e toilicht' dhol 's an t-sealladh
fhads a bhiodh anam sàbhailt'.

on the rafters in the back room;
he was pleased to get out of sight
[just] as long as his soul would be safe.

'Si' a bhalais' is an epithet for one of the crofters, Murchadh MacCoinnich (Murchadh Sheonaidh Alasdair Sheumais), whose speech was liberally peppered with the phrase, 'Siuthad a bhalaich!' ['*Come on boy!*'], said rapidly with a slight lisp. His son Iain, a noted piper, was given the nickname 'Seadan' in imitation of his father's rendering of *feadan* [chanter].

'Dunnchadh Beag' is Dunnchadh Peutan [Duncan Beaton], a small broad man who used to live in Siadar. He had a remarkable memory and could sing over a hundred verses of one of Dugald Buchanan's hymns from memory. He was one of Iain's closest acquaintances in Siadar and the two used to trade songs and humour with each other at céilidhs.

5. Ho-ró chan eil an smal orm

One favourite subject for a song was slighted love.

TM: Do you remember who that one was to?...

IM: O...té a bha shuas a's a' bhaile ann a' shiud, sa Ghleann, a thachair a bhith air chéilidh, fhios agads'. Siud a' chrìoch a bh'aig a' gnothach. Ach bha fear eile bha staigh, fhios agad, bha e 'g obair. Bha mise *supposed* a dhol suas ach ta, thàinig an gnothach, bha esan a-staigh. Cha robh càil ann, fhios agad, ach rinn mis' an t-òran; bha mise dìreach a' dol a shealltainn dhaibh aig an àm. Sin an aon *revenge* a bh'agad.

IM: *Oh, a woman who was up in the village there, in the Glen [i.e. Glen Hinnisdale], who happened to be visiting, you know. That was the end of the business. But there was another man who was in, you know, he was working. I was supposed to go up, but anyway, when it came to it, he was [already] in. There wasn't anything in it, you know, but I made the song; I was just going to see them at the time. That was the only revenge you had.*

Ho-ró chan eil an smal orm

1. Ho-ró chan eil an smal orm
   ged thug an òigh mo char asam;
   gur h-e na bh'innte dhen a' phròis
   nach fhaighinn còir dhol dhachaigh leath'.
   Ho-ró chan eil an smal orm.

2. An cuala sibh mar dh'éirich dhomh
   air oidhche 's mi air chéilidh
   far na thachair orms' an nìghneag òg –
   gun d'rinn mi còmhradh réidh rithe.
   Ho-ró...

3. Gad nach robh mi eòlach oirre
   gun d'shuidh mi greis a' stòraidh rithe;
   bhon bha coltas suairce ciùin oirr'
   bha mi 'n dùil gun còrdamaid.
   Ho-ró...

Ho-ró I am not gloomy

1. *Ho-ró I am not gloomy*
   though the young maiden cheated me;
   it is the overweening pride in her [that meant]
   I could not get a right [i.e. permission] to go home
   * with her.*
   Ho-ró I am not gloomy.   5

2. *Did you hear what befell me*
   on a night I [was] visiting
   where the young girl fell in with me
   and I made pleasant conversation with her.
   Ho-ró...

3. *Although I did not know her,*   10
   I sat a while chatting with her,
   since her appearance was mild and gentle,
   I was hopeful that we would come to an agreement.
   Ho-ró...

4. Gun d'thòisich sinn air cainntearachd
    's gun d'ruith an oidhch' go ceann oirnn,
    gu robh e teannadh ri tràth cadail.
    Dealachadh cha b'annsa leinn.
        Ho-ró...

5. 'S ann dh'iarr i duanag òrain orm
    gun d'ghabh mi dhi gu deònach e
    bhon bha mi 'n dùil ri faicinn dachaigh
    mum biodh geilt nam bòcan oirre.
        Ho-ró...

6. 'S an t-òran 's gann do chriochnaich mi
    na siud a-mach gu fiataidh i
    gun d'ghabh i fàth, 's ann air an doras,
    thàrr i ás mar fhiadh orm.
        Ho-ró...

7. 'S mar as math as aithne dhuibh
    siud as a déidh gun d'ghabh mise,
    ach 's beag a shaoil mi gu robh 'n eucoir
    fon an sgéith a' falach aic'.
        Ho-ró...

8. Is air a' starran thàrr mi i
    is thairis chuir mo làmh oirre.
    Gun d'bhoc 's gun d'leum i h-àirde fhéin,
    gun fhios 'am dé 'n ceann-fàth bh'aice.
        Ho-ró...

9. 'S ann thòisich mi ri ciallachadh –
    cha tug mi bheag de riasladh dhi,
    gun cluinneadh tu mac-talla chreagan
    a' freagairt a cuid sgiamhaichean.
        Ho-ró...

10. 'S a Mhàiri, chan eil diumb orm,
    gad a chuir thu cùlaibh rium.
    'S bhon a rinn thu ormsa tàir,
    gu bràth cha chuir mi ùidh annad.
        Ho-ró...

11. Cha tug mi gaol na gealladh dhut,
    gad a rinn thu mealladh orm.
    Bha 'n fhoill eadar thu fhéin 's mo nàbaidh
    's cha chuir càch às a' bharail mi.
        Ho-ró...

4. *We started to chat*
    and the night ran to an end on us,   15
    it was coming up to bedtime.
    Parting – we would prefer not to.
        Ho-ró...

5. *Then she wanted a little song-rhyme from me*
    and I sang it for her willingly
    since I was hoping to see her home   20
    in case she would be afraid of apparitions.
        Ho-ró...

6. *And the song, scarcely [had] I finished*
    when out she slipped.
    She took her chance, it was at the door
    she made off from me like a deer.   25
        Ho-ró...

7. *And as well you know*
    yonder I took off after her,
    but little I thought that there was deceit
    she had hiding under her wing.
        Ho-ró...

8. *And on the stepping stone I got her*   30
    and put my arm round her.
    She jumped and leapt her own height,
    I knew not what cause she had.
        Ho-ró...

9. *Then I started to calm her down –*
    I had not jostled her very much   35
    [and] you could hear the echo of the rocks
    answering her cries [because they were so loud].
        Ho-ró...

10. *And Mary, I am not offended,*
    though you turned your back to me.
    And since you rejected me,   40
    I will never show an interest in you.
        Ho-ró...

11. *I did not give you love or a promise,*
    though you deceived me.
    The scheme was between yourself and my neighbour
    and no one will put me from the opinion.   45
        Ho-ró...

6. A Mhàiri bhàn, tha thu lurach

TM: There's always another [song].

IM: Aye, oh there was.... [*laughs*] Och, [the songs were] something just to, pass the time.

TM: Is that the same Màiri [as in *Bidh mi cuimhneachadh is ag ionndrainn* (15)]?

IM: No, no. Different, oh no.

TM: [The songs were to a] different person every time.

IM: Every time yes, oh yes.

A Mhàiri bhàn, tha thu lurach

[séisd] A Mhàiri bhàn, tha thu lurach,
        flùr nan cruinneag gura tu.
    'S lìonmhor fear a tha an tòir ort;
        'na do bhòidhchead chuir iad ùidh.

1. Gad nach dug mi gaol thar chàich dhut,
   innsidh mi 's gach àit' do chliù,
   on ghabh thu a bhith coibhneil bàidheil
   rium gach tràth nuair ruiginn thu.

2. Tha do dhà shùil ghorm mar dhearcag,
   do shlios mar shneachda nam beann àrd'.
   Tha do dheud gheal cothrom snaidhte
   's do bheul as meacharra nì gàir'.

3. Tha gach maise ort mar dh'iarrainn,
   nàdar ciallach mar as còir
   's mi gun taghadh thu thar cheudan;
   chan eil d' fhiach an Tìr a' Cheò.

4. Bhithinn sona dheth na saoilinn
   gu faighinn le aont' ort còir
   's mi nach gearaineadh mo shaothair
   le dhol daonnan air do thòir.

Oh fair-haired Mary, you are lovely

[chorus] Oh fair-haired Mary, you are lovely,
        the flower of the young women, you are.
    There are many in pursuit of you;
        in your beauty they have taken an interest.

1. Though I did not love you above all others,   5
   I will tell of your character everywhere,
   since you were kind and gentle
   to me every time I would meet you.

2. Your two blue eyes are like berries,
   your form like the snow of the high mountains.   10
   Your even, white teeth are polished
   and your mouth the tenderest that ever laughs.

3. You have every grace just as I would wish,
   a discreet nature, as is right
   and I would choose you over hundreds [of others];   15
   you have no equal in the Land of the Mist.

4. I would be fortunate if I could imagine
   that I would, by consent, win you
   and I would not complain of my labour
   of continually courting you.   20

7. Tha mi fo thùrs' air bheagan sunnd

TM: Do you remember who this was to?

IM: ...Aye she was over in Kingsburgh, as a maid or something and we'd be going over there at céilidhs just...like that, you know. Maybe joking like that. And maybe she would be wanting [me] to compose for her too, and I would have it.... And she, och she wouldn't like it at all after that [and would say], "away with you". And that's how I ended it up you see.

Tha mi fo thùrs' air bheagan sunnd

1. Tha mi fo thùrs' air bheagan sunnd
   mun sgeul às ùr a fhuair mi
   mun chailin chiùin a thug dhomh rùn
   a' dùrachdadh nis fuath dhomh.

I am under a sadness and with little joy

1. I am under a sadness and with little joy
   about the latest rumour that I got
   concerning the gentle girl who loved me
   now wishing me hatred.

2. An Cinnseaborg tha i tàmh –
   an tràth seo tha mi luaidh air –
   gad thug mi dhi mo ghaol 's mo ghràdh,
   gu bheil i 'n dràsd' an gruaim rium.

3. Dèan innse dhomh a seo gun dàil,
   gu dé 'n ceann-fàth a fhuair thu
   na dé 'n nì chuala tu mi ràdh,
   nuair ghabh thu gràin cho luath dhiom.

4. Bu lìonmhor oidhche ruig mi thu
   gad bhiodh an dùbhlachd fhuar ann;
   gum biodh tu agam air mo ghlùin
   's mi 'n dùil gun dèanainn buannachd.

5. Ach on chuir thu rium do chùl,
   's nach diù leat anns an uair mi
   gu faigh mi caileag laghach shunndach
   a bheir rùn san uair dhomh.

6. Gun mhol mi thu air seòl na dhà
   bho d' cheann go d' shàil – gach buaidh bh'ortsa.
   Mas nì nach taitneach e ri d' chàil,
   gu bràth cha chluinnear bhuam e.

2. In Kingsburgh she dwells –   5
   this occasion I'm talking about –
   though I gave her my love and my affection,
   she is just now ill-disposed towards me.

3. Tell me here without delay,
   what reason did you find   10
   or what thing did you hear me saying,
   when you took a loathing to me so suddenly?

4. It was many a night I met you
   though it was cold winter;
   I would have you on my knee   15
   and me hoping I could win [you].

5. But since you turned your back on me,
   and [you think] I am beneath you just now,
   I will get a kind, joyful girl,
   who will give me love at once.   20

6. I praised you in several ways
   from your head to your heel – every virtue you had.
   If it's the case that it displeases you,
   it will never be heard from me.

TM: When did you make that one?

IM: Och some time ago. Just, I was only making more fun, mockery and things like that, you know. Maybe there was nothing in it, but just for the sake of composing and things like that. If you saw her speaking something circular [i.e. saying something evasive] or anything like that, you'd think, "Ach well, she doesn't care for me" and I would compose something like that, you know. Take it, sing it for her the next day [or] anytime I would meet her...again. That's all I would have [been] meaning. Mm. Aye.

8. Nuair a thòisich iad ri bùidsearachd

TM: Do you remember a song called *Nuair a thòisich iad ri bùidsearachd*?

IM: Oh-ho [*laughs*] that's myself again, aye, oh yes. Oh that was a night we were at an old soldier's house up at Gleann Hìonasdail there. [It was] about eleven o'clock [and he had] a tup. Well it was coming late in the year, you know, well you always kill them in the early summer because the flesh is getting...strong at that time on a tup. So there was a shepherd there and [a] few of us there and a céilidh, you know, and "Ohh," said the soldier "kill the [tup for me]".

"Och," they says. "Yes, why not". Well, as they were doing the thing, you know, I start[ed] singing and [as] we were discussing it, I started composing, you know, [about] what was going on,...putting [it] together.... And before they left I had the song made! [*claps hands and laughs*] "Oh well," he says, "it's a good recipe," he said to me. [*laughs*] That was the only thing he said about it himself, but the other boys were so vexed [at me for] composing that as they were doing it.

Nuair a thòisich iad ri bùidsearachd

1. Nuair a thòisich iad ri bùidsearachd,
   bha reithe bàn toirt shùrdag às,
   nuair a thòisich iad ri bùidsearachd.

2. Gur ann aig aon uair deug as t-oidhche,
   bha sinn cruinn an taigh an t-Saighdeir.
   Fhuair sinn gnìomh a bha glé oillteil:
   toirt a' cheann bho rùda dha.
      Nuair a thòisich iad ri bùidsearachd.

3. Gun deach na gillean ann an òrdugh,
   ma na casan chuir ad ròpan.
   Nuair a chaidh a' sgian 'na sgòrnan.
   thòisich e ri rùchdanaich.
      Nuair a...

4. 'S ann thuirt Màrtainn fhéin cho ciallach,
   "'S mór am beud gun d'rachadh sgian air.
   Chan eil a leithid as na crìochan;
   tha adharc bhrèagh' air tionndadh air."
      Nuair a...

5. "'S ann shaoileas mi gur tu bha gòrach,
   nach d'fhuair loidhn' thu bhon a' Bhòrd dha;
   gum biodh àl aige bhiodh bòidheach,
   gum biodh clòimh is rùsg orra."
      Nuair a...

6. "'S truagh nach dug thu chun an t-Show e,
   oir tha bodhaig air tha sònraicht'.
   Chan eil móran agus òirleach
   bhon an t-sròn go'n t-sùil aige!"
      Nuair a...

7. 'S ann thuirt a' Saighdear fhéin cho ciallach,
   "Chan eil ann dheth ach an dianag.
   Creidibh mi gur ceart mo bhriathran;
   's math ais fhiach a' sùgh a bh'aige."
      Nuair a...

8. "Gum biodh móran geir sa mhàileid;
   nì e maragan gun àireamh.
   Gum bi dòrlach air na h-àirnean
   's fràigidh mi an grùthan leis."
      Nuair a...

When they started to butcher

1. *When they started to butcher,*
   the white ram was struggling,
   when they started to butcher.

2. *'Twas at eleven o'clock at night,*   5
   we were gathered in the Soldier's house.
   We got a task that was quite horrible:
   taking the head off a ram for him.
      When they started to butcher.

3. *Then the lads got in order,*
   about the legs they put cords.   10
   When the knife went in his windpipe
   he began gurgling hoarsely.
      When...

4. *Then said Martin himself so sensibly,*
   "[It's] a great pity that he should be knifed.
   There's not his like in the region;   15
   there is a lovely turned horn on him."
      When...

5. *"I think it's you who was foolish,*
   that you didn't get a licence from the Board for him;
   he would have offspring that were beautiful,
   [and] there would be good wool and fleece on them."   20
      When...

6. *"It's a pity that you didn't take him to the Show,*
   since he has a body that is exceptional.
   There's little more than an inch
   from his nose to his eye!"
      When...

7. *Said the Soldier himself sensibly,*   25
   "He is only a two year old.
   Believe me truly, my words;
   his broth is good and well worth it."
      When...

8. *"There would be a lot of fat in his belly;*
   it will make countless puddings.   30
   There will be a handful [of fat] on the kidneys
   and I will fry the liver with it."
      When...

IM: By gosh, you have a lot of them [i.e. the songs]....

   [Re. lines 23–24] There's no much [more than] an inch between...the eye and the nose, that was the points of him being good, you know.

TM: That's a quality?

IM: Well, I don' know, but that was supposed to be [good] if the nose, you know, and...the eye [were] near one another. It was a good thing to see him that way. That was the point [*laughs*], whether I was right or wrong, I don't know....

Aye.... He got too much of [i.e. too many] boys doing it and I was by the fireside, listening [to] what was going on. And so when the tup was finished, you know, I had the song composed. [*laughs*] So he was saying there himself, "Oh well,...och you gave us a good recipe," he says. [I]t was!

TM: You made it right there?

IM: Yes! There and then, aye. I was just watching them what was going on and what, where they went to perform it, you know.... Aye it was eleven o'clock at night, aye that was right. It happened too!...

Màrtainn, that was one of the boys that was killing him.... [A] Morrison he was, aye; he was the shepherd, you know, at Kingsburgh [at] one time. He's not living now....

TM: Do you remember who else was there?

IM: Oh well, there's none of them living today, except myself, aye. There was Norman MacPherson there and Màrtainn Morrison and the soldier's boy too, John Beaton his name was, he was there along with them.... It was them that was there, but I didn't mention them [i.e. name] who they were, but just said...boys, you know? Mhm.... But you have the translation here too.... Mm. I don' know how you are able to do it.

9. An cuala sibh mun fhiadh

IM: This was [about] a stag that was coming into Gleann Hìonasdail.... Aye [he] just got up, off the mountain somewhere and he came down the Glen and he was making for the corn and took it.... Aye, aye. And they was chasing him, right enough, but no one would could get him, he was too quick for them. Only, you know, he was smelling them at least and he was away, but he would make quite [a lot of] damage on the stooks...at night and things like that, but if he heard you coming he would smell you in the distance and he was off again. They couldn't get him at all, he never got eat[en].... No, that's what I'm say[ing in the song], if they get a hold of him,...he would be divided between them.... Ah hah.

An cuala sibh mun fhiadh	Did you hear about the deer

1. An cuala sibh mun fhiadh
    bha air feadh a' bhaile?
'S mór a rinn e riasladh
    am measg a' bharra;
bha adagan gan riasladh
    's gan cur o chasan.
Bidh ad ann am fiachan
    man cuirear stad air.
	1. Did you hear about the deer
	    that was all over the township?
	He did a great deal of damage
	    among the crops;
	stooks were disordered 5
	    and put [i.e. trampled] under his feet.
	They [i.e. the crofters] will be in debt
	    before a stop is put to him.

2. Cha robh fios có 'm mèirleach
    bha dèanamh calla
gos do dh'inns' dhaibh Màrtainn,
    nuair a thug e 'n aire
gu robh damh na cròice
	2. No one knew who the thief
	    doing damage was 10
	until Martin told them,
	    when he noticed
	that the antlered stag was

air lón a' chreachail
's gu robh na deich meòir air,
  na corr a bharrachd.

in the hillocky water-meadow
and that there were ten points on it[s antlers], 15
  or even more.

3. Thàinig e air chuairt,
  gur ann uair an-uiridh
gun deachaidh a' ruaig air,
  cha d'fhuair e fuireach.
Ach bhon thill e 'm bliadhna,
  's e 'm bròd na culaidh;
tha gach fear gu dian dhiubh
  a-muigh ga fhuireach.

3. He came around,
  it was once last year;
he was put to flight,
  he wasn't allowed to stay 20
But since he returned this year,
  he is in top condition;
every one of them is eagerly
  awaiting him outside.

4. Tha gach fear san àite
  gun tàmh ga chaithris,
'n dùil gu faigh iad fàth air,
  's gun cuirear às dha.
Bidh iadsan a' liùgadh
  air chùlaibh adaig
le gunna làn de dh'fhùdar
  is luaidhe ghlas ann.

4. Every one in the place 25
  is sleepless watching for him,
hoping they will get a chance at him,
  and that he will be destroyed.
They will be creeping
  behind a stook 30
with a gun full of powder
  and blue-grey lead in it.

5. Ach chan fhaigh iad dlùth dha,
  bidh e air fhaiceall.
Bheir e dhaibh an dubhlan;
  chan fhaigh iad faisg air.
Thig e nuair as àill leis
  tràth 'sa mhadainn,
ithidh e làn-shàth às
  is nì e tarraing.

5. But they won't get near him,
  he will be watchful.
He will give defiance to them; 35
  they will not get close to him.
He comes when he likes,
  early in the morning,
he eats his fill from it
  and dashes away. 40

6. Ach nam faighte gréim air,
  readh a roinn gu h-ealamh,
siud far 'm biodh an aimhreit
  sa Ghleann ga fheannadh.
Readh móran a' fiadh oirnn
  dhe na balaich;
siud far 'm biodh an riasladh
  air feadh nan caileag.

6. But if a hold were gotten on him,
  he would be quickly divided;
what a contention there would be
  in the Glen [while] skinning him.
Many of our lads 45
  would go rampant;
that's where there would be great carryings-on
  among the lasses.

10. An cuala sibh mun ùpraid (Tarbh Eighre)

Iain made this song about an event in which he was not a participant, an example of the bard's eye for a suitable subject.

IM: Oh that was a mad bull that was in Eyre, up that way. Mhm.... They were going to try and get 'im and the bull was turning on them, you know. He was just put mad some way and had too many [peo-ple] about him and he was charging them here and there. So I've only heard about that, I was just composing as I was hearing about those people that was about there. Mhm.

An cuala sibh mun ùpraid

1. An cuala sibh mun ùpraid
      bha san dùthaich, 's chan annas,
   mun tarbh ghòrach bha 'n Eighre
      gun d'rinn iad chur cragte?
   Nuair thàinig fios bhon a Bhòrd
      gum bu chòir a chur dhachaigh,
   gun do dh'fhalbh iad, na seòid,
      air thòir leis na maidean
         ga chur fo smachd.

2. Gun do chruinnich iad còmhladh
      Clann 'IcLeòid is an Seathach,
   Clann 'IcRath is 'IcAoidh,
      's na daoine làidir a bh'aca.
   Gu robh Alasdair Mór Peutan
      ann e fhéin, 's e bha tapaidh
   cur nan ròpan an òrdugh
      gos an seòladh ma amhaich
         nan d'readh aig' air.

3. Nuair a chunnaic a' bhrùid ad
      's ann gan ionnsaigh a ghabh e.
   Nuair a dh'fhalbh e 's e bùirean
      gun do dhùisg e am baile.
   'S na gàrraidhean ùrach,
      bha e smùideadh le chlaigeann;
   gun do tharraing na diùlnaich,
      gach fear a dh'ionnsaigh a thaighe
         fo mhóran boil.

4. Thàinig Lighiche nam Brùidean
      ann an ùine glé aithghearr;
   gun deach e ghabhail 'na chùlaibh
      is chaidh a phunndadh an oisean.
   'S nuair a ghabh e ga ionnsaigh
      leis an t-sùil ghabh e beachd air.
   Gun duirt e ro dhiùmbach,
      "Tha bhrùid air dhroch cheartas
         o chionn fad'."

5. Gun do dh'aontaich e, an creutair;
      chuir e an X-ray air a mhalaidh.
   Rinn e innse gun bhreug dhaibh
      nach robh feum ann don bhaile;
   bhon a chaill e a reusan
      gu feumadh a cheannach.
   Cha biodh e 'na fhàbhar
      dhol ga fhàgail air machair —
         's e às a bheachd.

Did you hear about the uproar

1. Did you hear about the uproar
      [that] was in the country and it's not strange,
   about the daft bull that was in Eyre,
      that they made it go crazy?
   When a message came from the Board   5
      that it ought to be sent home [i.e. back to the Board],
   they went away, the heroes,
      to pursue it with sticks
         to put it under control.

2. They gathered together   10
      the Clan MacLeod and Shaw,
   Clan Macrae and MacKay,
      and the strong men they had.
   Big Alasdair Beaton was
      there himself, he was clever and adept   15
   putting the ropes in order
      in order to direct them around its neck
         if he could.

3. When the brute saw them,
      it's toward them it made.   20
   When it went away bellowing
      it woke the town.
   And the soil dykes,
      it was pulverizing with its skull;
   the brave men took off,   25
      everyone towards home
         in a great hurry.

4. The Beast Physician came
      in a very short time;
   he got caught behind it   30
      and he was pounded in a corner
   and when it charged towards him,
      with its eye it judged him.
   He said very indignantly,
      "The brute has been handled badly   35
         for some time."

5. It yielded, the poor creature;
      he put the X-ray on its brow.
   He told them without falsehood
      that it was no use for the township;   40
   since it lost its reason
      it must be sold.
   He would not be in favour
      of going and leaving it in the field —
         and it out of its senses.   45

6. Anns a' mhadainn, 'n àm éirigh,
    chaidh fios Dhùn Éideann le cabhaig
a dh'innse nach robh fon ghréin seo
    gu léir gheibheadh faisg air,
ach gun gabhadh iad fhéin e
    son feum an luchd-taighe;
bhiodh e math mun Fhéill Mhàrtainn
    on bha 'n t-àite gun sgadan —
    's nach robh e pailte.

7. 'S e Calum Hearach bha deònach
    gun d'readh còrdadh gu h-ealamh
bhon a bha aige bùtha;
    théid soidhn' a' Bhùidseir ri dharas.
'S nì e reic air a' phunnd
    's cha bhi unnsa gun phrofaid.
Bidh e math dhan an òigridh
    tha còmhnaidh sa bhaile
    go fàgail bras.

6. In the morning, at rising time,
    a message went quickly to Edinburgh
saying that there wasn't here, under the sun,
    a single one who could get near it,
but that they themselves would take [i.e. slaughter] it 50
    because of the need of the householders;
it would be good around Martinmas
    since the place was without herring —
    since it wasn't plentiful [in the sea].

7. It's Calum the Harrisman who was willing 55
    [and] it was agreed quickly
since he had a shop;
    the sign of the Butcher will go up on the door.
He will sell it by the pound
    and there won't be an ounce without profit. 60
It will be good for the children
    who are dwelling in the town
    to leave [them] bold.

IM: [Seathach was a Shaw]; Johnnie Shaw I would say [i.e. call] him. That was his name, Seathach.

TM: Iain Seathach?

IM: Iain Seathach, aye..., I didn't say Iain there, but I says "the Seathach". He was known as that, as I would be [known as] "the MacNeacail" or something like that.

[Alasdair Mór Peutan.] ...That was...Big Alec Beaton, you know.... Well, he was...bigger than any of them probably.

IM: ...That's it, aye aye.... Oh well you have them all [translated] there.

TM: This isn't a very good translation either.

IM: Oh well, you made them very good though I think.... You made it as good as anybody could. Mm.

TM: Well, I hope so.

IM: Ah yes, it'll pass alright; it gives me the meaning of what's there. That's all you need. Oh aye.

11. An cuala sibh an car a bha sa bhaile seo mun dannsa

Dòmhnall Saighdear [Donald the Soldier] took a great interest in community activities, but sometimes got himself into a fankle.

An cuala sibh an car a bha sa bhaile seo mun dannsa

Did you hear of the fiasco of the dance in the village?

1. An cuala sibh an car a bha
    sa bhaile seo mun dannsa:
    's e Saighdear thug tarraing air
    's cha toir e nis gu ceann e.
Cha robh de bhiadh na shiùcar ann
    am bùth a dhèanadh [?]taing dha;
    's e na caileagan bhios diùmbach dhiot,
    bha sùil ris fad a' gheamhraidh.

1. Did you hear [of] the fiasco
    of the dance in the village:
    it's the Soldier who suggested it
    and now he cannot bring it off.
There wasn't food or sugar enough 5
    for the job in any shop;
    it's the lasses will be cross with you,
    [they] were expecting it all winter.

2. 'S tu fhéin a rinn a' bhòilich uim',
   nuair a thòisich thu ri cainnt air,
   gun digeadh ad á Ròmasdal
   's na h-òg-bhean air làimh ac',
   gun cuireadh tu an òrdugh ad
   gach dòigh airson an dannsa;
   bidh platforms le còmhlaichean
   ri còrnairean an t-seann taigh.

3. Bhiodh tu ag innse fìrinn nis
   nach cinnteach bitheadh maill' ann
   gu faigheadh tusa fidhlearan
   is pìobairean gun taing dhaibh,
   's gun digeadh ad à Eàrlais
   às gach ceàrnaidh a thoirt taing dhut —
   's tu fhéin am measg a' chòmhlan
   's tu a' gabhail òrain Ghallta.

4 'S nuair théid [thu] chon a' phlatform,
   bidh màtag a' toirt làimh ann
   gu seall thu dhaibh mar steapas tu,
   's mar sheatas tu san dannsa:
   an Irish jig, 's a' Seann Triubhas,
   am Fling, 's an Claidheamh Danns' ann,
   gum bi do mhedals uileadh ort
   a bhuinnig thu air Galltachd.

5. Bidh iomadh sitheann shònraicht' ann,
   bhon a' smeòrach gon a' féasan;
   bidh taobh a dhamh na cròiceadh ann,
   'n tarbh gòrach a bha 'n Eighre.
   Bhon a bha an teas cho pianail air
   gun bhuail a' ghrian sa cheann e,
   bidh faiteachas is fiamh orra
   's cha mhiann leotha dhol teann air.

6. Bha cùram ort mar chòcairean
   nach robh gu leòr sa ghleann dhiubh.
   Bhiodh Calum, bhiodh Iain Phàdraig ann,
   bidh Màrtainn air an ceann-san.
   Nuair ruigeas ad am Brusach,
   bheir e cuideachadh nach gann dhut;
   bidh Dòmhnull Nèill 's Iain Tharmaid
   ad a' falbh ag iarraidh fry pan.

2. It's you who boasted about it,
   when you began to speak of it,   10
   that they would come from Ròmasdal
   with girlfriends on their arms;
   you would arrange them in order
   [and] in every way for the dance;
   there'll be platforms [made] with doors   15
   at the corners of the old house.

3. You were promising
   that there would certainly be no delay,
   till you'd get fiddlers
   and pipers regardless   20
   and they would come from Earlish,
   from every quarter to give you thanks —
   [and] yourself amidst the band
   singing Lowland songs.

4. And when you go to the platform,   25
   a mattock will lend a helping hand,
   till you show them how you step,
   and how you set in the dance:
   the Irish jig, and the Seann Triùbhas,
   the Fling and the Sword Dance   30
   wearing all your medals
   that you won in the Lowlands.

5. There'll be many a special meat there,
   from the thrush to the pheasant;
   there'll be a side of the antlered stag   35
   [and] the mad bull that was in Eyre.
   Since the heat was so excruciating
   that the sun addled his brain —
   they will be afraid and fearful
   and won't want to go near it.   40

6. You were worried about cooks,
   that there weren't enough in the glen.
   Calum and John (son of) Peter will be there
   [and] Martin himself in charge of them.
   When they come to the Bruce,   45
   he will give unstinting help to you;
   Donald (son of) Neil and John (son of) Norman
   yonder heading off to look [for] a frying pan.

12. A Bheileag, 's mór a chaidh do mhealladh

In 1932 or 33, Iain teased a would-be suitor to Isabel Gillies (now Ross) with this song. Four years after I first got word of the incident in a letter,[44] I was able to follow it up:

Peter Stewart: *He made two songs for Bella Gillies. That's the second one you have [*Thoir an t-soraidh seo bhuam* (13)]. She used to make songs herself: 'aoir',...miscalling, telling bad things about them.

When he was in Gleann Hìonasdail, Bella was up there too and she had relations up there....

He made a song about Duncan MacKinnon; he was going with Bella. Peter MacKinnon came over and Bella was going to go out with Duncan. They had her 'tied' to the séise [couch], one on either side of her and wouldn't let her go out to see Duncan. He was waiting outside all night! Peter told Sgiobair to make a song on Duncan.

Iain soon had the song made and sang it at the shepherd's house in Kingsburgh, the only one visible from the main road (it is no longer there).

I then decided to visit Isabel herself, hoping to gather enough clues to jog Iain's memory, as he could not recall the song when I asked about it. A little more research led me at last to Fortrose in the Black Isle where Bella lived with her husband Angus (son of Neil Ross, the shopowner mentioned in Ho-ró tha mi fo smalan dheth (1)). She said she would be glad to see me and so at the end of January, 1993, I stopped by for a visit.

She was lively, witty and engaging; she instantly dubbed our interview-to-come 'Sgiobair-gate', saying that Camilla Parker Bowles "*had nothing on this".[45] Not long into our tape recorded conversation, I asked about the songs that Iain had made to her. She first spoke of Bidh mi cuimhneachadh 's ag ionndrainn (15) and then A Bheileag:

IR: Agus rinn e òran eile oidhche a bha date agam ri – tha fear ris an canadh ad Dunnchadh – agus bha bhràthair air chéilidh cuide ris a' Sgiobair.

TM: Dunnchadh MacFhionghain?

IR: Dunnchadh MacFhionghain. Agus bha bràthair aige air a robh Peter. O cha mhór nach toirinn slap do Pheter, bh'e cho mìomhodhail! E-co-dhiù, bha date agam ri Dunnchadh. Agus...bha mise 'ga mo dhreasaigeadh, is 'cà robh mi dol' 's thuirt – bha piuthar Dhunnchaidh pòsd' aig bràthair mo mhàthar – agus dh'innis ise 's nuair chaidh mise mach, rug ad orm agus cha d'fhuair mise mach 's chaidh mo ghlacadh. Bha mi ann a' shin fad na h-oidhche!... So rinn e òran an uair sin, òran a' magadh.

IR: And he made another song one night when I had a date with – there's a man who's called Duncan – and his brother was visiting the Sgiobair.

TM: Duncan MacKinnon?

IR: Duncan MacKinnon. And he had a brother named Peter. Oh I almost slapped Peter, he was so impertinent! Eh anyway, I had a date with Duncan. And I was dressing, and 'where was I going' [Anna asked. She] said – Duncan's sister [Anna] was married to my mother's brother – and she told, and when I went out, they grabbed me and I didn't get out, I was caught. I was there all night long! So he [i.e. Sgiobair] made a song then, a mocking song.

Neither Bella nor Peter Stewart could remember the melody, but armed with the two verses that they recited to me, I asked Iain again.

IM: Tha Beileag Gillies a bha sin ann an Uige.... Bhithinn dol a-sìos a chéilidh oirre; bha mi eòlach...air a màthair 's air a seanmhair 's air daoine bha sin 's chaidh mi ann an oidhche a bha seo.... Och bha i ga cur fhéin air dòigh 's bha ga dreasaigeadh 's mar a b'fheàrr a b'urra dhi, 's cha robh i dol a dh'innse...cà robh i dol...na càil [?]ud....

   Chaidh mi fhìn sìos aig àm co-dhiù ['s]...nuair a chunna mi ise 'a cur air dòigh,...[dh'fh]aighnich mi càite robh i a' dol, 's o cha robh i ag innse dhomh cà robh i dol idir och bha fear a-muigh ga feitheamh, fhios agaibh.... Agus och

IM: It's Bella Gillies who was in Uig then. I used to go down to visit her; I knew her mother and her grandmother and [other] people there and I went [down] this night, but she was getting ready and dressing herself as nicely as she could and she wasn't going to tell where she was going, or anything.

   Anyway, I went down myself one time and when I saw her getting ready, I asked where she was going. Oh she wasn't telling me where she was going at all, but there was someone outside waiting for her, you know.

dh'fhalbh i co-dhiù agus [nu]air a chunna mi mar a rinn i... – chunna mi i falbh – rug mi oirre an uair sin 's thug mi air ais i agus,...cha leiginn a-mach cuideachd i.

Bha bràthair dhen a' bhean aig a h-uncle,...bh'e ann cuideachd, agus...bha esan, fhios a'ad, cheart cho déidheil ise a chumail a-staigh gos nach faigheadh am bràthair a-mach idir i agus dh'fhalbh mi fhìn agus, co-dhiù, rug mi oirre 's thug mi staigh i agus seo agad mar a thòisich mi ris an òran.

And, but she went anyway and when I saw what she was up to – I saw her going – I caught [up] with her then and brought her back and I wouldn't let her out either.

Her uncle's wife's brother, he was there as well and he was, you know, just as keen to keep her in so that the brother wouldn't find her out at all, and I went and caught [up] with her and, anyway, brought her in and this is how I started on the song.

A Bheileag, 's mór a chaidh do mhealladh

1. A Bheileag, 's mór a chaidh do mhealladh,
   cha d'fhuair thu raoir a-mach a' daras.
   Nach e Dunnchadh fhuair a lathadh,
   feitheamh fad' na h-oidhch' riut.
      A Bheileag, 's mór a chaidh do mhealladh.

2. Gun deach mi oirr' sìos air chéilidh,
   'n dùil gun deanainn còmhradh réidh riut,
   gu robh thusa trang gad èideadh –
   's dearbha fhéin bha loinn ort.
      A Bheileag...

3. Air m' fhacal fhìn gur tu bha deàlrach;
   b'ioghnadh liom nach d'bhrist thu 'sgàthan –
   air do sgeadachadh go d' shàil,
   cha robh san àit' cho spéiseil.
      A Bheileag...

4. 'S nuair a fhuair thu ann an òrdugh,
   'n dùil gu robh gach nì mar deòin leat,
   's ann a chuir thu ort do chòt',
   's tu falbh fo sgòd gun m' fhaighneachd!
      A Bheileag...

5. 'S a dh'aindeoin cho sgiobalta 's a bha thu,
   anns a' starsaich 's rinn mi d' fhàsgainn:
   's thug mi staigh thu 'n còmhair do shàil,
   's chaidh do chàradh air an t-séisidh.
      A Bheileag...

6. Gun deach Anna a thoirt làmh dhut,
   mur bu mhisd' thu i cha b'fheàirrde:
   chaidh ur leagail air a' làr;
   bha sibh gu h-àrd a' spréighlich.
      A Bheileag...

7. Bha e gad fheitheamh mun a' chruachan;
   's eagal orm gum mill am fuachd e.

Oh Bella, you were badly cheated

1. Oh Bella, you were badly cheated,
   you didn't get out the door last night.
   Wasn't it Duncan who got frozen,
   waiting for you all night long?
      Oh Bella, you were badly cheated.   5

2. I went down to visit her,
   hoping I would have a quiet conversation with you,
   you were busy dressing yourself –
   you were spruced up, right enough.
      Oh Bella...

3. Upon my word, it's you [who] was brilliant;   10
   it amazed me you didn't break the mirror –
   prettied up from head to toe,
   no one in the place was so dolled up.
      Oh Bella...

4. When you had got everything ready,
   thinking that everything was just so,   15
   and then it was on with your coat,
   and you were off under full sail without asking me!
      Oh Bella...

5. Despite how quick you were,
   at the threshold I grabbed you:
   I whisked you in heel first,   20
   [and] you were trapped on the settle.
      Oh Bella...

6. [Then] Anna went to give you a hand,
   if you weren't the worse for her [intervention, you] weren't
       the better:
   you both landed on the floor;
   you were tumbling frantically.   25
      Oh Bella...

7. He was waiting for you around the corn stacks;
   I'm afraid the cold will ruin him.

Ma nì crith mheileach ortsa bhualadh,
's feuch gu suath thu bhroinn aig'.
  A Bheileag...

If hypothermia strikes,
make sure you rub his belly [to warm him up].
  Oh Bella...

IM: Sin agad a bh'ann.... 'Crith mheileach',...tha fios agad dé th'ann...a fhuair thu air do lathadh. (TM: Ceart.) Gu faod thu bhith air lathadh, seo agad an ciùr, a bhith a' suathadh a' bhroinn aige. [laughs] O ghabh ad an cuthach, ghabh, och cha do ghabh Beileag cho dona e. Ghabh a h-uncle, o ghabh ise cuthach, o!

IM: That was it. 'Hypothermia', you know what that is, [it's] what you got when you were frozen. (TM: Right.) You could be frozen, here's the cure, to be rubbing his belly. [laughs] Oh they were furious, oh Bella did not take it so badly, [but] her uncle, oh he was furious!

When I talked to Bella about the song, she laughed aloud and said,

IR: Dhia, bha mi glé fhiadhaich, bha mi coma có aca, theab mi a ràdha, 'Sgiobair na sad'!

IR: Lord, I was completely wild, I didn't care, I almost said, 'Sgiobair the pest!'

13. Thoir an t-soraidh seo bhuam

Beileag was indeed indignant and there is a very real sense in which one can pay someone back with a song, as William Ross discovered in his own day.[46] Thoir an t-soraidh seo bhuam represents a form of apology for A Bheileag and was made in answer to a request from Beileag herself. At the time, she had returned to Skye and was working in Uig Hospital (where the Youth Hostel is today).

Isabel Ross: O sin agad, "...chun na rìbhinn as suairc". Nach eil i brèagha a-nist'! Feuch gun innis thu sin ann an New Hampshire! [laughs] Nach do chaill mi biod dheth? Gu bheil mi fhathast 'first class'.... 'S ann tha mi nist' a' fàs coltach ri Lester Piggott.... Co-dhiù, nuair a gheibh mi face-lift, bidh mi nas fheàrr.

Isabel Ross: Oh you have [it], "...to the gentlest girl". Isn't she beautiful now! Try to tell [them] that in New Hampshire! [laughs] Haven't I lost a bit? But I'm still 'first class'. I'm getting to look like Lester Piggott now. Anyway, when I get a face-lift, I'll be better.

Thoir an t-soraidh seo bhuam

1. Thoir an t-soraidh seo bhuam
   chun na rìbhinn as suairc
   air an tric bhios mo smuaintean an còmhnaidh.
   Gur òigh thu tha ciùin,
   a tha fìnealt gun smùir;
   bidh gach fear a' cur ùidh 'na do bhòidhchead.

2. 'Na mo dhùisg is 'nam shuain,
   bidh mo smuain oirr' gach uair;
   gu bheil àilleachd do shnuaidh a' toirt leòn
       dhomh.
   Bheileag òg an fhuilt dhuinn,
   's mór a dh'fhàs ort a loinn;
   tha thu gàirbheulach, aoidheil gun mhór-chùis.

Take this greeting from me

1. Take this greeting from me
   to the gentlest girl
   on whom my thoughts ever dwell.
   You are a young maiden who is gentle,
   who is handsome and fine without blemish;   5
   every man takes an interest in your beauty.

2. Awake or in deepest sleep,
   my thoughts are on her every hour;
   the beauty of your appearance is wounding me.
   Young Bella of the brown hair,   10
   great is the comeliness that has grown on you;
   you are laughing-mouthed, cheerful and without pride.

3. Tha thu sìobhalta, suairc
   's tu gun phròis na gun uaill,
   tha gun fhoill na gun ghruaim na gun
        ghòraich'.
   Do dhà shùil mheallach chiùin
   toirt dhuit àilleachd is mùirn,
   beul a' mhànrain bhon cùbhraidh na pògan.

4. Tha thu bho fhìor Chloinn 'Ill'-ìos' –
   bhon robh tàlant is rian –
   nach robh meat' ann an gnìomh ri àm
        còmhraig.
   Gheibh iad urram is cliù
   bho gach aon chuir orr' iùil.
   'S beag an t-ioghnadh 's ann liom gad bhiodh
        tòir ort.

5. Gur tu mo roghainn fhìn
   dhe na chunnaic mi 's a chì,
   ach, mo thruaighe, dé nì mi 's mi gun chòir ort?
   Gu bheil eagal orm, a ghaoil,
   gun toir càch thu a thaobh,
   oir bidh an tòir ort luchd maoin agus stòrais.

6. Ach mur bi e an dàn
   nach fhaigh mi thu air làimh,
   's e mo dhùrachd gu bràth dhut gach sòlas,
   gach beannachd 'nad dhéidh
   's gach cùis bhith leat réidh,
   ge b'e àite fon ghréin sam bi d' chòmhnaidh.

3. You are peaceful, kind
   and you, without pride or vanity,
   are without deceit, without sullenness or folly.   15
   Your two alluring gentle eyes
   giving you beauty and joy,
   a mouth of melodies from which the kisses are sweet.

4. You are of the true Gillies Clan –
   from whom there was talent and an even disposition –   20
   who were not cowardly about a feat in time of strife.
   They will get honour and fame
   from every one who makes your acquaintance.
   It's little wonder to me, indeed, that there would be suitors
        after you.

5. You are my own choice   25
   of those I have seen and will see,
   but my woe, what will I do, and me without a right to you?
   I fear, oh love,
   that others will take you aside,
   since you are courted by people of means and wealth.   30

6. But if it is not fate
   [and] I do not get you by the hand,
   my eternal wish is [for] every happiness for you,
   every blessing with you
   and that everything be smooth for you,   35
   whatever place under the sun your dwelling be.

What is so interesting about this exchange is that the teasing one-upmanship and friendly rivalry of youthful banter was carried on through the medium of song. Even now after nearly sixty years there is a good natured 'nippin and scartin' between the Sgiobair and Bella which they both relish by quoting the songs of their joint past. It is a thrust and riposte of tremendous wit, creativity and vitality. As my visit with Bella was drawing to a close, I showed her some of the Sgiobair's other songs on my computer.

IR: That's enough of them, now that I've seen my own, I won't bother with the rest.... They would only make me jealous! [laughs]

In these years between the wars the Sgiobair justified his nickname, serving occasionally as crew aboard Glenconon neighbour Iain Stiùbhart's fishing boat. According to Murdo, Iain Stiùbhart's eldest son who was also aboard, the Sgiobair and Murdo's brother Peter would often be at the songs: "*'Hut!' my father would say. 'Get up here and do some work!' and the Sgiobair would be down below learning songs to Peter!"

"My father's house was only just about three [hundred yards]" away from the Stiùbhart's croft, Iain recalls. "I could walk it in ten minutes, to the house."

IM: I would go out now and again.... Oh, he was able at the sea, you know, he was, he knew everything.... Oh yes, a big boat aye, he had that and he had Aonghas Phàdraig and all these people about with him, you know, and Angus Fletcher and these were his crews.[47] I would go out with him any-time I wanted to go out and you would be amazed! I'd never seen the size of herring. "How do you know there's a herring there?"

"Well," Stiùbhart says,... "Is the night yet out?" he says. "What's these white stripes?" White stripes in the sea, you know, when you're looking down. But it came at last, sheets of it! You couldn't see...the bottom but white: it was the herring!

According to Peter Stewart, the stripes below the surface of the water were the phosphorescent glow of plankton agitated by the motion of the herring shoal.

Nowadays, Iain says, the herring fishing has declined and has been replaced by trawling for prawn:

IM: Of course that's what's ruined all the other fishing, the prawns. Well you know, we used to get her-ring and things like that and cod, but there's nothing today but the prawns. And the trawling...on the beds what were put upside-down, mixed up. So you don't get this herring what [i.e. like] they used to have.

The herring fishery in its heyday was a major industry in the islands.

IM: Oh away! There was seven curers down at Uig pier then.... They were getting them from Lewis, from Yarmouth, people coming to gut the herring here.... I've seen my mother go too, yes and [Margaret Bennett's] grandmother [Flora MacKenzie] too, she would be down...at the time of the gutting.... I would go out now and again.... That was before World War, 19 oh 30...36, I believe. Aye, that was my last year, aye.

FROM FORESTRY TO THE FIELDS OF FRANCE

In 1936, after twelve years feeing in Gleann Hìonasdail, it was time for a change. The Mathesons' croft was no longer being kept up and Iain went to work for Sir John Stirling-Maxwell at his Corrour Estate on Rannoch Moor. According to Peter Stewart, "*many from Skye would go to Corrour in the spring, work through the summer, and return to Skye for the winter. The estate was *already* forested, but Maxwell had them planting more."

IM: Oh I was about thirty months there, or more.... Aye, two and a half years, aye.

TM: Was it all through the year, or did you come home in the winter?

IM: No, I was there in the winter too.

TM: So would you come to Skye for a couple of weeks in the summer?

IM: Oh-h, yes, yes. You would get a holiday every year, ten days or something like that.... Yes, I would go to Glenconon. We'd go back again to Corrour after my holiday. Yes, I was two and a half years there. Mhm.

The estate is still not accessible by road; it can be approached only by rail (on the Glasgow-Fort William line). Even upon arrival at Corrour Station, Corrour Lodge and the bothies in which the men stayed are at the far end of Loch Ossian, five miles away by a dirt track. Nights in the unheated bothies could be long and cold, but the more experienced workers soon shared their 'tricks of the trade': "*I had fifteen blankets on my bed.... I would put my overcoat over the bed and the woman [the cook] would think I was cold and give me another blanket, until I had fifteen! The other boys taught me that."

MacNeacail approved of Stirling-Maxwell himself ("Oh, a nice man he was too, real good man"), and the owner of the lodge, who kept it open and staffed all year round, but who came only once a year during the shooting season. He had more trouble, however, with his immediate bosses: "*The gentlemen would pass you by, say hello and keep walking without looking back, but the foremen would pass and keep looking back to make sure you were working." The lads were allowed a day off now and again when the weather was particularly bad, until one such day when the foreman caught several of them out fishing and said, "*If you can fish in this [weather], you can work. And that was the days off; we had to work then every day."

IM: [We were] planting trees, aye and drainage. And you were draining the land before you would plant trees,...when there was water running in it, you know, and you would put a [another] drain beside the drain again, because it was getting enough water from the ground the way it was.... Well you had the drains maybe three feet apart, lengths of it.... It was Douglas Fir and Spruce we were putting there. Aye.

*We worked all year long ditching and planting, whatever the weather. Even if the weather was nice, you'd get just as wet. Many's the time I was soaked through, because you were pruning all the trees to make them grow up instead of out and they were all covered with dew.

14. A's a' mhadainn 's mi 'g éirigh

This song perfectly encapsulates life on the estate.

Uilleam MacNeacail: Bu toil liom, 's dòcha gun gabh e fhéin e, ma th'e aige – bha e 'g obair sa Choir' Odhair,..."Coir' Odhar nam fiadh-bheann".... Ai, siuthad 's feuch air....

IM: O chan eil òran [ann].[48] [sings]

Uilleam MacNeacail: I would like, maybe he'll sing it himself, if he has it – he was working in Corrour, "Corrour of the wild mountains". Aye, go ahead, try it.

IM: *Oh [it's] not a song.[48] [sings]*

A's a' mhadainn 's mi 'g éirigh

1. A's a' mhadainn 's mi 'g éirigh
    's ann neo-éibhinn a tha mi;
   cha b'ionnan 's mar a b'àis' domh
    nuair a bha mi sa Ghleann.
   Bhon thàinig mi 'n taobh-sa
    's beag m' shunnd ri ceòl-gàire;
   tha eilean nan àrd-bheann
    gach là tighinn 'nam shùim.

2. Gur ann gòrach a bha mi
    nuair a smaoinich mi fhàgail –
    gur h-ann ann gheibhinn bàidh agus dòigh.
   Cead laigh' agus éirigh
    gun chùram fon ghréin dhomh;
    cha robh fàillinn na éis air mo lòn.

3. B'e Coir' Odhar nam fiadh-bheann
    dh'fhàg m' aigne cho cianail.
    chan eil iongnadh gad liathainn le bròn –
    gun nì air gach làmh dhiom

In the morning I rise

1. *In the morning I rise,*
    it's unhappy I am;
   it's not thus that I used to be
    when I was in the Glen.
   Since I came over here   5
    little is my inclination to light-hearted laughter;
   the island of the high mountains
    comes to my mind each day.

2. *How foolish I was*
    when I thought of leaving it,   10
    for it's there I would get kindness and courteous treatment.
   [And] leave to rise and lie down,
   without a care for me under the sun;
    there wasn't any lack or want in my diet.

3. *It was Corrour of the wild mountains*   15
    that left my spirit so melancholy.
    It is no wonder though I would grow grey with sorrow –
   with nothing on either side of me

16. Iain, Nurse Ironside and Simon Cameron, the Head Forester in Coire Odhar [Corrour], ca. 1938. The nurse had been called in due to an outbreak of measles among the workers. (MacNeacail collection)

ach coilltean is fàsach
    is monaidhean àrda fo cheò.

4. Tha mi faotainn gach riasladh,
    le droch shìd' agus siantan,
mach air frìthean na' fiadh,
    mi gun dìon na gun sgàil.
Mi sgìth air mo chasan,
    ri cuibhleadh a' bhara,
gu saoil mi le fadal,
    gur seachdain gach là.

5. 'N àm dhol dachaigh san fheasgar,
    bidh e drùidhte do m' chraiceann,
mo bhiadh cha bhi deasaicht'
    gad is beag dha mo chàil.
An fhàrdach bidh falamh
    gun cheò far an teallaich,
cha b'ionnan sna gleannaibh
    far na chleachd mi bhith tàmh.

6. Ach nuair a thig deireadh bliadhna
    gur ann luath nì mi triall às
air long-adhair na' sgiathan,
    nach till siantan a' Mhàrt.
Gu seòl mi leath' thairis,
    thar chuain is thar bheannaibh;
gun gabh mi gach aithghearr
    go eilean mo ghràidh.

IM: Sin agad e. [laughs]
UM: An cuala tu sin riamh?
MB: Cha chuala.
UM: Bha e aige ma-tha.
IM: Och. Ach tha mi air a dhìochuimhneachadh ge-ta. Chan eil guth agam an-diugh.
MB: O tha guth math [agaibh]....
UM: O tha e math air seinn, nach eil?...
IM: Tha mi fàgail móran....
TM: Cuin a rinn sibh an t-òran sin....
IM: O...tha mi cinnteach gu bheil...corr...is fichead bliadhna co-dhiù, aon pairt, tha.[49] O siud an aon chur-seachad a bh'againn.

---

but woods and wilderness
    and high moors under mist.   20

4. I am suffering every hardship,
    with bad weather and the elements,
out in the deer forests
    and me without protection or shelter.
I [am so] tired on my legs,   25
    with wheeling the barrow,
that I wish with longing
    that a week [passed with] every day.

5. At the time of going home in the evening,
    it [i.e. rain] will be soaking [me] to my skin,   30
my food will not be ready
    though little is my appetite for it.
The living quarters will be empty
    without smoke from the hearth,
not the same [as] in the glens   35
    where I used to be dwelling.

6. But when the end of the year comes,
    it's fast I will get away from there
on a winged airplane
    that the blasts of March will not turn back.   40
I will sail over with it,
    over ocean and over mountains;
[so] that I will take every shortcut
    to my beloved island.

IM: There you have it. [laughs]
UM: Did you ever hear that?
MB: No.
UM: Well he had [i.e. knew] it anyway.
IM: Och, but I have forgotten it anyway. I don't have the voice today [i.e. anymore].
MB: Oh [you have] a good voice .
UM: He is good at singing, isn't he?
IM: I am leaving [i.e. forgetting] a lot.
TM: When did you make that song?
IM: Oh, I'm sure it was more than twenty years [ago] anyhow, part [of it], yes.[49] Oh that [i.e. making songs] was the only pastime we had.

After two and a half years of service at Corrour, Iain went to "Sgoil na Craoibh'...ann a' Darnaway" ["Forestry School at Darnaway"] in Morayshire (on the river Findhorn, near Forres), where he passed as an Assistant Forester: "Fhuair mi dà chertificate a-mach as." ["I got two certificates out of it."] Following four weeks of lambing in Newtonmore, it was briefly back to forestry work.

IM: But the wages weren't there and the mists were so terrible and ach, I just made off to a contractor

[who] was working on the tars, working on the roads, and water, dams. Well, you were getting more wage there. As long as you were out, you were getting [a] wage [whether] it was wet or dry, but you had to be out.

15. Bidh mi cuimhneachadh 's ag ionndrainn

One night, at the end of a holiday from the forestry, Iain was visiting friends in Uig Hospital, where Isabel Gillies and her friend Màiri Lamont worked.

IM: O-o-o [chuckles], dithis caileagan, uel...bhon ospadal – far a bheil *hostel* agad an-diugh,...bh'e 'na ospadal an uair ud.... Agus bha dithis nighean ann, fhios agad. 'S bha mi falbh go ruige *forestry* làrna-mhàireach. O bha iad ag iarraidh orm, "Ach dèan òran dhomhsa, dèan òran dhomhsa."

"O thalla! O a shíorraidh, chan eil tìd' agam." 'S e *bicycle* a bh'agam an uair sin. Thòisich mi air man do dh'fhalbh mi; dh'fhàg mi ma aon uair deug. Beileag Gillies a bh'ann agus, bha an té eile, chan eil i beò 'n-diugh, Màiri a bh'oirre.... Thòisich mi smaoineachdainn air òran dhaibhse. Nach d'rinn mi 'n gnothach; co-dhiù, chaidh mi sìos an ath oidhche 's ghabh mi e. Dh'fhalbh mi rithist go ruige *forestry* làrna-mhàireach....

Cha d'rinn mi ach siud a dhèanadh ann an cabhag aig an àm.

IM: *O-o-o [chuckles] two girls, well, [I was coming] from the hospital – where you have the hostel today, it was a hospital then. And there were two young women there, you know. And I was going away to the forestry the next day. Oh they were asking me, "Ach, make a song for me, make a song for me."*

"Oh away! Oh eternity, I don't have time." It's a bicycle I had then. I started before I went away; I left about eleven o'clock. Bella Gillies was there and, there was another one, she's not living today, she was Mary. I started thinking of a song for them. Didn't I do it; anyway, I went down the next night and sang it. I went again to the forestry the next day.

I only made something in a hurry at the time.

Isabel was twenty-four at the time and thinks that Iain may have already been called up by the army:

Isabel Ross: Bha mi *nursadh* ann an ospadal – ...bha e an uair ad 'na ospadal *maternity* agus bha seann daoine ann a bharrachd. 'S bhiodh e [Iain] tighinn a dh'amharc air pairt dhe na seann daoine agus bhiodh an còcaire [Màiri Lamont] bh'ann aig an àm nuair a thigeadh e.

So bh'esan a's an arm aig an àm-sa, 's rinn e òran an uair sin dhomh fhìn 's do Mhàiri. Uel tha Màiri marbh an-diugh.

Isabel Ross: *I was nursing in the hospital – it was a maternity hospital at that time and there were pensioners there besides. And he [Iain] used to come to see some of the old folks and the cook [Màiri Lamont] who was there when he came.*

So, he was in the army at that time and then he made the song for myself and for Màiri. Well Màiri's passed away now.

Bidh mi cuimhneachadh 's ag ionndrainn

1. Bidh mi cuimhneachadh 's ag ionndrainn,
   na h-òighean ciùine tha mi fàgail,
   bidh mi cuimhneachadh 's ag ionndrainn.

2. Bidh mi cuimhneachadh nan caileag,
   gur h-e Beileag agus Màiri,
   air an tric a bha mi céilidh;
   's ann bhuap' fhéin a gheibhinn fàilte.
   Bidh mi cuimhneachadh 's ag ionndrainn.

I will be remembering and missing

1. *I will be remembering and missing,*
   the gentle young women whom I am leaving,
   I will be remembering and missing.

2. *I will be remembering the girls,*
   it's Bella and Màiri,
   whom I was frequently visiting;
   it's from themselves I would get a welcome.
   I will be remembering and missing.

5

3. 'S iomadh oidhche chaith mi ùine
   ann an sùgradh 's an ceòl-gàire.
   'N ioghnadh gad a bhithinn tùrsach
   deòir om' shùilean ga ur fàgail?
       Bidh mi...

3. *Many a night I spent some time*
   in sporting and light laughter.
   Is it any wonder though, [that] I would be melancholy   10
   [that there is] a tear from my eyes at leaving you?
       I will...

4. Mholainn Beileag gu sònraicht'
   bha mi eòlach ort 'nad phàisde.
   Chan ionghnadh liom thu bhith cho coibhneil
   's nach robh foill san t-sliochd on d'fhàs thu.
       Bidh mi...

4. *I would praise Bella especially,*
   I knew you [when you were] a child.
   It is no wonder to me that you are so kind
   since there was no deceit in the stock from which you grew. 15
       I will...

5. Chan fhàgainn Màiri air mo chùlaibh,
   bha i biùthaisteach is bàidheil.
   Chan eil aon a chuireas iùil oirr'
   nach toir cliù dhi anns gach àite.
       Bidh mi...

5. *I would not leave Màiri behind me,*
   she was of good renown and affectionate.
   There is not one who makes her acquaintance
   who does not praise her everywhere.
       I will...

6. Soraidh leibh is beannachd dùbailt' –
   gu robh cùisean mar as feàrr dhuibh,
   nuair a thilleas mi do dh'Ùige,
   tha mi'n dùil gu faic mi slàn sibh.
       Bidh mi...

6. *A farewell to you and a twofold blessing –*   20
   may things be as is best for you [and]
   when I return to Uig,
   I hope that I will see you both well.
       I will...

IM: Aye there was one or two verses [more], but I forgot them all. I can't get them, no, no. Ach that was enough anyhow. That's all they'd sing at a concert anyhow,...aye.

CALLED UP FOR THE SIX-WEEK WAR

MacNeacail was still working in Dalwhinnie for Balfour-Beatty when he was called up by the army in 1939, and, like many contemporaries, he did not feel that a war would last long.

IM: I could have been exempted if I had stopped [i.e. stayed] in the forestry, but I went to Balfour and Beatty.... They got me there. But...there was a man from Kingussie saying, "I'll exempt you yet.... I'll keep you out if you want to come...." But I thought, you know, the war was only going to last but five or six weeks or months at the time. Well it lasted six or seven years! So that's how they got me.

   But I could have been exempted [if] I wanted to, but I didn't [do it]. Ach well, I got out of it anyhow. That's how it was.

Back in MacNeacail's sitting-room, Margaret drew Iain's attention to a portrait of himself in uniform on a corner table. "Aye, it wasn't me that put it there. I told [Màiri to] put it in the fire.... Aye, aye. Oh I didn't want to mention that was there."

IM: O tràill obrach! [Oh *slave work!*]

MB: Was it awful?

IM: Awful? I wouldn't mind if I knew who I was speaking to but, "You're not here to think" and "We're here to think for you" and they couldn't think for themselves!

   Iain joined the *Royal Scots Fusiliers* and was sent for training on Ayr race course. Living conditions were, if anything, worse than in the mists of Corrour.

IM: I gave more, better food to my *dog* than I got there many a time. Oh we got pudding, potatoes, cabbages, everything mashed same as you would make a dog's breakfast. Mmhm, och I couldn't take it, there was sand and things like that in it, you know. It wasn't properly cleaned. Ah, I dumped it. "What," he says, "are you doing there? You're dumping good food,...when people is starving in other countries and here too!"

"I'm dumping nothing," I says. "It wasn't fit for anybody, not for a dog!"

Though the men were "not allowed to think for themselves," some were more independent than others.

IM: Many's the thing I got into hot water over...in the army. Ach, I was there one time and myself and an English fellow used to go out together and we had to sign out when we went out...and were signed to come in at twelve o'clock. [You couldn't stay later] unless you had a special pass.

The lads missed the deadline and earned a reprimand from the Camp Commandant.

Sometime later, when on regular sentry duty, MacNeacail routinely questioned a man's identity not knowing it was Drill Sergeant Owen. Owen promptly reported the Sgiobair for "molesting an officer" and he was brought up on charges of insubordination. They were quickly dropped, however, upon review by the Commandant, who decided that Skyemen simply "take a lot to do with other people's affairs."

IM: [*Heatedly*] Well, when I got out [from the Commandant's office], I cracked my fingers to [Owen]: "Come on now," I says to him, "you'll get plenty...out of it!" But he went to the Regimental Sergeant Major, [and] complained about me.

[The Sergeant Major] said to me, "Well Private Nicolson, I hear a lot of complaints about you with those people on sentry, that you molest them."

"I've done nothing of the kind Sir in any way."

"Well you know what [the punishment] is if you incite a mutiny?" he says.

"Oh, to be shot."

"Yes," he says [*as MacNeacail laughs*], "and take care!"

The Sergeant Major evidently did not take Owen's accusations very seriously, but MacNeacail does say quite gleefully, "I made myself a nuisance there. And there was a Welsh sergeant there [i.e. Owen], ach he was quite delighted."

MacNeacail eventually got some respite from the discipline of camp life when he was allowed to do some gardening on his leave days for Major Struthers in Glasgow.

IM: I went there to do the gardening for him.... And he had a wee daughter like that [*holds his hand to the height of a small girl, c. 1m.*] and oh, she used to come and play with me and things like that and be working in the garden, and I'd [be] showing her flowers.... And the Major's wife would come up and tell me to come up for a meal; I got my dinner, I got my tea at night, [and that] compared to what you would get in the camp!

When I went there [on my leave days,] he'd send me three pounds. I used to do the garden and things like that. Och and who came up [one day] but the Welsh officer [Owen, who had been] telling me to shut up.... However, I got this one [i.e. won this round]. "Look what the Major gave me now!" [*holds out his hand as if showing the money*] They never went near me anymore, [or] preferred charges or anything. They wouldn't do it you know, because I would have got away with it [with the backing of Major Struthers].

17. Iain in Swansea, awaiting posting overseas, ca. 1940. (MacNeacail collection)

16. Nochd gur luaineach mo chadal

After three months' training in Ayr, MacNeacail's battalion was sent to Europe. "Oh yes, I was in Germany, Italy and Brussels, Belgium and France," he says, his voice tinged with sadness. Those were "wasted, wasted years." He does not talk about them with ease, as he was in the thick of the conflict with the Fusiliers in his five and half years in the army.

There was little time for reflection and few fellow Gaels with whom to share a song. As a result, the war was not a productive period for MacNeacail where composition is concerned. "It's after I came back again I thought of them; there was nobody there." Fortunately though, we have one song that he did make: the moving *Nochd gur luaineach mo chadal* which describes the magnitude of the tragedy that was engulfing Europe and the world from the point of view of a soldier far from home.

IM: Ach I was just lying in the bunk there and on the ground there...many a time they'd plant us in the mud, you know, to keep the cows right out of it!

If the living conditions were hard, the combat was far worse. When I asked if he saw action, Iain replied sharply,

IM: Oh! [*pauses*] I don't talk about it. Did I not sing you the song, at all?

TM: No.

IM: Mm. Ah hah. [*sighs, tiredly*] Oh ho.

For him, the song says it all, and indeed it does:

IM: "Nochd gur luaineach mo chadal, fliuch fuar tha mo leabaidh...gun fhasgadh"...without a shelter on a field in France. Mhm. "'S gach cunnart is gàbhadh o tha mi a' tàrsainn bidh 'nam chuimhne go bràth fad bhios tàlant 'nam cheann." "As long as there will be talents in my head I will remember it!" That was the meaning of it, ach aye. You had to do something....

TM: What was happening...when you made that?

IM: Och, just bombing and planes coming down and from the skies...aeroplanes bombing here and bombing there, oh!... The way the blast came, you know, it would miss you and [cause] destruction up there. The walled huts were [blown] to the ground and you were only about ten yards away, but the way the blast went it just took a sweep and you were safe enough here. Strange,...how the blast goes like that. Oh it was terrific [i.e. filled with terror].

Nochd gur luaineach mo chadal

1. Nochd gur luaineach mo chadal,
   fliuch fuar tha .no leabaidh,
   's mi 'nam shìneadh gun fhasgadh
      air achadh na Fraing.
   Gach cunnart is gàbhadh
   om bheil mi a' tàrsainn
   bidh 'nam chuimhne gu bràth
      fad bhios tàlant 'nam cheann.

2. Mìle mallachd don Ghearmailt
   dhùisg an cogadh le farmad,
   nach déid leinn air dearmad
      gun bhith searbh dhaibh a réir
   'son na mìltean a mharbhadh

Tonight how restless my sleeping

1. *Tonight how restless my sleep,*
   wet, cold is my bed
   and me stretched out without shelter
      on a field of France.
   Every danger and peril   5
   from which I escape
   will be in my memory forever
      as long as there is sense in my head.

2. *A thousand curses to Germany*
   which awakened the war with envy,   10
   that we will not forget
      without being bitter to them according[ly]
   because of the thousands who were killed

de ar n-òigrigh bu chalma
    's bailtean móra bha dealbhach
        chaidh a spealgadh 's a chéil'.

3. 'S ann a thòisicheadh còmhraig
    ag iarraidh go Pòland
        'n dùil gu faigheadh iad còir
            na Roinn Eòrpa gu léir.
    'S gach rìoghachd 'nan crìochan
    gun dug iad gu strìochdadh,
        cur dhaoin' ann an iarainn
            's gam pianadh gu geur.

4. Gu bheil innealan sgriosail
    tigh'nn 's na speuran gun fhios oirnn
        air an talamh toirt clisgeadh
            's a bristeadh o chéil'.
    Longaibh adhair mar dhruidean
    feadh na h-iarmailt air uidil,
        's gu bheil deatach bho ghunna
            cur a dubhar air gréin.

5. Ach bròn de gach sealladh
    faicinn òigridh ga sgathadh,
        's iad leònt' air gach machair
            a' sileadh fon creuchd.
    Na raointean tha dathte
    le fuil chraobhach nan gaisgeach
        nach tilleadh le athadh
            ach chaidh gaisgeil san t-sreup.

6. Gu bheil móran rinn falbh dhiubh
    a Ghàidhealtachd Alba;
        b'iad taghadh ar n-armailt
            's a dhearbh e 'nan euchd.
    Ar nàimhdean bu gharga
    gun chuir iad gu farbhas;
        chaidh an sgapadh mar mheanbh-spréidh
            feadh gharbhlach an t-sléibh'.

7. Ach thoir beannachd go m' mhàthair
    's do luchd-eòlais 's do m' chàirdean,
        's dèan inns' dhaibh gur slàn mi
            gad is ànrach mo cheum,
    gun till mi rithist sàbhailt'
    nuair théid crìoch air na blàran,
        's a bhios sìth dhuinn air fhàgail
            's do gach àl thig 'nar déidh.

of our bravest youth
and towns that were picturesque;   15
    they were shattered asunder.

3. Hostilities were begun
[with their] moving toward Poland
in hope that they would get possession
    of the whole of Europe.   20
Every kingdom in their territories
they caused [them] to yield,
putting men in irons
    and cruelly torturing them.

4. O destructive machines are   25
coming at us from the skies without warning
making the earth shake
    and break apart.
Aircraft like starlings
through the sky flitting about   30
and the pall of gunsmoke is
    putting its darkness on the sun.

5. But the saddest of all sights
[is] seeing youth being destroyed,
and they wounded on every field   35
    bleeding freely from their wounds.
The plains are coloured
with the spreading blood of the heroes
who would not return with fear
    but who went heroically in the strife.   40

6. There are many of them who departed
from the Highlands of Scotland;
they were the pick of our army
    and [the ones] who proved it in their deeds.
Our fiercest enemies   45
they drove [them] headlong;
they were scattered like young cattle
    over the rough-ground of the moor.

7. But take a blessing to my mother
and to acquaintances and to my relatives   50
and tell them that I am well
    though wandering and weather-beaten is my step,
and that I will return again safely
when the battles are ended,
and peace will be left for us   55
    and for every generation that will come after us.

IM: Sin agad e. [*There you have it.*]

TM: Math dha-rìribh. [*Very good indeed.*]

IM: Well what was strange, I sent that away on a record. I composed it in Belgium again;[50] it landed in Glasgow in bits.

    I put [i.e. sent] them to Glasgow. My sister was there and she got it. Well…her son [William Grant] was a telephone engineer and he got the bits, put them together, bound them with Seccotine[51]…and they got the result…although there was a 'trak, trak'.

    Aye, but they got the results, aye. I beat the censor because they couldn't understand the words!… So the best thing [they could do, since] they didn't understand the Gàidhlig, you know, [was to] break it! Well that's what they did! Well I got it through, just the same. [*laughs*]

Iain is now a little unsure of the optimism expressed in the last verse of the song: "Aah, well I don't know what will happen again, if the next World War is coming, if it will." Many island communities have been changed forever by the loss of two generations, particularly as the Highlands had already suffered from emigration to the industrialised South and overseas and could ill afford further depletion.

Having the rhetorical package of the song as a point of discussion enabled me to elicit more specific information about MacNeacail's wartime experiences than would otherwise have been possible. The poetry serves as an entry point for both of us into areas of memory that are difficult to access.

Iain described another frightening incident while his battalion was encamped "near Paris somewhere":

IM: I was ten minutes after leaving the big mansion they had for the Colonels and Majors and everybody that was there…. I was just come down about fifty yards from there, this bomb came and demolished the whole building, I was there. There was thirty-three in it in all and what I was regretting, a wee toddle of a girl, oh she was lovely. I was going on the back with her;[52]…she was got among them. Oh, how my heart was sore when I heard that. All was dead there…. Might have been me. Oh, it was terrible, and it was only a few yards from our other place, but it got a direct hit.

At this point in our conversation Iain's wife Màiri approached to put another shovel-full of coal on the glowing fire. The Sgiobair moved the microphone stand and his warmly slippered feet to make room for her to pass and concluded, "That's how it was. You had to take it."

The soldiers never knew where they would be next, how quickly they would have to move there or what conditions would prevail. A sodden field in France was much the same as any other.

IM: Ach, again in Holland I was there. Och I've been there putting up [my tent] in the mud, you know. Oh everything was mud, [I was] putting branches to put my ground sheet on, [*laughs*] you would sink in the mud just the same! You would wrench [i.e. wring] your blankets at times. Wet? Augh! I don't know how people existed at all. But I've seen them there, going away and never came back again…. They just, well they just, perished. [*speaking quietly*]

Chapter Two

NUAIR A THILLEAS MI DO DH'UIGE – WHEN I RETURN TO UIG

HOME TO SKYE

After his discharge in 1945, Iain moved back to Glenconon for a time, where he shared work on the family croft with his brother. "Alec...was needing a horse to go along with his own to put out the potatoes", so Iain went to Cuidreach House, near Earlish, to ask Mrs. Ferguson, the then owner, for the loan of a horse. "'Oh' she says, 'I have only one horse, she says, but you can have it till you get your work done, because I'll be taken over to Talisker.'" Her brother, who lived in Talisker, had just died and left her his house.

IM: Of course she belonged to Talisker. At one time she had, I think, ten shepherds and [I don't know] how many people working the land.... But then...her husband died, she was only married four years (and she was a Cameron too by name).

But you know she was rather swell-headed and she wanted to thrive and be good [i.e. successful] and she took Linicro, Kilvaxter, Mogastad and Sgudiborg and all these places. Well, that was beyond him.... He hadn't got the money, but she wanted to do it. Well, I understand when he died he was nine hundred pounds in debt over the transactions he was making.... You know she was demanding this and demanding that, but he wasn't capable to it; he hadn't got the money to cover it.... Well, I understand anyhow, nineteen-ten or nineteen-nine, when he died,...they sold out Lìonacro and Mogastad and [?]Sgudiborg and he cleared [the estate].

Well,...Linicro was broken and Glenconon, in the same years [1910] and they was split up for crofting. That was the way [it worked] then and everybody was crofting down there.... Well, the crofts are now going derelict.... [People] are coming from England [and] everywhere now to to take up these places. To see a house empty is kind of a miserable sight.... That one on that side there [is empty] and up here too. [*gestures to croft sites around his present home in Cuidreach*]

Iain got the loan of the horse.

IM: "[Now] how much do I have to give you in satisfaction [i.e. payment]," I says.

"Well," she says "you could give me twenty days [of work for] twenty days of the mare and that'll square it up...." She wasn't very generous at all, you know.

Nevertheless, she was held in some affection by the locals and she threw a regular New Year's party in Cuidreach House.[53]

17. Lìon a-mach go bàrr na cuachan

IM: Oh aye, that's the one I made for Mrs. Ferguson who was up here [in the big house].

TM: Ah hah. Did she have any Gàidhlig?

IM: Yes, plenty, but she would never speak it. But she would say, "I hate these English songs. I prefer the Gàidhlig every time."... She had a gramophone and she used to give a party every New Year here, but...the party stopped at last, you know, and she says, "I've been rather poor, getting poor now," she says, "I can't afford to give it". I think they were dancing and they were breaking the...flax [in her carpets], you know dancing and all that...and she told them to put on soft boots. That was enough, you know, to tell them what they were doing, and she stopped it.

But I, myself and another, John Cameron (she was a Cameron herself to name, before she got married) and a Dugald MacLean, she would take us over at New Year, or three days after that or before that, to give us our New Year there and we'd be there till twelve o'clock and [she'd be] giving us drams and all that. That was the finish of us then [i.e. the end of the parties there].

18. Iain on the moor above Cuidreach House, probably in the 1950s. He is lifting the turf off the peat bank with a caibe-làir [flauchter spade] in preparation for cutting the peats themselves. (MacNeacail collection)

Lìon a-mach go bàrr na cuachan

1. Lìon a-mach go bàrr na cuachan!
   Òlaidh sinn deoch-slàint' an uasail:
   Bean na Cuidirich a chuir uaill oirnn,
       's lìonmhor uair nach gabh dhuinn cainnt.

2. 'S i 'n fhine Chamshronach gun mhòrchuis
   cùl-taic na Gàidhealtachd 'sa chòmhraig
   thug na naimhdean uil' go stòl
       a dh'aindeoin seòl sna bhuail ad lann.

3. Thug i 'm bliadhn' dhuinn cuirm bha sònraicht',
   bha de shòlas de gach seòrs' ann:
   cluich 's a' dannsa, gabhail òrain,
       's cha robh sòradh ann dhen dram.

4. Bha stuth Thalasgair a b'fheàrr ann
   'n tìr ar dùthchannan chaidh àrcadh.
   Fhuair sinn dheth gu robh sinn sàsaicht'
       cha deach ar tàlant leis a chall.

5. 'S e deoch cho sèimh 's cho blasd' 's a dh'òladh:
   chuireadh sogan air an òigridh,
   bheireadh seann duine go còmhradh
       gad a bhiodh a threòir car fann.

6. Cha robh mìothlachd measg a' chòmhlain,
   'n cridhe mireadh 's iad cho stòlda,
   h-uile nì cho math an òrdugh,
       mar a dh'òrdaich i gun mheang.

7. Bheir sinn taing dhi anns a' Ghàidhlig,
   h-uile beannachd bhith 'na fàrdaich,
   gach Bliadhna Ur a bhith mar bha sinn,
       is an àireamh dhinn bhith ann.

8. Lìon a-mach gu bàrr na cuachan!
   Olaidh sinn deoch-slàint' an uasail:
   Bean na Cuidirich a chuir uaill oirnn,
       's lìonmhór uair nach gabh dhuinn cainnt.

Fill up the quaichs to the top

1. Fill up the quaichs to the top!
   We will drink the health of the noble one:
   the woman of Cuidreach [House] who made us proud
       more times than we can say.

2. *The unassuming Cameron clan is*   5
   the support of the Highlands in the struggle
   [that] brought the enemies all to order
       whatever way they wielded a blade.

3. She brought the year [in] for us [with] a special feast,
   there was good cheer of every kind there: 10
   playing and dancing, singing songs
       and there was no grudging of drams.

4. The best Talisker stuff was there
   in the district of our lands it was corked.
   We drank of it until we were satisfied   15
       [but] we didn't lose our senses from it.

5. It's a drink as gentle and as flavourful as has [ever] been
   drunk:
   that would put the youths in good humour,
   [and] that would make an old man [take] to conversing,
       even if his strength were a bit weak.   20

6. There was no discord in the company,
   their heart[s] playful and they so well behaved,
   everything so well in order,
       faultlessly as she decreed.

7. *We will give thanks to her in Gaelic:*   25
   every blessing be in her home,
   every New Year be [with us] like we were [that year]
       and the [same] number of us be there.

8. Fill up the quaichs to the top!
   We will drink the health of the noble one: 30
   the woman of Cuidreach [House] who made us proud
       more times than we can say.

18. Spògan circeadh

One New Year, Iain received a curious parcel in the post: two chicken feet. He knew immediately that it was the maids at Cuidreach House who were responsible.

TM: Cuin a rinn sibh sin?

IM: *...Tha mi cinnteach [o chionn] leth-cheud bliadhna, [nu]air a bha na h-ighnean a's a' taighe-mhór, bha barrachd air sin. Uel, [thàinig] spògan na circeadh gam ionnsaigh aig a' Bhliadhn' Uir, fhios agads'. Agus cha robh fhios a'm có bhuaithe. Bha postmark air bho thimcheall à's an dùthaich. Thuig mise math gu leòr gura h-iad a rinn e. Sin agad e.

TM: *When did you make that?*

IM: *Fifty years ago, I'm sure, when the girls were in the big house, more than that. Well, the chicken feet came to me at New Year's, you know. And I didn't know who it was from. There was a postmark on it from somewhere in the country. I understood well enough that it was they that did it.*

Spògan circeadh

1. 'S ochoin a Rìgh,
     gur h-e mi bhios muladach
   ma théid mi dh'innse
     gach nì a chunnaic mi.
   Gad a rinn sibh fòirneart,
     an dòigh nach tuigeadh sibh e,
   dhearbh ur còmhradh
     's na spògan circeadh e.

2. Gad rinn mi 'n duan dhuibh,
     chan fhuath liom idir sibh
   on dh'fhalbh a' fuachd
     agus cruas mo thrioblaidean.
   Gu sìn an samhradh
     gun chall sa fhreasdail dhomh;
   gu bheil mi taingeil:
     thug ainneart leasan dhomh.

Chicken's claws

1. *Oh Lord,*
     how mournful I shall be
   if I tell [you]
     everything I saw.
   Though you did violence,   5
     in a way you wouldn't understand,
   your conversation proved
     and the chicken's claws proved it [i.e. your complicity].

2. *Though I have made this poem,*
     I don't dislike you at all   10
   since the chill
     and the hardness of my troubles has gone away.
   The summer shall begin,
     touch wood, without loss;
   I am thankful: 15
     the suffering taught me a lesson.

IM: Och, cha robh càil...den t-seòrs' sin, [ach] spòrs ann.... Cha robh ad ag innse có bhuaithe a bha ad, och...fhuair [mi] a-mach có bh'ann, fhios agad.

IM: *Och, there wasn't anything of that kind [i.e. malice], just fun. They weren't telling me who they were from, but I found out who it was, you know.*

Isabel Ross tells me that this was a regular trick: at Hogmanay you would maybe kill a few hens and send them to Glasgow to friends. Then you would send the *spògan circeadh* [chicken's claws] to someone for a laugh. Apparently, Iain was not fooled for a minute and sang the song at a local concert soon afterwards. Here is a couplet, as Isabel remembered it:

IR: 'S e Santa Claus a rinn an fhòirneart uile orm
     's a thug na spògan far eòin na Cuidirich.

IR: *It's Santa Claus who did all the violence to me*
     and who took the feet from the Cuidreach fowl.

Mrs. Ferguson would like to have kept Cuidreach House, but according to Iain,

IM: She couldn't get people to work for the garden and working out girls, you know, after the war. They wouldn't look at her wage of nine pounds a half year. [There] was no money at all for them, so she couldn't get anybody [and had to give up the house].

MacNeacail then had a chance to buy Cuidreach House and the hundred and fifty acre steadings with it for three thousand pounds. Unfortunately, that sum was beyond his resources at the time and the house was sold to two cousins, Miss Dorothea Mann and Miss Jennifer Mabel Anderson (a solicitor) for £3700.

19. A Mhàiri, a Mhàiri

At this time Iain was courting Mary Munro of Gleann Hìonasdail, seventeen years younger than himself.

IM: Bheir mi dhut òran a rinn mi dhan a' bhean,...Màiri, mun do phòs mi. [*I will give you a song I made to the wife, Mary, before I married.*]

TM: After the War then.

IM: Oh aye, oh I was home here anyhow. Mhm.

A Mhàiri, a Mhàiri

1. A Mhàiri, a Mhàiri,
      tha mo ghràdh ort is bidh;
   tha mo smuaintinn gach là ort
      nuair a tha mi liom fhìn.
   Tha mo ghaol ort, chan fhàilnig;
      chan àicheidh mi chaoidh
   gu bheil t' ìomhaigh is t' àilleachd
      gach là tighinn 'nam shùim.

2. Có an neach a chì t' aodann
      nach cuir aonta ri m' sgeul?
   Chan eil coir' ort ri àireamh
      ann an nàdar na 'm beus.
   Tha do chaomh-shlios mar eala
      no mar chanach an t-sléibh',
   pearsa dhìreach gun fhuarachd,
      gur uallach do cheum.

3. 'S iomadh aon do nach eòl thu
      bhios a' feòrach có thu,
   leis a' loinn tha gad chòmhdach
      ann am bòidhchead 's an cliù.
   D'aghaidh shìobhalt' cho nàrach,
      's tu 'nad nàdar cho ciùin —
   cha cheil mi air chàch,
      nach tu 's feàrr liom tha 'n Uig'.

Oh Mary, oh Mary

1. O Mary, o Mary,
      I love you and always will;
   my thoughts dwell upon you every day
      when I am by myself.
   My love is for you, [it] will not abate;   5
      I will never deny
   that your image and your beauty
      come into my mind every day.

2. What person who sees your face
      will not agree with my tale?   10
   You have no fault[s] to be enumerated
      in nature or in deed.
   Your gentle form is like a swan
      or like the mountain cotton-grass,
   an upright figure without coldness,   15
      graceful is your step.

3. Many a one who doesn't know you
      asks who you are,
   because of the distinction that surrounds you
      in beauty and in reputation.   20
   Your peaceful face so modest
      and you in your nature so gentle —
   I will not conceal from others,
      that it is you I like best in Uig.

19. Màiri Munro, ca. 1945, before her marriage to Iain. (MacNeacail collection)

4. Ach na faighinn mar 's deòin liom,
   gheibhinn còir ort dhomh féin.
'S mi gun dèanadh do phòsadh,
   chailin òg tha gun bheud.
'S tu a dhùisgeadh mo shòlas
   le bhith 'n còmhnaidh riut réidh:
blas na mil air do phògan
   bho bheul òg an deagh sgéil.

5. Bidh mi niste co-dhùnadh
   leis an dùrachd as feàrr
gu faigh mi, a rùin, thu
   le cùmhnantan gràidh,
is nach cuir thu do chùl rium,
   is nach diùlt thu dhomh d' làmh,
bho'n is tusa mo cheud ghaol;
   cha bhi té eile 'nad àit'.

6. A Mhàiri, a Mhàiri,
   tha mo ghràdh ort is bidh;
tha mo smuaintinn gach là ort
   nuair a tha mi liom fhìn.
Tha mo ghaol ort, chan fhàilnig;
   chan àicheidh mi chaoidh
gu bheil t' ìomhaigh is t' àilleachd
   gach là tighinn 'nam shùim.

4. But if I were to get as I desire,   25
   I would get a right to you for myself.
It's I who would marry you,
   oh young maid without defect.
It's you who'd awaken my joy
   by being always together with you,   30
the taste of honey on your kisses
   from the young mouth of the good story.

5. I will be concluding now,
   with the best wish
that I will get you, oh dearest,   35
   with pledges of love,
and that you will not turn your back on me,
   and you will not refuse me,
since you are my first love;
   there will not be another one in your place.   40

6. O Mary, o Mary,
   I love you and always will;
my thoughts dwell upon you every day
   when I am by myself.
My love is for you, [it] will not abate;   45
   I will never deny
that your image and your beauty
   come into my mind every day.

On November 20th, 1947, they were married in Portree, with a reception following at the Royal Hotel.

IM: Oh-h, there would be a hundred [there] anyhow, oh there would be, in Portree. Of course,...I butchered two sheep myself and put them up to the hotel because you wouldn't [i.e. couldn't] get meat at that time. But I had the sheep here, you know, and on the quiet [the sheep] went up there and they cooked them there [with] whatever they had over and above that.

TM: And that was the same day as the Queen got married, right?

IM: Aye, right! Aye, aye, the 20th of November. And the doctor and these people, aye, oh aye, [we had] plenty of a reception. But things wasn't so easy got then as it is now. The drinks were scarce at times. But I got so much [i.e. a certain amount], you know, on the quiet. Mm.

Oh yes, I had an anniversary here three or four years ago [in 1987], in Portree [laughs]. The boys [and] the girls faces! I was there, just the same. Well, it was all right [i.e. he enjoyed it].

TM: And I assume Màiri came along as well!

IM: Oh aye, aye, she was, oh she was; she would need to be....

TM: Were there a lot of Uig people at the [party]?

IM: Oh yes, quite a lot, yes. Well of Glenconon and...Earlish and Gleann Hìonasdail. Oh yes...we got plenty of telegrams and things like that, heaps of them there.

Shortly after their marriage, Miss Mann offered Iain and Màiri accommodation as caretakers of Cuidreach House itself.

20. Miss Dorothy Mann with her brother Col. Mann and their mother. Miss Mann, who lives in Oban today, owned Cuidreach House with her cousin Miss Anderson, a solicitor. Iain's and Màiri's second youngest daughter, Jenny Mabel, is named after Miss Anderson. (MacNeacail collection)

IM: "Oh yes," she says, "because we're away all the year round except for a few months [when] we'll be coming to the fishing of the Storr Lochs. So you can have the big house." So I had the big house and she was giving us rations sent down by the bus every weekend, our food. And she was giving [us] three pound a week, but I had to not rest, you know, on the stock [i.e. I had to work with the stock]; I bought the stock of Mrs. Ferguson. And I had the stock with...no expenses, there was no rent or anything.... So I stopped there three or four years in the big house. And I was well off there, you know, and I [had] no expenses, nothing at all, not for soup or anything you got. It was there and everything you wanted, and coals and all....

Well I went wrong, you know.... I should have taken the big house [*slaps hand on table*] when it went for three thousand! Because the man who got it, you know, he got it for that! [*snaps finger, i.e. for nothing*]... Well, he sold it for...twenty-eight thousand...three or four years after that.

TM: It must be worth much more than that now.

IM: Och yes! That's it, but there's no land with it now. That would be a stumbling block for the man that would take it, if he wanted land. They would have land anyhow, [unless] they wanted a [large] tract of it along with it.

When Miss Mann and Miss Anderson sold the big house, they offered the MacNeacails the Cuidreach House stables for conversion into a dwelling and it is there that Iain and Màiri have spent nearly fifty years.

It is here also that Iain composed a good number of songs.

20. Chaoidh cha phòs mi, tha mi 'n dùil

This song could easily have been made between the wars, as it was shortly after the First World War that bobbed hair made its first appearances in the Highlands. It was only after the Second World War, however, that it really began to catch on. Before then, it was customary for single women to wear their hair long and loose and for married women's to be worn tied up. It is also the norm for women to cover their heads in church in the Highlands.

I am very grateful to the late Murdo Stewart for remembering the first couplet of this song, which instantly triggered Iain's memory.

IM: [Nu]air a thàinig am *bob hair* a-mach,...bha a h-uile duin' a bh'ann a' bruidhinn 's a' càineadh na nigheanan, fios agad, gun do gheàrr ad a' falt diubh. Bha ad an toiseach suas go guaillean, uel nuair a thàinig am *bob hair* a-mach, chaidh a ghearradh suas mun a' chluais agus sin mar a thòisich mise...dèanamh an òrain.

IM: *When the bobbed hair came out, everyone was discussing and criticising the girls, you know, that they cut their hair off. They were at first down to the shoulders, well when the bobbed hair came in, it was cut up around the ear and that's how I started making the song.*

Chaoidh cha phòs mi, tha mi 'n dùil

1. Chaoidh cha phòs mi, tha mi 'n dùil;
   cha chuir mi m' ùidh sna caileagan:
   cha taitneach liom a' fasan ùr;
   cha diù liom e 's chan annas liom.

2. Gun d'rinn a' phròis dhiubh culaidh-bhròin,
   cha bhòidheach leat sealladh dhiubh:
   an cuailean chleachd a bhith 'na dhuail
   man cluasan tha e barraichte.

3. 'S ann a chì thu iad air sràid,
   gach té air fàs cho fearail dhiubh:
   an ceann cho maol ri mulchag chàis'
   gun nì cur sgàil air earrann dhiubh.

4. Gun d'dh'inns' am fàidh dhuinn o chian
   gur h-e mì-rian nan caileagan
   a chuireadh air an t-saoghal crìoch –
   's e sgeul tha fìor a dh'aithris e.

5. Ach a' seanfhacal seo nì mi inns' –
   feuch an tog e prìs nan caileagan –
   gur feàrr dhaibh a bhith a dhìth a' chinn
   's gach té bhith às an fhasan dhiubh.

I will never marry, I hope

1. *I will never marry, I hope;*
   I will never take an interest in the lasses:
   the new fashions do not please me;
   I don't care [for] it and [it] is no surprise to me.

2. *Their vanity has made them objects of pity,*   5
   you do not like their appearance:
   the curl that used to be plaited
   is cropped about the ears.

3. *You see them on the street,*
   each one of them becoming so masculine: 10
   their head as bald as a kebbuck cheese
   without anything at all covering some of them.

4. *The prophet told us long since*
   that it's the impropriety of the lasses
   that will bring the world to an end –   15
   it's a true tale he said.

5. *But this proverb I will tell you –*
   to try to raise their self-esteem –
   that they prefer to be without the head,
   every one of them, [than] to be out of fashion.   20

IM: They're better without the head to be in the fashion, you know?

21. Nach bòidheach Uige

This is another song, in a more serious vein, that could have been made either side of the war. In describing Uig in such loving detail, Iain demonstrates a bard's sense of place perfectly.

Nach bòidheach Uige

1. Nach bòidheach Ùige
      gur h-e tha cùbhraidh,
   le choille dhlùth-ghorm
      fo dhrùchd a' Chéitein,
   le eòin cho sùrdail
      a' seinn gun tùchadh
   's gach seòrsa ciùil ac'
      air bhàrr nan geugan.

2. 'S tha bheanntan àghmhor
      mun iadh an sàile
   ri cumail sgàil
      air gach àird bho séid gaoth.
   Tha fiamhan gràsail
      ri geamhradh geàrrt' ann
   tha gach lus a' fàs ann
      ri blàths na gréine.

3. Gu bileach snuadhmhor
      gach glac is bruachag
   le neòinein ghuanach
      's an tuar cho èibhinn.
   Ann an cois gach fuaran
      tha 'm biolair uaine
   's tha bada luachrach
      ri bruach gach féithe.

4. Tha dealbh a thràghad
      mar lorg a' chapaill;
   tha 'n cuan gu sàmhach
      cur àilleachd féin air.
   Gach allt gu siùbhlach
      a' ruith an cùrsa
   'n teis-meadhan ùrlar
      a' dol 'na chéile.

5. Tha chreagan uaibhreach
      mar bhalla suas ris
   ri freagairt nuallan
      nan tonnan beucach;
   thaobh obair nàdair
      chan fhaicear àicheadh
   gur àit' as àille
      'sa chruinne-ché e.

How beautiful Uig is

1. How beautiful Uig is;
      it is fragrant,
   with its dense verdant greenwood
      under the May dew,
   with birds so spirited   5
      singing without hoarseness,
   and they have every sort of music
      atop the branches.

2. *And its glorious mountains,*
      which the sea encircles,   10
   keep every place sheltered,
      whatever direction the wind blows from.
   There's a delicate touch of the sun
      during bitter winter,
   every plant is growing there   15
      with the heat of the sun.

3. *How beautifully verdant*
      every hollow and little bank
   with nodding daisies
      so delightful in their hue.   20
   At the foot of every spring
      are the green cresses
   and tufts of rushes are
      on the bank of every channel.

4. *The shape of its seashore is*   25
      like the [hoof]print of the mare;
   the sea is quietly
      putting its own beauty on it.
   Every stream wandering,
      running their course,   30
   in the very middle of the valley floor
      going together.

5. *Its proud rocks are*
      like a wall up against it
   to answer the bellowing   35
      of the roaring waves;
   regarding works of nature,
      [you] will not see the like
   it is the most beautiful place
      in creation.   40

6. Tha'n sluagh tha tàmh ann
      gu h-iochdmhor càirdeil,
   ri nochdadh bàidh
      ann an gràdh da chéile.
   Cha sgeul air thuairmeis
      a ta mi luaidh air;
   bidh eachdraidh buan
      fad bhios buar air sléibhtean.

6. *The people who are living there are*
      compassionately tender,
   revealing kindness
      in [their] love for each other.
   This is no unfounded tale   45
      that I am relating about it;
   its fame will live
      as long as cattle are on the moorland.

22. 'Illean, na biodh oirbhse smalan!

IM: O shiorraidh! [*Oh goodness!*]

TM: Now what was this one all about, *'Illean, na biodh oirbhse smalan.*

IM: Aye aye, going to Portree, aye, [to] take a dram...there.... Well, at that time, you know, there was no pubs in Uig then, and if you went up, you went in with some friends and all that....

TM: If you went to a cattle sale.

IM: Aye, then you would come and maybe you got...a bus [home] or something like that when you would come home, you know. Och, the rumours went about, "Oh they were up in Portree and they got drunk last night" and all that, you know. Well, it was a good subject to make a song on then.... And that's how I [did it].[54]

'Illean, na biodh oirbhse smalan

[séisd] 'Illean, na biodh oirbhse smalan,
       idir na biodh oirbhse gruaim,
       mas e nì gun gabh sinn drama,
       's ann uair ainneamh théid sinn suas.

1. Tha gach cailleach as an àite
   'ga ar càineadh feadh na tìr
   bhon a ghabh sinn smùid an ànraidh,
   latha a bha sinn am Port Rìgh.

2. Bidh gach ministear san dùthaich
   bhon a' chùbaid 'g radha rinn
   nach e balaich òg' Uige
   bhrist an cliù an arm a' Rìgh.

3. Their gach bodach as an àite
   gu bheil a' Sàtan air ar cùl,
   gu bheil sinn 'nar n-adhbhar nàire,
   mar a thachair sinn air cùrs'.

4. Sibhse 's motha nì de bhòilich,
   là ur n-òig bu ghòrach sibh.
   Bheil cuimhn' agaibh air bhith sna claisean
   'ga ur dalladh leis a' *spree?*

5. 'S ann their cuid gu bheil sinn cragte,
   's dòch' nach eil ad fada ceàrr;

Lads, do not be gloomy

[chorus] *O lads, do not be gloomy,*
        do not be at all sullen,
        if it be that we take a dram
        it's a rare time we go up [for a drink].

1. *Every old woman in the place*   5
   is slandering us throughout the land
   because we got riotously drunk
   one day that we were in Portree.

2. *Every minister in the country will be*
   saying to us from the pulpit   10
   isn't it the young lads of Uig
   who lost their character in the service of the King.

3. *Every old man in the place will say*
   that Satan is behind us,
   that we are a cause of disgrace   15
   as we happened on [our sinful] course.

4. *Most of you will do your haranguing*
   [about] the day you were foolish, our young men.
   Do you remember being in the ditches
   blinded by the spree?   20

5. *Some will say that we are crazy,*
   maybe they are not far wrong;

21. *Iain and Màiri with Dunnchadh, Mórag, Willie and John Angus at the gable end of the house in Cuidreach,*
ca. 1953. (MacNeacail collection)

| na faiceadh iad na chunnaic sinne, | if they could see what we saw, |
| am biodh iad idir dad na b'fheàrr? | would they be any better at all? |

6. Bheirinn comhairl' air gach cailleach,	6. I would give advice to every old woman	25
air gach bodach as an àit',	[and] to every old man in the place,	
gun iad bhith cruaidh air na balaich	that they be not hard on every boy,	
théid cho daingeann as gach càs.	who goes so bravely into every predicament.	

Verse two is pieced together from several slightly different versions. Iain also gave me an alternate first line for the verse.

IM: Well, there was another verse in it, you know, "Gu bheil ceisteir feadh na dùthcha," all the preachers, you know, feadh na dùthcha, "anns a' chùbaid ag ràdha rinn, nach e balaich òg Uige bhrist an cliù an arm a' Rìgh". [laughs] I put that in it!... As the minister was saying, you know, [they] lost their character in the service of the King.... They were saying that too.

But that was only my own imagination, but that she [i.e. the 'cailleach' in verse one] was there saying it. "Bidh gach ministear san dùthaich bhon a' chùbaid 'g radha rinn from the pulpit, saying to us, our "balaich òg' Uige, bhrist an cliù an arm a' Rìgh". [laughs] Aye. Aye, aye, that's it.

23. Tha sluagh òg air dhol gu aimbeirt (Oran a' veto)

TM: Now, Oran a' veto.

IM: Oh aye!

TM: That was before there were any pubs in Uig?...

IM: Aye, aye, well just they were starting it. They were out...to get the veto, you know.

John Angus MacNeacail: There was pubs in it, but they were trying to do away with it.

TM: Oh I see,...there already were pubs.

IM: They didn't get it sanctioned at all. It was by...the veto that was going to...sanction it [i.e. proscribe licensed pubs and close the ones already there]. "Tha sluagh òg air dhol gu aimbeirt" [reads the song] Sunday will no be with them, sin agad e. [there you have it.]

Tha sluagh òg air dhol gu aimbeirt (Oran a' veto)	**Young people have acted ruinously (The veto song)**	
1. Tha sluagh òg air dhol gu aimbeirt,	1. Young people have acted ruinously,	
tha sluagh òg air dhol gu aimbeirt,	young people have acted ruinously,	
'g iarraidh taighean òil an Uige	seeking drinking houses in Uig	
nì a spùilleadh is an creachadh.	that will spoil and ruin them.	
Tha sluagh òg air dhol gu aimbeirt.	Young people have acted ruinously.	5
2. Gu bheil corr is leth-cheud bliadhna,	2. For more than fifty years,	
bha iad dùinte 's cha robh deur ann.	they were closed and there wasn't a drop.	
'S adhbhar smaoin cho beag 's tha chiall	It is food for thought how little sense is	
aig an iarmaid tha ga thagradh.	in the paltry few who are demanding it.	
Tha sluagh òg...	Young people have...	
3. 'S iomadh mallachd a tha lùb ris,	3. Many's the curse that is involved with it,	10
chì iad sin ann an geàrr-ùine.	they will see that in a short time.	
Dh'inns am ministear bhon chùbaid	The minister reported from the pulpit	

22. Iain with his mother, ca. 1956. With them are two of Iain's and Màiri's children, Mórag and Dunnchadh. The child on the right is a cousin, Kirsty Russell. As can be seen here, the other dormer windows had not yet been added to the house. (MacNeacail collection)

gach mi-chliù aig mac na braiche.
  Tha sluagh òg...

4. Ge b'e dh'òlas dhen an druaip ad
   gos am bi an ceann 'na thuaineal,
   chan eil fàbhar bàidh na truas riuth'
     nuair thig àm go gluasad dhachaigh.
       Tha sluagh òg...

5. Cuid 'na sìneadh dhiubh sna cùiltean,
   cuid 'nan cadal-cha ghabh dùsgadh
   'S ann a dh'fheumas tu an tionndadh
     feuch faic thu a bheil annt' an anail.
       Tha sluagh òg...

6. Nuair a thig orr' oidhche h-Aoine,
   an cuid stòrais théid a sgaoileadh;
   bidh ad gan dalladh leis an daoraich;
     h-iad ga slaodadh anns na claisean.
       Tha sluagh òg...

7. Ged a dh'innsinn pàirt de 'bhuadhan',
   cha bhithinn buileach a' toirt fuath dha;
   nam b'e 's gun gabht' e ann a' stuamachd,
     cha bhithinn cho cruaidh ga chasaid.
       Tha sluagh òg...

8. 'S a' luchd-cuairt a thig don àite
   cha bhi 'n teistneas air mar b'àist daibh,
   faicinn miastadh na deoch làidir
     mar chaidh an t-Sàbaid chur à fasan.
       Tha sluagh òg...

every infamy that the son of malt [i.e. whisky] has.
  Young people have...

4. *Whatever they drink of yon dregs*
   until their head is spinning, 15
   there is no favour of mercy or pity for them
     when the time comes for moving home.
       Young people have...

5. *Some of them stretched out in the corners,*
   some sleeping cannot be wakened.
   You'll need to turn them [over] 20
     to try to see if there is a breath in them.
       Young people have...

6. *When Friday night hits them,*
   all their money will be dispersed;
   they will be blind drunk;
     [and] they dragging themselves along in the ditches. 25
       Young people have...

7. *Though I would recount some of its 'virtues',*
   I wouldn't be taking a total aversion to it;
   if it were taken in moderation,
     I wouldn't be accusing it so firmly.
       Young people have...

8. *And the travellers who come to the place,* 30
   their report of it will not be as it used to be,
   seeing the mischief of strong drink
     and how the Sabbath has been put out of fashion.
       Young people have...

24. Tha mealladh mór am measg an t-sluaigh

One day, after singing several other songs, Iain mentioned the travelling evangelists of the 1950s:

IM: It was pilgrims that were going about here and they were converting everybody.... And you know...the conversion would last about a couple of months and that's about all.... And of course I composed this – there was a fellow in Uig too who was composing a thing and he was praising them and so I got it the other way about. But I didn't refer [to] them personally unless they were that....

IM: Tha ad ann fhathast, feadhainn dhiubh; tha iad a timcheall uaireannan. Chan eil daoin' a' dol 'gan éisdeachd mar a chleachd ad sam bith idir.... O 's dòcha chonvertadh ad aon dusan, fad na seachdain bha iad a' searmonachadh; cha bhiodh iad mìos air falbh [nu]air a bha na daoine cho miosa riutha fhéin, agus sin agad an t-òran a bh' a'amsa.[56]

IM: *They are there still, some of them; they are around sometimes. People aren't going to listen to them as they used to at all. Oh, perhaps they would convert a dozen, all week they were preaching; they wouldn't be away for a month when the people would be as bad as them-selves,[57] and that's the song I had.*

IM: That's how I got at them, I [made] this, you know. Mm.
TM: And they went back to their old ways.

23. *Iain on the road just above the house, ca. 1980.* (MacNeacail collection)

IM: Aye, the old way.... It didn't come from the right spirit, you know. Mhmhmhm [*laughs*],...so that's how I composed this, you know, for them, aye.

Oh well, they're coming every year practically. And there's these Jehovah's Witnesses too, they're just the same, oh. And they come here to your door,...[they] open the Bible and take a verse out of here and there and trying to argue with you, you know. Oh I never have time for them at all, no. [*laughs*]

Tha mealladh mór am measg an t-sluaigh

1. Tha mealladh mór am measg an t-sluaigh
    le luchd-teagaisg thruagh gun éifeachd
   tha dèanamh uaill am briathran fuar
    toirt gràdh do dhuais na h-eucoir.
   Lem beachdan truaillt' a tha gun bhuaidh
    toirt sluagh a-mach 's an Eipheit
   bhith dèanamh bàthadh sa Mhuir Ruaidh
    le anma truagh bheir géill dhaibh.

2. Théid iad don chùbaid air bheag lùths –
    gun 'chùram' na gun ghràs annt',

A great deception is among the people

1. *The people are greatly deceived*
    by pitiable preachers with no real effect,
   who are boasting in cold words,
    giving love as the reward of wrong.
   With their corrupted opinions that are without virtue, 5
    [they are] bringing people out of Egypt
   to make a drowning in the Red Sea
    with [the] pitiful soul[s] who will succumb to them.

2. *They will go to the pulpit with little genuine strength –*
    without 'concern' and without grace in them, 10

ach briathran ciùin a tha gun sùgh
    tha ruith air cùrsa nàdair;
ad fhéin an dùil gu faigh ad cliù
    bhon chuid bheir rùn is àit' dhaibh,
gun aca fhéin ach cridhe cruaidh
    le spiorad suain a' tàmh air.

3. Ged a leughas iad am Bìoball,
    mìnichidh mar 's àill' leo.
Nì iad an t-slighe dhut cho dìreach
    le bhith dol clì san àithnte.
Cha toir iad géill do dh'fhocal Dhè:
    's e 'm beachdan fhéin as feàrr leo;
ma chreideas tu bhuap' brìgh na sgeul,
    gun dèan iad fhéin do thèarnadh.

4. Tha iad coltach ris na h-òighean
    aig robh na lòchrain thràighte
dol an coinneamh an fhir nuadh-phòsd'
    le còt' a' cur na sgàil orra.
Ach chuirear ad taobh a-muigh na còmhla,
    mar gheibh an còrr dhen àireamh,
mur bi aca càil de thròcair,
    na an creideamh beò bh'aig Abram.

5. Len inntinn fheòlmhor tha ad sàsaicht'
    's iad a-ghnàth gun 'chùram',
gun gheilt, gun sgàth orr' ron bhàs
    a ta gach là tighinn dlùth dhaibh.
'S ann their ad fhéin gu bheil ad sàbhailt'
    on tha an cogais mùchte;
cha d'fhuair ad ath-bhreith tro ghràs
    a bheireadh càil go ùmhlachd.

6. Ged fhuair iad gibht is tàlant cinn,
    gu bheil ad gun chridh' gun eòlas
air an fhìrinn a tha sgrìobhte
    a bhios 'na dhìteadh mór dhaibh.
Mas e 's nach creid ad anns a' là
    man téid grian nan gràs fo sgòth orra,
gum bi iad dùinte mach 's an Aros
    tha uile làn de shòlas.

7. Gu bheil an Fhìrinn fhéin ag inns'
    ron chrìch bi iomadh àmhghair,
aig ar dorsan th'e a' bualadh;
    cha tuig an sluagh gun ghràs e
gum bi na daoine taghte fhéin
    dol iomadh ceum air Aros,
ach tuigidh iad ro cheann na réis
    gur e fuil na réit' bheir slàinte.

only gentle words that are without substance
    that are running in the 'natural' course;
they themselves hope that they will get renown
    from those who will give regard and status to them,
without anything themselves but a hard heart   15
    with a dormant spirit dwelling in it.

3. Although they read the Bible,
    they interpret [it] as they wish.
They will make the way [to salvation] so direct for you
    by going wrong in the commandment.   20
They will not obey the word of God;
    it is their own opinions they prefer,
if you believe the substance of the tale from them,
    they themselves will save you.

4. They are like the [foolish] virgins   25
    who had the half-empty lamps
going to meet the the bridegroom
    with a coat shading them.
But they will be put outside the gate [of Heaven]
    like the rest of their number,   30
unless they have an iota of mercy,
    or the living faith that Abraham had.

5. With their carnal minds they are satisfied
    and they [are] ever without 'concern'
without fear [or] dread of death   35
    that is coming near them every day.
They themselves will say that they are saved
    because their conscience is smothered,
[but] they did not get rebirth through [the] grace
    that could bring anything to obedience [to God].   40

6. Although they got a gift and mental powers,
    they are without heart and without knowledge
of the truth that is written [in the Bible]
    which will be a great condemnation for them.
If it is the case that they do not believe it during the day   45
    before the sun of grace goes under a cloud for them,
they will be shut out from the House [of God]
    that is totally full of solace.

7. The Bible itself is telling
    [that] before the end there will be many afflictions,   50
at our doors it is beating;
    [and] the people without grace will not understand it:
that only the Elect will be
    going the many steps towards [the] House;
but they will understand before the end of the race   55
    that it is the blood of atonement that will bring salvation.

TM: That's a good one, I like this one.

IM: Do you? Oh well, I don't know. But...if you were right, it wasn't interfering with you....

TM: So a man like John Stewart wouldn't have been affected.

IM: Oh no! No, I wouldn't think so. He was a...quite a natural man, you know, in the sense of being a true worshipper. Mhm. But as long as they got praise for what they said and all that, and people believed they were so good. But still there was nothing in them. [Just] their own ways, mhm. That's it then.

25. O anma, feuch an dùisg thu

About the same time as the pilgrims were on the go, Iain made this song expressing his own evangelical call.

O anma, feuch an dùisg thu

1. O anma, feuch an dùisg thu,
     's tu dlùth do dhoras bàis,
   is dèan do roghainn dùrachdach
     do Phrionnsa mór na Slàint':
   's E theasraigeas o dhaors' thu
     's E shaoras tu bhon phlàigh';
   's E bheir don ionad naomh sin thu
     far bheil an gaol nach cnàmh.

2. Ta E toirt cuireadh fialaidh dhut thu
     go thighinn o Dhia nan Gràs –
   o'n tà an obair crìochnaichte
     's na fiachan uile pàight' –
   gu saorsainn choisinn Crìosda dhut
     's a thug riarachadh tro' bhàs;
   's a mheud a thig 's a dh'iarras E,
     cha dèan E orra tàir.

3. Ma théid thu chur dàil ann
     gum bi Sàtan air do thòir;
   bidh na h-ana-miannaibh nàdarra
     gad thàladh leis gach sgleò.
   Gabh an cothrom gu bhith sàbhailt'
     ann an gàirdeachas is glòir,
   far nach goid am meàirleach,
     's nach dig nàmhaid air do thòir.

4. Cha ghabh e cur am briathran
     meud na diamhaireachd a ta
   co-cheangailt' ris an ullachadh
     bha am fulangas A bhàis.
   Gun ghiùlain E ar n-euceart,
     chaidh A cheusadh air ar sgàth
   's gun d'rinn E sìth is réite
     's tro A chreuchdan thug E slàint'.

Oh soul, make sure you awaken

1. Oh soul, make sure you awaken,
     since you [are] close to death's door,
   and make an earnest choice
     [to follow] the great Prince of Life:
   it's He [who] will deliver you from slavery   5
     and He [that] will free you from plague
   and He [who] will take you to that holy place
     where there is love that withers not.

2. He is granting you a generous invitation
     from the God of Grace to come –   10
   since the work is finished
     and all the debts [are] paid –
   to a freedom Christ won for you,
     and gave satisfaction for, through His death
   and whosoever comes, and [whosoever] seeks Him,   15
     He will not contemn them.

3. If you proceed to any delay,
     Satan will pursue you;
   earthly lusts will
     entice you with every falsehood.   20
   Take the chance to be safe
     in joy and bliss,
   where the thief does not steal
     and no enemy pursues you.

4. It cannot be put into words,   25
     the magnitude of the mystery that is
   intertwined with the preparation
     that was in the suffering of His death.
   For sure He bore our wrongs,
     He was crucified on our behalf;   30
   and He made peace and concord
     and through His wounds He gave salvation.

5. Chan iarr E òr na airgead ort,
    chan iarr E seilbh na maoin,
ach thu thighinn gu dàna
    on tha A ghràs cho saor.
Tha thròcairean gun tràghadh orra
    gach là do chlann nan daoin':
gur sona dheth an àireamh ud
    a gheibh don Àros naomh.

6. O feuch gun cuir thu do dhòchas ann –
    's e Rìgh nan Glòir a th'ann:
's E theagaisgeas gu h-eòlach thu
    gad threòrachadh 's gach ball;
's E bheir a-null thar Iòrdan thu
    chum còmhnaidh ann is tàimh
far bheil a h-uile sòlas ann
    a dh'òrdaich E ro-làimh.

7. 'S gad bhios agad gàbhaidhean
    is sàraichean san fheòil,
bidh gheallaidhean 'nan àrach dhut
    gum faigh thu gràs gu leòr.
Bidh d' anam air a shàsachadh
    le sàth dhen uisge bheò
á tobraichean glan bàthtach
    's ad làn do na beòil.

5. He does not seek gold or silver from you,
    He seeks not possession[s] or wealth;
only for you to come boldly,   35
    since His grace is so cheap.
His mercies are without end
    each day for mankind:
how happy from it that number
    who reach the sacred House.   40

6. You must try to put your hope in Him –
    He is the King of Glory:
it's He [who] will teach you [all] knowingly,
    strengthening and directing you in every way;
it's He [who] will take you over Jordan,   45
    to dwell there and remain,
where is found every solace
    that he preordained.

7. And though you will have perils
    and oppressions in life,   50
His promises will nourish you
    until you achieve sufficient grace.
Your soul will be satiated
    by an abundance of living water
from clean, overflowing wells   55
    [that are] full to the brims.

26. An Eaglais Shaor an Steòrnabhagh

The Reverend Kenneth Macrae [1883–1964] was born in Dingwall and became a Free Church minister, serving in turn Lochgilphead, Kilmuir in north Skye and finally Stornoway, Isle of Lewis, from 1931 to 1964. (Thomson 1983:191) The *Diary of Kenneth Macrae, a Record of Fifty Years in the Christian Ministry* (Murray 1980) was published posthumously.

Macrae was always "preaching the gospel, and they were converting people here and there, everywhere.[58]... O 's e duine math a bha sin, ceart gu leòr." ["Oh, he was a good man, right enough."] He is still well remembered throughout the Western Isles as a forthright leader and preacher. Whole families of children, mostly born in the nineteen twenties, were baptised by him during his tenure in Skye, so it is no surprise that many continued to follow his career after his move to Stornoway in 1931. His congregations were so large that they appeared "a sea of black," to Glenconon natives Peigi Bennett (née Stiùbhart) and her brother Peter.[59] MacNeacail's biblical diction and tone in this elegiac song indicate his own regard for Macrae's presence and guidance as well as expressing the sense of loss and grief felt by many even today.

IM: Seo earrannan a rinn mi dhan an Urramach Coinneach MacRath a bha 'na Mhinistear ann an Steòrnabhagh. Bha mi eòlach air nuair a bha mi 'nam bhalach. Nuair a chuala mi gun do chaochail e, bha mi glé iomagaineach timcheall air a' ghnothach a

IM: *Here are some verses I made to the Reverend Kenneth Macrae who was the Minister in Stornoway. I knew about him when I was a boy. When I heard that he had died, I was very distressed about the business and I thought I would put these quatrains together, as a stone on the cairn.*

bh'ann agus smaoinich mi gun cuirinn na
ceathramhnan tha seo ri chéile, mar chlach air a
chàrn.

An Eaglais Shaor an Steòrnabhagh

1. Tha 'n Eaglais Shaor an Steòrnabhagh
   an-diugh fo bhròn 's i caoidh
   ag ionndrainn aon bu lòchran dhi
       bu threòir dhi ri àm teinn.
   Th'e nis air a dhol gu Pàrras
   gu àros an Ard-Rìgh
   far a bheil e aig a' làthaireachd
       gu bràth air nach dig claoidh.

2. Mhaighstir Mhacrath, bidh ionndrainn ort
   mar cheannard-iùil ar slòigh
   's tu shéideadh dhuinn an trùmpaid
       nuair bhiodh cùisean dol far dòigh.
   Do theagasg a bha cho drùidhteach
   gu bhith dùsgadh sean is òg
   bha móran air an tionndadh leat
       gu slighe dh'ionnsaigh Glòir.

3. Bu shaothaireach anns an fhìon-lios thu
   gach bliadhna bha thu san fheòil
   cur aolach ma na freumhan
       bha crìonadh 's ad gun deò.
   Thu tagradh gum biodh mìorbhail
   bho Chrìosda gan toirt beò.
   Bha coimhlionadh air t' iarratas –
       tha iarmad dhiubh an Glòir.

4. Tha cuid eil' air fhàgail dhiubh
   tha cràiteach as do dhéidh.
   Tha dòchas math tro Ghràs aca
       gun d'fhuair iad fàbhar Dhé,
   gu faic iad anns an là sin thu
   nuair ghabhar ris an treud,
   nuair nach sgar am bàs sibh
       gu bràth o aon a chéil'.

5. Thor liom gur mór de ghàirdeachas
   ann an Tìr Chanàain shuas.
   Tha do chomunn ris na fàidhean
       man tric a bha thu luaidh.
   Chan eil roinn na pàirtean ann
   gach aon toirt gràdh bith-bhuan
   don Tì bu charraig shàbhailt' dhuit
       san fhàsach rè do chuairt.

The Free Church in Stornoway

1. The Free Church in Stornoway is
   mourning today,
   missing one who was a [guiding] light for it
       and who was a strength for it in time of difficulty.
   He has now gone to Paradise   5
   to the abode of the High King
   where he is in the presence
       upon which no sorrow will ever come.

2. Minister Macrae you will be missed
   as a guiding pillar of our people   10
   you used to sound the trumpet for us
       when matters were getting out of order.
   And your teaching was so penetrating
   with a view to be waking young and old,
   many were turned by you   15
       [on]to the road towards Glory.

3. You laboured in the vineyard
   every year you were alive,
   putting manure about the roots
       that were withering and lifeless.   20
   You [were] pleading that there would be a miracle
   from Christ giving them life.
   It was fulfilled according to your wishes –
       some of them are in Glory.

4. Another portion of them are left   25
   who are racked [with sorrow] after you.
   They have high hopes through Grace
       that they [have] found the favour of God,
   that they will see you on that day
   when acknowledgement will be given to the flock   30
   [and] when death will not separate you
       ever from one another.

5. I think how great your joy
   in the Land of Canaan above.
   Your fellowship is with the prophets   35
       about whom you frequently spoke.
   There is no division or confederacy there,
   each one giving love eternal
   to the One who was a rock of salvation for you
       in the wilderness during your life.   40

6. Bidh cuimhne mar a' Fìrean ort
leis an linn a thig 'nar déidh,
gum b'e Israeileach da-rìr' thu
bha gluas'd an slighe Dhé.
Gur mór a bhios an dìteadh
do nach d'chreid bhuat brìgh na sgéil
bu chòir bhith dhuinn nas prìseile
na nì 'sa chruinne-ché.

6. *You will be remembered as a true [Christian]*
by the generation that will follow us,
that you were a true Israelite
who was moving in the path of God.
How great will be their condemnation of those 45
who did not believe from you the substance of the tale
which ought to be more precious to us
than anything in the universe.

IM: I suppose that was equal, as good one [as] I ever composed.... I knew him well in his day, but he was very tough on the Sabbath, strict and all that.... Oh he was dead on it.

I think Macrae's song was more truthful than any of them, you know. You were only just putting him as he was, explaining how he was....

TM: Well everybody remembers him too.

IM: Yes, they did at the time, aye. Yes, and still do too. I see there's [a] commentary on the subjects he has yet in the pulpit, aye. Well he's a good twenty-five years dead now anyhow. But [in the song] I refer to his saying what he said at one time. He was very popular that way, and what was very strange, it was Gàidhlig he learnt and he was preaching from it.

TM: Really?

IM: Aye aye, but to have in everyday conversation he wasn't very accurate at all.... To preach, he was as perfect in it, but...speaking about cattle and crofting and all that, he would be lost.

TM: So he would have to work on his sermon to get it just right.

IM: Oh yes, he would have, but his sermon morning and night in Gàidhlig was perfect, but if he was in the ordinary conversation on everydays he was lost! Well that is strange.... He was that because he came here and he was just learning the Gàidhlig when he came, but they took him on all right and he was a good preacher right enough and very attractive and he had a lot of communicants too.... Oh I believe he was a God-fearing man, if there ever was one, he was.

TM: Peigi and Peter [Stewart] were describing his communions in Stornoway being huge.

IM: Oh yes. Well that was the biggest [congregation that] was in Scotland, the church he had in Stornoway. Aye. Oh yes, oh he was [there for] forty years there anyhow, or more.[60] Oh yes, he would be.... I don' know, did he retire or not? I never heard of him retiring.

TM: [I don't think he did, but] he...died in 1964.

IM: Aye some time like that, but I don't think he retired at all, no.

TM: And there used to be services here twice a day?...

IM: Every Sunday and fast days, oh yes there would be that, aye. And communion services. Well he always had helpers with him then at the communions, another two along with him. Mhm. Oh he was...very popular everywhere he went. But I don't think he has been in many places but Stornoway and Skye itself in his day.

TM: I think he was in Lochgilphead for a little while.

IM: It could be.... He was about twelve years in Kilmuir anyhow. Then...they gave him a call in Stornoway. Well they were saying then he had the biggest congregation in Scotland, in Stornoway.

TM: How many people, do you know?

IM: Oh I can't tell you, there must be thousands. It would have been. But that was at the Free Church itself. Aye.

TM: Peigi was also saying that her whole family was baptised by him....

IM: Oh they would be, but you had to be very strict before he would baptise you.... Brought up, you know, in the way of the truth and all that, otherwise you won't get it.

27. The news we've heard from Waternish (A song for Johannes Hellinga)

In addition to songs about local characters and churchmen, Iain also made songs to other establishment figures. Such a one was Johannes Hellinga, a Dutch financier who came to Skye in the 1960s. He bought the Waternish Estates from Lord Godfrey MacDonald who was in debt due to the tremendous death duties that accrued on the passing of his father. See Chapter Five for more details on how and why this song in English, and the next in Gaelic, were made.

The news we've heard from Waternish

1. The news we've heard from Waternish
   has echoed through the Highlands,
   that the noble Dutchman
   has bought part of our island.

2. His name is Johnny Hellinga   5
   his fame has gone before him;
   from all that I have seen and heard,
   both young and old extol him.

3. He sailed across from Holland,
   with dollars and with guilders,   10
   he bought from the MacDonald laird
   his land, his stock, his buildings.

4. The crofters now are full of joy,
   the laird is on their side now –
   he gives them land as they desire   15
   no tax, no rent will bind them.

5. From Sgor a' Bhàigh to Geàrraidh,
   from Fàsach up to Triumpan,
   of land the finest anywhere,
   from Hàllainn down to Giùbaig.   20

6. Here the crops are heaviest,
   the cattle are the finest
   and when they go to market
   they're unequalled in the Highlands.

7. When Johnny comes to Triumpan,   25
   there will be celebrations;
   the taverns will be drained quite dry
   as he receives ovations.

8. In Dutch he'll drink a toast to them
   and they'll reply in Gaelic   30
   and though their drams would be one foot high,
   they'll drain them dry in Geàrraidh.

9. I end my song and wish him well,
    may peace and joy attend him,
    his stay with us be content and long,   35
    "Ceud mìle fàilt'" we'll send him.

TM: Whatever happened to him anyway?

IM: Och, he's at Staffin there about, he's going about.

TM: Really?...

IM: Well, I think he was last week, a fortnight ago anyhow. But he goes back and forward. He was married and I think he left the wife. He was married to a banker's daughter in Inverness and I think he was here once or twice.... He's quite all right, good English speaker too, och aye and money was no object to him. He gave it [i.e. land] away for five pounds the acre, well the people there took it and they built houses there and sold them for thirty and thirty-five thousand, houses on...plots he gave them. "Why did you," I said, "sell them?"

"Oh I thought I was going to die at that time," he says. "I weren't keeping well." That was his [?]excuse, but I don't know what was [the] idea at all.

28. 'S e seo a' sgeul tha taitneach leinn (Oran do Johnny Hellinga)

IM: I've seen him here, he bought my lambs, and he sold them in Portree for so much and he lost two hundred pounds on them. "Oh," I says, "Hellinga,...I'll need to make some of that up to you."...

"Away, be quiet!" he says, "I make...that in a quarter of an hour!"...

TM: You made a song on him [in Gaelic]....

IM: Oh I did, aye.

'S e seo a' sgeul tha taitneach leinn	*This is the story that pleases us*
1. 'S e seo a' sgeul tha taitneach leinn, nì thachair as an dùthaich gun deachaidh Oighreachd Bhatarnais a cheannach leis an Dùidseach.	1. *This is the story that pleases us,* *a thing that happened in the area;* *the Waternish Estate was* *bought by the Dutchman.*
2. Gun dàinig e bho'n Olaind, le chuid stòrais agus ionntais, 's a cheannaich e bhon Dòmhnallach gach òirleach bha de ghrunnd aige.	2. *He came from Holland,* 5 *with all his money and wealth,* *and he bought from [Lord] MacDonald* *every inch of ground that he had.*
3. 'S e an t-ainm dha Johannes Hellinga tha e bho chinneadh chliùiteach, 's their gach neach tha eòlach air gur h-e duine còir go chùl e.	3. *His name is Johannes Hellinga,* *he is of renowned ancestry,* 10 *and everyone who knows him says* *that he is a decent, honest man to his back[bone].*
4. Gu bheil na mìltean acair ann de dh'fhearann torrach sùghmhor le spréidh tha iad ag àrachadh: cha déid nas fheàrr gu bùidsear.	4. *There are thousands of acres there* *of fertile, moist land* *with cattle that they are rearing:* 15 *better [ones] will not go to slaughter.*
5. Na croitearan bidh uaill orra gu bheil uachdaran ùr ac'	5. *The crofters they will be boasting* *that they have a new landlord*

is tha fearann dhaibh mar 's deòin leotha
gun bòid bhith orr' na cùmhnant.

and land is [available] for them as they wish
without any need for a guarantee or account.   20

6. Crìochnaichidh mi 'n t-òran seo
   le deagh dhòchas agus deagh dhùrachd
   guma fada buan e còmhnaidh leinn
   's gach sòlas bhith 'na lùchairt.

6. *I will finish this song*
   with optimism and a good wish:
   long and harmoniously may he dwell with us
   and every happiness be in his mansion.

IM: I think there was more Gaelic than this,...I think there was, but I don't know. Mhm.... [*thinks*] I can't say it is [i.e. there is] now. Och I never forgot it [then], at the time it was alright.

"THEY REALLY ARE A REMARKABLE FAMILY"[61]

It is in the white-washed converted stable on the shores of Loch Snizort that Iain and Màiri raised their family and where they live today. They had "eight of children," just like Iain's own family: Duncan (b. 1948), Mórag (b. 1949), Willie (b. 1951), John Angus (b. 1952), Jessie (b. 1953), Jenny Mabel (b. 1954 and named after Miss Anderson of Cuidreach House), Stanley (b. 1957) and Isobel (b. 1964).

All of the married children are now scattered around the country: Mórag in Falkirk, Jessie in Inverness and Isobel, Jenny and Stanley in Aberdeenshire. The other three sons live mostly at home and work for various local concerns: John on the road crews, Willie doing construction work all over the Highlands (he has a reputation as a tremendous and tireless worker) and Duncan looking after stock in Gleann Hìonasdail as his father did over seventy years ago.

The MacNeacail household is a typical old-fashioned Hebridean home. Màiri looks after Iain throughout the day: cups of tea, sandwiches and the like, and keeps the fire well stoked, but it is in the evening, when the boys come in from work at five-thirty or six, that the pattern asserts itself – they sit comfortably reading newspapers or watching television while Màiri bustles about tending the fire, brewing them tea, laying the table and preparing their meals. When she calls them to the table, they respond and get up to take their food. Iain sits in his comfortable chair by the fire and gets tea and a sandwich or a boiled egg; at ninety-three, he has earned his relaxation. He can be quite authoritarian with his sons and with Màiri and has perhaps given the boys a model. They certainly take Màiri and her excellent care for granted.

In recent decades, MacNeacail's reputation as a song-maker has led to gratifying friendships with the Chief of Clan Nicolson and with the Edinburgh merchant banker and Gaelic enthusiast Sir Iain Noble.

TM: He was at your daughters' weddings.

IM: Aye. Aye, both of them.... Ach aye, it was very good that, you know, because it's very few you'd see of his kind coming to a wedding, or would be asked to come to a wedding. But he was so popular here, you know, that he was asked.... But in many other cases you wouldn't see many of Sirs, or anything like it, coming to a [wedding, nor the] ladies in the big house there.

Clearly, Noble values the Sgiobair's friendship a great deal and when Noble married in 1991, he was, of course, invited. The feeling of respect is reciprocated.

IM: I suppose the best thing to give him [for his wedding] would be an apple tree. He has plenty of money anyhow. [*laughs*]

TM: ...Where is this apple tree, you have this apple tree?

IM: She's in the room [up] there, I'll get them up sometime. Well if he's up...before February, because it's fixed in a pot and you keep water in and...you can put her in the ground...the way she is. But she's there alright... But I don't know when will I get up to see him unless he comes down himself. If he would, I would give it to him here, he would have to take it.

Interestingly, he has chosen an apple tree, one of the Celtic symbols of lineage and aristocracy, as "the best thing to give him": "*Bha sin a' ciallachadh gum biodh ad gu math *productive*! ["*That meant that they'd be very productive!*"]

29. 'S thoir mo bheannachd do dh'Eilean Iarmain

Sir Iain values the Sgiobair's talents and traditions a great deal and in the nineteen-eighties, Iain made this song to him. Noble has taken a great interest in the Gaelic language and culture and in addition to establishing Sabhal Mór Ostaig, the Gaelic business college, he hosts Còmhdhail nan Seanchaidh [*the Gathering of Tradition-bearers*], held bi-annually at his hotel in Eilean Iarmain, Skye. For more about their friendship and Sir Iain's request for a song on the occasion of his wedding, see Chapter Five.

'S thoir mo bheannachd do dh'Eilean Iarmain

1. 'S thoir mo bheannachd do dh'Eilean Iarmain,
   don dhiùlnach fiachail ud Iain Noble,
   thug cuireadh fialaidh dhuinn a chum dìota
   gu ceòl is sgeulachd san t-Sabhal Mhór aige.

2. Bha sean is òg againn cruinne còmhladh
   toirt fuaim air òrain 's toirt ceòl air teudan.
   Chaidh biadh air bòrd dhuinn dhen h-uile
          seòrsa;
       bha deoch gun stòradh toirt tuilleadh spéird
          dhuinn.

3. B'e fhéin an t-àrmann cùl-taic na Gàidhlig';
   's e thog an àird i na b'fheàrr na Mòdan.
   Bidh gach oisean sràide len ainm an Gàidhlig
       is air gach ceàrnaidh sna raithdean móra.

4. Ceann-iùil ar dùthcha gu robh ad diùmbach,
   ag ràdh nach b'fhiù leotha bhith 'ga h-òilein.
   Nan d'fhuair an dùrachd gun d'readh a
          mùchadh,
       's cha d'readh a h-ionnsachadh dha'n an
          òigridh.

5. Chuir e colaisde oilein an Eilean Iarmain.
   Thig iad o chrìochan na Roinn-Eòrp' ann
   's bidh Ghàidhlig aosda, 's i air a sgaoileadh
       air feadh an t-saoghail, le aont' is òrdugh.

6. B'e sàr-dhuin' uasal, 's ann dha bu dual sin;
   gur ann o uaisle a-nuas a dh'fhàs e.
   Bidh cuimhn' le mùirn air gu deireadh ùine
       airson an cùram – bha ùidh dhan chànan.

Take my blessings to Eilean Iarmain

1. Take my blessings to Eilean Iarmain,
   to yon worthy champion Iain Noble,
   who gave us a hospitable invitation to dinner
       and for music and story in his 'Great Barn'.

2. Our young and old were gathered together,   5
   giving voice to song and making music on strings.
   Food of every sort was put on the table for us;
       limitless drink was giving more energy to us.

3. He himself was the chief supporter of Gaelic;
   it's he who promoted it better than the Mods.   10
   Every street-corner will have its name in Gaelic
       and [they'll be] on the main roads everywhere.

4. The leadership of our country was contemptuous,
   saying they didn't think it worth their while for people to
          learn it.
   If [they] had got their wish, it would be choked,   15
       and it wouldn't be taught to the young.

5. He put an institute of learning in Eilean Iarmain.
   They will come there from the boundaries of Europe
   and ancient Gaelic will be broadcast
       throughout the world, by agreement and decree.   20

6. He was an excellent noble man, for him that was a birthright;
   it's from nobility he is descended.
   He will be remembered with respect to the end of time
       because of the care – his interest was in the language.

7. Guma buan thu an Eilean Iarmain;
  's e sin a dh'iarradh gach neach dhan eòl thu.
  Cha chualas riamh a's an Eilean Sgiath'ach
    fear sheas cho dian riut air thaobh na còrach.

7. *Long may you live in Eilean Iarmain;* 25
  that is wanted by everyone who knows you.
  There was never heard, in the Isle of Skye,
    one as steadfast as you on the side of justice.

CLACH AIR A CHÀRN

Only forty years ago Iain started out with Mrs. Ferguson's sheep and no house.

IM: There was fifty [sheep] then, but there's over a hundred and twenty odd now, so I have built it that much. Well, I was keeping a horse and three or four cows and a plough horse.... [Eventually] I was selling them...cause the boys are away and I'm not going to be harassing myself doing it. I'll be here forever, taking a long time [caring for them everyday]. I was thinking of going to Australia for a time to see the Clan Chief, but ach I thought in my head, when the boys are not at home, you know, when I would come back [there] will be no house here at all, I know.

As most of the children have grown up and left home, Iain and Màiri have found caring for all the stock too taxing. Those still living in Cuidreach – Willie, John Angus and Duncan – are all employed away from the croft and coping with the cattle, in addition to their full time jobs, is too much for them as well. At last, Iain and Màiri have retired from full-time crofting at the ages of ninety-three and seventy-six.

The Sgiobair is well known in Skye for making songs, but he is also famous the world round for a little incident which happened at the Skye Gathering. According to Iain, the athletes were having trouble with the caber and Colonel Jock MacDonald (of Viewfield House in Portree, presiding over the games) stepped in.

IM: "Well," says Colonel Jock, "take the light one then." Well, that's what they did.... So when they got all the thing past...just for curiosity to myself,...(I didn't think that anybody taking any heed of it), I went to see the caber, how [heavy] it was, and got it...balanced on my shoulder.... That's when the cameras went and all that. What all was said about it [at the time] I never heard a murmur. But they made it [up] themselves, they made up the story. And they said I had a few drams.... I did not! I never mentioned anything.

MB: They never even spoke to you?

IM: Not at all! No, but they took the cameras you know and...they were showing it in the Portree [paper, there was a picture of the] Cuillin Hills...all over Japan, China, everywhere. [Everyone was asking], 'Who was the little man?' Ah, it was nobody at all!... Well, anybody could do it. Well I don't know, would anybody.... Well, I think it was twenty-two feet long, aye and weigh[ed] about over a hundredweight anyhow, but it's the balancing on your shoulder.... But the big hefty bunch wouldn't have it, that's why I tried, [to see] what's up with it when they can't do it. I thought I would do it, so that's why I tried it. And I never thought they were going to get [i.e. photograph] me there, otherwise I wouldn't have done it.

For the most part, Iain's life has been a healthy one.

IM: Never a day [in] bed with illness or anything. And even in the army I seen them carried out and never came back. Many a time I wrenched the blankets over me,...you know, I put the ground sheet in mud and branches and anything I could get, to keep it out of the mud and [I was] lying on that. I don't know how I survived at all.

24. Iain at home in Cuidreach, Spring 1993. (T. A. McKean)

Even when I took the measles, I never had to be in bed among...my brothers there. But they [would] come and scold me, "What are you doing up...?" I went back there laughing to myself, taking the scolding.

Well I went...to the army then and...I was just the same. The only thing I had [was] chilblains on my feet you know. [I was] complaining like that. Ach there's no use complaining there. No, they wouldn't listen. You'd be a nuisance if you were going [on] too much.

So then I came home.... Now when they took me in the army, they went through me.... I don't know who the man was, but I said "He's away anyhow [i.e. he's crazy]," to myself, when I went there. "[You're] one of the strong men of the West," he said to me [and] that was forty years ago. But nine years [ago], I went to Doctor Ball, he went through me [and said], "What a remarkable ticker [i.e. heart]."

It's now I put weight on [i.e. gave credence to] the army surgeon, [and I] knew that he was right, but I didn't believe it at the time. Of course when you go into the army you're away anyhow.... That's how it was.

Well since then, you know, I had a [major] operation [in which a tumour was] caught in the bud.... But I was never sick, although it happened to me that way. That's the only...handicap I had in my life.

31. Should I have time available

In keeping with his tradition of honouring establishment figures, Iain's latest song is to his surgeon, Mr. Ball.

IM: I didn't know that he knew anything about me composing anyhow. Unless Dr. Macrae[62] or somebody would have told him, you know.

MB: And he told you to go and

IM: Aye, "Compose a song there," staying down in Broadford, looking through the window.

TM: He was pointing at the sunset?...

IM: Aye. He was pointing out the window down to where I would see a lot to draw my attention for composing. "I think," I says, "I'll compose one for surgeon Ball,"...and off he went, he left me there, you know. But I had no word[s] for that – on the tip of my tongue – at the time. So that's how that happened. Oh...I'm finished composing, I'm no use now; my memory is gone complete....

TM: How many days after that did you finish the song?

IM: Och there's no days in it, no. No, no.

Should I have time available

1. Should I have time available,
    I'd give in praise a song:
  to Mr. Ball the surgeon,
    who did my life prolong.
  He examined and X-rayed me   5
    had an operation done,
  to him I will be grateful
    all my days to come.

2. He came to Broadford Hospital
    from Swansea town in Wales,   10
  where I have happy memories,
    the time I there did stay;
  the people were so generous
    and kind in every way,
  what surgeon Ball inherited   15
    in his former days.

3. He is the greatest genius
    that has ever been to Skye.
  He has performed miracles
    by saving many lives.   20
  His name it is familiar
    throughout the Western Isles;
  he will be commemorate'
    as generations rise.

MB: And you think you might put more on it yet.

IM: I may, if I have something on my mind.

See Chapter Four for a detailed look at the composition of this song, his first in many years. He was long out of practice, and yet the song simply came to him. No doubt with a little practice, his accustomed fluency would return. It is sung, incidentally, to Iain's 'panegyric' tune, the one he used for *An Eaglais Shaor an Steòrnabhagh* (26).

TM: Well, it looks like you have many years ahead.

IM: Oh-h. Oh away, thank you very much for the compliment.... What are you, twenty-four?

TM: Twenty-seven.

IM: Are you? You don't look like that at all. Starting out. I hope it will be a good life for you.

In recent decades, MacNeacail has seen his beloved culture swept away by a flood of Anglicisation and modernisation. It "doesn't count among the young...they have no interest in it," a disregard for the past which makes him rather sad.

IM: Well yes, I would say that you're stupid if you don't take note of it. I'm thinking myself how stupid I was [that] I didn't take more interest in it because it goes a long way [towards telling you] how the world was run.... I'll regret the day I can't do nothing of it.

Chapter Three

THE POETIC TRADITION, THE *BAIRD BHAILE* AND THE *TAIGH CEILIDH*

Before looking at the social milieu in which the Sgiobair practised his art, it is in order to take a brief look at the traditional origins of the twentieth-century township poet.

THE POETIC TRADITION

> The human experiences of the Gaels can be traced in the instinctive, inveterate and spontaneous compositions of the bards;...they react to every major event affecting the lives of their community, and their songs mirror their folk-history. (Bloomfield and Dunn 1989:67)

Iain MacNeacail was born into a culture that places a high premium on verbal dexterity, observation and quick wit. He is one of the last of the *bàird bhaile* [plural of *bàrd baile*], the local poets who were often requested, indeed expected, to make songs, both serious and satirical, for the local *cèilidhean* [visiting sessions or informal house visits]. The *bàrd baile* was an important figure in Gaelic society for centuries and remained so until well after the Second World War. These unpaid, unofficial poets were the de facto spokesmen and women for their communities; as such, they wielded considerable power over their neighbours and public opinion. For this society a song was, and to some extent still is, a functional and practical piece, an essential element of communication seamlessly integrated with other types of expression.[63] To mainstream Western society on the other hand, a song, whether old or new, is well outside accepted norms of daily social interaction; to most, it is an anomaly, while to the *bàird bhaile* and their communities, it is not. Only in the present century has Gaelic society's ancient emphasis on song and poetry as an everyday form of emotional expression begun to break down. (See Chapter Five for the use of song in Iain's community.)

The roots of this functional oral song-making tradition in Scotland date back at least to the coming of the Gaels of Ulster to their colony of Dal Riada in South-west Scotland in the sixth century AD. The 'professional bard' or 'poet' in this early period was actually a song-maker, as most Gaelic poetry until the present century was meant to be sung. These highly trained and skilled song-makers composed orally, to extremely difficult metrical patterns.[64] (It is said that bards used to lie in the dark with a heavy stone on their stomachs as an 'encouragement' to composition.[65] Perhaps this was also a good incentive to finish.)

As far as we know, these professionals were always men, as composing poetry was not considered a seemly occupation for a woman. There are records of several women composing in the styles of these professional poets, most notably Màiri nighean Alasdair Ruaidh [Mary (MacLeod) daughter of Red(-haired) Alasdair] and the aristocratic Sìleas na Ceapaich [Julia (MacDonald) of Keppoch] in the seventeenth century.[66] Another one was Maighread ni Lachainn who was unable to compose out of doors (a curious echo of the bardic technique mentioned above[67]). Unfortunately, however, there are no known records that payments were made for their services in anything other than kind, suggesting that professional status was not conferred upon them. And even in this century there are several traditions, found in the Western Isles of Scotland, that Màiri and Maighread were buried face down (MacInnes 1968:41), an acknowledgement – or punishment – of their bardic (i.e. unwomanly) activities.[68] No doubt the professional educated poets kept very close tabs on who was or was not considered one of their number; even in those days, there was no equal pay for equal work. However, despite this professional prejudice, it must be pointed out that much extant Gaelic vernacular verse is thought to be by women (MacInnes 1968:36).

The most highly trained of the professional song-makers in the employ of a Chief were composers primarily of eulogies, elegies and other praise poems for the nobles of the clan. They were also, following the conflation of the different types of court officers of the Classical period, keepers of genealogical knowledge in the clan system.[69] Between these two duties of praise (implying present legitimacy of the ruler based on his heroic behaviour), and genealogy (implying historical legitimacy) the song-maker was in a unique position of influence outside the normal corridors of political power.

> The power of the bards was partly at least a temporal power, growing out of possessions, and often boosted by closeness to the Chief.... And the Scottish evidence itself points to conditions of comfort in the material sense and strong influence in a social and political sense. (Thomson 1973:12)

There was of course a danger that the song-maker would simply act as a sort of publicity agent since he was in the Chief's pay (Thomson 1973:12). In fact, it must often have been the bard who held the upper hand, so great was the Chief's fear of satirical condemnation in song. Public image was and is an important consideration for any leader, especially a Clan Chief. Technically his power was hereditary but, practically speaking, it was largely based on a good reputation among his subjects (a situation which still applies for some today, as the recent tendency to 'trial-by-tabloid' shows). A scathing, rapidly-spread satire was therefore a thing to be feared; consider how valuable a word-of-mouth recommendation must have been in the absence of academic transcripts, diplomas and other 'immutable' proofs of virtue we have today. Furthermore, the Chief's health was at risk as there are several reports in Scottish oral tradition of people breaking out in boils as the result of a satirical blast.[70]

The power of the poets was, however, severely curtailed in the seventeenth and eighteenth centuries by the degeneration of the Clan system, culminating in the disaster of the Jacobite defeat at Culloden in 1746. By this time there were almost no professional clan poets[71] and in the following centuries, the people's confidence in their own culture and language was systematically undermined through educational propaganda until, by the late nineteenth century, they themselves considered the Gaelic language a hindrance to upward mobility; to learn English and to leave the Islands was considered "what was needed to get on in the world". (Smout 1986:219) Gaelic society was methodically crushed by the British government in a concerted effort, the effects of which are felt throughout the Highlands today.

The Statutes of Iona[72] in 1609 and the much more explicit 1616 Education Act had required the Chiefs to educate their sons in Lowland schools and through the medium of English, so that

> the vulgar Inglishe toung be universallie plantit, and the Irishe [i.e. Gaelic] language, whilk is one of the cheif and principall causis of the continewance of barbaritie and incivilitie amongis the inhabitantis of the Ilis and Heylandis, may be abolisheit and removit. [sic] (Donaldson 1970:178–179)

And, as Derick Thomson says, in *An Introduction to Gaelic Poetry*, the later "schooling [of] potential chiefs and lairds in the caste-schools of England, came without benefit of legislation". (1974:116) By the early nineteenth century, therefore, the aristocracy were heavily Anglicised; they had become no more than absentee landlords (and English-speaking at that). The chiefs needed cash to maintain their newly acquired expensive London lifestyles; the people, no longer necessary for military purposes or as a measure of wealth and power, were systematically cleared from the land, making way for the more profitable (and less troublesome) sheep. Having been moved to the shore-line, the inhabitants were forced, by the need for cash, to gather and burn kelp for the landlords, who sold the resultant potash for use in English and Lowland industry. With the end of the Napoleonic wars in 1815, however, in-expensive supplies of potash became available from Spain and the kelp market collapsed. Cattle prices too, fell at the same time due to freer access to continental markets, leaving the crofters, newly con-verted to a cash economy, without a cash income and starved of land on which to grow their food. Emigration then became the landlords' new solution to the overcrowding caused by their own mis-appropriation of land.[73]

The chiefs could no longer afford to keep professional song-makers, even had they desired, and the makers themselves, no longer benefiting from a system of patronage, ceased to find praise poetry such an interesting form of composition. The emphasis of bardic vernacular verse shifted to Nature Poetry. The eighteenth century saw a great flowering of this genre through the efforts of ministers and other public figures and poets like Alasdair Mac Mhaighstir Alasdair [Alexander son of the Minister Alexander (MacDonald)], Dunnchadh Bàn Mac an t-Saoir [Fair(-haired) Duncan MacIntyre] and others, many of whom are now anonymous.

While beautiful and often technically brilliant, many of the later eighteenth-century and the nine-teenth-century Nature Poems talk in paradisiacal terms of the pre-Clearance Highlands and, unfor-tunately, blame the sheep for the devastation, rather than the tenants' own countrymen: the landlords. Part of this self-deception arises from the paternalism that had been inherent in the clan system,[74] but there were other influences at work, for instance the high-handed eviction of certain 'trouble-makers' which ensured that no momentum for change built up, and the teachings of the church, touched on below. In addition, the Gaels' self-esteem and the sense of their culture's value was by this time almost non-existent. Little wonder, then, that they did not rebel against both their blood ties and a system which taught that authority was right and beyond the question of ordinary folk.

This unprotesting mind-set held sway through the vast emigrations during the worst of the Clear-ances (ca. 1820–70), and the potato famines of the 1840s. A further shadow was cast over the free expression of Gaelic song-poetry by the evangelical revivals which swept the Highlands in the first half of the nineteenth century, reinforcing the idea of subservience to authority and teaching that this world was no more than a 'vale of tears' and song a 'mere vanity' therein.[75] As the modern Gaelic poet Somhairle MacGill-Eain [Sorley MacLean] put it, "Gaelic song poetry degenerated to a feeble wail and to a feebler pietism".[76] (1985:107–8)

The middle of this devastating nineteenth century, however, brought the dawning of a new age; a little vigour returned to Gaelic verse as poets like Dr. John MacLachlan of Rahoy and especially Uilleam MacDhùnleibhe [William Livingston] put a new spirit in the poetry.[77] For popularity and influence, however, the composer of the nineteenth century who undoubtedly stands out is Mary MacPherson, or Màiri Mhór·nan Òran, as she is known throughout the Highlands. About nine thousand lines of her poetry (including stinging anti-landlord criticism, belying the common criticism that she was too deferential to the gentry) were noted down from her recitation by John Whyte and published in 1891. The editor, Alasdair MacBheathain [Alexander MacBain], says in his introduction that though she

> can read her own poetry in print, she cannot write it.... And she has at least half as much more of her own, and twice as much...floating [i.e. then current in oral tradition], unpublished poetry, mainly that of Skye and the Western Isles. (MacBheathain 1891:xiii–xiv)

Clearly, her memory was astonishing and MacBheathain's mention of it is an indication of the value that Gaelic society places on a good memory.[78]

Crofters' conditions improved slightly with the 1886 Crofters' Holdings Act (Scotland), by which crofters were granted such basic rights as security of tenure. The focus of the Gaels' land agitation was then no longer so sharp, and the poetic outcry against the profiteering landlords abated to some extent.[79] Filling this relative void of poetic activity, a new tradition appears: the aforementioned *bàird bhaile*. Local bards were not, of course, a new development, but a perceived upswing in the activity of the tradition can be traced to three factors: (i) the absence a strong formal tradition which might have overshadowed the work of these less-established local poets; (ii) the establishment of the Mòd competitions in 1892 in which they were provided with a more public platform for their material than in the village céilidh house; and (iii) the appearance, following the clearance of the rural Highlands, of large numbers of Gaelic speakers in cities such as Glasgow, providing a new synthetic community in which the local poet's observation was welcome.[80]

This urban population also had access to the large numbers of Gaelic books that began to emerge in response to the spread of literacy. By the nineteenth century, many rural villages in the Highlands had a voluntary schooling programme run by the church, which taught reading and writing in Gaelic for the purposes of religious education. "At this time," wrote the Swiss traveller Louis Necker de Saussure in 1822, "there is scarcely a village in the Highlands where the children do not learn to read and write in Gaelic and the Holy Scriptures are in the hands of every Highlander". (p. 90) The Free Church of Scotland opened many schools in the nineteenth century, but unfortunately, with the coming of the Education (Scotland) Act in 1872, they were "more or less destroyed, or made redundant". (Smith 1981:35) Thereafter, children were normally taught to read and write only English and by the late nineteenth century, "the Highlander himself was strongly and consistently against the use of Gaelic as a school language". (Durkacz 1977:19)

Late in the last century and continuing into this one – despite prohibitions against, and in some cases corporal punishment for, using Gaelic – a number of young scholars applied the same basic principles learned in the reading of English to the Gaelic of the Bible, small books of spiritual songs and the Gaelic newspapers and periodicals that were becoming available in inexpensive popular editions. A new, literate class of Gael had been created.

THE *BAIRD BHAILE* AND THE *TAIGH CEILIDH*

In this century, there have been a number of good collections of *bàird bhaile* poetry and they continue to appear.[81]

Unfortunately, collections like these and those of professional bardic poetry usually elucidate only the factual background to the bards' topical and occasional songs. They almost wholly neglect the social function of the songs and the thought processes of their composers. Russian scholars realised the importance of context as early as 1926 and "established early the value of performer and repertoire studies.... Only in recent decades has their importance been recognised in Anglophone scholarship". (Buchan 1992:248) Scottish Gaelic song scholarship is still many years behind in this repect. Musicologist Thorkild Knudsen's *Calum Ruadh, Bard of Skye* (1978) made a start at redressing the balance, with its emphasis on the bard's impression of his own technique, but, while this is a valuable contribution, a fuller investigation of the living song-maker in Gaelic tradition is long overdue.

To narrow the topic of this book down to a single song-maker, Iain MacNeacail, let us begin to focus on the Isle of Skye. A look at Gaelic literature through the last few centuries will show that the island has produced its share of well known song-makers: the lyrical Uilleam Ros, Niall MacLeòid, Màiri Mhór nan Oran (whose village, if she were to be called a village bard, would have to be the entire *Gàidhealtachd* [Gaelic region] or the whole Isle of Skye, at least).[82] Less well known, and more in the bàird bhaile mould, there have been Bàrd Ghrialain [the Bard of Grealan (near Staffin)], Calum Ruadh Nicolson of Braes, Sgiobair himself and Aonghas Fleidsear.[83] There have also been modern 'art-poets' such as Somhairle MacGill-Eain and Aonghas MacNeacail.

Iain is one of the last of the village bards. Now in his nineties, he is still making songs. He made his first song at the age of fourteen and can still sing most of it. "I thought anybody could make a song, but I didn't know," he says, not so much belittling his talent, as indicating how natural he considers a life of which song is an integral part. Song was certainly, and to some extent still is, a pervasive part of Gaelic society and so MacNeacail has become well known in his native village, and beyond, as a bard.

Between the wars Iain often made a new song, sang it at a céilidh or two, and then it would be forgotten as it ceased to be topical or a new issue presented itself; "They were for the time being, just." Since the topics were usually ephemeral, a song often had a short working life. Sometimes, however, it would prove popular and be taken up by local people and learned, sung, traded and taken to other parts of Skye and further afield (for example, *Nochd gur luaineach mo chadal* (16)). But these songs were not made in isolation. For Iain they are not book-bound static documents, but a living means of communication. Until the breakdown of the social structure of this community and the drastic reduction in house-visiting, they were made for both himself *and for a local audience*.

In discussing song and story, or indeed any aspect of community life in Uig with Iain, one is inevitably brought round to the subject of the céilidh. It was *the* context for social interaction, especially of the kind I usually have with MacNeacail (i.e. discussions about songs, local history and characters), so it is no wonder he is often reminded of them during our visits. To a village bard like the Sgiobair, who spent six nights a week in one of the *taighean céilidh* [visiting houses], they are inseparably intertwined with community identity. Indeed, I think it is hard for him to conceive of the community without them as they provide the environment for which the bard composes and in which he performs. Conversely, the bard serves as a mouthpiece for the céilidh and, by extension, the community, expressing many people's thoughts and emotions through his songs. Compositions are made specifically in and for this milieu; outside of it they do not exist in the same sense. They are different creatures out of context, not without their intrinsic merits, but different and lesser nonetheless. Ask when he heard a tradition, or where he started learning songs and he is likely to say, "Ach, bhithinn gan cluinntinn a's na taighean céilidh 's an àitean dhen t-seòrsa sin." ["*Ach, I used to be hearing them in the céilidh houses and places of that kind.*"] Iain's own songs must therefore be examined in context and to facilitate that we must build up a detailed picture of the céilidh and how it worked in Uig society.

The céilidh house has been described many times in literature and scholarship through the ages, from scenes of storytelling in old Irish sagas to vignettes set down by modern folktale scholars. J. F. Campbell's *Popular Tales of the West Highlands* (1890) gives several descriptions based on the notes of a number of his collectors: Hector Urquhart (iv–v), Hector Maclean (vi–vii) and John Dewar (li). Other accounts may be found in MacInnes' *Folk and Hero Tales* (1890:ix–x) and *Carmina Gadelica* (Carmichael 1928:xxii–xxiv). Frank Vallee's 1954 study, *Social Structure and Organization in a Hebridean Community*, gives a view of what went on at a more formal mid-twentieth-century gathering (26–9). The Irish situation is well covered in Delargy's "The Gaelic Story-teller" (1945:182, 192–95 and throughout) and Ó Suileabháin's *Storytelling in Irish Tradition* (1973:10–12 and throughout).

Much of this community social structure, the céilidh society, is now gone, but before the Second World War it was still largely intact in Scotland and Gaelic-speaking Ireland, as well as in emigrant communities in Canada.[84] In fact, in many ways the twentieth-century céilidhs that most resemble those of MacNeacail's youth in Skye may be found in Newfoundland, Quebec, Cape Breton and Prince Edward Island in Eastern Canada.[85]

Bennett, MacNeill and MacQueen aside, most published accounts of the céilidh houses concentrate on the telling of the long wonder tales and in the shuffle, the basic function of the gatherings is lost – they are basic building blocks of community identity, not exceptional sessions of back-to-back international folk tales. Undoubtedly, tales (long the subject of comparative scholarship) were told at many a céilidh, but generally as part of an astounding range of news, songs old and new, jokes, history, anecdotes, gossip and the like, of which the tale, as a sort of cinema or high art of the day, is only a part.

IM: Aye but that was the custom you know.... Y'had nights in the house. You'd always be there and somebody would have something queer [i.e. funny] to say and you would get at them for doing it.

The exchanges characteristic of the *taighean céilidh* were the life-blood of the village and reflected a living community. News was passed, people gently ribbed and satires exchanged, relieving many of the pressures that build up in a small self-contained community – essential in a society that relies on co-operation for survival. Curiously enough, in many small rural communities there is no anonymity, no hiding from the public eye, no personal 'space' to cool off, as there is in a large city. Social pressures must therefore be released before devastating feuds and libellous gossip arise that could severely damage crucial interpersonal relations. I would suggest that in a lot of modern communities, this catharsis is achieved through the use of alcohol. Whatever the case, the question of how social tensions are relieved in the village and in the city merits further investigation.[86]

TM: How often would you go to the céilidh house?

IM: Well I would be here tonight and another house tomorrow, you got...round the place y'know...and the rest of the boys would be following suit.

MB: Every night?

IM: Every night.... Aye except Sunday. Oh yes, well, we had church on Sunday. We had...to go there anyhow.

25. Iain with Maighrearad nighean Pheigi Iain Phàdraig (Margaret Bennett), *whose great-grandfather's house was one of the great* taighean céilidh [*visiting houses*] *in Glenconon. Sgoirebreac, May 16, 1992.* (T. A. McKean)

Well, I think it [was] Pàdraig Stiùbhart's house [it] was mostly. Yes, and Dòmhnull Oighrig's.... Well yes, Seonaidh Mór too, when he was there, John Anderson. Yes, [*laughs*] I used to go there for tales and yarns, he was very good at the yarns, you know.... Aye, old stories, aye.

MB: What kind of stories?

IM: Oh, you don' know where [i.e. whether] they were true or not!

MB: Ones like Gilleasbaig Aotrom? [*Foolish or light-headed Archie*]

IM: Aye, aye, aye, oh yes.

(See accompanying CD and Appendix Three for Iain's telling of the story, the text and background information.)

Iain draws a distinction between houses where one would go for the 'crack' and those where one would go for 'old stories'. Several neighbours were well known for stories, for example Murdo Siadar (mentioned above) and Katie MacKenzie, but the Sgiobair's interest was clearly in the songs and news side of house-visiting. An amplified distinction between types of céilidh house is made by Joe Neil MacNeill in Cape Breton:

They always would gather in a place where there was a lot of oral tradition, and, in the neighbourhood where I was it was Michael MacLean's house that was the best for lore and songs. And when people wanted to hear tales, it was Archie Kennedy's house; that was the house for tales, for if there was any entertainment at all there the tales would prevail. To be sure, if people came visiting who were good singers they would certainly sing songs at Kennedy's and tales would not be so well represented; and so if we were looking for a tale, we would be somewhat disappointed if many people came to the house and there was a lot of conversation and songs. (1987:30–1, translated from the Gaelic by Dr. John Shaw)

MacNeacail has never explicitly referred to the classic wonder tales in my presence and I do not know whether this is because they were mostly gone in Trotternish by the early part of this century or because he simply didn't take a great interest in them (a reason he has given for not learning other people's songs; the same may apply here).

The summer days, long and filled with farmwork had little time for the diversions offered by the céilidh houses, but in the winter (with nights as long as sixteen hours), the entertainment would start early and sometimes continue until dawn.

IM: Well, [on] the winter nights, you...wouldn't mind walking a couple of miles over to a house in Earlish or something like that. Somebody else would come here the other night and maybe three or four or five or six, maybe eight at times, according to what would be going on. That was...the ways of the Highlands, of the islands all through. It was mostly in the...Islands, that was...the customs. Mhm.

Many local characters, such as Dòmhnull Saighdear [Donald the Soldier] and An Sagart, would be there.[87]

TM: And they'd be telling stories as well?

IM: Oh stories, and things that happened and things like that you know.

Also discussed would be historical characters like Gilleasbaig Aotrom and the great Lochaber drover John Cameron, known as Coire Chuinnlidh.[88]

IM: Well I heard [about Coire Chuinnlidh] at céilidhs long ago of the old folk....

That was the way people were at that time, you know, tales at night, winter nights when they'd come from the labouring and they would be [at] a house here and a house there tomorrow night and these were the cracks [i.e. conversations] that were going on, you know, about people that existed in their own time and before then.

TM: So they were often stories about real people?

IM: Oh yes! Oh yes, well, you know, it was from mouth to mouth, you know. There was no writing or anything putting down then, but since then you know, they've got a lot of it in writing now, you know, what happened, but I don't suppose you'd get all the things that was there [in the céilidh houses] in writing at all.

Oh he was a noted drover anyhow. One farmer went and told one of Coire Chuinnlidh's men, "Come and see the flock of sheep I have here." Oh, he went to see them. "What do you think of that now?" There was a big flock of sheep.

"Och," he says, "I've seen more die with Coire Chuinnlidh with braxy"[89] than the farmer had [laughs]. So it tells you what kind of man he was, he had a vast area for cattle and sheep.

TM: [Did they tell stories of] other local people...at the taigh céilidh?

IM: Yes, that would have been the kind of talk they would have. That's how details went from one mouth to another, you know, and they came to me here from the old generations, you know. Maybe my grandfather would, he would be living at that time anyhow, [or] my father would tell so much about it and just from mouth to mouth,...everything like that.

Though he took a great deal of interest in local tradition and history, MacNeacail was not terribly interested in 'traditional' songs.

IM: But I never took much to do with others' songs at all....

TM: Why is that?

IM: I don't know, I wasn't just interested in [them]. Well of course I heard them often enough, but I wasn't taking the notion of them. I would rather be composing myself,...but I'm finished at that now.[90]

This self-confessed lack of interest may appear odd in a song-maker, but as a composer he naturally emphasises his own need to compose (and it is as involuntary as that) over learning the efforts of others. Despite this disclaimer, he has continually acquired songs, almost inadvertently by osmosis, both orally and from the printed page. Once, for example, I asked him where he learned *Feasgar Luain*, part of which he had just sung.

IM: Och cha robh mise seinn riamh ach mar seo fhéin: measg dhaoine eile, mar seo ag obair, any old way.

IM: *Och I wasn't ever singing [it] except like this: amongst other people, working like this, any old way.*

MacNeacail only occasionally sings songs by other poets, and never sings *puirt-a-beul* [mouth music] or *òrain luaidh* [waulking songs], though he certainly knows about them and would have heard plenty of them in the céilidh houses. Nevertheless, he constantly surprises one with quotes from songs one didn't expect him to know, in view of his avowed lack of interest in such material. Often, when I mention a song about which I am curious, he knows it and can recite or sing it. On one occasion he recited four verses of the nineteenth-century emigration song *Nan ceadaicheadh an tìde dhomh*, which he had only heard a few times on the radio and yet knew. In some cases, no doubt, he would have heard a song in the céilidh house, remembered part of it, or at least the melody, and reinforced the words by reference to the printed page. This is undoubtedly the case with some songs by his favourite song-makers, such as Dunnchadh Bàn, Màiri Mhór, Niall MacLeòid and Uilleam Ros, but it must be emphasised that he also has many songs and epigrams attributed to them and traditions concerning them which are not to be found in the books he possesses.

To return to the examination of village life between the wars: in addition to informal house céilidhs there were occasional village dances.

IM: There used to be two or three or four every winter there, but not now, unless they have one in summer or maybe when tourists are about. They have concerts and dance then. Aye that's all they have.

Several times a year the villagers would organise a formal public 'céilidh' more along the lines of our present-day expectations.

IM: Well, you had the song or you wrote [one, and], if you were a bit of a singer, you were called out to the platform and you would go there at a concert. They would select so many here and there. There was a committee who would be taking names the week before, you know, of all to perform the concert and make a sketch[91] of something, you know, and...that's the way they were.

Isabel Ross, brought up in Earlish, tells of the local céilidhs and the humorous sketches:

TM: Innis dhomh beagan mo dheodhainn[92] na céilidhean a bh'ann.

IR: Uel, innsidh mi an fhìrinn dhut, cha b'e bean-céilidh a bh'annamsa ann. Cha robh móran ùidh agam ann an òrain is rudan mar sin riamh ach bu thoigh liom eagalach rud ris an can ad *humour*, dìreach *laugh*, fhios agad, seòrsa dìreach de spòrsa.

TM: Airson spòrsa.

IR: Airson spòrsa, 's...cha robh mi...riamh trom air dhol air chéilidh na rud [?]mar sin, ach bu toigh liom, can, leithid a' Sgiobair, na Uilleam Iain Chaimbeil, sin eile bha fear [sic] a bhiodh a' gabhail òrain *comic*, agus dìreach dèanamh òran ma rudan a thachair,...na [rudan] *comic* mar sin.

Och na céilidhean a bh'ann an uair sin, 's bhiodh ad a' dol san taigh sgoile, 's bhiodh. Tha cuimhne a'm – a-nist, Aonghais, bha thusa aig fada bharrachd dhiubh sin – bha fear ann ris an canadh ad Duncan Corbett aig àm a' chogaidh, 's bhiodh ad a' dèanamh *sketch* air Hitler. 'S bha fear eile ann, có bha dèanamh Goering?... Bha Hitler co-dhiù, 's e *chauffeur* aig an dotair a bh'ann.[93] 'S cha robh e ach a' bruidhinn 's ùmadaraich[94] mu Churchill...a' spùtaireachd..."Gheibh sinn Eàrlais, 's gheibh sinn Calum Beag," ma b'fhior gu robh Hitler ag ràdh rudan mar s[in]. Bhiodh *sketch*-ichean ann, 's bhiodh òrain ann,...'s dòcha gu robh 'n *accordion* a' dol 's bhiodh danns dòcha as a dheodhaidh. Ach cha robh mis' ach dà chas cheàrr orm, 's cha robh mi math ann an dannsadh riamh.

TM: *Tell me a little about the céilidhs.*

IR: *Well, I'll tell you the truth, I wasn't much of a céilidh-goer at all. I never had much interest in songs and things like that, but I really liked what they call [i.e. you'd call] humour, just a laugh, you know, just sort of fun.*

TM: *For fun.*

IR: *For fun and I wasn't ever very big on going visiting or anything like that, but I liked, say, the like of the Sgiobair, or William John Campbell, that's another who was one who'd be singing comic songs, and just making a song about things that happened,...or [something] comic like that.*

Och, the céilidhs that were around then, they would be going in the school-house, yes. I remember – now Angus, you were at far more of them – there was a man there they called Duncan Corbett at the time of the war, and they would be making a sketch about Hitler. And there was another man there, who was doing Goering? There was Hitler anyway, it's the doctor's chauffeur who [played] him.[93] And he was just speaking and blustering about Churchill and spouting, "We will take Earlish and we will take Little Calum [MacDonald, from Idrigill]!" as if it were true that Hitler was saying something like that. There would be sketches, and there'd be songs, maybe the accordion was going, and there would be dancing perhaps after it. I only had two wrong legs on me and I wasn't ever good at dancing.

Murdo Stewart has similar memories:

MS: *Oh-ho, [laughing] I remember him in that one. Corbett was like Hitler, right enough. [laughs] He had a wee moustache and he used to take his hair down like this [pretends to pull his hair over part of his forehead]. The one who played Goering, he was a man from Ròmasdal, near Kensalyre. 'Laddie' they called him. Oh he was funny right enough! Laddie was a tall man and Corbett wasn't; they were a sight!

Between the work cycle of the year and the nights' entertainment, there was clearly no lack of activity, intellectual or physical. Another event where traditional songs could be found was the *luadh* [waulking], which still went on in Iain's youth.

IM: Luadh? O Dhia bha.

TM: Nuair a bha sibh òg?

IM: Bha agus nuair a bha mi sean cuideachd; chan eil cho fad' o'n a bh'ann. Uel, tha mi cinnteach gu bheil coig bliadhna

IM: *Waulking? O God yes.*

TM: *When you were young?*

IM: *Yes, and when I was old[er] too; it's not so long since there was [one] here. Well, I'm certain that twenty-*

fichead, bha feadhainn ann. Bha na h-ighnean a siud 's bhiodh iad a' luadh a' chlò, ach dh'fhalbh na breabadairean....

TM: O dh'fhalbh.

IM: Chan eil ad ann an-diugh, ach bha seanmhair Màiri, 's e breabadair a bh'innte, dhèanadh i plangaidean is clòimhean is eile.

TM: Bheil òran luaidh agaibh?

IM: [*laughs*] O chan eil! Cha robh thu a' gabhail ach dà loidhne dheth siud. 'S cha robh e cho fad' ri ceathramh idir, ri òran eile.[95]

TM: Nach robh sibh aig luadh idir?

IM: Och bha, bha. Bhithinn ann an còmhnaidh, bhiodh a h-uile duine ann. Bhiodh ad a' cruinneachadh air an oidhche ann, fhios agad; 's ann air an oidhche bhiodh ann. Bhiodh boireannaich ann 's na gillean òga a' dol dachaigh leotha, fhios agad, as déidh a' luadh.... O bha, bha sin.

five years ago there were some. The girls were there and they'd be waulking the cloth, but the weavers are gone.

TM: *Oh yes.*

IM: *They're not there today, but Màiri's grandmother, she was a weaver, she would make blankets, other cloth and things.*

TM: *Do you know any waulking songs?*

IM: *[laughs] Oh no! You weren't singing but two lines of it there. And they weren't as long as a quatrain at all, like other songs.[95]*

TM: *Were you ever at a waulking?*

IM: *Oh yes, yes. I would often be, everyone would be there. They would be gathering at night there, you know; it's at night [it] would be. Women would be there and the young lads going home with them, you know, after the waulking. Oh yes, yes.*

Most reports from the Outer Isles indicate that waulkings were for women only. Interestingly, in Skye, males seem to have been included, as they were in Nova Scotia and Newfoundland (Bennett 1980); perhaps the 'young lads' would simply come along at the end to walk the ladies home, as MacNeacail suggests.[96]

Hebridean lifestyles have undergone a dramatic metamorphosis. The depopulation that began in the aftermath of the '45, and which continued for a century and a half with the Clearances, has gone on unabated. And though the reasons for the exodus have changed, the net effect has not: a crippling of the native people's cultural (and financial) self-confidence. In the early days of the Clearances, the destruction of the clan system, followed later by the institutionalisation of a hostile education system, undermined the people's confidence in their own culture. In this century, the World Wars compounded these blows, altering the future of the islands through war losses,[97] and the changed expectations of many of the returning soldiers. Many moved to urban areas and many others became acculturated to an urbanised cash economy, both of which have contributed to the people's devaluation of their own traditional folkways.

MacNeacail, one of the older generation of Islanders, still has an unshakable belief in his own culture.[98] As for local social tradition, when I asked if the céilidhs had stopped, he was quick to respond:

IM: Oh they never stopped yet! Well they're not what they were, you know, television and everything has brought things to a halt now. Because that was the only way you had for going without a wireless or anything, you know.

The proliferation of radio and television has considerably altered daily patterns of social interaction and therefore the very fabric of island life, probably forever. This is a trite explanation for the demise of traditional cultures, but it is undoubtedly part of the reality, and one to which Iain himself draws attention. The rich oral culture of the Gael was quickly jettisoned in favour of these modern delights, which the people were 'educated' into valuing by exposure to more 'progressive' society (during war service, for example). Nevertheless, some house-visiting does still go on.

IM: Oh well, that's been going just till [recently]. Well, we get occasional...céilidhs,...not many, but maybe two or three comes and [visit] here.... We see quite a lot here at night, in wintertime.

The MacNeacail household is one of the few céilidh houses left. Often when I come to visit there are several visitors in for a crack and the atmosphere of the old céilidh is recreated. The visitors may be relatives, such as Iain's two sisters down from Siadar or old friends, such as Murchadh Sgudiborg, who grew up in Glenconon, and shared many a good night with the Sgiobair in the céilidh houses between the wars.

IM: They just [come] to pass the time, come all the same. And I would go over to the hotel and...make a night. [And] somebody else would come here just the same. That's how things were working. That was the customs, they were quite happy at that time.... They weren't rich financially in any way, but they had so much they did and were quite happy with it. Not what they are today.

Iain often laments this dramatic change in values that the community has undergone since his youth.

IM: Well, that was only entertainment you had;...people would come to your house and two or three of them...and I would go away the next [night] somewhere else myself, and maybe there were some [visiting] in here when I was away. That was the custom in the Islands all throughout, Lewis and Harris and everywhere. Aye.

But it's not...similar now with television and things like that and pubs. The pubs has brought a lot of destruction...here in Uig;...they're in the pub [now] when they...used to be in my house or your house or anywhere. Och aye. It's a change of life! Change of atmosphere. That's how it is.

Even Iain's reminiscences of twentieth-century céilidhs portray an almost idyllic picture of Highland life, recalling, as they do, the people's recreation during winter months. The spring, summer and autumn months allowed little time for socialising, as there was so much work to be done while the good weather and long days lasted; a crofter's life was, for the most part, harsh and unforgiving. If, from the perspective of the urbanised late twentieth century, this pre-industrial, rural life appears utopian, it was cultural traditions such as the céilidh house that made it bearable.

It is in this social context of hard work and community interaction, full of lively and witty verbal exchange, that MacNeacail has spent his life, composing songs and trading news with his fellow villagers.

On November 14–17, 1991 I attended Còmhdhail nan Seanchaidh at Iain Noble's hotel in Eilean Iarmain, Skye. One of the great benefits of the weekend conference is that it gives older tradition-bearers like MacNeacail a chance to get together and recreate a real old-fashioned céilidh. I felt privileged to be part of such an event and was delighted to see the sort of exchange of stories, jokes, songs, history and witty repartee that the Sgiobair has told me about in such detail. One memorable moment arose during a discussion on clan and place-name history: when the MacNeacails or various locales around Trotternish were mentioned, the Sgiobair would come to life, move to the edge of his chair, listening intently and periodically supply some information on Caisteal Uisdein or Coire Chuinnlidh. It was wonderful to see him in his element, his piercing blue eyes alive with the excitement of being transported back to the environment of his youth.

PART II

PRELUDE

There have been many, many Highland song-makers through the centuries and yet very little information exists on what stimulated them to compose in the first place. Even in recent decades, when Gaelic scholars have had access to the latest technology and to international scholarly writings on the subject, the tendency has been to publish text after text without adequate context of this sort. This section aims to provide some of that information about one traditional song-maker.

To describe a thought process is, at best, a difficult undertaking. Describing a creative endeavour as individual as song-making is even more so, since we must include matters such as context, motivation, 'audience' expectation and technique.

Over the years, there has been considerable conjecture in world song scholarship about how song-makers and singers work. David Buchan summarises the effort and skill needed for such study:

> Performer and repertoire study in historical perspective makes considerable demands, requiring as it does both solid detective scholarship to build up the picture of the performer, the social context, and the cultural context, and sensitive textual analysis to triangulate the performer, the contexts, and the performed text in order to arrive at the whats and whys of function and meaning. (1992:248–9)

Even as this passage notes some of the challenges, it reveals an omission of consultation, namely that with the singers and – in the case of Iain MacNeacail – the composers themselves. Sometimes, scholars confuse the concept of the performer and the creator, but, as E. D. Ives points out, "it seems a mistake to set 'folk' tradition apart from other artistic traditions as being one in which the two kinds of creativity are the same or of equal importance – or even one in which the former is less important than the latter." (1978:423) To make such a mistake is to neglect first-hand interpretations of social function and the song-*makers'* thought processes.

No doubt the prevalence of this approach is largely due to the fact that much work on individual song-makers and singers has been done posthumously: for example, collections such as *Dòmhnall Ruadh Chorùna* (Dòmhnallach 1969) and Dòmhnall Ruadh Phàislig's *Sporan Dhòmhnaill* (Mac an t-Saoir 1968), and studies such as David Buchan's *The Ballad and the Folk* (1972). I hasten to add that Buchan would certainly have been keen to interview Mrs. Brown, the subject of his study. In many cases, it is not through lack of desire, but of opportunity, that this gap in song scholarship exists.

In recent years, folklorists have shown a great deal of interest in informants and their backgrounds. Items of lore are now only rarely studied in isolation, due to the general ascendancy of context in folklore studies. *Lawrence Doyle: The Farmer-Poet of Prince Edward Island* (Ives 1971), *Folksongs and Their Makers* (Browne 1970), and Breandán Ó Madagáin's "Functions of Irish Song in the Nineteenth Century" (1985), and others, have made detailed studies of creativity and the function of singing in *context* (though still often after the fact). In Gaelic song scholarship, however, the social context of the *bàird bhaile* has been almost completely neglected. The rest of this book helps redress that balance by examining the bard's catalysts for composition and how 'lore' is used in the context of an informant's life.

To set the scene, I begin with a conversation I had with MacNeacail in June of 1992, in which he recaps some of the points discussed above and touches upon many of the ideas I will discuss in more detail in the following chapters. (See also CD track 1.)

IM: Ach 's e siud an aon dòigh a bh'againn an uair ad air cur seachad na tìde; cha robh telebhiseain, 's cha robh wireless, cha robh càil ann ach dol air chéilidh a's na taighean air an oidhche, 's a h-uile fear a ghabhadh òran, na dh'innseadh stòiridh 's air rudan a bh'ann, 's rud a thachair. "Seo am fear ann bha fad air falbh," 's thigeadh iad 's dh'innseadh iad, uel, eachdraidh 's mar sin. Sin mar a bha.

TM: Agus an dèanadh tu òran ùr a h-uile latha, no a h-uile seachdain?

IM: O uel, dòcha nuair a bhithinn a' coiseachd a' rathaid mhóir, thigeadh e gam ionnsaigh. Cha robh mi bodraigeadh an sgrìobhadh idir, cha robh càil. 'S dòcha gum bithinn a' coiseachd a' rathaid 's gu faicinn rudeigin, fhios agad. Bhiodh sin ag obair orm gos an dèanainn beagan air choreigin, agams'. Cha robh mi feuchainn mór sam bith bhith 'ga dhèanadh, ach dìreach nuair a bhuaileadh ad mar siud 'nam inntinn. Cha robh mi glé mhath air bàrdachd ann gad a bha mi ris, sin agaibh, cha robh! Ach [nu]air a chì mi na seann bhàird a bh'ann 's a' Ghàidhlig a bh'aca, chan eil càil an diugh coltach rithe. Och, 's e chuid as miosa nach eil mi cluinntinn na h-uimhir dhiubh air a ghabhail nis, na feadhainn aig Dunnchadh Bàn 's Uilleam Ros 's na daoine a bha sin.... Agus gheibheadh tu breithneachadh eagalach math aig Dunnchadh Bàn is a' chànan aca, a's a' Ghàidhlig a bh'aca. Uel chan eil Gàidhlig dhen seòrsa sin a' dol an diugh, chan eil, chan eil. Ach bha fios aca, 's e chuir an t-ioghnadh ormsa, nach eil dath a bh'...air an t-saoghal nach robh aca,...air a chur sios a's an òran mu dheighinn breac,

Bradan tarrgheal sa choire gharbhlaich
    's a' tighinn bhon fhairge bu ghailbheach tonn,
air buidhean buirb is e leum cho foirmeil
    'na éideadh colgail le ghormghlas druim,
le shoillsean airgid gu h-iteach meanbhbhreac
    gu ballach deargbhallach earball slìom.[100]

Thug e ris 'a description', mar a chanadh sibh, air a' bhreac ann a' shiud, ann a' faclan, 's cha leughadh e, 's cha sgrìobhadh e fhéin! Ta, bha fhios aig' air a chuile càil a bha siud, rud nach eil fhios a'masa air càil ma dhéidhinn!

TM: Bha thu gam innse stòraidh bheag mu dheòghainn Dunn-chadh Bàn agus...leabhar.... Cha [b']urrainn dha leughadh idir.

IM: Cha b'urrainn, cha b'urrainn, ge-ta bh'e aig' air dòigh eile....

IM: Ach, that was the only way we had then to pass the time; there was no television, there was no wireless, there wasn't anything at all but going on visits in the houses at night, and every one would give a song, or tell a story about something that was there, and thing[s] that happened. "Here's a man who was far away" and they would come and they would tell, well, factual stuff of all sorts and [things] like that. That's how [it] was.

TM: And would you make a new song every day or every week?

IM: Oh well, maybe when I would be walking along the big road, it would come to me. I wasn't bothering to write them at all, not a bit. Perhaps I would be walking the road and I would see something, you know. That would be working on me until I made a little bit of something or other, to have for myself. I wasn't making any big effort to do it at all, but just when they would hit me in my mind like that. I wasn't very good at composing although I was at it, there it is, I wasn't! But when I see the old bards that were there and the Gaelic they had, there's nothing like them today. Och, the worst part is that I'm not hearing the number of them sung now, those of Duncan Bàn and William Ross and all that crowd. And you'd get fearfully good imagination from Duncan Bàn and their language, in the Gaelic they had. Well, there's no Gaelic like that going today, no. But they knew, I'm amazed, there isn't a colour on earth that they didn't know [i.e. didn't have language for], as was put down in the song [by Duncan Bàn] about a trout,

A white-bellied salmon [is] in the rough corrie
    And coming from the sea of the stormy waves,
On the raging [? —] and he is leaping briskly
    In his martial armour with the blue-grey back,
With his silvery glitter, [and] finely speckled fins
    and his spotted red-speckled sleek tail.[100]

He gave a description to it, as you would say, on the trout there, in words, and he couldn't read and he couldn't write himself! But he knew about everything that was there, things which I know nothing about!

TM: You were telling me a little story about Duncan Bàn and a book, [that] he wasn't able to read at all.

IM: No, no, but he had it some other way.

TM: Dé thachair le Dunnchadh Bàn agus a' leabhar?

IM: Oh uel [bha duine] a' bruidhinn ris, gu robh a' leabhar aige ceàrr. "O" ars es', "sgoilear math, chan eil dol ag amharc ciamar a th'aige, gun leughadh e dòigh sam bith e", ge b'e dé an dòigh a bhiodh aige, sìos no suas, up or down. Bha e math gu leòr, fhios agad, mur robh thu 'nad sgoilear math 's gu leughadh tu e. Och cha dèanadh e sin idir, cha chreid mi gun dèanadh e sin.

TM: Cha robh e go diofar do

IM: Cha robh e go diofair dha, cha robh e dèanamh uaill dha fhéin air dòigh sam bith, ach bha e smaoineachadh dìreach gun dèanadh siud an gnothach, mar a bh'e fhéin ga ràdh. Rinn e móran de dh'òrain mhatha. Agus 's e obair nàdair bu mhotha bha e ag obair air.

TM: 'S e. Agus dé bha Màiri Mhór ag ràdh mu dhéidhinn òrain agus cuimhneachadh?

IM: O bha i ràdh, nuair bheirear i dhachaigh leis a' bhàs, bidh ar n-àl ga seinn. Thuirt i sin ceart gu leòr.

TM: Bidh na h-òrain ann.

IM: Uel bithidh, tha mi cinnteach, ach bha i minigeadh, tha mi cinnteach, na h-òrain aice fhéin....

TM: Uel tha iadsan gan seinn fhathast.

IM: O tha, tha barrachd 'n diugh...na latha a bha i beò. Tha, tha. Cha robh i cho iomraiteach...nuair a bha i beò 's tha i an-diugh dir, cha robh idir.

TM: What happened with Duncan Bàn and the book?

IM: Oh well, a man was saying to him, that his book was wrong [way up]. "Oh," he said, "a good scholar is not going to look how [i.e. which way up] it is, he could read it any way at all", whatever way he'd have, down or up, up or down. He was good enough, you know, if you were a good scholar you could [still] read it. Oh he couldn't do that at all, I don't believe that he could do it.

TM: It didn't matter to

IM: It didn't matter to him, he wasn't boasting about himself in any way at all, but he was thinking just that that would do the business, as he himself was saying. He made many good songs, and it's mostly the natural world he was working on.

TM: Yes. And what was Màiri Mhór saying about songs and remembering?

IM: Oh, she was saying, when she will be borne home by death, our generation will be singing them [i.e. her songs]. She said that right enough.

TM: The songs will be there.

IM: Well they will, I'm sure, but she was meaning, I'm sure, her own songs, that they would be sung.

TM: Well they're singing them still.

IM: Oh yes, more of them [now] than when she was alive. Yes, yes. She wasn't so famous when she was alive as she is today at all, not at all.

Chapter Four

THE SONG-MAKER'S ART

I thought anybody could make a song, but I didn't know.

THE BEGINNINGS OF INTEREST

The role of the *taighean céilidh* in transmitting rural Highland culture cannot be over-emphasised. As outlined in Chapter Three, it was by far the most usual (and natural) environment for oral entertainment traditions, providing endless information about the community, whether through songs, sayings, stories and legends of the past, or news and gossip of the present. From his earliest days Iain was a keen participant and it was there that he first began to take an interest in songs.

TM: If you heard a song that you liked [at a céilidh], how would you learn it?

IM: Och,...just from you or from somebody else, he had it and you would learn it from him.

TM: Just one or two listenings?

IM: Oh well maybe, and maybe no. If you wanted to get it you would, but...[you'd say to yourself], "I'm going out to get that song off him." I would learn from you, or I would scribble [it] down in my own way. I would concentrate on [i.e. study] that again, so I had it. Oh aye. That was the only way you had.... Mhm. Aye, that's the way.

In this highly oral culture, it is interesting to note that, though MacNeacail generally did not write down his own songs as an *aide memoire*, he did learn some traditional ones in this way.[101]

Mostly, Iain learned songs through repeated hearings, but with the near cessation of house-visiting in recent years, he does not often get a chance to hear singers. When he does, however, he can still pick up a song quite quickly.

TM: Last night you were saying that you like Christine Primrose's singing... and you recited a song she sang.

IM: Aye, aye.

TM: By MacKenzie was it? Who went to Canada?

IM: Aye, aye, he was a Leódhasach, a Lewisman, aye he was [from] Cnoc Chùsbaig in Lewis, that's where he lived, but he went to Canada and that's why he made [recites]

Nan ceadaicheadh an tìde dhomh

1. Nan ceadaicheadh an tìde dhomh,
   gun innsinn air do chàch
   mar a mheall a' saoghal mi
   le faoineasan gun stàth;
   Nuair a bha mi 'n toiseach m' òige,

If the time were allowed me

1. *If the time were allowed me,*
   I would tell to others
   how the world deceived me,
   with worthless vanities;
   when I was at the dawn of my youth,   5

bha mo theaghlach òg a' fàs,
mar a chaidh a sgapadh bhuam,
  le freasdal is le bàs.

Aaa, o chan eil càil, chan eil e agam idir, chan eil
cuimhne 'am air ge-ta. [continues to recite]

2. Mo chridhe gheall e sòlas
     nuair a bha mi òg is maoth.
   Gheall e iomadh seòrsa dhomh
     do shòlasan an t-saoghail.
   Gheall e, nuair a phòs sinn,
     gum bitheamaid beò go aois
   's gum bitheadh gach nì mar dh'òrdaicheadh
     's mo chòmhnaidh ri mo thaobh.

3. Ach chaidh an t-àm sin seachad,
     chaidh e mar fhaileas bhuam.
   Na sòlasan chan fhaic mi ad,
     tha iad a' falach bhuam.
   Mo theaghlach air a sgapadh bhuam
     is...fear dhiubh nach eil buan;
   rim bhean gum b'fheudar dealachadh
     chaidh eadar mi 's an uaigh.

4. 'S nuair a chì thu clann gun phàrantan,
     gun càch a' gabhail sùim,
   a dh'aindeoin dé cho àlainn
     's an t-àl nuair a bha ad cruinn,
   nuair a chuimhnicheas mi air Màiri
     bha cho gràdhach air a' chloinn,
   chan ioghnadh ged a dhrùdhadh
     air mo shùilean bùrn mo chinn.

Aaa, o chan eil e agam idir, chan eil cuimhne 'am
air ge-ta.... Sin agad e,...cuimhn' agam e co-
dhiù.

my young family was growing,
how they were scattered from me,
  by fate and by death.

Ahh, oh there's nothing, I don't have it at all, I don't remember
it anyway. [continues to recite]

2. My heart promised happiness
     when I was young and tender.   10
   It promised to me many kinds
     of the world's comforts.
   It promised, when we married,
     that we would be alive to [old] age
   and that everything would be as wished for [by me]   15
     and my wife by my side.

3. But that time passed,
     it passed like a shadow from me.
   The comforts, I cannot see them,
     they are hiding from me.   20
   My family [is] scattered from me
     and one of them who is not living;
   that we had to separate
     went between me and the grave.

4. And when you see children without parents,   25
     without anyone taking care [i.e. showing concern],
   despite how beautiful
     the family [are] when they are gathered,
   when I remember Mary
     who was so loving to the children,   30
   no wonder flows
     the water of my head [i.e. tears] from my eyes.

Ahh, oh I don't have it at all, I don't remember it anyway. That's
it, what I remember [of] it anyhow.

TM: So you learned that one just from listening to Christine.

IM: Aye aye, och yes. Yes well, I heard her, I think, on the wireless there a few times, you know, aye. Yes,
     but I didn't learn it all, there was a lot more on it, oh yes. Oh she's a good singer.

TM: Yes.

IM: Oh she's good. Oh yes, she used to go up to Iain Noble['s] there, Sir Iain. Every year we're going
     up there for a céilidh there.[102]

A visit to Iain Noble's is a true house-visiting situation for MacNeacail as he is able to hear songs in the
old way: "*I heard it from her, just. I heard it from her a few times and learned it." Hearing the song
on the radio several times after the céilidhs would have reinforced it, much like repeated hearings in the
local céilidh houses of his youth.[103]

Iain obviously has a retentive memory for songs and poems, a talent that also extends to local history and characters. It is worth noting how much background information he usually supplies for anything he tells me about, whether it be a traditional song, an anecdote about the drover Coire Chuinnlidh or one of his own songs. Such an insistence on the correct context and origin for a song or piece of tradition is well established in Gaelic oral tradition (Thomson 1983:79).

BOOK LEARNING

In addition to the lively atmosphere of the céilidh house, the Uig children also heard songs on a more formal basis, in school. "We'd usually have singing classes in school you know, before Mòds or any [Highland] games." Iain draws a distinction between school learning, where the teachers were there to "keep them right", and the less formal process of osmosis in the céilidh house. To him, the word 'learning' has connotations of formal instruction, indeed when speaking English, he sometimes uses the word 'learn' in place of 'teach', following the usage of Gaelic *ionnsachadh* which serves for both.[104]

Though English was the language of education, pupils were taught to sing in their native language for local events.

TM: But you'd be singing in English in school surely?

IM: Oh yes, but we had Gaelic[-speaking] teachers, you know, but it wouldn't do for us to have...an English[-speaking] teacher.... You had the Gaelic here, so that's how it...worked.

MacNeacail shows an inborn faith in the validity of his language and culture, as if it were no more than the children's due that they got Gaelic songs in school. Indeed it *was* no more than their due, but his assumption is uncharacteristic of a time when having Gaelic taught in school was far from being considered a right. Teachers in Highland schools at this time were often monoglot English speakers, though Uig school was fortunate in this regard. Theirs were usually Gaels and, while they did speak exclusively English in the classroom, they allowed and even encouraged the children to sing in Gaelic for Mòds and village céilidhs. In addition, there was an itinerant music teacher who saw to the more formal side of the scholars' musical education. In Iain's day this was the redoubtable Ethel Bassin, who was unusual in her respect of native traditions.[105] Nevertheless, Gaelic was struggling for a place in the educational system, as it continues to do today:

> The school in Gaelic Scotland has perhaps failed so far to promote an education which enables Highland people to conserve and develop their cultural and physical heritages. (MacKinnon 1972:385)

Fortunately, oral tradition has proved to be remarkably resilient, giving the present revival of language and culture a firm foundation upon which to build.

THIGEADH AD GAM IONNSAIGH

In Iain's youth, song was an everyday form of expression, and was seen as the natural vehicle for a bard's feelings, thoughts and opinions on virtually anything. To a great extent, therefore, all *bàird bhaile* song-poetry arises directly out of the 'need to react'. This idea will be touched on in more detail in the next chapter about the function of song, but let us look first at how he composes.

The phrase "thigeadh ad 'gam ionnsaigh" ["*they would come to me*"] has come up on numerous occasions in seven years of interviews with Iain. While being a very simple, and in some ways singularly unilluminating phrase, it does tell us several things about how a traditional song-maker works. Firstly, the songs come unbidden, sometimes unexpectedly. Secondly, in some ways, he feels that composition has nothing to do with him; the songs come to him, rather than him making them. They require no effort to compose. Thirdly, there is a sense of physicality about song-making; "they would come towards me" would be a more literal translation of the phrase. In one conversation, he described himself as very passive in the situation and used an even more physical description: "Cha robh mi feuchainn mór sam bith bhith ga dhèanadh, ach dìreach nuair a bhuaileadh ad mar siud 'nam inntinn." ["I wasn't really trying to do it, but just when they would strike my mind like that."]

Iain made his first song while still only a teenager, as we saw in Chapter One: "Ach I haven't got it today." Actually, he remembered Ho-ró tha mi fo smalan dheth (1), and sang nearly all of it immediately after this disclaimer. So, while still in school, MacNeacail had embarked on a life of song-making. He did not deliberately try to make them at first, but they came nevertheless.

IM: Well yes, now and again if something would come, but they were forgotten. [They were] only for the time being just.

Iain says that poets are born, not made, and he did not think of his own talent as anything unusual. This is reflected in his astonishment that others are not as capable: "*I asked the minister down there could he compose, and he couldn't do it!" This assumption of ability and an unquestioning acceptance of his skills has meant that he has not fully thought out how he composes; it simply happens. Over the years I have been interviewing him, however, I have asked him about how he makes the songs, trying to draw out how he thinks about it, even if he does not have the reflexive critical vocabulary of a modern-day literary poet.

Bha e furasda dha

From the beginning, song-making was a completely instinctive process.

IM: Oh yes, well it was coming to me, you know. I was passing by the road and something would come on me and I would maybe have passed by and then it would come to me again and would keep on. At the time I would never think of making...a song.

This is spontaneous composition; the song rushes in suddenly and builds up until finished or the muse departs. It is a sort of serial inspiration. One such occasion was the killing of the tup in Glen Hinnisdale, Nuair a thòisich iad ri bùidsearachd (8).

IM: Well as they were doing the thing, you know, I start singing and [as] we were discussing it I started composing you know.... And before they left I had the song made! [claps hands and laughs]

Spontaneous composition like this was not a unique occurrence, of course.

IM: I've seen, coming from Uig...Hospital to here, I was going for the forestry next day and I was in the hospital with Beileag Gillies out there, and she was there as a nurse, and Johnny Alec Tobhtscòir [MacDonald],...they were pair of them then.[106] Oh, they were asking me to compose a song before I would go and all that. Well, I was on the bicycle, then, coming here [?to Glenconon], so when I left the hospital I started pondering it and before I reached here I had it! It was coming to me, easy, you know.[107]

When Iain was at his most active, many songs came this easily. Three of them — A Bheileag 's mór a chaidh do mhealladh, Thoir an t-soraidh seo bhuam and Bidh mi cuimhneachadh is ag ionndrainn (12, 13, 15) — were addressed to Isabel Gillies, now Mrs. Angus Ross, who has known him for over sixty years:

IR: If he met, say, Mórag [my daughter] – she was a very bonny girl – he would compose a song just [like that]. I suppose he had an interest in poetry and in bàrdachd and he just seemed to get the word and then another word would follow.

This concurs exactly with Iain's own description:

IM: Gheibh thu facal an uair sin,...rud den t-seòrs' sin. Can gun do thachair rud a-raoir agus...dh'fhalbh mi suas a dh'Eàrlais no àite dhen t-seòrs' sin, 's dòcha bhithinn air a' rathad, bhithinn a' smaoineachadh air na faclan 's bhithinn gan cur ri chéile.

IM: You will get a word then, something like that. Say something happened last night and I went up to Earlish or some place like that, maybe I would be on the road, I would be thinking about the words and I'd be putting them together.

In this way, songs were made in an evening, in an hour, in a day, for nearly any event, occasion or occurrence. Many of these songs were also very short lived, however, due to their topicality, "*I'd make one and keep it for two weeks and then it would be forgotten;...they were for the time being just."

Considering the 'Occasional songs'[108] that have survived – which affirm that he did make this sort of song – it is safe to say that there were many more than the dozen or so complete ones presented here. His own estimate is well over one hundred.

TM: And how long would it take you to make a song like [Tha mi fo thùrs' air bheagan sunnd (7)]?

IM: Ach I don' know, it would come just mebbe quick to me at times, at other times no.... It all depends on how it was I would get the words to rhyme. If they were corresponding their own words to one another.

It appears that songs came in several different states of completion. Sometimes they would flow quite quickly, like Bidh mi cuimhneachadh is ag ionndrainn (15), and other times they would need more pondering.

Though many Occasional songs came without much effort, they were well made and worked on (as are other traditional song-makers', cf. Ives 1964:166, 128). They were not composed as they were being sung, but were often made very quickly. Mrs. Ross:

IR: Och bha fhios a'masa gu robh Sgiobair a' dèanadh òran ann a' priobadh na sùil....

Och 's e duine tàlantach a bh'ann ann am bàrdachd airson cha robh e go diofar, co-dhiù, 's e sgeula faoin dh'fhairich e, no rud annasach a thachair, na co-dhiù 's e cuidiche a's na ghabh e iùl – nuair a chaidh e dhachaidh 's bhiodh òran aige deiseil as madainn na màireach.

IR: Och, I knew that the Sgiobair could make a song in the wink of an eye.

Och he was a talented man at poetry because it didn't matter at all whether it's a foolish bit of news that he observed, or something unusual that happened, or whether it's a hint from which he took a lead – when he went home he would have a song ready the next morning.

TM: Bha e furasda dha.

IR: Bha e furasda dha. Agus a's a' linn a bh'ann, chanainn gur e duine breithneachail a bh'ann. Dh'fhàg e sgoil, tha mi cinnteach, nuair a bha e ceithir bliadhn' deug, sin mun àm a bha sinn uile ga fàgail an uair sinach. Uel cha chuala mi riamh gu robh e aimhreiteach;...cheasnaicheadh e a-mach rud gu faigheadh e brìgh a' rud. Sin a' seòrs' nàdair a bh'aige. An ann mar sin a fhuair sibh fhéin e?

TM: It was easy for him.

IR: It was easy for him. And at that time, I would say that he was an astute man. He left school, I'm sure, when he was fourteen, that's about the time we all left it then. Well, I never heard of him being quarrelsome; he would ferret out a thing till he'd find the substance of it. That's the sort of nature he had. Isn't that how you found him [to be]?

Now and again if the muse would come

Iain sang his songs in the céilidh houses of Uig, Glen Hinnisdale and Earlish, quickly gaining a reputation in the area.

TM: Did anyone ever ask you to make a song for them?

IM: Asking me? That's how they're there! I wouldn't have...ever thought of them.

TM: Really?

IM: Aye, but young girls and such like [and] all these people, you know, and something curious happening in the place.

TM: And they'd ask you to make a song about it?

IM: Aye, aye. Mhm.

A request for a song, as discussed above, does not always yield results immediately, but might start a train of thought leading to the creation of one. It depended largely on whether the muse was co-operating.

Recently a request from Sir Iain Noble for a song went unfulfilled because, "*Cha dàinig ad gu nàdarrach." ["*They didn't come naturally."] Evidently, the process could not be forced or hurried: "No, but it might come to me then." Another traditional composer, Calum Ruadh of Braes in Skye, felt the same way: "It came to me then, as if I was...being inspired all along, but some unseen, unheard of feeling came over me, and I had a verse done." (Knudsen 1978:11b)

The image drawn by these two makers of Gaelic songs is echoed by an Eskimo song-maker, of all things: "And then it will happen that the words we need will come of themselves." (Rasmussen 1931:321, quoted in Merriam 1964:175) Not only was a song uninvited, but there was very little MacNeacail could do to prevent its arrival, not that he would have tried.

It is said that emotional periods of life can also be times of great creativity (Miller 1981:198) and there is little doubt that MacNeacail's most productive period was between the wars, when he was in his late teens, twenties and thirties. There were numerous songs, many of them addressed to young ladies in the Uig area. As Isabel Ross said, "Och,...rinn e òran dhan a chuile nighean òg mun àm sin a bha san àite." [laughs] ["Och, he made a song to every young girl in the area at that time."]

The making of songs – whether by craft or inspiration[109] – was not difficult, as long as he was in practice.

IM: Cha d'rinn mi ach siud a dhèanadh ann an cabhaig aig an àm.... [Nu]air a...tha thu ag obair orra, mar a thigeadh ad gad ionnsaigh cho luath. Och, tha mise a' faireachadh cho *stale*.

TM: O?

IM: Tha, tha falbh cho *stale* dhomh. Nuair a bha mi a' cleachdadh a bhith ga dhèanadh,...cha robh taidhe sam bith agam, thigeadh e gam ionnsaigh.... O cha déid an-diugh. O tha mi gu math *stiff* an-diugh,...gu 'n cuimhnich mi.

IM: *I only made that [and it] was done in a hurry at the time. When you're working on them [i.e. composing a lot], they come to you so quickly. Och, I'm feeling so stale [about composing].*

TM: *Oh?*

IM: *Yes, yes, [it's] gone so stale for me. When I used to be doing it, I didn't notice at all, it would come to me. Oh it doesn't go today. Oh I'm very stiff today, till I remember.*

Walking the road

IM: When I used to be composing, it was walking the road and things would come to my mind. There was no word of writing it or anything, I couldn't do it. That was the custom, but when you were at it regular, everything was coming to you so natural some way. You would get some words coming in, but that was only just for the time being and it was finished, forgotten again, maybe for a night or two in a céilidh in ordinary houses about, that was the custom.

TM: Would you be thinking about a particular subject?... Would you be thinking about something as you walked along?

IM: No I would not!

TM: About a neighbour of yours or,

IM: No, but probably there was something that [would] draw your attention, it would be nice to compose a song for that. If it would come to you, then you would start on making, you know,...how you would put it and getting words to comply with that, och aye.

Again Iain connects motion, such as walking or cycling (as in *Bidh mi cuimhneachadh* (15)), with composition, an idea that is found in several areas of Gaelic tradition, most obviously in *òrain luaidh* [waulking songs] where extemporaneous verses are said to have been added to extant songs by members of the gathering (particularly at the end, in the *òran basaidh* [clapping songs], which teasingly paired villagers off with each other).[110]

To return to the connections between visual stimuli, motion and rhythmic composition, Aonghas Dubh, though he does not make songs, echoes several of the Sgiobair's thoughts. (Note his use of phrases very similar to Iain's (my italics)).

AM: I suspect there would also have been times when, you know, heading for the céilidh house, and maybe having *seen something in the course of the day or...as you're walking along the road* there'd have been [something] a bard would be liable to put his mind to.[111]

I mean I found myself recently...composing short pieces on my way down to pick the wee fellow up from nursery, 'cause I walk down, it's maybe [a] fifteen minute walk and,...by the time I get there I've got maybe just eight short lines of verse [and] I may elaborate on them further.

That's three or four pieces I've written in two months so it's not as if it's happening every day,...but surely [for] a young man who was a bard, who had that particular skill, [it] is a perfectly natural thing for the bard to do....

TM: I suppose if somebody was used to making up verses as he was walking along, he could hardly help it after a point.

AM: Well exactly.

The catalysts of location and motion serve as compositional stimuli on both subconscious and conscious levels.[112]

Iain's concern with rhythm extends even to reading his own songs in Catrìona NicGumaraid's booklet *Orain Aonghais agus An Sgiobair* (1980a):

IM: You [would] know by the way I was saying it, there was a slip, you know, and it was...some other word that was put instead that was breaking the contract, the rhythm;...the word wasn't coming to the syllables.[113]

MELODY MAKING
The question of melodic invention is more problematic than the creation of lyrics.

IM: Cha robh music a'masa dhaibh gad [a bha mi] gan chur ri chéile. Bha mi coma fhad 's a bha...ad a' dol ann an rhythm. O cha robh music agam...idir.... Chuirinn na faclan ri chéile ceart gu leòr air bha ad correspond-adh,...facal leis an fhacal eile,...och a chur ann am music, bhiodh e eadar-dhealaichte, mar a tha fhios agaibh fhéin....

TM: Is caite an d'fhuair sibh am fonn?

IM: Och chan eil fhios am, cha robh mi ach dìreach a' smaoineachadh...a bha ad a' rhyme-adh,...bha na faclan a' rhyme-adh, bha mi ga chur air a'...rhythm a bha sin. Cha robh fonn agam dha na càil.

IM: *I didn't have music for them, although I was putting them together. I was happy as long as they were going in rhythm. Oh I didn't have music at all. I would put the words together right enough till they were corresponding, one word with another, but to put them to music, it's different, as you know yourself.*

TM: *And where did you get the tune?*

IM: *Och I don't know, I was only just thinking that they were rhyming, the words were rhyming, I was putting it to the rhythm there. I did not have a tune for it at all.*

This implies that the melody itself grows from the way the words fit the rhythms, and his casual, off-hand manner makes it sound as if producing complex internal rhymes was effortless.

J. L. Campbell maintains that in the Scottish Gaelic tradition, the melody to the waulking songs could be extemporaneous as well as the text (Ó Madagáin 1985:159). This is surprising given, as we shall see below, that most traditional song-makers use extant tunes. Perhaps this opposition can be resolved by a redefinition of composition along the lines suggested by Anne Dhu Shapiro, who says that the creation of variants in the process of recomposing words is composition in the world of the traditional song-maker (1985:411).

Certain types of 'strophic metre', some of the songs of Eachann Bacach (Ó Baoill 1979), for instance, seem to call, or at least allow for, melodic creation in order for the composer to reach the pre-determined long last line of the verse.[114] The structure of Iain's *An cuala sibh mun ùpraid* (10) may hark back to this form of poetry, though he clearly uses a pre-existing melody in this case.

TM: Would you pick a tune that you knew already? A melody?

IM: Well, as long as they were agreeing, the words with one another. I was humming it, just to make it sound [like] something [i.e. like a tune he knew].

No, I had no tunes really...of my own, but I was just quite near another tune or something like that.

TM: Whatever tune seemed to fit the rhythm that you were working with.

IM: Aye, aye, aye, aye, that's it, if the rhythm was, if they were corresponding [to] the words, they would follow. You would...hum the way. Mhm. Aye, that's how it was. Mhm.

The idea that the song should be sung, though not necessarily to a unique tune, could be compared to reading a play to oneself as opposed to seeing it *performed*: the text is the same, but the rendering is unique, individual and in line with the author's intentions. For a song to live up to its maker's intentions, then, it must be sung.[115]

Iain does feel that there is a 'correct' melody for each song, as is shown by his saying that he doesn't 'know' certain songs, even when he is familiar with the words. Correct in this sense, however, refers to its rhythmic and emotional appropriateness, rather than to specific progression. One afternoon, after he sang me *A Mhàiri, a Mhàiri* (19), I asked if he had made the tune as well.

IM: Och cha d'rinn.... Bha mis' ag iarraidh *tune* sam bith,...mu facal tighinn ann a' *rhythm*, fhios agaibh, go *sound*-adh ad mar sin. Sin a bha mi ag iarraidh.

IM: Och no. I was wanting any tune at all. [I think] about word[s] coming in rhythm, you know, till they would sound like that. That's what I was wanting.

So the tune must go properly with the words, rhythmically and emotionally speaking, in order to be 'correct'.

It is interesting to note that if he does not know the melody of a song by another song-maker, he will set a tune to it as he goes along and sing it, rather than simply read it aloud from a book. He did this with Uilleam Ros', *Ged is socrach mo leabaidh (Cumhadh a' bhàird airson a leannain)* (MacChoinnich 1834:106–11):

IM: B'urrainn dhomh a ghabhail 'nam dhòigh fhìn ach chan eil mi ag amharc leis a' *music* idir.... *[I could sing one, in my own way, but I don't keep to the music at all].* [sings]

That's a love song for you!...

TM: Right!... Where did you get that tune?

IM: I had it just going to rhythm.

TM: Mhm.

IM: I only just have to make [sure] the words are corresponding to rhyme, to rhythm.... I put them [like] that. I have no tune for it at all, I have nothing at all....

Tha fear no dhà agam mar sin.... Tha feadhainn, ach còrr dhiubh, chan eil ad an *rhythm* idir dhomh. Tha mi ['g]a *rhyme*-adh, go *sound* adh.

I have one or two like that. Some are [in rhythm], but more of them, they aren't in rhythm for me at all. I rhyme [i.e. recite?] them until they sound [right].

This implies that a song is "in rhythm" if he knows a melody for it.

Even Dunnchadh Bàn receives the same melodic/rhythmic treatment. I asked if he would like to sing one.

IM: I don't know what one...[maybe] *Praise of Beinn Dòbhrain*. But that was for...pìobaireachd, it was for dancing and things like that.... [sings]

TM: When you would read Duncan Bàn...would you know a particular tune?

IM: No.

TM: Would you just pick a tune that fit?

IM: No-o. Well, I just [had] a tune that would suit myself according to the rhythm of the words,...that were, you know, corresponding in sound.

A song's rhyme also depends ultimately on rhythm.

TM: When you're making a song yourself,...do you try to rhyme in certain ways?

IM: Oh aye, I would, aye.

TM: Or does it just come out?

IM: Putting it in rhythm, aye.... Well, then I ponder it and I...make it similiar [sic, similar+familiar?] to a tune I heard or...some[thing] like that. No, but [if] it's not to the music...they [i.e. the céilidh-goers] would soon check you on that.

Here we see the audience conditioning the bard's efforts by demanding a certain standard and aesthetic. This is another aspect of the two-way communication between a bard and his public touched on in greater detail in the next chapter.

Chuirinn rudeigin eile ann

To some extent, Iain uses the words rhythm and rhyme interchangeably, with the implication that a word in rhythm *is* in rhyme. Rhyme to him is more than a simple alliteration; it is a confluence of rhythm, assonance, stress and melody, elements which come together to make a good line of poetry. If this confluence is not present, as is sometimes the case when we are going over a song he made seventy years ago, the rhythm is "broken" or the line is "not complete". "Tha rudeigin ceàrr ann a shin," ["*There's something wrong there,*"] he will say, mulling over the line until it comes right in his head.

Sometimes, the word "rhyme" is used to mean recite, meaning that he goes over a song until he irons out the irregularities. Speaking the verses is the exception rather than the rule, however, as he only does so when illustrating a point or going over the finer points of my transcriptions.

As can be seen from Iain's use of English loan-words in discussing his songs, these concepts are probably not ones that he has articulated before, even to himself. His exposure to this kind of analysis has been through the medium of English, so that he needs to borrow the terms.

Obviously, the need for rhythmic completion and a totally controlled verse form is a very strong one for MacNeacail, as indeed for Gaelic artists through the ages (Thomson 1974:159). For Iain, this need even extends across decades; when he is proofreading with me and sees a problem with the rhyme or rhythm of a song, he has a very strong urge to correct it.

IM: What['s] that. Something wrong there....

> Ho-ró tha mi fo smalan dheth,
> 's mi an còmhnaidh air an allaban,

aye [*reads on, trying to remember*]. What could I put there?

Bhithinn 'gan *recite-adh* rium fhìn, fhios agad, gos a' faicinn gu robh ad a' *rhyme-adh*, fhios a'ad, bha *rhythm* a' ruith ceart; mura robh chuirinn rudeigin eile ann. Sin mar a bha e.

I would recite them to myself, you know, till I'd see that they were rhyming, you know, [the] rhythm was running right; if it wasn't I would put something else in. That's how it was.

Even though the last two lines were there in the transcription we were reading, they did not sit well with him and he saw a need for improvement. In those days, he once told me, "*Cha robh tìde agam mar bu mhath liom e, gan dèanamh ceart!" ["*I didn't have [as much] time as I would have liked to make them right.*"]

Recasting traditional melodies

As we have seen, Iain is not so concerned with a specific melody as with its interaction with the rhythm. A song, therefore, has a 'correct' tune for him only to the extent that the air's rhythms and emotional pitch match those of the song, not that its melody is necessarily unique. The perception of whether a tune and the emotional pitch of the words match or not is, of course, a very personal one. In addition, serious songs can be set to light-hearted melodies and vice-versa, opening them to widely differing interpretations, from the solemn to the comic. Nevertheless, I stand by the point that Iain selects a tune, consciously and unconsciously, that suits the tenor of the lyrics he is composing (or rendering from memory, if he is singing a song that he does not 'know' from a book). He does not deliberately compose original melodies; his tunes are usually reworkings of traditional melodies that undergo a subtle recomposition during the process of song-making.

It is the norm for traditional Gaelic song-makers to make new words to old tunes. One has only to listen to Aonghas Fleidsear's songs (NicGumaraid 1980b) to realise that he and the Sgiobair shared a body of tunes upon which they drew when making new songs. On a larger scale, a look at almost any collection of traditional-style Gaelic songs such as Niall MacLeòid's *Clàrsach an Doire* (1893), Rob Donn MacKay's *Songs and Poems in the Gaelic Language* (1829), or Sinclair's *The MacLean Songster: Clàrsach na Coille: A Collection of Gaelic Poetry* (1881) will show that this was the case for most song-makers – nearly every song is preceded by the words "air fonn..." ["to the tune..."], followed by the name of a Highland or often a Lowland melody. In Ireland the situation is the same: "It was to a ready-made tune that the poet composed his verses." (Ó Madagáin 1985:158) Across the Atlantic, the practice has continued among emigrant Gaels who, according to Bloomfield and Dunn, make new songs "cast in the old pattern and set to old tunes". (1989:68)

This is also the case for Scots- and English-language song-makers; a glance at the songs of Robert Burns, or almost any broadside from the British tradition will reveal "to the tune of..." or "sung to the air..." beneath the title of the 'new' song. Even English-speaking North America is no exception: according to Ives "a traditional song-maker creates new words to old tunes." (1964:159) He goes on to say that,

> the maker of traditional song...does not think in terms of metrical scansion, but in terms of a tune he wishes his words to fit: the stanza forms and metres he uses will be dictated by the stock of tunes at his disposal. (1964:154)

This is too extreme: Iain does not select a tune beforehand. Instead, he has a song *text* in mind which serves as a rhythmic – and *by extension* melodic – model. His stanza forms and metres are therefore dictated by the stock of poetic models at his disposal, not the body of tunes he has to work with. (Of course, the models may have been originally defined by the forms, metres and tunes. We cannot categorically state which defined which in earliest days of Gaelic song-poetry.)

On very rare occasions, Iain creates a stanza form variation within a single song, as in verses two and three of *A's a' mhadainn 's mi 'g éirigh* (14), where he shifts from eight line verses, with two stresses per line, to six line verses in a repeated 2-2-3 pattern. As one would expect, the words and melody fit the modified rhythm perfectly, the whole combination lending an extra edge of emotion to his voice.

As may be seen in some of the Sgiobair's songs, he occasionally takes a common tune and totally reworks the rhythm for his own use (for example, *Loch Lomond* for *Tha mealladh mór am measg an t-sluaigh* (24)). This technique was noted by musicologists Melville and Frances Herskovits:

> Not all melodies are rephrasings of old ones. Sometimes a tune heard...can be "swung" into a desired rhythm, with perhaps a change of a few measures, or no change at all.... Many times this is done half-consciously, or unknowingly. (Herskovits 1947:277 and quoted in Merriam 1964:178)

Sometimes, of course, the melody in its renewed form has been in Gaelic tradition for years, so Iain is simply using a tune which is in effect traditional.

Brendáin Ó Madagáin says that the Irish composer's choice of tune is sometimes consciously made (1985:158); MacNeacail's is rarely so, if ever. He does not pre-select a tune to which he will fit words, although the basic contours of his melodies are drawn from a pool of songs that were popular on the céilidh scene between the wars (many have appeared in the *Còisir a' Mhòid* series of books as well, not that MacNeacail could read music). In his composition, the melody arises as a derivative of the rhythms of the words; it is a re-creation using the contours of a particular traditional tune as the point of departure. This is not re-creation in the Parry-Lord sense, in which the song(text) is re-created with each singing, but a one-time re-creation which takes place only during the process of composition.[116] Very occasionally, when he is having trouble remembering the 'right' tune to a song (his own or someone else's), Iain will 're-compose' a melody as he sings. To some extent, to call this composition or *re*-composition is a matter of semantics, but the fact that he does it both exemplifies a traditional style of melody composition and also reveals how important it is that the song be *sung* rather than spoken.

To Iain himself, the question of whether or not he has composed a particular melody from scratch is unimportant. Sometimes he says that he tried to make a tune "similar" to another one he knows, but on the whole he is just as likely to indicate that he made it. For instance, he says first that he made the melody to *A time will come, a time will go* (30), which is recognizably related to *The girl I left behind me*, and then that he "had no tunes" of his own, indicating that he does not compose melodies, nor does he think of them as independent entities; they really exist only as frameworks for songs.

IM: If the words were coming to the rhythm, you know,...I would put them [like that], if they would sound that way.

TM: ...So they'd fit with the tune?...

IM: Aye, aye,...as long as the words... – I would hum it like that – ...were coming in metre, you know.

Iain's attitude to melodic originality is echoed in another exchange in which I asked him to sing one of Màiri Mhór's songs from a book. He did, and when I asked him about the melody he used, he said he did not know the 'real' tune to the song, but that he had chosen this one because it fitted.

TM: Is that the same tune you used for *Nuair a thòisich iad ri bùidsearachd* (8)?

IM: Ah,...I don't know, could be.

TM: They're quite similar....

IM: 'S dòcha gu bheil, chan eil fhios 'am air sin. [*Perhaps it is, I don't know about that.*] [*pauses and thinks*] Aye, aye. Aye, aye [Màiri Mhór's song] *Nuair a chaidh na ceithir ùr oirre*, aye aye, it could be, mhm.

This is a revelation of sorts for Iain, who does not usually think along comparative lines melodically, although he often compares the text, language and rhymes of songs. Here, he himself makes a connection between his own song and the model he unconsciously used for it. Even though he ends up by saying "it could be", this is the only time he has ever named a source tune for one of his compositions. (The song bears no other resemblance to Màiri Mhór's; Iain has only used the melody and hence the verse structure.)[117]

Iain also sometimes uses one melody for several songs, seemingly unaware, until pressed, of their similarity. The tune, therefore, is not central to a song's identity in his mind, though I would not go as far as Ives in saying that there is no connection at all (1964:159).

In her article, "Scottish Regional Song Styles" (1985), which includes fieldwork done with MacNeacail, Anne Dhu Shapiro proposes the existence of several melodic shapes indigenous to the Isle of Skye. These she labels "Skye contours" and suggests that Skye song-makers unconsciously follow them when composing their own songs. As evidence, she compares the melodic contours of two of Sgiobair's songs with one by Màiri Mhór nan Oran and one by Uilleam Ros. The similarities are certainly there, but it is difficult to say whether this proves the contour's existence, or simply that Iain often uses Skye songs (including those of Màiri Mhór) as melodic models for his own.[118]

Given the creation, re-creation and re-working of original and traditional melodies in this type of song-making, the origin of a particular melody is a very subtle question indeed. From MacNeacail's perspective, he is making a series of subconscious decisions while making a song, so that the music "goes with the rhythm, with the syllables". As Somhairle MacGill-Eain, a modern European poet thoroughly conversant in Gaelic song tradition, has so neatly described it, "the song-poet is walking the tightrope of metre without being conscious of it, [making] ineffable melodies rise like exhalations from the rhythms and resonances of the words." (1985:112 and 106)

MacGill-Eain's description refers to the great anonymous songs of the sixteenth and seventeenth centuries, but the idea that the melody grows out of and with the song makes sense in the context of MacNeacail's modern songs as well. I have thought this for some time and recently Aonghas Dubh made the same connection regarding the Sgiobair's songs: "*Sorley talks about the total marriage of song and tune. The old Border ballads have that quality as well." Later, when discussing *Nochd gur luaineach mo chadal* (16), he again talked about the unity of words and melody and how, if a song is well-made, even a borrowed melody can seem unique to it.

AM: It just becomes [the song], when you hear it sung. It doesn't matter where the melody came from,
    it just becomes so much a part of...the song that it's as fresh as if you'd never heard the melody before.
TM: Maybe because the song wasn't *set* to the music, it all came at once.
AM: It all came together, yes. Uh huh. I think *Oran Uige* (20) has the same kind of quality.

Using an abstract, theoretical approach to the creation of melody – and keeping in mind Iain's focus on diction – we could say that the song-maker begins the melody wherever he or she likes, and is then faced with a limited number of choices for the next note, according to the ground rules of traditional melody (the traditional modes, habitual intervals, common cadences, etc.). The next note brings fewer options, the next even fewer and, by the time the first line is complete, he or she is practically locked into the rest of the song.[119] There is almost the sense of a 'tone language' type connection between certain syllables and the pitches to which they are sung. In other words, the choice of vocal sound and rhyme scheme virtually demands certain pitches and progressions. "I just [had] a tune that would suit myself according to the rhythm of the words,...you know, *corresponding in sound*."[120]

To put the same system in different and perhaps more acceptable terms, the composer knows a basic body of tunes (covering the various types and moods of song, such as lament, or praise), one of which is (unconsciously or consciously) selected as suitable. At each stage of composition, then, the song-maker further modifies this melody, bringing it closer to one of the recensions of these basic tunes until, by the time the second line is reached, the tune is 'made' or 're-made' (depending on the degree of modification demanded by the developing song).

> In the aesthetic world of the traditional singer, this is indeed composition; refashioning the Gaelic tune to fit the new text makes a completely new entity.... In fact, the use of old tunes with new texts may well be one of the principal means by which, over time, whole families of related tunes are spawned. (Shapiro 1985:411)

This seems a very likely solution to the problem of the origins of the enormous 'tune families' found in British Isles' and related song traditions.

THE SINGING IMPERATIVE

As we have seen, melodic originality is not an important characteristic of traditional song. We may therefore conclude that the measure of creative tradition for MacNeacail and his audience, the aesthetic upon which the song-maker is being judged, is the creation of lyrics (which includes the bard's treatment of his subject and the skill shown in fitting the words to the chosen melody, whatever its cultural origin).[121] This is not to say that the traditional composer disregards the tone and atmosphere of a melody as it relates to the subject matter of the song, but to Iain the music is not a *separate* concern. It is not the primary concern, but it is an essential one; what is crucial is that the song be *sung*.

MEMORY

I do not have room here to treat the subject of memory in any depth, but would like briefly to touch upon some of the main aspects of it (I will go into more detail in a forthcoming article on recovering *Tarbh Bhràigh Ùige* (4)).

How does a man of ninety-three remember a song that he made nearly eighty years ago and, when he cannot quite remember it, how does he reconstruct, and in some cases recompose, the song? The songs of most other local poets, such as Calum Ciorstaigh [Malcolm (son of) Kirsty] – "a great man for songs" – and Uilleam Iain Chaimbeil [William (son of) John Campbell], have been lost. With the breakdown of the old ways, the chain of memory has been broken.

IM: Och there was nobody there that could write then, so you had to take it in the book of memory. That's the only way you could have it then. If you could memorise them the son to the father down onward, that's how they were carried out. They hadn't got the advantage here [of writing].

The teaching of Gaelic did not start at Uig school until approximately a decade after Iain left, so he has had to teach himself to read and write the language. That he has done so indicates the depth of his commitment to maintaining access to his beloved song-makers and bards; their songs, with the demise of the rich oral world of the céilidh house, are accessible only through books.[122] Undoubtedly, this latter-day reliance on collected editions has some effect on his own poetry, but literacy is neither a prerequisite nor a hindrance to traditional composition, as Derick Thomson archly puts it:

> Illiteracy in a literal sense can co-exist with a high degree of "oral literacy", and this phenomenon has been strikingly present in the Gaelic area. Highly literate bards can write in the song tradition, and a variant of the bardic tradition can be found in the work of poets who were probably not literate in a literal sense. (1974:99)

I have never seen a manuscript of any of Iain's songs, except the two in English written out by Iain's sister Mary (*The news we've heard from Waternish* and *A time will come, a time will go* (27 and 30)). I am told that the late Hugh MacKenzie, of No. 6 Glenconon, would also occasionally write songs down for him. Iain has taught himself to read Gaelic well, but his writing is not as fluent and a postmistress and a schoolmaster were ideal candidates to serve as scribes. Hugh and Iain had been acquainted since youth and both he and his late brother – Murchadh Sgudiborg – used to céilidh frequently in Cuidreach.

The book of memory

In what was essentially an oral culture, repetition was the usual method of remembering a song, but with the demise of the céilidh house, opportunities have dwindled. Occasionally, MacNeacail would have someone write the songs down for him but, more usually, he would rely on his remarkable memory: "Once I got it together you know, it would be there."

Nor does Iain consciously make changes after finishing a song, as he considers them temporary creations: "They were only just for the time being and that was all forgotten you know." Many very topical songs were left by the wayside as the occasion passed and the details ceased to have relevance for both the singer and his audience. Indeed, the details of the song to Mr. Ball (31), discussed below, were forgotten almost immediately.

IM: They're all mixed up with me now. I never practise them now, you know, and they're gone dead. At one time, when you were young and your memory is active, it was going every night and everywhere somewhere, so you had it that way. Mm.

TM: Does it seem strange to see them in print?...

IM: [laughing] Yes well, I haven't got them myself, you know, where are they? Although I was composing them at the time, they were gone and after years of not being put in practice,...that's how they went....

The one I made in France [Nochd gur luaineach mo chadal (16)],...you have that one, have you? Well that was quite popular at one time, but I'm forgetting them now, you know. 'Cause they're past now and there's no word of it. But it was quite popular at the one time when I came home after the war.

Retrieval

For the most part, then, the songs which have survived are the ones preserved in Iain's mind.

IM: You had to take it in the book of memory.... If you could memorise them the son to the father down onward, that's how they were carried out.

Nowadays, there is no one to teach the songs to until I began this project. The first twenty-five or so songs were relatively easy to record, but recovering the last few has thrown some interesting light on the workings of the human mind.

The first challenge in retrieving songs that Iain has not sung for two generations is knowing what to ask for. One method is of course to say, "sing me a song you haven't sung for seventy years," a rather crude but occasionally effective method of retrieval. It only works, however, when he is aware of a song that he has not sung in a while. The songs that were most difficult to collect were the ones he did not even remember making and it is here that a catalyst to memory is vital.

This is the case with most fieldwork actually; it is therefore essential at least to know what you are looking for, preferably better than the informant himself. Without this knowledge you are unlikely to plumb the deeper levels of memory. The downside to having this knowledge is the tendency to pre-judge, giving a biased view of an informant's repertoire and world-view.

In the case of my work with MacNeacail, I am specifically concentrating on his own composition, so my fieldwork is deliberately biased towards that. In conversation with other villagers, neighbours and relatives of his generation, I have got hints of the existence of other songs. These range from phrases such as, "Rinn e òran eile mu dheodhainn na Pilgrims" ["He made another song about the Pilgrims"], to actual fragments of songs:

Isabel Ross: Rinn e òran mu dheodghainn tarbh a bha an Ùige: "Thug gach fear dhiubh ris a' mhonadh/ mun toireadh e an t-anam beò dhiubh", bha sin ann. O bha siud éibhinn. Is bha fear eile ann a rinn e dha na nigheanan a bha ag obair a's an taigh mhór. Chuir ad spògan circeadh...a's a' phost, mar fealla-dhà 's bha fhios aige 's rinn e òran man deodhainn: "'S e Santa Claus a rinn an fhòirneart uile orm/ 's a thug na spògan far eòin na Cuidirich."

Isabel Ross: He made a song about a bull that was in Uig: "Every one of them took to the hills/ lest it took their very lives", that was in it. O that was funny. And there was another one he made to the girls working in the big house. They sent some chicken's feet in the post as a joke, and he knew and he made a song about them: "It's Santa Claus who did the violence to me/ and who took the feet from the Cuidreach fowl."

Once armed with hints like these, I can prompt him, which sometimes works spectacularly well as in the case of *Tarbh Bhràigh Ùige* and *Chaoidh cha phòs mi tha mi'n dùil* (4 and 20). I mentioned the subjects and quoted the couplet I had and the songs, of six and five verses respectively, came tumbling out. Luckily I had the tape machine running, because, on some occasions since then, he has not been able to bring them to mind. Memory is truly a fickle thing, all the more remarkable, then, that he was able to summon up these verses at the drop of a hat, given the correct question to elicit them. How many songs and stories have been missed over the years through not asking the right questions?

Sometimes even a couplet hint is not enough to retrieve a song. In the case of *Spògan circeadh* (18), I recited the couplet and retold what I had heard of the circumstances of its composition. Iain remembered the event but not the song. This illustrates well the extremely temporal nature of much township poetry; the songs were very topical and as Iain says himself, they were "for the time being just". A few months later, the two verses came to mind when I prompted him again with Mrs. Ross' couplet.

Melodic catalysts to memory

In my experience with Iain, melody plays a central role in the recollection of songs. Earlier this year I was going over some songs with him. When he would stick at a line, he would pause until it or a passable substitute, came to mind. Eventually we reached an impasse where he knew there was a missing line and following that, a missing verse. At this point, his son Willie suggested that Iain sing through the verses, that that might help him recall the words. Indeed it did, and as he sang the song most of the difficulties disappeared. Memory, especially when tenuous, needs a certain momentum to maintain its flow; the melody provides that.

In this situation, I have watched as Iain recomposed lines and even verses, probably as close as I shall ever come to actually seeing him make a song.

Occasionally he would stop his singing or reciting as he reached a line that did not sit well. He would repeat the line until an inspiration came and then recite or sing the whole verse. Still the line would not sound right to him and he would say, "O tha rudeigin ceàrr ann a shin" ["*Oh there's something wrong there*"], and ponder the line until the right one came. Although in remembering a line he will sometimes say, "Cha chreid mi nach eil sin math gu leòr a' sin" ["*I think that's good enough there*"], or "that'll do", he is definitely looking for a 'right' way.

To some extent, this re-composition of lines is a formulaic reconstruction of the original, with the formulae being a combination of the metric and the poetic that one might expect in such township poetry.

The songs don't come as easily as they used to:

IM: O thigeadh e gam ionnsaigh.... [laughs] Ach [air son] beagan bhliadhnachan, cha bhiodh guth a'masa orra, fhios a'ad, dh'fhalbhadh ad.... [Tha mi] a' call mo mhemory. Och tha cuimhn' agam air rudan nas fheàrr, fhios agad, a bh'ann o chionn fad' na th'agam air an t-seachdain seo chaidh. Sin agad e.

Chaill mi, fhios agad, an art orra oir nach eil mi gan gabhail na càil. Gad a rinn mi aig an àm e, bha e math gu leòr; och cha robh an còrr ma dheodghainn, fhios ad. Sin agad...mar a chaill mi ad.

Cha chreid mi nach eil sin [an t-òran] math gu leòr a' sin.

IM: Oh they would come to me, anyway. [laughs] But for a few years, I haven't had the voice for them, you know, they've gone. I am losing my memory. Och I remember things better from long ago, you know, than what [happened] last week. That's it.

I lost the art of them, you know, since I'm not singing them or anything. Since I did it at the time, it was good enough; och there was no end to it, you know. That's how I lost them.

I think that [the song] is good enough there.

This is undoubtedly an echo of the days when the songs would come to him quickly, as he was walking the big road.

IM: Och 's dòcha gur ann coiseachd a' rathaid mhóir...gun digeadh rudeigin 'nam chlaigeann, fhios agad, nuair a bha mi oidhche mach còmhla ri cuideigin eile,...gum bithinn dèanamh [spòrs].

IM: Och maybe it was walking the big road that something would come into my skull, you know, when I was out one night with a few others, and I would be making fun [and having a laugh].

HE'S MADE A NEW ONE

Now in his tenth decade, Iain feels that his composing days are over.

IM: I'm finished composing, I'm no use now; my memory is gone complete.

MB: Oh, I don't know about that.

IM: Oh yes, yes.

The occasion on which he made these protestations, however, was only a few days after he made a new song (in December of 1990), so perhaps there are a few more songs to come yet:

Margaret and I had arrived for a visit shortly after Iain had returned home from the hospital where he had had a serious operation. He was sitting by the fire, dressed as usual in twill trousers, a white shirt buttoned to the top, maroon carpet slippers and a dark blue serge waistcoat with watch chain. His son John Angus was there and from here I will let my fieldwork notebook take up the story:

"He's made a new one," says [John Angus]. We asked [Iain] about it. It was to the doctor who did an operation on him.... Màiri said she tried to get him up on Friday and he wouldn't get up. Then she and [Jessie, one of their daughters,] tried to get him up and he wouldn't. Later he got up [at 2 p.m.!] and had the song made. Màiri said that was why he wouldn't answer and wouldn't get up – he was composing the song! Iain denied that that was when he had made it up.

Despite this denial, the echo of Martin Martin's description of the traditional bardic method of composition, lying down and in the dark, is striking (1884:116).

The composition of this song is a rare case where MacNeacail did make notes to himself: as he said on another occasion, "scribble [it] down in my own way," though, as will become clear, this was no more than a rough guide.

The song was on two sheets of [crumpled] steno[graphy] paper, three verses, English. Iain jr. was very proud of it. "It's good, eh?" He took it from Iain and showed it to us. Then we asked him to sing it, which he did — *changing some of the words to rhyme (and adding a few) as he went along!*

As he sang, with the papers on his knees, I looked on from beside him and I could see that he was not singing what was on the paper. The gist was certainly the same, and the words largely the same, but the way the lines ended was radically different. The rhymes in the sung version worked rather better than the ones on the page. Sometimes he sang the written words, but re-ordered, indicating that the writing was a sort of code to remind him of some of the words, but not really the song text per se.

The tune was the same one as he used for *An Eaglais Shaor an Steòrnabhagh* (26), another praise song. About twenty minutes later, when we had brought in recording equipment, we asked him to sing the song again. We gave him back the words, but he *did not recognise* the song, and sang it hesitantly and to a different tune; apparently it was not yet fixed in his mind.

Unfortunately, we had a problem with the microphone cable and the first recording was unsuccessful. When he sang the song for a third time, he was back to the first melody (the one that he had obviously composed the song to) and deviated from the written text in the *same ways* as before. On playing the song back to him, he mouthed all the words as he listened, then folded the paper and placed it on the mantelpiece at his side.

Perhaps that moment between not knowing at all and knowing by heart is just two singings and a listening away.

As we were leaving, much later in the evening after more recording, going over song texts and visiting, he lifted the paper off the tiled mantelpiece, slowly folded it over and over, bent to the fire, lit it and, between phrases of conversation, held the burning text to his pipe to light it. Usually, he reaches for some old newspapers tucked behind him in his armchair, but this time the handiest piece of paper was the song, no longer needed for its original purpose.

Compose, sing 3x and destroy original. When he used to do it often, it would come more easily (and stay better no doubt).

During his recovery in the hospital ward, Mr. Ball had practically demanded that he compose a song, "But I had no word[s] for that, on the tip of my tongue, at the time. So that's how that happened." It is clearly an unusual feeling for Iain to be unable to compose something on the spot; not only has he mentioned how easily the songs came in the past, but he remarks here how that ability has deserted him (probably through lack of practice as well as ageing and in this case having to compose in the medium of English for Mr. Ball). Nevertheless, *Should I have time available* (31) was finished in short order, despite the protestations to the contrary.

TM: How many days after that did you finish the song?

IM: Och there's no days in it, no! No, no.

The song may not have come as quickly as in the old days, but it appears to have been less than a day.

MB: So...you're still composing.

IM: Ach no, for a long time I haven't done anything at all.... The only one I did there, was this. Mm.

Despite MacNeacail's sense of finality, he admitted that he might add to the song: "I may, if I have something on my mind. It may come to me like that you know," so perhaps the situation is not as bleak as he first painted it. His memory, at age ninety-three, is still remarkably sharp. These days, however, the mental exercise and exchange found in a lively céilidh house is increasingly hard to find.

IM: O, [laughs] tha mi gan dìochuimhneachadh, a bhalaich. Chan eil mi gan cumail a' dol ann, fhios agad, tha mo chuimhne a' falbh. [sings]

IM: Oh, I am forgetting them, laddie. I'm not keeping them going, you know, my memory is going. [sings]

Songs that Iain has sung frequently and consistently do not appear to suffer so much from the vagaries of memory. Perhaps songs like Nochd gur luaineach mo chadal (16), made during the Second World War, and Nach bòidheach Ùige (20) are more universal in appeal and subject matter and therefore would have been sung more often, thus reinforcing them. Whatever the reason, versions of these songs recorded in 1951 and 1989 differ very, very little, whereas versions of songs less often sung and some still not fully retrieved show verses ordered differently, lines changed, refrains changed, used and not used, and, on one occasion, a different melody.

This last case is very unusual for, as we have seen, the melody is an organic part of the song as MacNeacail makes it. In this case, as he is retrieving and remaking the words of the song, he does the same to the tune. They were created together and are being re-created together.

One of the crucial features of these songs was their transience, a concept that is hard for most Western Europeans to grasp, used as we are to the permanence of the written word. They were oral both in use and in nature and were never meant to be written. By being transcribed, they have been so divorced from their function that they are transformed into different entities and judged by inappropriate criteria. It is time now to take a look at how the songs function in the social fabric of a Hebridean community.

Chapter Five

THE FUNCTION OF SONG
IN A HEBRIDEAN COMMUNITY

There is probably no other human cultural activity which is so all-pervasive and which reaches into, shapes and often controls, so much of human behaviour [as song]. (Merriam 1964:218)

There is a proverbial saying in Gaelic that testifies to the importance of song in the lives of the Gaels.

IM: "Mairidh gaol is ceòl;" *when the world will end,...love and music will last....*

TM: O chuala mi sin ach

IM: Chuala sibh e? Uel, chuala mi – tha Dòmhnull Nicolson ag ràdh gur e Màiri Mhór nan Oran thuirt e, chan eil fhios a'masa, ach tha e coltach gu leòr, co-dhiù; cha chreid mi nach eil. Bha siud a' dol co-dhitù: 's bha e riamh 's bithidh.

IM: *"Love and music will survive;" when the world will end, love and music will last.*

TM: *Oh I heard that but*

IM: *You heard it? Well, I heard – Donald Nicolson says that it's Màiri Mhór nan Oran who said it, I don't know myself, but it's likely enough anyway; I think it is [her]. That was going round anyway: it ever was and will be.*

Song is central to Gaelic culture and will outlast anything on this earth.

THE FUNCTION OF SONG

Having discussed how Iain made songs, let us now look at why he made them, and how they worked in his life and that of the community: the function as opposed to the use (a useful division drawn by Merriam (1964:218)).

Township poets like MacNeacail, whose witty, intelligent repartee was so popular at céilidhs, composed songs of love and emotion, songs about local history, elegiac songs and biting satires that, without naming names, left no one in doubt as to who was being lampooned. "They were feared of me making a song to them," says Iain. "Maybe myself and a neighbour were cast out on [i.e. disagreeing or feuding about] something, and that was enough."[123]

While satires and humorous songs were certainly a release for potentially damaging tensions in a small island community, those songs and the exchange of *aoir* [a satirical song or rhyme] were tempered by the many other types of song, such as songs of exile, like *A's a' mhadainn 's mi 'g éirigh* (14) about his years working away from Skye on the mainland; songs of love, like *A Mhàiri, a Mhàiri* (19), or songs about local events, like *Lìon a-mach go bàrr na cuachan* (17). Between them, MacNeacail and Aonghas Fleidsear, seven years his senior, made songs about the iron horse (in this case a bicycle), local and national political questions, affairs of the heart, amusing local occurrences, and even myxomatosis.[124] Each of these was "a good subject to make a song on...and that's how I did it". Many of these songs were, of course, exercises in composition, making Iain and Aonghas vernacular versions of the court bard.[125]

The very structure of the songs themselves indicates their function as carriers of local news, a point highlighted by the frequent opening line, "An cuala sibh..." ["*Did you hear...*"]. This is typical of township poetry; the listener is invited to become 'in the know', one of the entertained rather than the subject or victim of the song. Occasionally, Iain will close with a formulaic phrase like "Bidh mi niste co-dhùnadh..." ["*I will be concluding now...*"], indicating to the audience that the song, and the message contained in it, are coming to an end. These features, which may seem awkward in a reading context, are typical of oral township poetry (Thomson 1974:117).

While these songs are about issues and events, they are usually not narrative songs in the Anglo-American ballad sense. There is a story *behind* each song, as we have seen in Iain's desire to set the scene for each one, but they largely depend on the audience knowing the story and the characters already. Narrative is important, but it is taken for granted.[126]

According to Somhairle MacGill-Eain, "all poetry reflects social phenomena," (1985:48) but to MacNeacail and the older generation of islanders, a song is as much a personal expression of emotion and the need to communicate. It is used, as Ó Madagáin says, referring to both Irish and Scottish Gaelic song, "on occasions when feelings were such that ordinary speech was inadequate".[127] He goes on to state that this function has "largely been lost to characteristic Western society". (1985:143) MacNeacail, however, retains it as part of his everyday life for which it provides "a vehicle for the expression of ideas and emotions not revealed in ordinary discourse". (Merriam 1964:219)

Given that Iain could and did make songs at the drop of a hat, what were some of the different catalysts which would lead to, or even demand, a song? Since a song "never has a single function, but several simultaneously (usually including the aesthetic)," (Ó Madagáin 1985:214) the breakdown of catalysts and functions that follows is artificial; MacNeacail makes no such categorical divisions in thinking about his song-making. For the moment, however, the unnatural separation will serve as a framework upon which to hang some observations and points of discussion. In general, the further down the list, the stronger the drive to produce the song and the more obvious function it has as a response to a personal or community need.

THE NEED TO REACT

A' dèanamh spòrs – making fun

Many of Iain's songs were simply made in fun, to have a laugh, often at someone else's expense. Foolish deeds or fiascos would quickly make the rounds in the community and locals did not like to be caught out in one of his compositions, feeling that it showed them up, as in *Nuair a thòisich iad ri bùidsearachd* (8):

IM: "Oh well," he says, "it's a good recipe," he said to me. [*laughs*] That was the *only* thing he said about it himself. But the other boys were so vexed [at me for] composing that as they were doing it!

Another, more extreme anecdote from Murdo Stewart concerns *Tarbh Bhràigh Uige* (4): Duncan Beaton, 'Dunnchadh Beag' in the song, heard Iain singing it and, grabbing him by the collar, threatened to throttle him if he sang it again. This was, no doubt, largely in fun, because the two were great friends, but it does demonstrate the sort of reaction a township poet's incisive satirical observation could evoke.

In addition to the general *raison d'être* of making fun, there are specific catalysts which lead to the composition of a song.

Response

Most of MacNeacail's songs were made during or after events of which he was a part and are about his own reactions to them. A few others tell of events about which he heard, but of which he was not a part. Such songs are reports of things that 'really happened' or at least that the song-maker thinks happened; they are a representation of truth (Ives 1978:404). This type of song in the Sgiobair's repertoire ranges from songs of major occurrences, the effects of which he has seen (such as *A time will come, a time will go* (30)), to humorous songs about local events (such as *An cuala sibh mun ùpraid* or *An cuala sibh mun fhiadh* (10 and 9)).

IM: I've only heard about that; I was just composing as I was hearing about those people that was about there.

These songs of reconstructed events emphasise the function of 'song as response' in his life; it is the appropriate acknowledgement of an occurrence and, for the village, a marker of local happenings, history and the passing of time. They account for less than one third of the repertoire that we have today, but there were certainly many more over the years. Perhaps the reason more do not survive is that, being topical, they date more quickly than some of his songs on more eternal themes. They are a reflection of, and a personal comment upon, events that affected his life at the time; when the event is over the need for the response passes and the song is forgotten. To a great extent, *all* song is response, arising as it does in answer to a need of whatever description.

To view a song as the appropriate acknowledgement of an occurence leads to the next level of 'song as response'; often a song would be made in answer to direct questions or a pressing situation. *A time will come, a time will go* (30), appears in this category as well, as it arose in answer to repeated requests from visitors for information regarding the recent history of Skye and the Gaels (see case studies later in this chapter). Another example is the pair of songs, one Gaelic, one English that MacNeacail made for the Dutch landlord Johannes Hellinga.

IM: Well I didn't meet the man to know who he was, but...I was on the phone [i.e. Hellinga phoned] and he was having a night over there – however he got my name I don't know – but I didn't go at all, because, well, I thought he would be coming and she [Màiri] told me,

  "You better do something for him. If he comes, you have nothing to say to him." So that's how I was thinking.

Both Sgiobair and Màiri felt that he should have a song to give Hellinga in response to his expected query as to why MacNeacail did not attend the party. (Although Shapiro says that Hellinga actually requested the song himself (1985:410).)

TM: And why did you compose this one in Gaelic afterwards?

IM: Aye, likely I [would] like to have it both ways [or] something.

TM: Have you ever done that with other songs?

IM: No I didn't, but...I thought he may not understand this, but still he could interpret from the English one.

Request

This brings us to the directly elicited response, the requested song. Iain says he would never have thought of them, if people had not asked for songs. This is perhaps overly deferential as he would certainly have made many anyway. Isabel [Bella] Ross, to whom he made several songs in the 1930s, has told me that he required little or no provocation to make a song and in the twenties and thirties, the requests came thick and fast.

IM: Oh it was always the case they would be at you for doing it: "Do a song for me," from them, wherever they were, you know.

This is even reflected in one of his songs, *Ho-ró chan eil an smal orm*: "'S ann dh'iarr i duanag òrain orm/ gun d'ghabh mi dhi gu deònach e." (5:ll. 18–19) [*"Then she wanted a little song-rhyme from me/ and I sang it for her willingly."*]

IM: They would like to have something,...but there was no many, you know, composing there at all. But Fleidsear, he would be there.

TM: But everybody wanted one....

IM: Oh they would be! Aye. But many a time you didn't bother with them; you couldn't.

There were too many requests for him to keep up with them. Isabel, born in Earlish in 1915, remembers those days.

IR: An t-òran a rinn esan 'san Ospadal bha, Màiri Lamont, an cocaire, "Feuch a-nist an dean òran dhuinn," thuirt Màiri sin ris ach bha fhios amasa gu robh Sgiobair a' dèanadh òran ann a' priobadh na sùil.

IR: *The song that he made in the hospital, Mary Lamont, the cook, [said], "Go on, make a song for us now," and Mary said that to him, but I knew well that the Sgiobair was making a song in the wink of an eye.*

Many people asked for songs about anything at all, knowing that MacNeacail needed little stimulus.

TM: Really?

IM: Aye, but young girls and such like [and] all these people, you know. And something curious happening in the place.

TM: And they'd ask you to make a song about it?

IM: Aye, aye. Mhm. But I thought anybody could make a song, but I didn't know. Aye.

The songs came so easily and about any event that captured people's attention.

There was, as Iain indicated, no guarantee that a request would lead to a song. Even nowadays, when requests to compose are not as numerous as they once were, MacNeacail is circumspect about taking on a commission.

TM: Iain Noble asked you to make a song in English and Gaelic, didn't he?

IM: Aye aye. Och. That's impossible.

TM: Which you haven't done before.

IM: Oh no, I didn't.

TM: Except the odd word like 'guaranteed' [in *An cuala sibh mun ùpraid* (10)].

IM: Oh aye, aye. Oh well, I mean, he thinks [if] I put it in English and Gaelic she [his wife] would understand it, because she only speaks English, but he would understand [the] Gaelic right enough. But I can't make a mixture like that, och I can't do that! I'll have to say...something like that.... Aye well, aye, I'll say to him just that I was in hospital and I forgot all about it; so I did.

Though MacNeacail says it is an impossible task, he has made Gaelic and English versions of some of his own songs and has used the odd English word in a few of his Gaelic compositions. In addition, he is certainly aware of the great macaronic song tradition.[128] No doubt he finds the request itself a little mystifying, as macaronic song is almost exclusively used for humorous, satirical and bawdy compositions. As such it is, by definition, not suitable for an epithalamium.

He is quite coy about refusing Noble's commission, however, and indeed I feel that in earlier days he might well have taken on the challenge as a matter of course and of pride. A different possibility, that of class deference, emerged at another point when we discussed the request.

TM: Well, you could do like you did with John Hellinga and do one in Gaelic and one in English.

IM: Aye, I did, right,...but I had more scope there, I didn't care...who I was speaking to, but now she's a Lady! She married Sir Iain. Well she's going to inherit [the title of] a Lady now.... She'll be now Lady Noble. I [*laughs*] can't go about the like of that at all. If she was a common girl it was different.

TM: You wouldn't mind composing a song to her then?

IM: No, [if she] was common, but I don't know how I would go about it, the like of that kind, but he wants it.

TM: I'm sure he does...

IM: Oh yes, yes!

To people of noble birth, or social status such as Mr. Ball the surgeon, MacNeacail does show a sort of deference, but even this does not necessarily lead to his fulfilling the commission:

IM: "Ach no," I says, "I can't."...

"Och," he says, "you'll do it all right, you're a genius."

"No, I'm no," I says, "if I was I wouldn't be here!" So I never composed anything for him yet.

Obtaining a song from MacNeacail, then, is not as easy as it used to be. He may also see requests as impertinent in some way and beneath the dignity of his calling. Perhaps he always took commissions with a grain of salt, preferring that the muse of his own inspiration dictate when, how and for whom he makes a song.

IM: Iain MacInnes [i.e. Dr. John MacInnes of the School of Scottish Studies] was telling me to make a song for him, but I never did.

MB: You don't make them to order....

IM: No, I [don't], but it might come to me then.

Here again, if the muse cooperates, a song may be forthcoming, but the results cannot be guaranteed and the song may not be at all along the lines imagined by the person commissioning it.

Just such a case was Surgeon Ball's virtual demand for a song (discussed in detail in Chapter Four). Without realizing it, Ball had trespassed on the bard's prerogative to choose his own subject, a theme that runs through these anecdotes about requests. The fulfilment of the requests is another matter, however. For the song to Mr. Ball, an individual vision came to the bard and two days later the song was made, not on the subject Ball requested, but as it came to the composer. Song-makers are an independent-minded lot and if one asks for a song, one had better be prepared for the result. In the end, when I offered to play the tape or send the song to Mr. Ball, the Sgiobair declined, feeling, I believe, that it was not up to his usual standards. This shows that pleasing the audience is a concern, but it is not the major one – the major concern is the exercise of composing itself.

Adversity

The next form of response is in answer to adversity, such as a public slight. These are not revenge songs exactly, but are nevertheless a means of public retaliation. Song in the face of adversity is best exemplified for MacNeacail by Màiri Mhór nan Oran who was wrongly accused and convicted of stealing. He has related this story and its poetic consequences to me several times:

IM: Well,...she was so desperate and against the big people...that was in authorities.... She was all out...to get [them] because they did so bad to herself, you know.

    She was working in the house [in Inverness] and...there was a garment.... It was put into her chest and it was done by another maid that was in working in the house that had some grudge against Màiri Mhór. And when the ransacking [i.e. the search] came, you know, they found it in Màiri Mhór's chest and she was convicted and she got four months [in jail].

    But I think Teàrlach Friseal Mac an Tòisich – I think he was an M.P. – he paid the fine and she got only four months for the suit and...bha i ràdh [*she was saying*]:

> 'S e na dh'fhuiling mi de thàmailt   *It's the injustice I suffered*
>   a thug mo bhàrdachd beò.   *that brought my poetry to life.*

In telling this story, he acknowledges that such adversity can lead to a natural reaction in song.

IM: And that's what made her start, you know, she was that disgusted with her [?]fate and things that she never did and she was putting down on these people and you know, how they gave her injustice.[129]

TM: Did she make a song about that?

IM: Oh aye, there'll be...songs about it, you know.

Revenge and protest – sources of catharsis

E. D. Ives draws a distinction between songs of protest and of satire. The former draws attention to harmful conditions and social injustice in the hope of some redress, while the latter is spiteful, vengeful and not generally desirous of creating change (1964:181). According to this distinction, the Sgiobair has made both types of song, though far fewer of the latter. Examples of his songs of protest would be Tha sluagh òg air dhol gu aimbeirt (23), warning of the consequences of licensed pubs in Uig and Tha mealladh mór am measg an t-sluaigh (24) which warns against itinerant evangelists, in the hope that people will see through false promises of salvation. Several more of his songs which may fit into this category were made retrospectively (such as A's a' mhadainn 's mi 'g éirigh and A time will come, a time will go (14 and 30)) and therefore were not expected to bring about a requital, but serve instead as a record of discontent or injustice. Probably the best recent example of protest song from Uig is Fleidsear's Oran Dotair Green which castigates the absentee landlord of Raasay House for his neglect of the property (NicGumaraid 1980a:24–5).

    Frederick Lumley, in Means of Social Control, defines satire as "an unanalysable mixture of humour and criticism" (quoted in Ives 1964:167). This definition would certainly apply to some of Iain's songs, but in the realm of observation and comment (as opposed to love and nature), his song-making tends to the humorous rather than the critical. Numerous people acquainted with him for decades have said that he is far too nice a person to be capable of such vitriolic songs. As far as the satire/revenge song is concerned, then, we have mostly mild public rebukes, rather than the scathing songs we usually associate with the genre.[130]

One such public scolding was *Ho-ró chan eil an smal orm* (5): "Sin an aon *revenge* a bh'agad." ["*That's the only revenge you had.*"] 'Revenge' is not meant in any very sinister way, only, as I said before, as a means of exorcising one's own humiliation. The use of song in this way, "as therapy," is a "highly important aspect" of traditional composition (Thomson 1974:82).

A poet was not condemned for these retaliatory songs; they were the natural reaction of the song-maker. Perhaps this aura of immunity owes something to the legendary *leabhar nam bàrd* [the book of the bards]. According to this tradition, a poet, if he or she was officially regarded as such,

> enjoy[ed] a kind of diplomatic immunity. There are numerous anecdotes told in connection with this – always involving the composition of satires, frequently addressed to girls who had spurned the bard's advances. (MacInnes 1968:41)

And yet this sort of complaint in song is a curiously humbling way to get even, as the details of the event become known to everyone through the song. The making of the song is therefore more of a catharsis and a 'laying to rest' of a grievance than a real retribution or punishment.

Iain himself has used the word revenge on occasions other than the recording above, though still not in a sinister way.[131] I asked him if he had ever been kept out of a house for his song-making, following a lead from Peter Stewart about such an event (see songs 12–14).

IM: No I don' think, I don' think that ever happened.... No, I never heard of that, no. No, they never put me out of the house anyhow. I'm sure of that, because they knew...if they did, probably there would be a revenge in a song! Oh they wouldn't do that.

Villagers were clearly wary of crossing the Sgiobair, or even drawing his attention, or there would be a song about them in short order.

TM: And some people...didn't want [a song] but you made one anyway.

IM: Oh well, if you're going to miscall them, as long as it was good, you know, it were alright, it would suit them fine.

TM: Did you make many like *An cuala sibh mun ghàrlach ud?*[132]

IM: Oh no....

TM: How many of those?

IM: No, one or two, but I wouldn't, you know, they were too filthy. Aye, aye.

In his latter years, MacNeacail views such songs as a product of the volatility of youth. He expresses some regret and would like to see this particular one suppressed. Nevertheless, they obviously fill a need in the community for the censure of those who transgress certain boundaries. Other villagers could also make good use of the song by singing it to its target. At the very least, listening to it would be cathartic.

IM: Oh they were happy with it, aye. Ach aye,...they would be, they would be casting it up to him, you know. Aye.

It appears that the criticism was accepted as deserved, or at the very least entertaining, if the song was well made ("as long as it was good"). Clearly, this harks back to the earlier bardic idea that if a satire was unjust, or went too far, it would either lose efficacy or rebound upon the composer; "satire was a double-edged weapon which could injure him who used it as well as his enemies." (Matheson 1938:xx) For the Sgiobair, the song would castigate the guilty and exonerate (or at least by-pass) the innocent, as he reveals in discussing his song *Tha mealladh mór am measg an t-sluaigh* (24) about the travelling evangelists.

IM: If you were right, it wasn't interfering with you, but if you weren't, that's [i.e. the song is] to your condemnation. Aye, that's how I took [it]; I wasn't making them going to be good when they weren't!... If you're good, it doesn't interfere with you, but if you are bad, this [*tapping the song text in front of him*] judges you.

...I mean where there was a real person [i.e. true Christian], he was preaching it right and, well he was alright. But if they were going to convert me and convert you and all that, within a fortnight they were back to their old ways. Well that's no conversion at all!

TM: Well their emphasis was on converting you right then.

IM: Aye that was it.

TM: As quick as they could.

IM: Aye that's [it]! Aye and they did it. You know, it wasn't left to God or grace to come to do it then; it's them that was doing it, see. Well, if they were not that type, this [song] didn't affect them, you know what I mean?

Note his insistence above that the *song* not the *song-maker* judges a person, which may be the basis for the long-standing bardic immunity mentioned earlier. (See case studies below for more discussion of revenge and satire.)

Competition

The ultimate in artificial catalysts for song must surely be organised competitions. In a sense, they are a formalised and logical extension of the flytings that sometimes took place between two bards well into this century, according to Aonghas Dubh MacNeacail.

AM: I know of a man down in Sleat, Aonghas Dhunnchaidh [Angus (son of) Duncan], Angus Mac-Donald,...who will quote you little flyting exchanges between bards, a local bard and a visiting bard, that he remembers. Whether they're from his own time or from an earlier time [I'm not sure], but they were there, that kind of extempore exchange. I think Angus was talking about seeing it happen. That sort of thing was still... happening,...people took it for granted,...well into the twentieth century. We may see 1900 as a time of great change, but it didn't bring electricity, it didn't bring radio, it didn't bring television.

So in Iain's youth, such exchanges would have still been going on.

AM: And he might be going into a situation where he would have to extol the virtues of the North-end bard over the South-end bard, who happens to be in the village or whatever, you know,...or a Staffin bard is over céilidhing [and] there'd be odd wee flytings that would, as a lot of the waulking songs did, take on local contemporary topical detail.

This competitiveness can be seen in *Tha mealladh mór* (24), where Iain was provoked into composition by another local song-maker: "There was a fellow in Uig too who was composing a thing and he was praising them and so I got it the other way about." One can also see the good-natured rivalry between Iain and Aonghas Fleidsear in their songs about the continuation of licensed pubs in Uig (see *Tha sluagh òg air dhol gu aimbeirt* (23) and Fleidsear's *Oran a' veto* below.

Competition, in the form of flytings, or women trying to out-do each other composing at the waulking board, had been part of Gaelic society since the early days of the bards. And even in the early twentieth century, Marjory Kennedy-Fraser heard of a song-contest at the end of which "the vanquished singer dropped senseless from chagrin". (1926:137) The field was therefore ripe for the formal competitions brought in by the Mòd in 1892. Local Mòds sprung up all over the Gàidhealtachd, and even much of the Lowlands, encouraging competitions for singing; MacNeacail himself won several prizes at the Portree Mòd.

IM: Oh I got a...couple of prizes there, right enough, [for songs] of my own composition and...other songs.

In later years, there have been other types of competition too, such as the newspaper announcement that led to the composition of *An Eaglais Shaor an Steòrnabhagh* (26):

IM: Bha mi eòlach gu leòr air an duine, fhios agad, agus bha Hughie MacKenzie – b'e maighstir sgoil' an uair ud – an oidhche bh'ann, fhios agad, chaochail MacRath [?]'s bha mi bruidhinn ri Uisdean, agus...bha Uisdean...airson rud a chur air falbh airson *competition* a bh'aca. 'S cha b'urrainn dha càil a smaoineachadh na b'fheàrr na dhèanadh òran do MhacRath. Thòisich mi air an oidhche sin fhéin!

IM: *I knew the man well, you know, and Hughie Mac-Kenzie – he was the schoolmaster then – that night, you know, Macrae died and I was speaking to Hugh and Hugh wanted to send something off for the competition they had. And he could think of nothing better than to make a song to Macrae. I started on it that very night!*

The competition was the catalyst, but, interestingly, MacKenzie's natural response to this emotionally pitched issue was to ask Iain to make a song. This idea – of song being the appropriate medium for the expression of such grief – was borne out by the public response to the song.

IM: O fhuair mi *demand* gu leòr air òran 'acRath, fhios ad. Bha ad cho eòlach air a[nn an] Leódhas. Bha litrichean 'gam bhombardadh ann a' sheo.... Bh'ad a' sgriobhadh go Fred Macaulay, feuch a faigheadh ad an t-òran a bha seo....

IM: *Oh I got plenty of demand[s] for Macrae's song, you know. They knew him well in Lewis. Letters were bombarding me here. They were writing to Fred Macaulay [of the BBC], trying to get the song here.*

Recreation – passing the time

"A chur seachad na tìde" ["*To pass the time*"] is the single reason Iain most often gives when asked why he made a song:

IM: Och cha bhithinn ach dèanamh rud, fhios agad, rud dhen seòrsa ud, airson feuch chur seachad na tìde, aig an àm [nu]air a bhiodh *céilidhs* a' dol air an oidhche ann an tighean mar a bha seo.... 'S bhiodh dùil aig duine, 's ma bha *notion* agad do dh'òrain, bhiodh tu 'g obair orra mar sin.

IM: *Och I would only be making something, you know, something of that kind, to try to pass the time, at the time when there'd be céilidhs going at night in houses like there were here. And one would expect, if you had a notion for songs, you'd be working on them like that.*

It is probably true to a great extent and, as he says, before television and radio, "Siud an aon chur seachad a bh'againn!" ["*That's the only pastime that we had!*"]

For both the composer and his fellow villagers, then, making songs (and house visits) was largely a pastime, rather like watching television or pursuing a hobby is for some today. Even when asked about the background to a song, such as one to a young woman in Kingsburgh, he reiterates the point. "Ach bha...rudeigin de seòrsa a chur seachad na tìde [*Ach, it was something of the kind to pass the time*], when you'd come home."

To stop at this would be too simplistic, however, because song-making, learning and singing were such a part of daily life that they also functioned on many other levels. This is not to belittle the need for pastimes in any way – all societies need their recreations – but simply to note that MacNeacail, as part of the community, may not see some of the other ways the songs work; he is unable to gain an objective perspective (and it probably does not occur to him to try).

Here the study of context comes into its own. Examining a whole body of bàrd baile poetry such as MacNeacail's must be a two stage process of (i) defining the song-maker's perspective and (ii) using this perspective to interpret his world *from his point of view* to see the interactions between his inner world and his outside world for what they are.

A means of expression

Much of the time, as MacNeacail says himself, the songs were simply made for fun:

IM: Oh well, how silly. Words, eh? But it was just amusing to have at the time and that was all that's in it. They would be forgotten. I never thought we would have this [i.e. tape recording and my transcriptions].

TM: Well you remembered [*Oran an tombaca* for me] two years ago. [*I hand him a transcription of the song*]

IM: When I got it here before me, it comes to me, but to tell me to [sing it and], I wouldn't have it, but I saw this now, it comes to me.... That's how I was, just putting it in my own way. [*sings more*]

He draws attention here to the composer's own vision which leads him to express through song in his "own way". The songs have a more central role in MacNeacail's internal life than he has been letting on and, by extension, in the life of the community of which he is a part. This brings us to the idea of individual vision and expression.

Expression through poetry is one of the few ways in modern Western society that people (though only select persons, such as poets and other 'artists') may still display raw, deep, undisguised emotion. Furthermore, such poetic expression is generally considered 'purer' and more direct and personal than expression in prose. Usually, this kind of emotional release is socially acceptable only at events specifically arranged for such a purpose, like poetry readings, where people are predisposed to accept a different level of emotional exposure and personal communication than they are used to in their daily lives. It is a specially orchestrated moment where interaction is expected according to non-usual codes.

MacNeacail's world of song-making and singing, while on one level about entertainment, is also about the regular, usual and unremarked expression of widely varying levels of emotion. The heightened speech of a song makes the emotional content more easily acceptable.[133] It is as if poetry readings were as unremarkable and regular a pastime for average Western society as breakfast table conversation or reading a newspaper. In this context, the poet's individual vision revivifies the poetic process with each composition, reaffirming the medium as a vehicle of expression.

To the poet, this vision will have its own internal logic, reference and validity as "any work of art is a distortion, a reshaping of reality for an aesthetic end". This reinterpretation of reality is also shaped by the tradition in which the song-maker works (Ives 1978:405–406). It is this internalised model we are trying to understand through examining MacNeacail's songs and his world in such detail. I believe that this perspective is the core of the folkloric study of context; it is as central to the artist's view as an outsider can get.

Though MacNeacail would not, of course, use these words to describe it, he is certainly aware of the importance of this individual perspective. This is clear from a story he tells about Dunnchadh Bàn Mac an t-Saoir, which shows how remarkably aware he himself is of the dichotomy between what the outsider hears and what the poet knows:

A man criticised Dunnchadh Bàn's *A Mhàiri Bhàn Òg*:

IM: "Uel, chan eil mi smaoineachadh," ars iadsan...ri Dunnchadh Bàn, "gu robh 'Màiri bhàn òg' cho bòidheach 's bha thu ràdh idir."[134]

"O cha b'e mo shùilean-s' bh'agad idir," arsa Dunnchadh Bàn. "It wasn't my eyes you had!" No, you couldn't beat them. Sin agad e, bha esan moladh,

> A Mhàiri bhàn òg, 's tu 'n òigh air m' aire
> ri m' bheò bhith far a' bithinn fhéin,
> on fhuair mi ort còir cho mór 's bu mhath liom
> le pòsadh ceangailt' o'n chléir,
> le cùmhnanta teann 's le banntaibh daingeann,
> 's le shnaidhm a dh'fhanas, nach tréig:
> 's e t' fhaotainn air làimh [le gràdh gach caraid]
> rinn slàinte mhaireann am chré.[135]

O bha e math air a dhèanamh. Ach bha fear eile 'ga chriticisadh. "O," arsa Dunnchadh Bàn, "cha b'e mo shùilean-s' a bh'agad idir."

IM: "Well, I don't think," they said to Duncan Bàn, "that 'young fair-haired Mary' is as beautiful as you were saying at all."

"Oh it was not my eyes that you had at all," said Duncan Bàn. "It wasn't my eyes you had?" No, you couldn't beat them. That's it, he was praising,

> Oh young Fair-haired Mary, you are the maiden I have noticed
> to be where I would be all my life,
> since I won a right to you, as much as I would like
> by the bonds of marriage from the clergy,
> with a firm covenant and with fortified banns,
> and with a knot that will endure, that will not yield:
> it is gaining you by the hand [with the love of every friend]
> that made health [for me] that will survive creation.

Oh he was good at doing it. But another man was criticising him. "Oh," said Duncan Bàn, "it was not my eyes that you had at all."

He had an answer for him. Dunnchadh Bàn was right; he saw it in a different view than him – "It was not your eyes I had."

TM: So his song was his view of it.

IM: Aye, that's it. It was his eyes, so you are seeing it that way, not the other man['s]. So he gave a good answer, you know.

TM: So a different person's song on the same subject...would be different.

IM: Oh yes, it would be probably.

TM: Like Angus Fleidsear's veto song.[136]

IM: Aye, aye.

TM: Completely different.

IM: Oh different aye.

There is no question in his mind that each song-maker is possessed of an individual perspective, which makes his compositions unique. Whether those compositions measure up to MacNeacail's standards of poetry is another matter, but the validity of a particular composer's vision is unchallenged.[137]

Why song?

What makes someone express themselves in song? For the Sgiobair, coming as he does from a society in which song was an accepted daily form of communication, it is a natural response. Should one desire to express something, a song was considered the proper medium in which to do it:

IM: Oh well, that's the only thing that I think,...because [if] you were inclined to give a description on anything, you would like to have it in a song. And you were just giving, commenting on the way it was, similar to that [i.e. describing it just like it was].

TM: That would be the way you'd describe something?

IM: Aye, the way you thought of it.

Song-making leads the maker to experience life differently, for he is already filtering reality through the aesthetic of his art.[138] And the subject is chosen partly according to how good a song could be made from it.

Conversely, a good song is one that comes closest to the marrow of the subject:

IM: I think Macrae's song [*An Eaglais Shaor an Steòrnabhagh* (26)] was more truthful than any of them, you know. You were only just putting him as he was, explaining how he was.

Song is at its best when it bears out the truth of its subject and the truth is best served when expressed in a song, the apogee of personal expression: "You would like to have it in a song."

This idea is borne out throughout MacNeacail's life. One can see it in daily conversation, where he will frequently answer a question with a quote from a song or with an epigram from one of his favourite song-makers, especially Dunnchadh Bàn Mac an t-Saoir, Uilleam Ros, Màiri Mhór nan Oran or Niall MacLeòid. To him the most concentrated form of information, or answer, is a song and he always refers to one for accuracy and validation when a point of discussion is at hand, much the way others sometimes use proverbs.[139]

Ephemeral creations

Motivations and subject matter aside, these songs were, more often than not, ephemeral. Frequently, they would arise out of a brief encounter with someone at a céilidh, be sung a few times and then forgotten, for example *Tha mi fo thùrs' air bheagan sunnd* (7). "[I would] take it, sing it for her the next day or anytime I would meet her again.... That's all I would have [been] meaning. Mm, aye." This gives a sense of how 'occasional' these songs were, much like the bardic compositions of the past, which were made for a particular event and then sung and discarded, their content perhaps too topical and quickly outdated for them to last long. It is this quality which makes the songs so hard to separate from their function; no doubt in Iain's mind they never were so divorced.

IM: I was only making more fun, mockery and things like that, you know. Maybe there was nothing in it, but just for the sake of composing and things like that.

I believe that this touches upon the central function of these songs in the bard's life. "Just for the sake of composing.... Just putting it in my own way" and "You would like to have it in a song" show that song-making is more than an activity. The songs define him, as he defined them, throughout the course of his ninety-three years (so far).

CASE STUDIES[140]

Any number of the categories presented above may apply to a given song to various degrees and in any combination. Let us now look a little more closely at some of the ways certain songs function. All of

Iain's compositions could profitably be examined in this way, but, because of limited space, I present just two of these 'case studies'; others will appear in print shortly.

(i) Debate and exchange through song – two local poets in opposition

Until recently, céilidh-goers in Trotternish would have been able to hear exchanges between many local song-makers. The *bàird bhaile* would be expected to make up songs of teasing, satire (both gentle and strong), one-upmanship and wit (the flytings referred to by Aonghas Dubh). This sort of exchange was undoubtedly commonplace and certainly served to "pass the time". Nevertheless, the songs performed a more complex function in the life of the community – they were a means of debate, a forum where certain issues were presented in different ways, according to the vision of each song-maker. Often a village such as Uig had several bards who would, inevitably, often disagree. The villagers could then hear several perspectives, and assess the issues in light of them.

Generally, the bards' compositions expressed their own points of view, defining the community by the topics they chose. But they could also express public sentiment by reflecting villagers' opinions. In this way, the community also defines the bard by providing his compositional agenda (through their actions and by their judgement of his songs).

In either case, the songs provide some interesting options for the listeners: (i) they can sing or applaud the songs which support their own views, bolstering their confidence, or (ii) they can choose not to sing them and/or withold approval when others sing them. If they did not sympathise with a song's sentiments, they simply wouldn't sing it (Ó Madagáin 1985:176). The bards do the work and the people get the information. By choosing a 'side', the villagers lend several levels of approval or disapproval to the issues touched on. Through song, therefore, people are able to express opinions they might not otherwise be able to articulate (cf. Ó Madagáin 1985:185). And even if they could express them, the bards do so more eloquently due to their facility with words.

In singing or simply responding to these songs, villagers also benefit from a measure of deniability. If challenged they can truthfully disclaim responsibility of authorship, thereby distancing themselves from the content in much the same way as a Gael could sing a pro-Jacobite waulking song (see Campbell 1933), or a bothy man in the North East of Scotland, a scurrilous bothy ballad (see Henderson 1971). The formal rhetorical package, in which the message is transmitted, allows the singer or listener to distance his or her self: 'It's just a song,...I didn't make it up,...I was just singing it.' This distancing occurs in the story-telling tradition as well, as is indicated by the classic closing line: "Ma's breug bhuam e, is breug ugam e." ["*If it is a lie from me, it is a lie [that was told] to me.*"] (Nicolson 1881:305)

The song and the sentiments can, if necessary, be blamed on the bard, who becomes the scapegoat or the spokesman for the community, depending on your point of view.

> In due course, the song passes into the entertainment repertoire and acquires a permanent vitality by becoming a symbol which singer and listeners can identify with and so give indirect expression to their emotions. (Ó Madagáin 1985:185)

Even as late as the 1960s, the use of song in public debate was still functioning in Uig, concerning the heated controversy over whether to allow pubs to continue trading in Trotternish. Several communities held votes on 'the veto', as it became known and which, had it been passed, would have made the villages in question officially 'dry'. The early decades of this century saw a licensed bar in the Uig

Hotel, but the local landlord had let the licence lapse in the 1920s as it was very expensive. According to Iain, he wanted the tenants to have more cash in hand, thus allowing him to raise the rents. Thus Uig was virtually dry until the 1960s, when several pubs had opened and the issue arose again.

There were fervent and protracted arguments with plenty of support on both sides of the issue. In general, the village was divided by age, with the older people feeling that pubs were not a good idea and that they would lure youth away from the church, home and their work. They worried that drink would become a focal point of life and that too much money would disappear down the throats of an already cash-impoverished population. The young, as ever, were eager for change and demanded their right to a licensed pub. Pressure from the outside world to be up to date with urban culture was tremendous and younger Gaelic society, 'educated' to abandon its roots and island culture, yearned for all the accoutrements of modernity. They were becoming discontented with their local céilidh scene. Firmly straddling this debate were the two song-makers, MacNeacail and Fleidsear. Each made several songs about the veto, but on opposite sides of the issue. Throughout the campaign, they sang them at céilidhs and to any interested listeners, giving us a rare contemporary view of public debate through traditional song.

The veto is by no means the only situation in which MacNeacail made a song opposing someone else's opinion, for he was ever independently minded. Another instance concerns the 'Pilgrims', the itinerant evangelists who came door-to-door around the island in the 1950s and '60s. Such 'travelling salesmen' of the soul have appeared periodically for centuries and continue to visit island homes, much to Sgiobair's disapproval. "There was a fellow in Uig too who was composing a thing and he was praising them and so I got it the other way about," he says, as noted above. In part, the Sgiobair felt challenged, as a bard, to make a song of opposite opinion to this "fellow in Uig" and was not afraid to do so, since he did disagree philosophically with the other song-maker (see *Tha mealladh mór am measg an t-sluaigh* (24)).

The veto issue was more publicly debated than the 'Pilgrims', however, as there was to be a vote on the matter.

TM: Would people expect you to make a song about something like this?

IM: No they wouldn't, but there was nobody do[ing] them.... But when you saw that was...a good subject for a song, [you made one].

MacNeacail is being overly modest in asserting that the neighbours would not expect a song; my conversations with other villagers show that such songs were expected at the drop of a hat and on just about any subject.

TM: So people would listen to the song that they liked, the song they agreed with.

IM: Oh they would [?]use them, but aye, they would have it from both of us. Aye, they didn't mind, you know, as long as it was just there, aye, if they get it, if it was there.

Here we see that people took it for granted that a song would appear. "As long as it was just there," he says, people did not make a fuss.

TM: But you and Angus Fleidsear would make songs about things.

IM: Aye, Angus Fleidsear had one too.... Aye, but he was praising it though, where I was against it, see.... Contrary. Mhm. [*laughs*]

In addition to his disagreement with Fleidsear over the veto issue, the Sgiobair also relishes a healthy devil's advocacy role.

For his part, Aonghas was sure that he was right.

Aonghas Fleidsear: Bha latha ann a' Snitheasort,...bha deasbad mhór ann...ma dheodhainn, co-dhiù, bu chòir na taighean-seinnse a bhith fosgailte...na an dùnadh uileadh. Nise, rinn mi an t-òran seo ma dheodhainn 's cha chreid mi nach tuig sibh e. Och bha fear eile shuas anns a' Chuidirich, fhios agad, An Sgiobair, bha esan a' smaoineachadh dòcha gu robh sinn ag òl cus. Och tha mi smaoineachadh gur e mis' a bha ceart!

Angus Fletcher: There was a time in Snizort, there was a big debate anyway about whether pubs ought to be open or if they would be closed entirely. Now, I made this song about it and I think you'll understand. Och, there was another man up in Cuidreach, you know, the Sgiobair, he was thinking maybe we were drinking too much. But I think it's me that was right!

Oran a' veto

1. 'S tha 'n tìd' againn bhith smaoineachadh
   ciamar théid an t-aonadh;
   tha buidheann air gach taobh a tha dalma;
   's e veto a thuirt aon diubh
   a fhreagradh air daoine,
   ach feuch nach gabh sibh 'n daorach g'a
      dhearbhadh.

2. 'S e veto tha cur cùram
   air Snitheasort 's air Uige,
   thubhairt ad às a' chùbaid gu falbh e;
   ach tha uisge-beath' is leann ann
   cho math 's tha san dùthaich,
   's bidh sinn uile diùmbach e dh'fhalbh às.

3. Nuair a bha ar sinnsir
   a' fuireach a's an tìr seo,
   siud agaibh a' linn a bha calma,
   le sùgha glan an eòrna –
   's e chleachd ad leis a' bhròthas –
   chan iarradh ad ri'm beò chur air falbh ás.

4. Och ma théid a' veto
   an aghaidh luchd na spree-adh,
   théid sinn a Phort Rìgh ann an carbad;
   tha cuid a ghabhas pinnt ann,
   tha cuid a ghabhas spree ann
   cuid eile dhiubh nach till mar a dh'fhalbh ad.

5. Och ma gheibh ad am Port Rìgh thu,
   théid thu dhan a' phrìosan;
   cuiridh iad am breather ga dhearbhadh;
   théid e ma do shròine
   's bidh t' anail a' record-adh
   cia mheud glainne dh'òl thu mun d'fhalbh thu.

6. Ach 's ann bhios a' spòrs againn
   nuair a thig latha bhòtaidh,
   bithidh na taighean-òsd' air an dùnadh;

The veto song

1. Time for us to think
   how the agreement will go;
   there's a band on each side who are obstinate
   it's a veto said one of them
   that would suit some people,   5
   but see that you don't get drunk testing it.

2. It's the veto that is causing anxiety
   for Snizort and for Uig,
   they said from the pulpit that it [i.e. whisky] will go away,
   but there's whisky and ale   10
   as good as any in the country,
   and we will all be indignant [to see] it go.

3. When our ancestors were
   living in this land,
   that's the race that was robust,   15
   with the pure sap of the barley –
   which they used with the brose –
   they would not ever want to put it away.

4. But if the veto goes [through]
   against the spreeing folk,   20
   we will go to Portree in a vehicle;
   there are some who'll take a pint there,
   there are some who'll go on a spree there
   [and] others of them who will not return like they left.

5. But if they get you in Portree,   25
   you'll go to prison;
   they'll put a breather to test it;
   it will go around your nose
   and your breath will be recording
   how many glasses you drank before you went.   30

6. But we'll have fun
   when voting day comes,
   the hotels will be closed,

ach air chùl na còmhladh,
nach bochd nach robh sinn còmhl' riutha,
gos an d'readh na bhòtan a chùnntadh.

but behind the outer doors,
isn't it sad that we weren't with them, 35
till the votes would go to the count.

7. Och na dèanaibh bòsdadh
mun rathad chaidh a' bhòtadh;
tha feadhainn air an dòigh 's cuid tha diùmbach;
och, 'illean, nuair a dh'òlas sibh
na bheil 'na ur pòcaid,
's e 'n dealan th'air a' chòmhlaidh ur cùrsa.[141]

7. But do not boast
about the way the vote went;
some are contented and a portion are discontented;
but, lads, when you drink 40
that which is in your pockets,
it's the bar on the door [that] is your route.[141]

(NicGumaraid 1980b:A2. This rendition of the song is on the accompanying CD.)

An Sgiobair, as noted before, was in favour of the veto; he felt pubs would lead to further excess. In the interests of space, I will not reproduce his song here, but refer the reader to *Tha sluagh òg air dhol gu aimbeirt* (23). Even the Sgiobair's melody sounds disapproving, with its lugubrious timing and subdued contour as opposed to Aonghas' light-hearted melody (the dance tune *'S mór tha mi smaoineachadh*). It will be noted that MacNeacail's song is not *totally* disapproving: he admits in verse seven that drink may have some virtue if taken in moderation.

In the end, the veto failed by a few votes and the pubs were allowed. As it turns out, according to my own observations, the older generation was largely correct. Whisky has always been available in Portree, even in the days before licensed pubs in Trotternish, and MacNeacail approves of a dram taken in moderation: "*There's no better way to show a welcome, than to offer a dram. But that's all, just as a welcome." To the older generation it was, and still is, a sign of hospitality and part of many rituals in the cycle of life, such as births, christenings, weddings and funerals (see Bennett 1992). To the young, however, it has become a focus of social life and an escape from modern post-industrial rural poverty and joblessness.

As far as the function of song is concerned, what is at issue here is not the outcome of the debate itself, but the fact that the villagers, even as late as the 1960s, looked to their local bards for perspectives on an issue and for articulation of their own feelings. The local song-maker retained this crucial role in Gaelic society as both a medium of and a catalyst for public debate until very recently. He serves as a record of opinion, like the bards of classical Gaelic society, and also expresses his own biases in song. His opinions are often given more credence than those of a 'normal' (i.e. non-song-making) citizen, as he had a reputation for thought, cleverness and eloquence. Ethnomusicologist Alan Merriam maintains that "social institutions are validated through songs which emphasise the proper and improper in society, as well as those which tell people what to do and how to do it". (1964:224–5) The exchange of songs between Aonghas and the Sgiobair, however, draws attention to both the proper *and* improper simultaneously; it is up to the villagers to decide which song represents which.

In later years, as a range of modern changes comes to rural Gaelic Scotland, the local song-maker is viewed as more and more of an oddity by the younger generation (see Chapter Six). Even so, many of the young people still appreciate that a talent for song-making is rare and that the bard may be capable of a more direct access to emotion and the expression of it than they are. These two song-makers are part of a centuries old dialogue that has been and still is indispensable to successful village life.

(ii) A Gaelic song-maker's response to an English-speaking nation

In recent decades, as Skye has shifted from a crofting economy (largely dependent on subsistence farming and barter) to a cash economy (increasingly dependent on tourism) and the number of English-speaking incomers has increased to flood proportions, MacNeacail has seen his village, his island, his language and his culture overcome by a tide of Anglicisation. Tour buses, Members of Parliament, Lords and Clan Chiefs all weave their way down MacNeacail's mile long side-road (often getting stuck in his driveway) to visit him in his role of 'Bard to the Clan Nicolson'.[142] What are the implications of these changes in the fabric of society to a man for whom song is such an essential form of everyday expression?

Recently, in response to English-speaking incomers' queries about the content of his Gaelic songs, and about the history of the Gaels and the Isle of Skye, MacNeacail has started to respond in English, but in the medium in which he feels most comfortable – that of song. To date, he has made two types in English: praise (a type often found in Gaelic tradition) and protest.

For centuries, "the painful experiences of the people who emigrated from the Highlands and Islands during the eighteenth and nineteenth centuries [have been] minutely recorded in song" (Bloomfield and Dunn 1989:67). Little wonder then that MacNeacail should avail himself of this medium; it is a language of daily communication in which he is fluent, rather than the set piece it is for most singers and listeners in Western society today. It has been a primary mode of social interaction in MacNeacail's culture for centuries.

A time will come, a time will go (30) fulfils an important role in MacNeacail's life. Through songs like this, *Nochd gur luaineach mo chadal*, *Lìon a-mach go bàrr na cuachan* and *A's a' mhadainn 's mi 'g éirigh* (16, 17 and 14) to name a few, significant events in his life are remembered, re-created and commemorated. The songs serve as *aides-mémoire* and informative set-pieces to be delivered in response to enquiry about the past (his own or his people's). This aspect of tradition pervades every level of his life. In daily conversation, queries are answered with verses or epigrams by song-makers (whether himself, for example, 'as I said in the song...', or his favourite composers of the past). To him, the poets said it best and their verses are mines of information.

Iain's English songs hold a distinctive place in his song-life. By answering questions in song he is, in fact, closer to his beloved eighteenth-century bards in motivation and skill than he will ever acknowledge. Not only is he performing much the same social function, but he is doing it in a foreign language and culture. Here he explains why he made *A time will come, a time will go* (30) in English:

IM: Well, there were so many coming about here and asking questions, about things like that, you know, and 'Did I know anything about the Highland Clearances?' They come from Canada, New Zealand too, and Australia, and they were asking,...'How did this happen?' and things like that.... Well, I was putting things like that together,...what I heard of old people.... Well, I heard quite a lot from my father, you know. In age now he would be over a hundred and fifty anyhow.[143] Well, he remembered quite a lot of the Clearances then, because his own aunties...went over to Canada, [they] had to go. Well, some of them stopped of course that couldn't; they were removed. So that's how I thought of putting that together.

"As a rule, the Gaelic poet of the Clearances is a Gael speaking to Gaels, but sometimes he addresses the rulers of the Empire." (MacGill-Eain 1985:65–66) MacNeacail does just this in this song and in English reminds them that, "the men that made our nation great,/ gain nothing but remembrance." (ll.

31–32) Unlike some of the makers of the often spineless 'Clearance Poetry' of the nineteenth century, he lays the blame directly at the feet of the landlords and politicians responsible for the crofter's plight:

...no more evil could befall our race,
by devilish type of landlords.

Prime Minister Gladstone was to blame
with his evil clique around him,
sent one thousand marines to Skye,
the people there to hound them. (ll. 11–16)

Even his beloved Dunnchadh Bàn, in the eighteenth century, laments the passing of the deer forests, rather than the clearance of the people (MacGill-Eain 1985:131), but the Sgiobair tells the Skyemen's story in heroic terms, as befits the descendants of a warrior race.

The Skyemen gallantly did stand
as always did to foe-men
and didn't yield an inch to them
but routed all before them. (ll. 17–20)

Through oral tradition, the story of the Clearances continues to have a firm hold on the psyche of the Highlander and Iain's sense of personal loss and wrong comes through with great poignancy:

Though wounds may heal the scars remain
and so it's with the Highlands;
the men that made our nation great,
gain nothing but remembrance. (ll. 29–32)

Apart from its function as response, this song is also interesting on a linguistic level, for though it is in English, we must look to Gaelic intonation, phrasing and poetics to more fully appreciate its complex character. MacNeacail has, with his distinctive dialect, unconsciously developed his own form of Highland English poetry. This incorporates linguistic features common in Gaelic verse, particularly assonance between long vowels in opposing lines. This is rare in an English song, as length is not considered a feature of most speech in that language.

Melodically, lines one, two and four of *A time will come, a time will go* are closely related to the chorus of *Té bhàn an achaidh luachrach* [*The fair one of the rushy meadow*], a song well known in Skye in the first half of this century (there are eight renditions by different Skye singers in the School of Scottish Studies archive). *Té Bhàn* itself appears to be based on *The girl I left behind me*. Where the tune varies it is in response to the dictates of Gaelic phrasing and assonance, having been modified through Iain's rhythmic composition system discussed in Chapter Four.[144]

By virtue of being in Highland English, which reduces some of the intimidation of listening to a foreign tongue, this song allows the monoglot Anglophone to appreciate some of the aural subtleties of Gaelic song-poetry otherwise missed by non-speakers of the language. Most translations of Gaelic songs by less traditional poets than MacNeacail are heavily content-oriented and though they may, in spirit, be accurate reflections of the poet's original concept, they rarely convey a poem's aural feel to the listener.[145] MacNeacail has grafted aspects of his fast-disappearing song tradition onto the incoming culture. His expertise in his native idiom colours his poetry in the language of another culture, even when the language, culture and idiom are as unrelated as those of English and Gaelic.

Over the last few centuries, the concept of linguistic inferiority has been both figuratively and literally beaten into the psyche of the Gael. Its influence can be seen in much of this century's Gaelic poetry, in the assumption that the culture's poetic tradition must somehow 'catch up' to developments in modern European poetry, even to the extent of changing its very nature.[146] In one sense, MacNeacail challenges this idea that the Gael's language must adapt to English, whether to survive or simply to die gracefully, by continuing to use song as a medium for direct communication. Conversely, he also exemplifies it by making the basic concession of language.

In either case, Iain has no inferiority complex. Perhaps a bard performing his traditional community function is less susceptible to majority propaganda, because he is expected to be (and is) a little outside the usual (see Chapter Six for more on this point). Through his songs, he is a source of change and comment, but also a barometer of them. He, like many other bards, also benefits from a wide knowledge of the wealth and depth of his tradition and he therefore knows that feelings of cultural inadequacy are without foundation.

While he considers himself to have only a shadow of the virtuosity of the older bards, aspects of his art are comparable, and the obstacles just as daunting. Where the eighteenth-century poets' world was being physically dismantled by the Hanoverian army, Iain's is undermined daily by an insidious cultural imperialism. On the surface, his use of English may be interpreted as a concession to English incomers, but it is, for all that, a rather subversive contribution as the aural feel of the poetry (and the use of the medium of song itself) comes from Gaelic tradition. MacNeacail, by his confidence in that tradition, shows us that it has a great deal yet to offer to European culture and is far from the "broken tradition" cited by Marjory Kennedy-Fraser to justify her lyric experiments (1926:147–148).

We have already seen that Iain does not consider most modern Gaelic verse-makers poets at all, as the concepts of poem and song are still largely identical to him. He applies this same unity of song and poem to English, redefining and enriching the interface between the languages. In the process of creating this middle ground of Highland English song-poetry, he gives new life to aspects of both poetic traditions, including his own endangered one. Perhaps even more important, culturally speaking, is the idea of the 'song as response' – Iain draws on a centuries-old tradition of song-making as an essential mode of social expression.[147] And as he sings his own song, or quotes his revered poets, the songs become a means of direct expression again, as they were at their creation (cf. Ó Madagáin 1985:186). With *A time will come, a time will go* he makes his oral world more accessible to us and, in the process, restores some of Gaelic Scotland's lost confidence and pride in the face of rapid cultural change.

Chapter Six

THE SONG-MAKER'S AESTHETIC

THE BARDS OF TRADITION

The cleverness of bards

Unsurprisingly, one of the qualities the Sgiobair particularly appreciates is a readiness of wit. A bard in Gaelic society has been "known for his way with words [and] his witty, sharp retorts" for centuries (Bennett 1989:72). Anyone, but especially bards, could be measured by their ability to respond cleverly to a challenge or situation, just as MacNeacail himself would be in the céilidh house. Some of these stories are of the archetypal variety, for example, some of his anecdotes about Gilleasbaig Aotrom, the 'wise fool' who roamed the north of Skye in the early nineteenth century, living off his wits (see accompanying CD and Appendix Three) or a version of 'the Lawyer's Mad Client' (AT1585). Others are simply anecdotes about witty or pointed retorts to foolish questions. My tapes and fieldwork notebooks are full of stories like this, a few of which will give a flavour of the spontaneous cleverness which the Sgiobair relishes. I have heard many of these anecdotes about witty or clever people from him and I have also heard him trading such stories with others, both at his own house and elsewhere, showing the important place they have in his mind.[148]

At the end of Còmhdhail nan Seanchaidh 1991, I had the pleasure of overhearing the Sgiobair trading stories about 'an Dotair Beag' ['the Wee Doctor'] from Glen Hinnisdale, with another Skyeman and longtime resident of Uig, Murdo MacLean. Both men were remembering the doctor with affection and clearly enjoying themselves a great deal; the anecdotes kept coming for quite some time.

IM: Oh yes, he was a witty fellow. A wee Doctor he was.

TM: What was his name?

IM: A MacKinnon he was aye, mhm: Doctor MacKinnon....

He was just in [retirement], you know, and going about the way. He was a doctor,...broken off by the Board of Health;...he couldn't be allowed to drink and all that, but he was a good doctor just the same, you know, when you got him right....

He was herding the cows in the morning [and met a man who asked], "What are you doing about here?"

"I'm herding the cows."

"And what other job do you do?"

"I do a lot of jobs about here."

"Where you ever in school?"

"Yes, I was," [said the Doctor].

"And can you count?"

"Oh yes, and write. I do a little. Mhm."

"And how many of us are here?"

"A hundred."

"A hundred? No-o-o, one, two."

"Yes," he says, "I'm one and you're...two nothings." [*laughs*] He had them! Oh you couldn't speak to him! He was a very outspoken, you know, out right away with it. No time to consider.

On another occasion, the Sgiobair was in court giving evidence on the Wee Doctor's behalf. Duncan Corbett, a local character and hire-car driver, was there.

IM: And that's when Duncan came to me and says, "Cha déid bàrd gu ruige Nèamh gu bràth!"... ["*A bard will never reach Heaven!*"]

"Och a Dhiabhail," ars an Dotair Beag, "An deachadh Daibhidh ann?" ["*Och, the Devil*," *said the Wee Doctor*, "*Did [King] David go there?*"] Did David go there? [*laughs*] He had them, you know. [*laughs*]

TM: He had the answer.

IM: Aye, the answer. "Och saoilidh mi gu robh Dàibhidh ann" ars an Dotair Beag, mhm. ["*Och, I wonder if David was there.*"] [*laughs*] ...Oh he was very witty.

TM: Mhm.

IM: Mhm. And the minister was passing by there and [said], "Were you in church today?"

"Yes," he answered.

"What did you learn today?"

"Oh I took the wrong book, it was *J. D. Williams*[149] I should take. He was only speaking about the fashions." You know [*laughs*], likely the minister would speak about people and fashions and short skirts and they 'couldn't sit on them' and all th[is] bobbed hair, you know, 'they could sit on the hair [in the past, but] not now'.... That's what they would be preaching at times and that's what he got here. "Oh," he says, "I took the wrong book." [*laughs*]

And I think the minister said to him one day, he complained of the rain.... "O," the minister says, "nach math nach eil e tighinn ann a' shin." ["*Oh*," *the minister says*, "*isn't it good that it's not coming in there* [i.e. through his long coat].*"]

"Uel, nam b'e sin a bh'ann, a Mhinisteir," ars an Dotair. "Cha sheasadh an còta...agadsa fada ris!" ["*Well*, [even] *if that were the case, Minister*," *said the Doctor*. "*The coat wouldn't stand long against it* [i.e. the fires of Hell]!*"] Your coat wouldn't stand long with you if it was fire, through the fire, you know. He said to the minister, aye! Och he was so witty, you know, he didn't care who he spoke to. But he had his word, mhm. Och shìorridh [*Oh goodness*], I knew him well. Aye he was a cousin of Peter Martin over at Cuidreach there, aye. But he was clever, clever...as a doctor too. Mm. Aye, aye.

Another story told with relish is about John Stuart Blackie, the professor responsible for the setting up of the Chair of Celtic at the University of Edinburgh.

IM: Agus bh'e tidseadh, ag ionnsachadh sgoilearan agus chuir e sios air a' bhlackboard, tha "*Professor Blackie intends to meet his classes at eight p.m. tonight*" a' sin. Thàinig na *students* a-staigh a sheall as a' rud agus bha iad smaoineachadh gu robh ad *clever*, thug ad as a' 'c'. Thàinig Professor Blackie, 's chunnaic e siod,...thug e as an 'l'. 'S e "*Professor Blackie intends to meet his 'asses'...tonight.*" [*laughs*] ...He had them! Oh you can't beat the education, eh? Och bha

IM: *And he was teaching, teaching students and he put down on the blackboard*, "Professor Blackie intends to meet his classes at eight p.m. tonight" *there. The students came in to investigate and they were thinking they were clever, they took out the 'c'. Professor Blackie came and he saw that, he took out the 'l'. It's* "Professor Blackie intends to meet his 'asses' tonight." [laughs] *He had them! Oh* duil ac' gu robh e clever ach cha robh, robh ad ealanta ma tha.

you can't beat the education, eh? Och they were think-
ing it was clever, but it wasn't; [they were thinking]
they were ingenious anyway.

Yet another favourite story, this time about another local song-maker, is about Bàrd Ghrialain, Archibald MacLeod of Grealan; MacNeacail particularly enjoys telling and hearing about clever bards. Such stories operate on several levels. Most obviously, since they are about song-makers, they are about people like himself, having a good laugh at the expense of another. In this way, he can identify with their cleverness. On a more general level, they are about the local man triumphing over the outsider and in this particular story, there's a piquancy in the triumph as the victim is a Leódhasach [Lewisman], which plays on the rivalry between the islands. Interestingly, the story is set on the neutral territory of the mainland.

IM: So there was a Leódhasach, a Lewisman, and a poet from Skye, Bàrd Ghrialain, he was a MacLeod. He was a good bard too, but...his songs didn't go very far at all, but he did quite good songs, if they were got today. But nobody was taking note of them then, but just...orally by mouth.... He met a Leódhasach and they were both working....

"Ah, where have you been?" he says. Well, there's a place at Fort William, down there, they call it Sròn na Bà, 'The Cow's Nose', but it's known as Sròn na Bà in Gàidhlig and in English....

"Ah well," he says, "tha mi aig Sròn na Bà." ["I am at 'The Cow's Nose'."]

"O ma tha, chan eil thu móran nas fheàrr na mi fhìn, tha mise air mo rathad 'Tòn an Eich'," bha esan a' ràdh. [laughs] ["Oh well, you're not much better [off] than me, I'm on my way [to] 'The Horse's Arse'," he was saying.] He was at a horse's arse working, in the stable, you know. So the one got the other [man].... Oh aye, he was from Staffin, well he's dead too.

But I mean, what I say, how quickly he got the answer to the Leódhasach.

MB: They were witty.

IM: Of course. Aye, but the Leódhasach said it genuine, you know, he was at Sròn na Bà, "Cait a bheil thu?" ["Where are you?"]

"Aig Sròn na Bà." ["At 'The Cow's Nose'."]

"O tha mise aig Tòn an Eich!" ["Oh, I'm at 'The Horse's Arse!"] Where [it is] I don' know, but he was very witty![150]

A quick response of this sort was typical of the *bàrd baile* and the level of mental acuity expected of him.[151]

Anecdotes such as this were the meat of the céilidh houses and were traded between the Sgiobair and people like Murchadh Dhòmhnaill Mhàrtainn [Murdo (son of) Donald (son of) Martin] and Dòmhnall mac Phàdraig [Donald son of Peter], the soldier in *An cuala sibh an car* (11).

IM: Och well we were discussing and things like that, you know, and I was just equal to him and him to me, but he would have something more, [more] news than I would have. Yes, oh he [was] very good, you know, what like of that. And that was the custom at the céilidhs at one time when we would gather in houses: cracks of old things like that and those people that was in Waterloo and Crimea and oh aye, aye, aye.

They asked Dòmhnull Saighdear [who] was up there, "What was the toughest battle you were in?"

"Blàr clach an teinntein, blàr clach an teinntein agus teanga nam boireannach." [laughs] ["The battle of the hearthstone, the battle of thc hearthstone and [the battle of] the women's tongue[s]."] ...He had more quarrels...

at the fireside and the tongue of the women. Dòmhnull Saighdear, bh'e a' fuireach 'san Gleann Hìonasdail. Bha e a's a' Chrimea. [*Donald the Soldier, he was living in Glen Hinnisdale. He was in the Crimea.*] ...Aye, and he was in...Sebastopol too. Mm [*laughs*] Aye, aye., but he...went that way. [*taps his head with a finger*] ...Oh he had a tough time of it. But they were soldiers then.

This appreciation of quick thinking is clearly evident even today when I céilidh on the MacNeacails in Cuidreach. With some of the boys living at home, this house is a non-stop, old-fashioned *taigh céilidh*, where the old sort of teasing and give-and-take still go on. As I wrote in my field note-book:

> While Willie was eating and cracking jokes, he would make a crack and then look at his father as if challenging him to respond. Well, [Iain] gave as good as he got and was quick too. Willie would then laugh appreciatively at the speed and accuracy of Iain's response.
>
> Sometimes, Iain would say something and look at me or Margaret and wink broadly, acknowledging that it was all in fun and that this one would really get Willie going. There was such a lovely twinkle in his eye and a smile on his face as he made the next crack.

Spontaneous composition

A more demanding manifestation of a ready wit is off-the-cuff composition, a skill which MacNeacail certainly has (see Chapter Four). He is very appreciative of others' abilities in this line, recounting several examples for me, including this one from Màiri Mhór.

IM: Aye, they told her just to give a description of the Island of Skye and she...looked about her and she said,

Nach bòidheach riamh an Cuilthionn,	Isn't the Cuillin ever beautiful,
's cho laghach am measg nan neòil	and so lovely amongst the clouds,
Glàmaig, Beinn Bhuirbh,	Glamaig, the Mountain of Borve,
Eilean Thuilm is Leac a' Stòirr	Tulm Island and the Slab of Storr
gu ruige Rubha Hùnais,	up to Rubha Hunish,
gach glac is cùl is fròg,	every hollow and corner and nook,
'n taobh eile sealladh aoibhneach	on the other side, the lovely view
de Mhaighdeanan MhicLeòid.	of MacLeod's Maidens.

Chuir i, mar a chanadh sibh, ann an *nutshell* e.... Agus rinn i glé mhath e. Agus thug i leatha an t-eilean uile.

She put it, as you would say, in a nutshell. And she did it very well. And she took in the whole island.

This verse of Màiri Mhór's *Eilean a' Cheò* (Meek 1977:57-61, ll. 17–24) may have been made extemporaneously, as MacNeacail says, and later used in the song. The important point is that Iain admires the verse for being off-the-cuff.

Description

The story about Màiri Mhór's place-names rhyme also brings us closer to understanding another one of MacNeacail's criteria for a good song:

IM: The best song she made?... I think it's "Soraidh leis an àite san d'fhuair mi m' àrach òg", I think that that's very good.

TM: Why?

IM: Well she give description of every place,

Seall fo Chaisteal Uisdein,
   [feasgar ciùin gun cheò]
buar a' dol go suas
   go Bòrd uain' 'icLeòid.[152]

See below Castle Uisdean,
   a gentle, mistless evening
cattle climbing up
   to green MacLeod's Table.[152]

And all that. Agus Cuith-raing. Is Sròin Bhaornaill, [*And the Quiraing. And Sròin Bhaornaill*]...the winds of Norway blowing over Sròin Bhaornaill, where the princess was buried there.[153] She gave a lot of description of those things that happened in that song. Mhm.

But they were saying...that...she was saying herself that [*Moch 's mi 'g éirigh*] was her best song. Well there's no much [description] in it but...she gave more description in [the song she made] when she was going to Glasgow,...*Soraidh leis an àite*, when she made that one,

[Soraidh leis an àite]
   san d'fhuair mi m' àrach òg,
eilean nam beann àrda
   far an tàmh an ceò;
air am moch a dh'éireas
   cluain nan speur fo ròs
fuadach neul na h-oidhche,
   shoillseachadh a' Stòirr.[154]

A blessing to the place
   in which I was reared in youth,
the island of the high mountains
   where the mist dwells;
early will rise
   the field of the sky under a ros[y light]
banishing the cloud of night,
   to illuminate the Storr.[154]

She took out a good description of all these things, but they were saying *Moch 's mi 'g éirigh* was quite a good song too [that] she got in Os. She was there with Bean Ois [*the Lady of Os*]...for a time. Description, then, is a notable feature of a good song, as will become obvious when Iain discusses Donnchadh Bàn.

The Gaelic language

One of the most important criteria upon which a bard must have always been judged is the quality of his Gaelic. The Gaels are, in general, unusually aware of linguistic competence and are quick to assert the superiority of a particular speaker, tale-teller or even a particular dialect over another. Such people and dialects are measured against a theoretical ideal, but as Nancy Dorian points out, "no one perfectly embodies that ideal at present, if indeed anyone ever did". (1981:116) MacNeacail, on the other hand, measures himself against the bards of old and so, for him, an 'ideal' does exist. Others may not measure him against this same ideal, but many have commented appreciatively to me about his diction and the quality of his Gaelic (see below).

MacNeacail is unassuming in his estimation of his own command of Gaelic, but much less so when singing the praises of the language itself. He often offers a verse from Duncan Bàn MacIntyre opining that Gaelic was the language of the Garden of Eden:

IM: Is that right?... Well it's difficult to argue with it, you have no foundation to say it wasn't. But it's like this, it must be so old that nobody knows. But Dunnchadh Bàn says,

IM: 'S i chainnte bh'a's a' Ghàrradh,
      's a dh'fhàg Adhamh aig an t-sluagh,
   a bhruidhinn anns an fhàsach,
     'n àm tràghadh na Muir Ruaidh;
   a' chainnt a bh'aig na fàidhean
     thug fios Phàrrais dhuinn a-nuas
   's gun d'dh'fhàg aig an àlach i
     tha làthair anns an uair.[155]

'S e a' ràdh a-rithist,

   Nach i a' chainnt a bh'aig Noah
     nuair a sheòl e a's an àirc?[156]

[laughs] Chan eil a leithid ri Dunnchadh Bàn ann a' sheo.... But where did they get it?... Cha b'e sgoilear a bh'ann Dunnchadh Bàn idir, cha sgrìobhadh e ainm fhèin!

IM: It's the language that was in the Garden
     and that Adam left for the people,
   that was spoken in the wilderness,
     in the ebbing of the Red Sea;
   the language of the prophets
     who brought knowledge of Heaven down for us
   and who left it with the generation
     that is now here.[155]

It's he who said again [i.e. elsewhere],

   Wasn't it the language of Noah
     when he sailed in the ark?[156]

[laughs] There's not the like of Duncan Bàn around here [today]. But where did they get it? Duncan Bàn wasn't a scholar at all; he couldn't even write his own name!

These verses are never far from the surface of MacNeacail's mind, and he will recite them to anyone who will listen, including the local minister, who, the Sgiobair gleefully adds, has not been able to offer any proof to the contrary.

Màiri Mhór, he continues, had something to add on the matter, as well.

IM: Thubhairt Dunnchadh Bàn sin. Ach chan urrainn dhut a ràdh gu robh e ceàrr.... Thubhairt Màiri Mhór nan Oran a-rithist,

   Thug Professor Blackie comhairle àraidh
   air a bhith cumail suas na Gàidhlig,
   oir 's ann leatha labhair Adhamh,
   "Ciamar a tha thu?" ris a mhnaoi.[157]

IM: Duncan Bàn said that. But you can't say he was wrong. Again, Màiri Mhór nan Òran said,

   Professor Blackie gave special counsel
   to keep up the Gaelic
   since it's with it that Adam said,
   "How do you do?" to his lady [i.e. Eve].[157]

So there must be something in it.... Ah? I don' know, but it's so, so old that nobody can go into it, how old it is. But it's a very expressive language.[158]

Many cultures have made claims of this sort over the centuries. For some people, however, MacNeacail's discussion of this topic may make him seem at best an anomalous naïf, at worst a cultural chauvinist. Both of these assessments have a certain validity, but they entirely miss the substance of the man and the sincerity with which the observations are offered. The Sgiobair brings this subject up largely in order to express his wonder at the knowledge of the bards of old. He lives in a Gaelic cultural past where poets have the same sort of elevated status that most people, including himself, accord churchmen or university lecturers. His entire world-view is filtered through the glass of song, so it is little wonder that his primary models in life should be song-makers such as Dunnchadh Bàn.

According to Iain, Gaelic is unmatched for expression of emotion and precision of thought and it is more accurate in speech than English. In its use of adjectives, this may well be true; there is a dearth of exact equivalents for many Gaelic adjectives. Often a single verse of poetry will be packed with them, expressing subtle shades of the same meaning. To translate such a verse into English accurately often requires a paragraph of English prose and even resorting to the dictionary (usually Dwelly's) for each adjective frustratingly yields the same English word over and over again.

IM: But what is very strange, you can't get...the interpretation of the Gàidhlig in English. You can't do it!

TM: Mhm.

IM: You have the Gàidhlig there, but you can't make it rhyme the same, no. But you can give exactly near the meaning of it, what he means, but you'll not get the word for word....

TM: It doesn't sound the same.

IM: No it doesn't sound [the same];...chan eil fhios am. [*I don't know.*] Mhm.

MacNeacail says that Gaelic is "one of the world's five pure languages," along with Chinese; he has not said what the other three are. Certainly Gaelic is one of the oldest European languages and possesses an ancient written tradition as well.

Iain's note of triumph and pride in his native language and culture is undoubtedly chauvinistic and, though he left school at the age of fourteen, there is a note of truth, and internal logic, in all he says about it. To me, as an outsider observing the aftermath of the Clearances and the results of a hostile education system, it is refreshing to see a Gael so openly displaying such a tremendous pride in his birthright.

The Gaelic of the poets

For MacNeacail, the language of the eighteenth-century poets is the ultimate in expression.

IM: Ah, they say Dunnchadh Bàn, he was giving a description of the *bradan*, or the *breac*, the salmon. He would say "am bradan tarrgheal":

> [Bradan] tarrgheal sa choire gharbhlaich
> 's a' tighinn bhon fhairge bu ghailbheach tonn,
> air buidhean buirb is e leum cho foirmeil
> 'na éideadh colgail bu ghormghlas druim,
> le soillsean airgid gu h-iteach meanbhbhreac
> gu ballach deargbhallach earball slìom.[159]

He gave a description of the salmon there.

I have heard Iain recite this verse many times to illustrate Dunnchadh Bàn's fine command of language. On this occasion, he translated some of it for me, including the missing couplet: "Le luinneis mheanmnach a' ceapadh mheanbhchuileag/ Gu neo-chearbach le chamghob crom." (MacLeod 1952:168, ll. 44–5) I include our discussion below to show how Iain, a man fluent in nineteenth-century poetic styles and vocabulary, copes with the language of his most admired eighteenth-century poet.

IM: Well,...tell it to anybody here and they wouldn't understand a word of it. Well, it's easy enough:... "Am bradan tarrgheal", 'tarrgheal' is whitish and mixed.... "A's a' choire gharbhlaich", the 'coire',...the stream is coming down, you know.... "Coire garbhlach", rough. "A' tighinn bhon fhairge",...scurries down from the waves, the currents of the waves.... "Air...buidhean buirb e" is jumps, I don't know what 'buidhean buirb'[160] is, but it's something that he's keen to do.... "E leum cho foirmeil", 'foirmeil', 'e cho foirm', firm in his jumps, the way he jumps.

TM: Muscular?...

IM: Aye, aye, aye, "foirmeil, bu ghormglas dhruim, le shoillsean airgid", is glittering, a silvery glitter....
"Meanbhbhreac",...mixed, you know, white and black, as you say. "A' ceapadh mheanbhchuileag",
catching the wee fly, the midges with his "camghob crom", with his snout bent,...agus "earball
slìom",...his tail is going down with a cast in it.

MacNeacail's text is not the same as that in the book. Either he has re-composed the verse in his own
mind, or this is a version he heard in the céilidh houses. In any case, we are left with an oral version
(even if it does turn out to have an intermediate source in print) which indicates his delight in the linguistic capabilities of the older poets. The verse carries meaning and performs much the same function
for him as the written text, confirming his belief in the brilliance of Dunnchadh Bàn's linguistic capabilities. To some extent, there is status in the mere fact that Dunnchadh Bàn's language is difficult and
almost opaque to many speakers of today. (Certainly poets such as Mac Mhaighstir Alasdair have been
much admired over the years for using obscure vocabulary in some of their songs.) MacIntyre is also
appreciated for the very fact that he is non-literate.

IM: Well, look at the description and that man couldn't read or write his Gàidhlig!... But...where'd he
get it? And...then he says, he says again [recites Dunnchadh Bàn's verse about language in the Garden of Eden (see
above), and continues:]

> 'S i ceòl na pìob 's na clàrsach   It [i.e. Gaelic] is the music of the pipes and the harps
> 's luchd-dàna dhèanamh dhuan.[161]   and versifiers who used to make songs.[161]

Well, you can't,...you can't say they were fools!

TM: No.

IM: Oh hm-hm-hm [laughs], I wish I was one of them! If I was I would be safe [for posterity].

He evinces a keen desire to be amongst the old poets and I have no doubt that he would feel at
home there; he already lives with one foot in their world. He would gladly trade places if it meant the
preservation of some of his poetry. I also have a sense from his last statement above, that he feels out
of his element in the modern world and that he'd be 'saved' from this by being back in time with the
eighteenth-century masters.

MacNeacail's favourite poets

There is no question but that Duncan Bàn MacIntyre is the poet against whom Gaelic oral song-makers
and tradition-bearers like the Sgiobair measure other bards. His language is very consistent and his
description is of a very high order indeed. His songs are also far more singable than those of many
others, perhaps because they were created by a non-literate person; it is not for nothing that he was
known as Dunnchadh Bàn nan Oran [Fair(-haired) Duncan of the Songs].

The paradoxical point here is that few of MacIntyre's poems actually survive in oral tradition. Perhaps, as John MacInnes suggests, the tradition that he was the best poet is passed on, rather than the
songs themselves (1968:30). In his own lifetime he published several editions of his poems and toured
extensively around Scotland presenting his songs. It may be that books like Sàr-obair nam Bàrd Gaelach
(MacKenzie 1841) lent added status to his poetry by making printed versions easily accessible (though
why Duncan Bàn's reputation should benefit more than others' is difficult to say). On the other hand,
it may be that editors like MacKenzie made their selections from the songs that were popular at the
time.

26. The waterfall on the Conon, just above the site of the original cemetery washed away in the flood of 1877. (Reproduced with permission from the George Washington Wilson photographic archive, Aberdeen University Library, C4385)

Another likely possibility is that this regard is partly due to MacIntyre's very illiteracy; his long complex poems were composed entirely orally, as he was not able to read or write.[162] That a non-literate bard should win greater respect from tradition-bearers than any other, including the highly literate Mac Mhaighstir Alasdair, is perhaps a testament to the premium that Gaelic song-tradition places on a good memory and the 'singability' of songs.

At one point, curious about his never having mentioned Alexander MacDonald to me, I asked Mac-Neacail what he thought of him and his poetry.

IM: *Oh Alasdair Mac Mhaighstir Alasdair was more learned than Dunnchadh Bàn, but everybody prefers Dunnchadh Bàn.... Alasdair Mac Mhaighstir Alasdair was quite good too, [but] they were saying that Dunnchadh Bàn was better on natural things.

Here is a very clear admission that MacDonald was better educated, and yet MacNeacail prefers Dunnchadh Bàn's eye for natural beauty, which is indeed renowned throughout the *Gàidhealtachd* for its dramatic realism and imagery. Some of the Sgiobair's preference may also be due to the relative scarcity of printed versions of MacDonald's work (though they were available in *Sàr Obair* as well). In any case, the Sgiobair is certainly far more *au fait* with Duncan Bàn's poetry.

TM: So where did you learn the Duncan Bàn songs?

IM: Oh, well I heard that [i.e. them] before I ever got this book, you know. Among the community, they had them here. How late...that was, I don't know.

Evidently the songs could be found in oral tradition until quite recently, though just how recently he is unable to say.[163]

Despite the emphasis on Dunnchadh Bàn, there are many other song-makers whose work the Sgiobair also appreciates, such as Uilleam Ros [William Ross]. He does not fully approve of Ros's rhyme schemes, however. To him they do not measure up to most *bàrdachd bhaile* [township poetry].

IM: Oh well, he was quite good.... Ach I have his book there, but...nobody here has...the music of them, so you're lost.

Again, we see confirmation here that for poems to live in the community, they must be sung.

IM: But even [then] they're not rhyming at all the way you get them here with me or anybody else,...the one word rhyming to the other one.... But they still...work with music all right. Mm.

TM: So they're better sung...than spoken?

IM: Oh yes. Mhm. Ach they are. Aye, aye.[164]

Ros is another poet whose songs MacNeacail prefers to Màiri Mhór's.

IM: I wouldn't say that she was anything like...Uilleam Ros or Neil MacLeod, aye I wouldn't class her to be as good as them.

MB: Which ones of Uilleam Ros's, or Neil MacLeod's are you

IM: *Feasgar Luain* [was] a very good one,..."'s mi air chuairt, chuala fuaim nach b'fhuathach liom." ["*A Monday evening and me abroad, I heard a sound that did not displease me.*"][165] Aye, he's in the book there. I have his book there, Uilleam Ros.... Oh he was good and of course he was a good scholar with English, Latin and Greek; he had the advantage over them. But still, I think Dunnchadh Bàn would be better than him,...on the average.

MB: Have you got a favourite of Dunnchadh Bàn?

IM: "Mhàiri bhàn òg, 's tu 'n òigh air m' aire," ["*O young fair[haired] Mary, you are the maiden I have noticed,*"] I think that's his best.[166]

Though Dunnchadh Bàn is his most admired poet, Iain probably quotes Màiri Mhór nan Oran more often than any other. While she is not his favourite poet, her mother's people were from Idrigill and, according to both Iain and Angus Fleidsear, she herself was born there; only after that did her parents move to Skeabost.[167] She was also well known to Iain's parents as she had relatives in Siadar at that time, and often took lifts between Portree and Uig from his father, Uilleam. Iain frequently refers to her conversations with his parents, quotes her songs and discusses her life.

For someone growing up in the north of Skye in the early years of this century it would have been impossible to be unaware of her towering presence. Somhairle MacGill-Eain notes that her poetry has "not received anything like its due except in popular esteem," (1985:72) and that

> it is difficult for any Skyeman, who has a strong feeling for Skye and a certain conception of it, to speak coldly of Màiri Mhór, for her native land was in her blood. (p. 71)

MacNeacail, though he does not ever speak coldly of her, does not shy away from criticising her either. To him, she is, though outstanding, only one of many local poets roughly contemporary with his youth and the few decades before.

IM: Ach cha robh ainm sam bith dhi fhad' 's a bha i beò, ach tha e an-diugh dhi agus tha sin mar a dh'éireas. Thuirt i fhéin sin, nuair a bheirear i dhachaidh leis a' bhàs, bi ar n-àl 'ga seinn. 'S chaidh barrachd a ràdh ma déigh' an-diugh 's a bha ann nuair a bha i beò....

A[ch] chuala mise m' athair 's minig a thug e lift dhi a Phort Rìgh. Bhiodh i dol suas a Phort Rìgh 's 's e carriage horse 's each is machine a bhiodh aca, no dog-cart a bhiodh aca an uair sin. Bha i faotainn lift suas mar sin comhla ris.

Ach bhiodh i measg nan daoine móra, fios agad, uile-gu-léir. Cha chuala tu cur móran air duine mór riamh i, oir bha na daoine móra math dhi, oir bha eagal aca [?]roimpe; mura dèanadh ad sin, bha an t-òran a chuireadh sìos iad. 'S cha robh sin a' dol a fhreagairt orra. Agus bha i na b'fheàrr air taobh an duine mhóir, 's bha na daoine móra math air a taobh-sa cuideachd. Agus sin a dh'fhàg ise cho iomraiteach, fhuair i staigh air na daoine móra. Och chan eil fhios am ciamar a tha iad ag obair an diugh, ach bha i iomraiteach latha a bh'ann a's an eilean.

IM: But she didn't have a name [as a composer] while she was alive, but she does today and that's how it happens. She said that herself, when she will be borne home by death, our offspring will be singing them. And more is said about her today than was when she was alive.

But I heard my father [say], many's the lift he gave her from Portree. She would be going up from Portree, and they used to have a carriage horse and a machine, or dog-cart that they had then. She was getting a lift up with him like that.

But she used to be amongst the nobility, you know, completely. You never hear of her putting [i.e. composing] much on the nobility, since the nobility were good to her, because they were afraid of her, that if they didn't do that, it was the song that would put them down. And that wasn't going to suit them. And she was better on the side of the nobility, and the nobility were good on her own behalf as well. And that's what left her so well known; she got in with the nobility. Och I don't know how they are working today, but she was well known in the island in the past.

Though Màiri Mhór was undoubtedly 'in' with such members of the upper classes as Fear Sgèabost, the owner of Skeabost House, she was also well known in her day as a campaigner for crofters' rights. MacNeacail is certainly aware of some of the renown she attained in her own lifetime, as he has recounted several stories of her ecstatically received appearance at the 'Skye Soiree' in Glasgow. Perhaps, since song-makers in those days were not as rare a breed as they are today, Màiri did not stand out so prominently in his mind. His opinion of her arises partly out of his great familiarity with the details of her life and person from a very young age; this would preclude the sort of reverence that many develop for her (and the sort that he holds for Dunnchadh Bàn).

Perhaps he also knows that her songs are not really in the same céilidh style as his own, hence his comment comparing her to Neil MacLeod.

IM: Ach cha dèanadh i càil do Niall MacLeòid, cha chreid mi, air na h-òrain. Rinn Niall MacLeòid orain glé mhath,

> Chì mi an Cuilthionn
> 's leóghainn gun tioma,
> le fhiasag de'n shneachd'
> 	air a phasgadh m'a cheann;
> a ghruaidhean a' srùladh
> le easanan smùideach
> a' tuiteam 'na lùban
> 	go ùrlar nan gleann.[168]

Och bha Gàidhlig mhath aig Niall MacLeòid agus bha Iain Dubh a bhràthair fada na b'fheàrr na e.[169]

	...Uel fhuair mi leabhar aig Niall MacLeòid, tha e agam fhathast,...Clàrsach an Doire.... Gheibhadh sibh eachdraidh Gilleasbaig Aotrom a's an t-seann fhear, nam faigheadh sibh aig MacLaren an Glaschu e.

IM: But she didn't make anything like Neil MacLeod, I don't think, for songs. Neil MacLeod made very good songs.

> I see the Cuillin,
> a lion without softness
> with a beard of snow
> 	wrapped about its head;
> its cheeks rushing
> with misty cascades
> falling in curves
> 	to the floor of the glens.[168]

Och, Neil MacLeod had good Gaelic and his brother, Black(-haired) John, was much better than him.[169]

	Well, I got Neil MacLeod's book, I still have it, The Harp of the Grove. You'll get the history of Simple Archie in the old one, if you could get it at MacLaren in Glasgow.

According to Derick Thomson, Neil MacLeod, "more than any other of his time," became part of the popular culture for his céilidh songs in "very unexacting" metres (1974:232). He also accuses MacLeod of spurious emotion and invented detail and harbours grave doubts about his artistic integrity (1974:225), but admits that "he was a competent craftsman with a strong musical quality" (1983:184). Perhaps MacLeod does not measure up to Thomson's standard of a "hard" cast of mind, but his musicality led to a great popularity with 'the folk' which surely goes some way to exonerating him from accusations of inexactitude. In their day, the songs filled a necessary niche as undemanding entertainment and were probably not regarded in the same light as the intellectual or literary effusions of the bards of earlier centuries. This, at any rate, is part of the Sgiobair's perspective on them.

IM: Oh-h Neil MacLeod was good, oh yes, there was nothing like him, no. Except Dunnchadh Bàn and he's, well, who can step with him? Nobody. [laughs]

The aesthetic upon which he judges MacLeod's poems is, largely, how well they can be sung. This becomes clear by contrast when I ask him about more modern poets such as Murdo MacFarlane of Lewis, who has "*not one line rhyming with the other! [But]...he was good at...a description of things." Part of the Sgiobair's definition of the term rhyme, however, is that a song must flow smoothly and rhythmically off the tongue and MacFarlane does not always measure up. I think the Sgiobair views him as transitional and sees in his work the beginnings of a shift away from céilidh-songs and sung poetry toward verse that is primarily for reading and recitation, such as that of MacGill-Eain: "*It's not for singing, it's bàrdachd [poetry]. Songs and bàrdachd are two different things." These latter statements are the sort of criticism he applies to most of the modern Gaelic poets we have talked about.

Curiously, even Calum Ruadh Nicolson's songs (see MacNeacail 1975, Knudsen 1978), though often in styles older than his own, do not meet his standards (which after all are seventeenth/eighteenth-century ones).

IM: No, I didn't approve of them at all.... They're not poetic at all; they don't rhyme or anything. Mind you he was making probably a bàrdachd of it, but that's no songs at all.

TM: So they're better for reading than singing.

IM: Oh yes, they will be. Well you could read them, but still you didn't get much...in them. No.[170] Of course it was this *Gairm* [the Gaelic magazine] that was going about, that did the publishing for them and of course they will likely [be] glad to get anything, but I wouldn't say they're...with Màiri Mhór or Niall MacLeòid. Màiri Mhór was more popular than any of them.

TM: Well she published six thousand lines of poetry when she was still alive.

IM: Oh yes, she did. Yes, but there's some of them that wasn't great.... Aye but...at that time, there was a lot of poets going at her age [i.e. in her day], aye. Mhm.

TM: There were a lot of others when she was alive?

IM: Oh yes, plenty, oh yes, quite a lot. Mhm. Oh yes, but not since then.

MacNeacail has now brought us back to the idea that there was an abundance of song-makers in his youth. In the early decades of this century, Màiri Mhór had only recently passed away and the céilidh houses were still filled with the new songs and daily anecdotes of a vigorous *living* tradition. I would argue that there was a brief period of living tradition after her death, but before the imminent breakup of her cultural tradition, in which there would hardly have been an opportunity to dwell for too long on her songs which we can now, in hindsight, assess as the flower of their era.

It is interesting that Iain considers a number of little-known song-makers to have been as good as Màiri Mhór. Perhaps in many ways they were, but we are left with a relatively small number of texts from North Skye song-makers of this period with which to make comparisons. We can probably put down the loss of these songs to the circles in which these local poets moved: (i) they were not among the Gaelic-literate classes, meaning that their songs would not have been written down; and (ii) they did not become widely known in their own day, as Màiri Mhór did, which might have led to a literate outsider taking an interest and publishing editions of their works. The influence of a sizeable volume of collected poems cannot be overestimated. It lends great status to a poet in a society that has enormous respect for the written word. And to book-oriented scholars, from the perspective of the late twentieth century, a volume of collected works denotes legitimacy. Having published, the author becomes revered to a degree not necessarily commensurate with a close reading of the poems.[171]

In the absence of a larger body of the local poets' songs, then, we must defer to Iain's judgement of them to some extent. He admires many of them, such as Uilleam Iain Chaimbeil, Seumas Iain Sheumais, Neil Gow in Staffin, Calum Ciorstaidh and others that I have mentioned before.[172] Here he talks again of Bàrd Ghrialain:

IM: Aye, he was a MacLeod from Staffin, aye. They called him Bàrd Ghrialain.... He was known as a bard, but he composed good songs.... They weren't many, but he was known as a bard at the time. There was few that would compose like him, you know, but he was known as a bard, but there's none of them now going, no.

TM: Do you think those people were comparable to Màiri Mhór?

IM: As good as Màiri Mhór? Och yes. Och yes, but of course she was following the big bugs of the place, you know,...and she always made good songs for them.

As for contemporary composers, their work does not accord with Iain's conception of poetry. Poets as different from each other as Calum Ruadh and Somhairle MacGill-Eain do not meet with his approval, though they compose in radically different styles (the former in older traditional styles and the latter in twentieth-century European styles, albeit influenced by a wealth of traditional knowledge). In fact, neither poet speaks MacNeacail's eighteenth to late nineteenth-century poetic language; their songs are therefore, by definition, not poetry to him. This may be seen as a parochial opinion on his part, but there are none so able to judge what they like as the folk themselves. And from within Iain's own aesthetic, this opinion brooks no argument; what passes, under the rules of tradition, has an innate validity that no amount of 'educated' critical judgement can deny. It would be unjust to interpret MacNeacail's dismissal of some of the modern poets as real disdain, for they compose to a different aesthetic. It is therefore not possible that their songs should meet with his full understanding or approval. As he said so picturesquely about Dunnchadh Bàn, sub-consciously echoing his own technique of composing while walking up the road, "Who can step with him?"

The dramatic changes that have taken place in Gaelic society over the last half century have been very difficult for MacNeacail to bear. He laments the lack of witty and lively repartee described at the beginning of this chapter and in Chapter Three. There is great sadness in his voice as he closes his reminiscences of those days and characters with, "Ah, but all these people are gone now, you can't beat them!"

AN SGIOBAIR, THE BARD

> The belief that a poet is born, not made, is extremely strong, and a curious aspect of the belief is that very often a bard will stress the fact that his gift comes to him from his mother, or from his mother's people, sometimes even when his father's family seems also to have included bards. (MacInnes 1968:40)

John MacCodrum maintained that he inherited his poetic gift (Matheson 1938:xix) and even a modern poet like Somhairle MacGill-Eain states that his poetic ability comes from his Nicolson mother's side of the family. Iain too, feels that his talent is inherited: "*You can make a piper, but you can't make a poet." I have also heard the same said of pipers, that they are born not made, so I suspect that whichever skill the tradition-bearer possesses is considered to be a gift and that of others, mere learning.[173] Curiously, Iain's saying runs contrary to the ancient tradition of the rigorously trained classical bard, but the Irish scholar of bardic poetry Osborn Bergin backs him up by saying that a poet had to be "both born and made" (1970:5). Perhaps an innate ability was in-bred, but further training was needed to polish it into professional skill.

Màiri Sgiobair [Mary (wife of the) Skipper] says that their son Willie is good at composing, and though I have recorded him singing one or two songs, I have not yet elicited a verse of his own composition. Iain says he makes the odd line or verse, but that he does not follow them through to completion.

It is said that a real talent for composition skips a generation, though, according to Iain, none of his own forebears made songs.

IM: Cha robh duine a's an teaghlach againne ri òran ach mi fhìn, fhios agad air a' sinach, 'gad a bhiodh ad 'gan gabhail nam b'urra dhaibh. O cha robh duine a's an teaghlach agam fhìn a bhiodh ga dhèanamh. O cha chreid mi nach robh e...as *generations* air ais gu faigheadh ad cuideigin a bha gu math càirdeach, [?fhios ag]ad, a's a' robh e an uair sin.

IM: *There wasn't anyone in our own family making song[s], but myself, you know, at that time, though they were singing them if they were able. Oh there wasn't anyone in my own family who could do it. Oh I think it was generations back before you'd find any who were related, you know, in which [composing could be found] then.*

If composition does run in families, none of Iain's own descendants has yet picked up the torch. This may, of course, be due to his own presence; it would take a bold and perhaps slightly disrespectful versifier to "step with him". In addition, the children have grown up in a post-war culture where song was less usual than it was in the Sgiobair's youth; there were not as many composers around and, in the way of children, they would have thought their father anomalous and not followed his model. That said, several of the children now appreciate his skill and are quite proud of some of his songs.[174] MacNeacail himself, like many other song-makers, considers his skill to be a gift and in his youth was not aware that he was possessed of anything special (see Chapter Five).

The song-maker on the outskirts of society

Many societies have come to view the song-maker as a little out of the ordinary, or at least eccentric. The image of the artist as a "kind of supernaturally-inspired madman" has been around for centuries, but it is only in recent times that "the artist began to feel himself separated from, and at odds with, his world" (Nash 1961:85). Before this separation occurred, the poet in traditional Gaelic society would have had a respected place in the hierarchy below the chief. He might be considered a little fey and perhaps, at times, he encouraged the idea that he had supernatural powers, but he played an accepted role, and was probably not "at odds" with his world. Even in the post-Culloden era, and all that that entailed, the village song-maker was still part of the fabric of society, outcast only to the extent that people kept him at a distance fearing his satirical skills.

In this century, however, the song-making personae of people such as the Sgiobair (and Larry Gorman, for that matter, cf. Ives 1964:29, 133) have been increasingly marginalised by the changing culture around them, which no longer has a central role for the township poet. By my observation, even MacNeacail's children have seen him as a little unusual, though this attitude has been changing gradually as they have seen me and others repeatedly visiting him. They have, I think, noticed and appreciated the effort (and therefore the implied respect) that I have given the work of transcribing his songs and thoughts.

Living in Cuidreach in the post-war years, MacNeacail has been physically distanced from the céilidh haunts of his youth, and many younger Uig folk, such as Aonghas Dubh, the Gaelic poet, grew up feeling that the Sgiobair was in some way different:

AM: The impression I grew up with was of his being somewhat eccentric, or being seen as somewhat eccentric, I should say.... I think that may have arisen out of a sort of attempt to distance people from him. They would not be unfriendly with him if they met him, but...those that didn't know him so well perhaps, kept themselves at a distance by defining him in such a way, and that in a sense insulated him...

TM: [They kept their distance] for safety's sake.

AM: I think there might have been an element of that, which you would get with any bard. I mean, curiously, his fellow bard of the time was very much a humorist, Angus Fletcher, maybe not a satirist, but I think that was the difference. The Sgiobair was more a serious bard and therefore potentially more dangerous were he to take to...accusing anyone in verse.

TM: Do you know of any specific occurrences of that?

AM: I don't actually, no.

Though the Sgiobair has made very few songs of this nature, he had a reputation as someone who could and might do so. This was enough to cause some folk to keep their distance.

In part, this impression of him being in another world may have been justified; he would often have seemed distracted when inhabiting his world of song-making imagery. On the other hand, he was able to make the transition between distraction and involvement very smoothly, as we saw with the composition of *Nuair a thòisich iad ri bùidsearachd* (8), where he removed himself from direct participation in the proceedings to compose his song. This introspection, so necessary for creativity, may yield impressions of eccentricity, which could, in turn, lead to a distancing between the song-maker and his own community.

AM: He was always thinking and...because he wasn't, strictly speaking, a humorist, that also put him a wee bit at a tangent with the rest of society, because with the likes of Angus Fletcher, you knew that [as he] drew his breath to launch into a song, you were going to have a giggle, or a belly laugh even, but you didn't have that assumption with the Sgiobair because he was much more liable to touch on serious aspects of life.

TM: But I suppose if somebody was used to making up verses as he was walking along, he could hardly help it after a point.

AM: Well exactly.

For Iain, making songs is almost involuntary. As such, it is also crucial to his definition of self. It therefore makes little difference what others think of him, especially if the persons with whom he compares himself are the eighteenth- and nineteenth-century bards. Perhaps he has developed his keen sense of the past in *response* to the marginalisation discussed above, but I suspect the reverse it true; his song-making persona has evolved from his reverence for the great poets of the past.

I hasten to point out that in discussing marginalisation in this way, I do not mean to imply that Iain is in *any* way a social outcast in terms of daily life, far from it; his home is still a busy céilidh house and an evening seldom passes without a visitor.[175]

THE COMMUNITY SPEAKS

In general, how good a song-maker is in local terms may be judged by how their songs are received "at the time and by the audience for whom they were created" (Ives 1978:413). I will now turn to "the audience for whom they were created" and present some assessments of the Sgiobair and his songs through the eyes of a number of fellow villagers and fellow Gaels.

One generalization may be made from the start and that is that folk do not judge the songs on their melodic content, as I have shown above. The measure of his creativity within tradition, the aesthetic upon which he is being judged, is the creation of lyrics and the fitting of them to the chosen melody (whatever its origin), but not the melody itself.[176]

Peigi Bennett and her brother Peter Stewart of Glenconon (now of Balquhidder)

Some of the Sgiobair's songs were "quite popular at one time", especially *Nochd gur luaineach mo chadal* and *Nach bòidheach Uige* (16 and 21). Peigi Bennett used to sing the latter at local céilidhs, and wrote it in her small black book of songs (Bennett 1950), so the songs did have a certain currency before the society veered too far away from its cultural basis of song.

"*He had very good Gaelic, the Sgiobair," says Peigi. "He used words that were uncommon." I have heard such statements from many people, not that he used unknown words (as Mac Mhaighstir Alasdair is famous for doing), but simply a heightened register of language slightly above the everyday. "*Now that's great poetry, Peter," Mrs. Bennett continued, speaking to her brother Peter about *An Eaglais Shaor an Steòrnabhagh* (26) as she was assisting me with the transcription. Peter agreed, thereby confirming that the song-maker is being assessed largely on his text. Perhaps this judgement is based partly on subject matter, as well as the fine control of language. There is a sense that the Sgiobair could really rise to an occasion, such as the death of Kenneth Macrae, to make a particularly outstanding song like this one. He himself has said that his songs were better when he took a little more care, rather than making them relatively quickly for one night in the céilidh house. His more remembered and respected songs are, for the most part, the ones over which he has taken the greatest care. "*Oh yes, he was a good bard," added Peter.

Murdo MacLean (nach mairean), Portree, Uig and North Kessock

Murdo MacLean was born in Portree, but knew the Sgiobair since the 1930s. Shortly after the Second World War, MacLean moved to Uig where he lived with his wife Effie and their family until the late 1960s. There was an obvious rapport between the two men when talking about people they both knew and about the old days in Trotternish (see the opening of this chapter).

"*I thought there was more depth to the Sgiobair's song's [than Fletcher's]," said MacLean. "*Oh he was good." (interview 29.1.93) Again we see that the Sgiobair, though perfectly capable of humorous and 'throw away' songs, also had a reputation for more serious compositions. Interestingly, MacLean used the word 'depth' in his qualitative description.[177]

Murdo and Teenie Stewart (nach maireann), Glenconon

Often, while researching this book, I would stay at Murdo's and Teenie's house at No. 10 Glenconon. Through talking to them and being there, I gained a great insight into traditional life in the glen that has helped me put Iain's songs into their proper context of the crofting community.

Murdo had a great appreciation of Iain's use of language and situation and also took a great interest in this book. I remember talking through the songs with him, hearing his memories of the events they portray and his tears of helpless laughter as he recalled Dunnchadh Beag's reaction to *Tarbh Bhràigh Uige* (4).

One night after talking like this, I went to bed at around one a.m. From the other end of the house, I could hear Murdo laughing heartily to himself as he continued to read through my thesis. I later found that he had stayed up until about five, reading and remembering the history of his glen told through Iain's songs.

That night, he also cleared up a number of transcription problems for me and came up with several couplets from Sgiobair songs I had not yet come across. I was then able to use these clues with Iain and recover the songs.

Both Murdo and Teenie called Iain a clever man, but perhaps the most touching testament to the high regard in which his work is held in his own native glen is the contents of their bookshelf in the kitchen at No. 10:

Seven bibles (two English); One Gaelic poetry book; Two church magazines; Two collections of churchmen's letters; Three collections of Gaelic sermons (the earliest is 1859); One pair of spectacles; One Stornoway Gazette (1974); One cookery book; One photo: "At the fank, August, 1939".

And last but not least: One copy of the Sgiobair's booklet of songs, *Orain Aonghais agus an Sgiobair*.

Isabel Ross (née Gillies), Earlish/Mogastad (now Fortrose)

Mrs. Ross has known Iain since her childhood (1920s), when Iain would visit her father's house to sing his latest composition. She and her brother, Norman, are cousins of Iain's wife Màiri. On one occasion, Isabel remembers her father laughing until he had tears running down his cheeks listening to *Tarbh Bhràigh Ùige* (4), because he knew all the people Iain was lampooning, could imagine the scene and their reaction to the song.

We have already seen how she and Iain sparred verbally, in songs 12–14 and the two still enjoy teasing exchanges on the rare occasions they see each other. But Isabel has made songs too, such as the humorous one about her husband sailing to America in a rowboat. She also recited songs by several other local song-makers, such as Uilleam Iain Chaimbeil, and gave me the first clues which led to the recovery of *Tarbh Bhràigh Uige*. Her excellent memory and sense of humour bring to life the vigorous song-making tradition with which she grew up and helped provide context for Iain's songs. Her opinion of them is therefore well-informed and from within the tradition.

TM: You were saying that the Sgiobair [was] better at making more serious songs.

IR: Yes, I think, the Sgiobair was ahead of even Fletcher too, but I suppose that's a matter of opinion.

But say there was a feud between you, he would try and settle it by negotiation, but...in an argument, well he wouldn't change his opinion.... He's got his opinion and you wouldn't shift him. But haven't we all. [*laughs*]

...He has a big heart and he's very, very kind and so is Mary. And he's really most enjoyable. Oh well I was there, remember Angus [my husband],...and he came home and Mary was teasing him.... Oh, he got really annoyed with Mary over something and I forget what his wife said to him, and I was teasing him [too]. And he says, "Right," he says, "when I go,...you don't know what you're saying,...I'm going to leave my money to an old folks home." [*laughs*]

She also notes with pleasure that the he is the Bard to the Clan Nicolson.

Norman Gillies (Tarmad Ruairidh), Lìonacro

Norman, Isabel's brother, crofts in Lìonacro, a few miles north of Uig. He is also a lay-preacher who takes the Gaelic services at Uig church nearly every Sunday. Norman has a great appreciation for *bàrdachd* old and new, clever wordplay and has even made a few songs himself.

Like his sister, he has known Iain for years.

NG: Cha do choinnich mise ri gin dhe na gillean a bh'air falbh a's a' chogadh ann a' shin nach dug dhachaigh uiread de chànan ris a' Sgiobair.... Canaidh e rud beag a's a' Ghearmailtis is...rud beag a's a' Fhrangais dhaibh, agus na cànanan a tha sin. Thog e faclan a' siud 's a' seo....

Bha visitors againn an a' sheo air chuairt agus...'s ann as a' Ghearmailt a bha ad. Thuirt an Sgiobair facal no dhà...as a' chànan aca fhéin riutha. Chòrd e riutha cuideachd.... O 's e duine modhail tàlantach a bh'ann.[178]

NG: I didn't meet one of the lads who'd been away in the War there who didn't bring home as much language as the Sgiobair. He can say a little in German and a little in French to them, and those languages [of Europe]. He picked up words here and there.

We had visitors here on a tour and they were from Germany. The Sgiobair said a word or two to them in their own language. It pleased them too. Oh he was an amiable, talented man.[178]

I went on to ask Norman about *An Eaglais Shaor an Steòrnabhagh* (26).

NG: O uel, gur e direach air a chur air a chéile go h-onarach, urramach.... Cha dèanadh duine gun tàlantan leithid a chur ri chéile, cha robh. A bharrachd air gu robh bàrdachd air;...bha móran rudan co-cheangailte rise, bha.

Bh'e fhéin measail air a' mhinistear a bha sin.... Bha ùidh aige sa rud a bha am ministear ag ràdh. Bh'e saoiltainn móran dhen a' mhinistear; bh'e a' toirt urram dhan a' mhinistear os cionn móran eile.

NG: Oh well, just that it's been composed with integrity and respect. Someone with no skills couldn't have managed a similar composition, no. Not just because there was poetry in it [but] there were many things related to it, yes.

He was respectful of that minister. He was interested in what the minister was saying. He thought a lot of the minister; he gave preference to the minister above many others.

The bard's detailed interest in his subject is reflected in the depth and substance of the song.

TM: An e fìor bhàrd a th'ann?
NG: O uel! 'S e! 'S e, 's e fìor bhàrd a th'ann gun teagamh.... Chan e mhàin gu bheil...a' rud an t-altaibh a chéil' aige, och tha brìgh a's a' rud a tha e ag radha.... Bheir e dealbh air a' rud leis a' bhàrdachd aige, agus tha bhàrdachd aige glé choimhlionta. Tha bàrdachd mhath aige, gun teagamh, tha.

TM: *Is he a true bard [or poet]?*
NG: *Oh well! Yes! Yes, he's a true bard without a doubt. It's not just that he put the stuff [i.e. the song] together, but there is meaning in what he says. He creates an image of what [he's talking about] through his poetry, and his poetry is very accomplished. He composes good poetry, without a doubt, yes.*

Iain, of course, has also made humorous songs, "Ach 's ioma fear a rinn e de dh'fheodhainn éibhinn, tha mi creidsinn tha'n duine air a dhìochuimhneachadh an-diugh." ["But he's composed many funny ones, I suppose, that the man's forgotten now."]

We also spoke of songs by other local composers such as Uilleam Iain Chaimbeil, from whose satire, *Òran na bachelors* [*The bachelors' song*], Tarmad quoted.

NG: Cha bhiodh a' Sgiobair cur rudan dhe'n t-seòrsa sin idir ann. Cha bhiodh e cur càil ann a bheireadh oilbheum do dhuine sam bith, a' Sgiobair. Orainean glana bh'aig a' Sgiobair as a h-uile gin a bha e dèanamh. Bha rian orra.

'S e duine glan 'na nàdar a bh'as a' Sgiobair cuideachd.... Cha robh dìth-mothaiche sam bith ann, ach bh'e ri bàrdachd ...dìreach,...sin agad a' rud a bh'e ris.

NG: *The Sgiobair wouldn't include anything like that. He wouldn't include anything that offended anyone, the Sgiobair. The Sgiobair composed straightforward songs, each one he made. They were good-natured.*

The Sgiobair was a straightforward man by nature, too. It wasn't that he lacked insight, he composed poetry, simply that's what he was about.

Iain Peutan [John Beaton] (nach maireann), Glenconon

The late Iain Peutan was born in 1900 and I asked him when he first met Iain: "Thachair ann a' 1909. O...gille beag laghach a bh'ann[s] an Sgiobair. O rinn e...de òrain glé mhath, rinn. ["[We] met in 1909. Oh, the Skipper was a lovely wee boy. Oh he made some very good songs, yes."]

Iain then referred, jokingly, to Sgiobair's series of songs to young women, made when both of them were in their teens and twenties. "O bha boireannaich gu leòr aige gad is e Màiri a phòs e!" [laughs] ["Oh he had plenty of women, though it's Mary he married!"] Beaton obviously enjoyed watching the bard's early social life unfold in song.

Aonghas MacNeacail (Aonghas Dubh), Uig (now Edinburgh)

AM: To me the man he compares with who was capable of satire, but also capable of the most marvellous poignancy is Iain Dubh Dhòmhnaill nan Oran [Black-(haired) John (son of) Donald of the Songs, and brother of Neil MacLeod], you know from Glendale,...the mariner bard who had a wonderful capacity for composing striking songs in very ordinary language. On one level, his songs were like conversation; on another level there was such an economy to them and such precision to them.

TM: You were mentioning that earlier,...talking about how, in many ways, it's quite ordinary...language, and yet quite precise and controlled.

AM: Yes, it is extraordinary that language can be used in such a way. It's [a] juxtaposition of words and images;...it's very hard to explain, it's a quality.

TM: It sounds like speech, but it's very deliberate and exact.

AM: Absolutely, yes. And...full of assonances and all sorts of the trickery of the bard that you don't get in normal speech, but...the rhythm of it is both flowing and fluid...as verse and yet has the ease of normal speech as well.

When you think of the translations that have been made of Gaelic poetry over the years and how sort of 'soft-edged' it can seem.... The reality of Gaelic poetry is very different;...it may deal with sentimental subjects sometimes, but always, I feel, unsentimentally.... The language transcends...the sentimentality.

TM: It's usually quite stark in a way.

AM: It is yes.... One of the songs I was reading was [Màiri Mhór's] Òran Beinn Lì...wonderful, wonderful, which again carries that quality of the simplicity and the striking...and...the Sgiobair is very much in that tradition.

Aonghas draws particular attention to Iain's careful diction, for example in line 25–6 of Nach bòidheach Ùige (21).

TM: Just the phrase 'lorg a' chapaill', you know, is more lyrical than it needs to be, but it's not effusive....

AM: No, absolutely not.... If you said in English, "Its beach is like a horseshoe," it would be pretty banal but...in Gaelic it isn't, particularly because you can make that choice of using the older word for a horse.... I think it would be 'poetic',...but...it also balances with 'tràghad', there's an internal rhyme there, "Tha dealbh a thràghad mar lorg an eich", wouldn't have the same sense at all.

Uilleam and Iain Aonghas MacNeacail and Màiri NicNeacail [William and John Angus Nicolson and Mary Nicolson], Cuidreach

Uilleam and Iain are the Sgiobair's sons who are most often present when I visit. They have a great appreciation for both Gaelic songs and traditions and their father's work as well. Initially, I was not sure that they shared his interest in history and local characters, but as I have got to know them, I see that they respect his knowledge and talent in those areas as well. They listen when I record and add further particulars or correct Iain's memory if he misremembers a detail.

John Angus has assessed more than one song as "good" and takes quite an interest when I am record-ing. Willie often compliments his father's singing, "O tha e math air seinn, nach eil?" ["Oh he's good at singing, isn't he?"], as well as frequently suggesting a song for Iain to sing to me: "*Gabh Nach bòidheach Uige, tha sin math." ["Sing How beautiful Uig is, that's good."] He has also made helpful suggestions about how to recover more of such fragmentary songs as Tarbh Bhràigh Uige (4).

Sometimes the brothers appear to tire of Iain's old-fashioned world-view, but as I have got to know them, I realise that this is primarily an opportunity for a good-natured argument. Willie, in particular, enjoys a good scrap and both he and his father will say things designed specifically to get each other going, often winking laughingly at me across the room and waiting for the reaction. Recently, however, while looking at his father, Willie said to me, "*O bha fhios aig na seann daoine air a h-uile rud a bh'ann. Chan eil a' leithid seo an diugh. ["Oh the old men knew about everything. There's no one like that today."]

Their mother Màiri enjoys the songs, and the stories from her lifetime, but does not share Iain's intense interest in the old bards of tradition. She is therefore sometimes concerned lest I record some of the "rubbish" that makes up the previous five chapters (and that she has heard for the last fifty years).[179]

Màiri and Iseabail NicNeacail [Mary and Isobel Nicolson], Siadar

The Sgiobair's sisters, Màiri and Iseabail (who is five years older than the Sgiobair) still live in their native glen of Siadar and regularly come down to Cuidreach for a visit. Màiri is known as Màiri Uilleam [Mary (daughter of) William] to differentiate her from the Sgiobair's wife, who is known as Màiri Sgiobair [Mary (wife of the) Sgiobair].

Both of the sisters are dedicated church-goers and are fairly strict on such matters as keeping the Sabbath. Màiri and Iseabail, like their brother, feel that Gaelic is important and that children in Skye should grow up with the language. They do not wholly approve of initiatives like Gaelic road signs, however, sometimes characterising them as frivolities. Despite this attitude, they do appreciate the Sgiobair's talent for song-making. Probably their favourite song is An Eaglais Shaor an Steòrnabhagh (26). The reason Iseabail gave for this is interesting, as it coincides with his own assessment (see below) of the strengths of the composition about Macrae: "*The song is just like him too."

Other tradition-bearers

I have spoken to Gaels from all over Scotland who have come across Iain's songs and their usual response is "O bha e math air na h-òrain", or "Rinn e òrain glé mhath" ["Oh he was good at the songs", or "He made good songs"], or some such phrase. At the Bughmore Home in Portree, I heard a whole roomful of men extolling Iain's skill in just these terms.

At the Comhdhail nan Seanchaidh in Sleat, I have conversed with other *seanchaidhean* [tradition-bearers] from all over the *Gàidhealtachd*. Over the years that the Còmhdhail has run, the *seanchaidhean* have got to know each other quite well and I decided to elicit some of Iain's contemporaries' and peers' impressions of his work.

I first spoke to Seasaidh Chamshron from Lewis, about *A Mhàiri, a Mhàiri* (19), which the Sgiobair had just sung, "*'S e òran snog a th'ann." ["*It's a nice song.*"] A woman with whom she was sitting replied, "Nach eil e brèagha!" ["*Isn't it lovely!*"]

Anna Dhunnchaidh [Anna (daughter of) Duncan (MacDonald)[180]] was another participant in the Còmhdhail. She had a fund of lore about Fionn MacCumhail and his band and I asked her what she thought about the Sgiobair from her perspective of some of the older Hebridean traditions: "*O tha e gu math fiosrachail." ["*Oh he is very intelligent and well informed.*"]

"O tha, tha," ["*Oh yes, yes,*"] answered Dòmhnull Dunnchadh Dòmhnallach [Donald Duncan MacDonald], seated at her side.

I then asked Anna about the songs themselves: "O tha ad uamhasach math! An cuala tu òran a rinn e, *A Mhàiri, a Mhàiri*? (19) Tha e misneach." ["*Oh they are terribly good! Have you heard [the] song he made, Oh Mary, oh Mary? It is spirited.*"]

Other public and media recognition

In recent decades, with the advent of inexpensive recording techniques, MacNeacail has been recorded extensively by me and others, such as the BBC, Cailean MacGill-eain, Anne Dhu Shapiro, David Clement and Jonathan MacDonald. In 1980, Catrìona NicGumaraid produced a cassette and booklet made up of some of the Sgiobair's and Aonghas Fleidsear's songs. It is interesting to see these modern poets, scholars and broadcasters appreciate the Sgiobair's work, perhaps as a genuine unbroken link with the past and perhaps simply because some of his best verse has a timeless quality and mastery about it. In a way, many modern Gaelic poets have been cut off from this past and so have had to start again using book-learned foundations.

Iain's compositions fit 'the tradition' perfectly, for they have been created by, and for, 'the folk'. To some, the only true test of such a song is acceptance into oral tradition, which assumes, among other things, a *healthy* oral tradition and a serendipitous meeting of tradition-bearer with interested learner(s). These conditions were sadly not in place for MacNeacail. Moreover, the *bàrd baile* tradition, as we have seen, was one of transience, yet Iain's songs are remembered with affection and respect by local residents and those further afield (and some did gain oral currency). But for the folk-song scholar, it is really the process and function of song-making, rather than the product, that is the defining characteristic of the genre.[181]

A CREATOR WITHIN THE TRADITION

MacNeacail, for all his knowledge of his inherited tradition, was always more interested in creating within it: "I wasn't taking the notion of them, I would rather be composing myself." It is this connection with a living tradition that makes the Sgiobair, and the few remaining bards like him, so important to Gaelic culture today. Aonghas Dubh:

AM: We really are the first generation where the living tradition isn't as healthy as it could be.[182] Which
     makes someone like the Sgiobair even more precious, that he doesn't just represent the tradition that
     these people recounted, he has been a creator in the tradition.

For his part, Iain sees his talent as a gift, but does not see himself as a composer of any note compared with the great bards.

IM: Well,...when I go into the language of Dunnchadh Bàn and William Ross here, no there's no
     comparison! I knew, I know...what a fool I am, compared to them.

MacNeacail both appreciates the efficacy of an oral education, and wonders that it worked so well. There
is also an element of self-deprecation here, reminiscent of Mac Mhaighstir Alasdair's claim in *Guidhe no
Urnaigh an Ughdair do'n Cheòlraidh* [*Entreaty or Prayer of the Author to the Muses*], to be skill-less and unschooled
(MacDonald 1924:10–15, especially ll. 67–80). Perhaps there is an unspoken code of self-assessment
to which artists are expected to adhere.

    I asked Iain if he made a deliberate attempt to compose like the old bards, for example in the use of
difficult words.

IM: Ah well, no but I want to go as deep in them as I can. But if I did so local[ly] here, they wouldn't
     understand it, because they [are] only working on the surface of Gàidhlig here, compared to what
     these bards were. They were going and there weren't a vegetable [i.e. plant] in the field, or a fish in
     the sea, or anything that, that...could compare with them!

Again the word 'depth' is used in relation to a poet's language. These bards knew the names of the very
building blocks of the earth.[183] Obviously, MacNeacail does attempt, within the limits he perceives himself to have, to emulate them in language at least. He implies that he *could* compose in a manner more
like the old bards than he does, but that as a contemporary poet he must modify his poetic 'ideal' to
keep in step with his audience.

> For a composer's music to be socially significant, it must carry some meaning to an audience.... If one's
> contemporaries do not understand or like one's music, there is little chance for it to become a part of
> the culture. (Nash 1961:93)

The audience is, after all, the final arbiter on whether his songs gain currency and whether he himself
reaps resulting approval in the community.

    Despite MacNeacail's undoubted bardic skills (which he often belittles), he does not expect his own
songs to live on:

IM: Yes, yes, yes, well Màiri Mhór [said], "Nuair bheirear dhachaigh leis a' bhàs mi, bidh ar n-àl ga
     seinn," ["*When I am borne home by death, our generation will be singing them,*"] but not any of them.

Had he been born earlier, I believe that more of Iain's songs would have survived. Màiri Mhór left her
songs to a culture with a fully functional oral tradition which allowed frequent transmission in a céilidh
setting. As we have already seen, several of the Sgiobair's songs were sung in the declining house-
visiting culture of the fifties and early sixties. Màiri Mhór, and Dunnchadh Bàn before her, were also
relentless publicists; their tours in combination with the publication of their songs during their life-
times gave them very high profiles in the Gaelic world. Perhaps as I have recorded and transcribed more
and more of Iain's songs, he has begun to believe that they too will live on.

    In the Sgiobair's perceptions, as we have seen above, Dunnchadh Bàn Mac an t-Saoir is a bard, *sui generis*. By this definition, therefore, he himself is not a true bard, by his own definition, though he holds the ceremonial title.

TM: Did you consider yourself a bard?

IM: No! But I'm known as that, in Australia, New Zealand and everywhere. They got that name and…I
   get [called in] Australia, the 'Bard of the Clan Nicolson'.

To him, the work of a bard and the ceremonial office that he holds are two different things. He does not consider himself to be on the same plane as Dunnchadh Bàn and therefore does not use the word "bard" in relation to himself, though he does gain some pleasure out of the recognition of his talents that the name implies. That he holds the office, in name anyway, is due to a suggestion from Aonghas Dubh to the Australian Chief of the Clan Nicolson: "*Somhairle [MacGill-Eain] seemed quite content to take the honours for the Clan MacLean, so I thought it would be nice to offer [the Sgiobair] something." (Interview 2.3.93) 'Sgoirebreac', as the Chief is called, was enthusiastic and arranged the matter immediately.

In May of 1992, Margaret Bennett and I had the honour of accompanying Iain to the Clan Gathering, which took place in the Cuillin Hills Hotel in Sgoirebreac. The Chief and his wife were over from Australia (probably, they said, on their last visit to Scotland) along with their son, 'Mac'. Also in attendance were Nicolson clansmen from all over the world. The Sgiobair, dressed in his kilt of Nicolson tartan, took part in the procession into the hall and I was pleased to see him seated at the head table in conversation with the Chief; he values his friendship with the Chief and is content enough to play the role of the Clan Bard at formal occasions every few years. In some ways, MacNeacail's situation parallels Màiri Mhór's when she was rubbing shoulders with "the big bugs", to use his phrase. On the other hand, he has not made a single song to or about the Chief or the Clan and those that he has made to the 'upper class' (such as *Thoir mo bheannachd do dh'Eilean Iarmain* (29) and *'S e seo a' sgeul tha taitneach leinn* (28)) have not gained him any form of patronage or sponsorship. Several people present (such as the Chief, Dr. Alasdair Maclean and others) told me they were very pleased that someone was collecting his songs and working with him in such detail. They value his compositions and probably the ancient image of the Clan Bard, too. The appreciation of 'educated' people like them would no doubt be a source of satisfaction to him.[184]

After the formal part of the evening was over, we spent quite some time in conversation with the Sgiobair and 'Mac'. Iain was honoured to be in conversation with the son of the Chief and commented later what a nice and ordinary person he seemed. The assumption that he might be otherwise shows that the Sgiobair is still quite deferential to people of social standing, whether they be doctors, lawyers or especially Chiefs. To him, since the Chieftainship itself went overseas, it was not to blame for the Clearances. For his part, 'Mac' was charmed by the Sgiobair and his poetic achievements and fascinated by the integration of song in his culture. He was also touched, flattered (and probably made a little self-conscious) by his old-fashioned respect and loyalty.

IM: Oh I never think I'd have the office too. No I don't, not, not! No, but…I could compose, you know,
   but being a bard, oh the like of Duncan Bàn MacIntyre…and these. Oh they were…the best bards….
   Dunnchadh Bàn,…you know him?

TM: Yes.

IM: He's the man!

Iain speaks as if 'mere' composers, such as he, were common. Certainly, there is more to being a bard than simply making songs, but I believe the Sgiobair's achievements in this area are not to be under-

27. *An Sgiobair* with the Clan Chief, Iain MacNeacail, at the Clan Gathering in Sgoirebreac near Portree, May 16, 1992.
(T. A. McKean)

28 and 29. *Iain* at the Clan Gathering in Sgoirebreac, May
16, 1992. (T. A. McKean)

assessed (as he would have us do). As I said at the end of the case studies, I believe that aspects of his art are comparable to those of his favourite bards, and the world he lives and works in more hostile to the practice of that art.

I haven't got them myself, you know

MacNeacail's own favourite songs are those that go to the heart of the matter, such as *Nochd gur luaineach mo chadal* (16), which simply "told it as it was". Another of his favourite songs of his own is *An Eaglais Shaor an Steòrnabhagh* (26), because it was "more truthful than any of them" and "put...him as he was". This offers an insight into why MacNeacail so values description as a measure of the success of a composition: to describe a subject well in song was to hit upon its pith, "brìgh a' rud" ["*the substance of the thing*"], as Bella Ross puts it.

These days, many of Iain's songs and those of other local song-makers have been lost, their topicality, humour and functional environment passé. Still others have been forgotten due to old age.

IM: Yes well, I haven't got them myself, you know. Where are they? Although I was composing them at the time, they were gone and after years of not being put in practice...that's how they went.

Nor is composing the involuntary, instinctive process it once was. He sees modern poets making a living from their work and, more importantly, becoming known and respected as poets. This highlights one of the main regrets of his later life. Aonghas Dubh recalls an evening in The Ferry Inn in Uig with the Sgiobair and one of his sons:

AM: The Sgiobair turned to me and said "Well," he says, "Angus, if I had known when I was your age," or "when I was young," in fact, "[that] people would take my poetry as seriously as they do now, I would have taken it much more seriously myself." And I thought it was a...wonderfully vulnerable and in some ways, maybe not quite tragic, but it was a sad recognition for a man to make who was, by then, well into his seventies.

TM: Sort of after the fact.

AM: That's it.... He was acknowledging that he was the kind of bard he was with the kind of output he [had]. I happen to think he's a very, very fine poet in his own genre. I think his poem to Uig [*Nach bòidheach Uige* (21) and his...war poem [*Nochd gur luaineach mo chadal* (16)] are very, very fine song-poems I suppose you can call them.

MacNeacail has expressed these regrets to me himself on several occasions.

IM: But how things are, you know, if I was at one time thinking that what was going on today [i.e. recording and publishing], I would have something to be of more merit than it is. I would have made them proper and more qualified than I am.

TM: Well, there are quite a few good ones.

IM: Ach I don't know, but I would have more...Gàidhlig words, better Gàidhlig in it than I have, no no, no no no.

In a way the Sgiobair has been caught in a hiatus of poetic patronage; he was born at the wrong time, with an 'out of date' poetic aesthetic. Had he been born much earlier, he would have been living in a society where expression in song was still the norm and where a man of his talents might have held some official poetic office, leading to patronage, formal training and more time to devote to his craft. At least he would have received more formal and community recognition of his skill and possibly some form of remuneration, all of which would have given him a higher status in society. On the other hand, had he been born a little *later*, when poetry, albeit in a different form, has once again become a means of making a living (or at least a recognised and acceptable role/profession with a certain social status), he could perhaps have been a poet in the modern sense. He was born at the tail-end of the validity of his own aesthetic and too early to acquire the pan-European assumptions that underlie most Western poetic aesthetics today.

The rapid cultural change taking place around MacNeacail in the latter half of his life has swept away the foundations of his pre-First World War aesthetic. The twentieth century was brought forcibly and suddenly to island communities.

AM: As you say, the war was a crucial time of breakup. There was no longer the sense of going to a house to hear the old stories or to hear the poems.

TM: And I suppose radio would have come on strongly after the war, as well.

AM: I was about twelve when radio came on, so in my teens, the time when I might have developed an interest in tradition, instead I was developing an interest in wondering why my...preferred version, the Carl Perkins version, wasn't given the same prominence as the Presley version of *Blue Suede Shoes*.

By the time this cultural invasion was happening, local school-children would have been coming home to an English-speaking environment, whereas in the Sgiobair's day, both home and the playground were entirely Gaelic-speaking and both were fertile nurturers of tradition.

A PERMANENT RECOGNITION

One of the most moving events for the Sgiobair in the last few years has been the erection in Sgoirebreac of a cairn to the Nicolsons evicted in the Clearances. Along with all the other names on the cairn, appear those of John and Mary Nicolson. Their parents were not cleared, but in a sense, the Sgiobair was evicted from the inheritance of the bardic tradition, and therefore the status that might have been his, had the enormous social and cultural upheaval of the Clearances never taken place. In the dedication of the cairn, MacNeacail sees some redress for these wrongs and a place in posterity for himself and Màiri.

IM: The Clan Chief put that there and he put my name there and Mary's name there, but there's no other name there but ours, giving Cuidreach, you know,...from all the other colonies that was there. The[ir] name was there, but no address. But we are,...John and Mary Nicolson, Cuidreach! [*slaps pipe on hands for emphasis*] Well, they know who would be there at Cuidreach. While that *càrn* is there it'll be there! That's what I was saying, I needn't have any memorial stone on me...in the church, in the graveyard, when I had it up there; they'll know who I was, there.

TM: But see, then they'll know that you're the same one who made the songs.

IM: Well, that wasn't put on it at all, but he only put down 'the Clan Nicolson Bard'.

Perhaps having his name written in stone on the cairn and in ink in this book will go some way to re-enfranchising MacNeacail in his own and others' eyes.

Chapter Seven

CONCLUSION

SONGS: THE DISTILLATION OF EXPERIENCE

I set out to investigate the relationships between a song-maker and his songs, his songs and his world-view and his community's perception of him in his role as a composer. Comparison with other folk song cultures for which in-depth studies exist, lead me to believe that a degree of inter-dependence can be expected. As this book shows, the integration of song in Iain's daily life is complete for, in his youth, matters of even passing significance were recorded in song. Songs that deal with important watersheds in his life, however, are more firmly remembered and more frequently sung, for they are teeming with associations and images of the past. In singing them, he reaffirms the information and the emotions expressed. They are his units of memory and, due to the nature of song, much of his emotional life is therefore on public display.

The traditional composer gains two kinds of release through song. Expression through *composition* and expression through *singing* a song are both cathartic; the former achieves release through a creative act and the latter through performance. To compose a song is to give free rein to expression, but to sing a song that is already made immediately narrows the range. In the twenties and thirties, MacNeacail participated fully in both these phases of his art, but in recent decades the environment in which such expression is customary has disappeared. The internal release of composition is still available, but the world of daily informal song and story that formed the second stage of expression is gone. To him, song is communication, the purest form of it, and though villagers today do not speak his language of song, the *potential* for renewed emotional release remains, at some level, so long as he is alive.

Iain's songs were not always expressions of deep emotion. They were often made as much for the exercise of composing and to "pass the time" as anything else. Some of his early courtship songs reflect this (as opposed to being accurate reflections of intense emotional involvement). Also, the roles of expectation and demand must not be overlooked in this type of song-making. A bard must have a response to every challenge, whether it be a song refusing a request or a revenge in the form of a satire. A reaction was expected and the very fact that he did react *proved* that he was a bard.

As exercises in the seemingly effortless use of language, many of the Sgiobair's Gaelic songs are exemplary. They flow smoothly and conversationally and yet his diction is undoubtedly heightened above that of everyday language without being especially formulaic. The Sgiobair is judged by his fellow villagers on his creation of lyrics and how well the song is put together; they particularly appreciate his command of language (for example, the description in *Nach bòidheach Uige* (20)) which, while easy to understand, is beyond their own creative capabilities. On the whole, the language is rigorously controlled, polished and well put together. Emotional involvement, when presented with such apparent ease, does not intrude upon the listener, for the message is contained in a framework within which such displays are expected; the expression is therefore seen as natural.

30. *Iain looking through a draft of this book, the first time he had seen so many of his songs collected together, Spring 1993.* (T. A. McKean)

THE VILLAGE SONG-MAKER AND HIS ENVIRONMENT

Today, a village song-maker is viewed by the younger generation as a little old-fashioned (though they appreciate that a talent for song-making is rare). In addition, the songs' native environment of the *taigh céilidh* is no longer easily found. Both the songs and the song-maker therefore have no natural setting and have ceased to be the carriers of direct expression in the community. Song still has a function in the village, of course, but primarily in the formal céilidhs which took over from spontaneous house visits after the Second World War. In this context, songs are not seen as personal statements. The singer may, by choice of song, reflect thoughts and emotions, but it is not the first-hand expression that composition is.

In many ways, the song-maker had more freedom to express opinions and emotions than most people, because song was accepted as an appropriate medium. The song-maker's semi-official role as a social commentator also meant that he could say things that might have caused offence coming from other mouths (in satires, for instance). The conventions of the medium itself allowed him direct access to emotional expression, simultaneously providing him with protection behind the persona of the song-maker and the heightened language of poetry.

In fact, villagers could expect the song-maker to deliver his reactions on a whole range of local matters. From the villagers' point of view, when he 'makes a song on' an occurrence, he acknowledges its importance; the event and the villagers gain status from being enshrined in a song, rather like an announcement in a newspaper which formally records something as having 'happened'. In this way, the bard defines the community's identity by his choice of subject, just as they define his by providing fodder for his compositions.

Many traditional composers make their songs almost exclusively for entertainment, but for a natural bard like the Sgiobair, the use of song is scarcely a choice; it is a requirement which arises out of his need to communicate. In a society accustomed to song, the use of verse, as opposed to prose, alerts the listener that he is receiving a distilled message. The custom that most traditional song-makers follow, of using a familiar tune for a new composition, may actually allow easier access to this message, for the listener need not come to terms with the melody before taking in the content. And the same may be said of stanza forms and linguistic formulae as well.

In addition, the melody (and possibly form) is selected (consciously or subconsciously) by the song-maker because of its associations. The audience is therefore predisposed to the tenor of the poet's message. To demand a fresh melody for each song would be to apply a modern 'art' music aesthetic and to imply that a song is primarily an artistic rather than a functional, emotional and communicative creation. In order to communicate at this level, the message *must* be sung to be in the register in which such communications are expected to be coded. It is clear from a number of references he has made to modern Gaelic poets that this is true for the Sgiobair. It confirms that, in his eyes, to be a true poet you must make songs: "You can't sing a single one of his songs, how can he be a poet!" [185]

In his youth, MacNeacail did not view his song-making as anything special. Undoubtedly the presence of other song-makers in the area – Uilleam Iain Chaimbeul, Seonaidh Aileag Chamshron, Bàrd Ghrialain and Neil Beaton in Staffin, Aonghas Fleidsear in Siadar, Calum Ciorstaidh (and others) – made him feel less unusual than he is today. Moreover, songs were a part of regular everyday life, and as such were not considered worthy of the same notice as we give them. The everyday occurrences in society are often overlooked and irrevocably lost before we realise that they were unique and worthy of interest and preservation. This is the case with MacNeacail's songs; as he has said himself, if he had known that tape recorders would become available and that poets like Somhairle MacGill-Eain and Aonghas MacNeacail would be making a living from versifying, he would have taken a great deal more care in both making and preserving his songs.

IM: They were only just for the time being and that was all forgotten, you know, but till just recently,...then this recording and such came and I took more interest in it. If that was done, say, thirty years before now, I would have made something worth of it, but I didn't.

A WORK IN PROGRESS

Inevitably, while engaged in an undertaking of this sort, I have gathered far more intriguing information than can be used in a single project, and Iain is not finished with me by any means. Each visit I make to Cuidreach reveals more lore, more poetry and more of the sort of knowledge that would have been expected from an old-style *file*: hill and field names, local and family histories and traditions.

A graphic example of such 'new' material – which I *have* been able to include – is the recent retrieval of *Tarbh Bhràigh Uige* and *Spògan circeadh* (4 and 18), Sgiobair songs that previously eluded me. Iain had mentioned them, but could not recall the verses. Over the years, however, other people I interviewed, such as uncle Murdo or Isabel Ross, would remember a couplet or two. I was then able to jog Iain's memory and hardly was a line out of my mouth, when he would say, "Oh aye", and reel off half a dozen verses. I had not even heard of these songs in our first few years working together and yet, after the smallest of hints, he remembered large tracts of them. Minutes later he sometimes cannot recall them as fluently, only to do so at a later date; memory is indeed a mysterious faculty.

Iain's mind is still brimming with tradition and lore, much of it still unrecorded. I look forward to following up other leads as time allows.

'LAST LEAVES' AND THE CREATOR WITHIN THE TRADITION

I hope that this project will be seen as saving some of the 'last leaves' of the *bàrd baile* tradition, both the songs themselves and the all-important context which allows us to reconstruct how and why a township poet goes about his business of making songs. But while it is certainly a matter of preservation, there is much more to be learned from the life and work of Iain MacNeacail than just the bare bones of his art. To claim to be 'saving' a tradition is unrealistic, for it implies (i) that the collector has the omniscience to preserve something in its entirety which, even with modern technology, is still impossible and (ii) that the tradition actually is on the verge of extinction. To suggest that a culture or tradition is so static that it will either live or die in a matter of years is to sound its death knell straight away, for only by adapting can it continue to be relevant to people's lives. This is the problem built in to the 'preservation' school of collecting, which practically condemns the material to immediate obsolescence, the subject of academic study in libraries, archives and museums alone. I would argue that the complete death of a tradition or a culture is actually a very rare occurrence.[186] They almost invariably adapt and undergo whatever transformation is necessary for their survival. Take for example, the British ballad tradition which had been described by collectors as moribund or non-existent for centuries. Then in the 1950s and 1960s came the discovery of the traveller traditions and thereafter the 'folk revival' which took over and adapted much of the travellers' living song tradition. It is certainly not the *same* tradition, but it is clearly a descendant which ensures the survival of a vast body of traditional song.[187]

For Gaelic tradition and culture, which is continually pronounced dead or dying, MacNeacail is an important symbol of the role adaptation has to play in cultural preservation. Traditional Gaelic society today has broken down so far that radical change may break apart what remains. It therefore needs change from within and confidence in order to survive. The Sgiobair has provided this himself by retaining the Gaelic tradition of song as communication, though now through the medium of English (see the end of Chapter Five). He does not just preserve the past, but re-casts it in a new and still living way, for he is a creator fully within the rules of a traditional aesthetic.

SONG AND THE SELF

At first glance, Iain may appear an ordinary individual leading an average crofter's life. Throughout this book, however, we have seen him in many guises: crofter, composer, soldier, father, humorist, poet and village song-maker to name a few. Closer inspection has revealed a combination of events, personality and culture which show him to be unique and aspects of his life experience to be powerful and moving. The intimate understanding of his world allows us to understand the role of these songs in this man's perception of self and environment and how the two interact. Such is the importance of context to the study of the individual; without it, one is left discussing 'the folk' or 'the people' collectively, losing touch with the power of individual experience.

The Sgiobair's songs function on several different levels: personal expression (for example, the songs of courtship); community expression (*Tha sluagh òg air dhol gu aimbeirt* (23), for example); national or cultural expression (*Nochd gur luaineach mo chadal* (16) or *A time will come, a time will go* (30)). Each song has intrinsic aural and literary qualities which can be appreciated by any listener or reader, who will pick up most of the content-based meanings within the songs. But to understand them as MacNeacail does and as he knew his fellow villagers would (sharing a common local culture as they do) we have had to understand the circumstances of their composition. Once this is done, we can begin to see the pervasive role they play in the persona of the Sgiobair, the song-maker.

> Nothing else he did in his life mattered to him as much as his poetry. To think of [him] as anything but a poet, then, is to miss the whole point of his character, for that is not only the way his contemporaries saw him, it is the way he saw himself. (Ives 1964:187)

For seventy-nine years (so far), MacNeacail has chosen to express and therefore to define his public self through song. His subject matter has ranged over the total human situation: songs of love, humour and grief; songs about personal and cultural history; songs of homeland and war (and even tobacco, for that matter), all expressed in different registers of language skilfully adapted to the matter at hand. Such was his urge to compose that he has exposed his innermost thoughts and emotions to the scrutiny of others in a way that many would shy away from. Of course he is partly insulated from the repercussions of these revelations by the persona of the poet discussed earlier.[188] The first-hand testimony in this book is perhaps an extension of his willingness to undergo this type of exposure. Through song, his private self has become public.[189]

How then does this definition of public self come about? To a large extent it grows from the need for response discussed in Chapter Five. For the person who is born a song-maker, song is the vehicle for personal information, the natural form of response to his own emotions and others' requests. For Mac-Neacail, a song reflects truths about its subject, whether it be the elegiac *An Eaglais Shaor an Steòrnabhagh* (26) or a vituperative squib about a local character. The poet is therefore immune to any accusations of invention or maliciousness. He says, in turn, that if you want to express something properly, whether it be love, or an appreciation of beauty, "you would want to have it in a song"; it encapsulates the essence of its subject. For the Sgiobair, song is an everyday register of speech, but one which communicates on a level that no other does. This idea is sustained throughout MacNeacail's long life, most obviously in daily conversation in which he quotes from songs and epigrams of his favourite bards. To him, information in song is pure – almost Biblical in veracity. Song is how he orders and formalises his vision of himself and of the outside world. For MacNeacail, song is wisdom encapsulated in an easily remembered and delivered 'meta-language'. His own songs certainly function in this way and in daily conversation he quotes those of the old bards to much the same effect.

BARD, POET, SONG-MAKER

In Iain's younger days, composing was instinctive; he could not help it. Nowadays, when the making of songs does not come as easily to him as it once did, he still quotes his own and others' songs in the uninterrupted flow of his speech. He is a poet, a song-maker, a bard. The words of Dunnchadh Bàn, delivered by Sgiobair with a glint in his eye, hold as true for him as they did for the great eighteenth-century poet:

31. Iain and me in Cuidreach, March 14, 1992. (*Margaret Bennett*)

IM: Uel, bha ad a' ràdh,...nach dùineadh tu beul bàird gun a theanga a thoirt às! *You had to take out his tongue before he would close his mouth!* Hmhmhm. [*laughs*] 'S bha ad ag ràdh nach do dhùin am bàs fhéin e!

IM: *Well, they were saying that you couldn't close a bard's mouth without taking out his tongue! You had to take out his tongue before he would close his mouth! Hmhmhm.* [laughs] *And they were saying that death itself didn't close it!*

AFTERWORD

It is with sadness that I reach the end of this project. At the start, I thought I could not even learn the language well enough to converse with Iain, but as he remarked early on, "*If I were at you with a new word every day, you would soon learn it." This entire book has been rather like that, a word or aspect of it handled and dealt with bit by bit until at last it was all there (after the deadline, of course).

I cannot begin to express what Iain has given me; as I said in the introduction, this project represents an opportunity of which most folklorists only dream – I pay tribute to his immense wealth of tradition, generosity, talent and humanity.

The most memorable trip to Skye in the whole of my acquaintance with Iain so far was on the 16th of May, 1992 when Margaret and I took him up to Siadar to see the place where he was born over nine decades ago. On the way, he kept up a running commentary about who lived where and what they were like, or were well known for: Murchadh Dhòmhnaill Mhàrtainn, Dunnchadh Beag, An Sagart, Aonghas Fleidsear. The entire glen was peopled with personalities. As we approached Baile nan Cnoc [the Township of the Hillocks] he began to name each little peak and valley, "gach glac is bruachag", as he says in *Nach bòidheach Uige* (21). Then he told us to pull over to the edge of the road and almost before either of us knew it he was out of the car and walking down the slope, stick in hand. As I recorded in my fieldwork notebook that night,

> We all climbed out and the old boy took off down the path off the road. It must have been about 200 yards over rough ground, tractor ruts, boggy places, through a gate and down a steep bit too [1:3]. He didn't hesitate a second, but took off like a *gille* [laddie], straight to the *tobht* [foundation]. There wasn't much left but the left-hand [North] end, in which the cows [had been] kept. About 3/4 of the *tobht* had been bull-dozed away to make a way through for tractors. He told about moving across the river to No. 15 Glenconon. They simply carried everything across (including a small dresser) as the Conon is quite [shallow] there. All the children but Màiri were born there in that house [in Siadar]. The [ruins of the] neighbour's houses were only fifty feet away and their walls are standing quite high and complete still. There was a big rowan tree growing at the end wall of the house.... Then we walked back up the slope.... It had been *years* since he was last there and there wasn't much to see. I wonder how he felt, I wonder where he played. What's it like going back to the house you were born in 89 years ago and left 82 years ago!

He seemed both excited and sad to see it all. I could clearly imagine him as a *gille beag* [little lad] running to and fro, and walking down to Uig past the Sagart's.

My acquaintance with the Sgiobair has been awe-inspiring in some ways, for through him I have a conduit back through nearly two hundred years of folk-memory, to his grandfather Alasdair Chaluim. It is, as Laurie Lee put it,

32. *Iain and me on the way to the làrach [ruin] of the house in Siadar. The remains of the front wall can just be seen at the base of the tree. Across the glen are the houses of Glenconon, where the family moved in 1910; Iain was seven. May 16, 1992.*
(*Margaret Bennett*)

like a deep-running cave still linked to its antic past, a cave whose shadows were cluttered by spirits and by laws still vaguely ancestral. This cave...looked backwards through chambers that led to our ghostly beginnings; and had not, as yet, been tidied up, or scrubbed clean by electric light, or suburbanised by a Victorian church, or papered by cinema screens.

It was something we just had time to inherit, to inherit and dimly know – the blood and beliefs of generations who had been in this valley since the Stone Age. That continuous contact has at last been broken, the deeper caves sealed off for ever. But arriving, as I did, at the end of that age, I caught whiffs of something old as the glaciers. There were ghosts in the stones, in the trees, and the walls, and each field and hill had several. The elder people knew about these things and would refer to them in personal terms, and there were certain landmarks about the valley – tree-clumps, corners in woods – that bore separate, antique, half-muttered names that were certainly older than Christian,...names which are not used now any more. (Lee 1984:95–7)

The parallel with the Sgiobair's naming of the hills of Baile nan Cnoc is exact.

And so, to Iain Uilleam Alasdair Chaluim 'ic Fhionnlaigh às a' Chuidirich, mìle beannachd, is guma fada buan thu còmhnaidh ann.

ACKNOWLEDGEMENTS

Naturally, with a project of this scale it is impossible to thank everyone adequately, but here goes.

First to my mother and father for their patience, faith and support of every kind through this long haul. And also to my family and friends for not being too sceptical along the way.

To Professors Susan Semel, Peter Saccio and Laurence Davies for believing that I was a 'risk worth taking'. And to Marion Singleton who taught me to keep on asking why.

Having arrived in Edinburgh, I was cast upon the imaginations of my supervisors, Professor William Gillies and Dr. Margaret Bennett. To them, all my thanks for their encouragement (subtle and otherwise), faith even in the darkest hour and sense of humour (including the promised orange wig, produced at last at my viva). They worked very well as a team; I do not think they ever duplicated each other's comments. And a special acknowledgement goes to Margaret for entrusting me with the project of a lifetime. I know it took a great leap of faith and she took it. I hope it was justified.

Thanks to all my kind informants for their valuable time and their hospitality to an interviewer with cold feet. First and foremost of course, to Iain MacNeacail for his enthusiasm and unstinting generosity in sharing his world with me. I hope this work is a fitting tribute to him. And to Màiri and the family for their patience. Thanks are also due to these other invaluable informants: Murdo and Teenie Stewart, Peter Stewart, Peigi Stewart, Isobel and Mary Nicolson, Isabel, Angus and Mórag Ross, Murdo and Iain MacLean, Margaret Bennett, Catrìona Fleidsear and Aonghas MacNeacail. Thanks also to Flo MacKenzie for allowing me access to her late husband's tapes and thanks to Iain's nephews, William and Peter Grant, for giving me the records made by the Sgiobair in Belgium during the War; I am honoured and delighted. Incidentally, the company in Brussels that made them also made Django Reinhardt's first recordings.

For patient and enthusiastic assistance with Gaelic (and sometimes English!) transcriptions over the years, and for their sharp eyes and ears, thanks go to Peigi Bennett, Professor Donald Meek, Donald Archie MacDonald, Peter Stewart, Mórag MacLeod and, more recently, Dr. Meg Bateman, Eachann MacCoinnich and Dr. Richard Cox.

I am very grateful to Dr. John MacInnes for his interest and enthusiasm for the subject, for his painstaking, on-going scrutiny of the songs and for knowing everything.

My thanks also to Marie Salton for her very helpful suggestions and critical eye. To Fred Kent and Neil MacQueen for technical support and advice, to Joan MacKenzie for being a voice of reason and knowing where everything is, to Ian MacKenzie for the great last minute photographic work, to Fran Beckett for always being helpful (and cheerful) and to Jim Wilkie for lightening the mood.

A thank you also goes to Sandy Ives for his perceptive comments on the dissertation which preceded this book; I have even managed to act upon some of them. Also to both Sandy and Bobbie Ives for inspiration, encouragement, warmth and two good senses of humour – a paragraph by themselves.

I gratefully acknowledge the American Friends of the University of Edinburgh for their generous scholarship award when I was writing the Ph.D. and the Carnegie Trust for the Universities of Scotland and the University of Aberdeen Faculty Research Committee for jointly funding the CD which accompanies this book.

Finally, before this begins to sound like an Academy Award acceptance speech, this book is dedicated to Iain MacNeacail and to Maighrearad nighean Pheigi Iain Phàdraig, without whom it could never have happened.

Thomas A. McKean
March 1997

And to H.F.M. with love.

Appendix One

METHODOLOGY

SOURCES

Most of the interviews were conducted with Iain MacNeacail at his home in Cuidreach, Skye and were recorded on a Uher open-reel machine at 7.5 i.p.s.

The tapes are lodged in the School of Scottish Studies' S(ound) A(rchive) at the University of Edinburgh and are cited in the appendices and notes as (SAyear.tape#.item#). The following are the tapes I have used extensively.

Tape Number(s)	Informant	Fieldworker(s)
SA1986.85–86	Iain MacNeacail	John MacInnes and Margaret Bennett.
SA1988.63–66	Iain MacNeacail	T. A. McKean and Margaret Bennett.
SA1989.25–28	Iain MacNeacail	T. A. McKean.
SA1990.104	Iain MacNeacail	T. A. McKean and Margaret Bennett.
SA1990.105–108	Iain MacNeacail	T. A. McKean.
SA1992.61–62	Iain MacNeacail	T. A. McKean and Margaret Bennett.
SA1992.63–65	Iain MacNeacail	T. A. McKean and Margaret Bennett. (These tapes were recorded on a Nagra full-track machine and consequently have only one side; citations therefore do not list side 'a' or 'b'.)
SA1993.2–3	Aonghas MacNeacail	T. A. McKean.
SA1993.4	Isabel Ross	T. A. McKean.
SA1993.15–16	Iain MacNeacail	T. A. McKean.
SA1995.50–51	Murchadh MacCoinnich	T. A. McKean and Margaret Bennett.
SA1995.52	Iseabail NicNeacail	T. A. McKean.

The following tapes are from my own collection, made on a Sony D6 after I left the School; they are not yet lodged with an archive and so are prefixed by TM. They are cited in the same way as the tapes above.

TM1994.1–3	Iain MacNeacail	T. A. McKean.
TM1994.4–6	Iain MacNeacail	T. A. McKean.
TM1994.7	Iain MacNeacail	T. A. McKean.
TM1994.8	Iain MacNeacail & others	Uisdean MacCoinnich (courtesy of Mrs. Hugh MacKenzie).
TM1995.1–3	Iain MacNeacail	T. A. McKean.

The following non-SA tapes were also used:

T1185: A recording made by David Clement in 1981 for the Place-name Archive at the School of

Scottish Studies. It consists of Iain MacNeacail singing various songs of his own and others' composition.

An Sgiobair is Mórag: A twenty-minute video interview of MacNeacail in Gaelic, by Mórag MacLeod of the School of Scottish Studies at Comhdhail nan Seanchaidh, Tigh Òsda Eilean Iarmain [the *Gathering of the Tradition-bearers*, Eilean Iarmain [Isle Ornsay] Hotel], ca. 1981.

An Sgiobair at Uig School: A cassette of the Sgiobair's visit to the school to talk to the children in English. Made in the mid-eighties by Mórag Henriksen, the Head Teacher at the school.

Other sources cited are:

Uig School Register, cited as (USRyear:page) or (USRday.month.year).

Fieldwork notebook (sometimes kept on computer), cited as (FWmonth.day.year:item#).

Books and papers listed in the bibliography, cited according to the Harvard convention (Author year:page).

TAPE TRANSCRIPTIONS AND CITATIONS

Virtually all transcriptions are verbatim from my tapes, with assistance from the individuals named in the acknowledgements. Extracts preceded by an asterisk (*), while not verbatim, are as close as I could note to the informant's original diction and syntax. The initials of the speaker are along the left margin.

In general I have used standard Gaelic orthography except when MacNeacail's dialect rendition is particularly distinctive. I have not used apostrophes before verbal nouns which appear without their particles, but I have used them to indicate elisions, particularly in the definite article. In addition, I have chosen to retain the acute accent, and have continued to spell the central lax vowel with a 'u', e.g. Pàdruig, when the pronunciation calls for it.

I have shown general features of MacNeacail's dialect in these transcriptions, though not, to any great extent, his idiolect. The following are the prominent forms represented:

- 'gad' and 'ged' depending on register and his pronunciation.
- 'gu' for adverbial forms, otherwise, 'go'
- 'ad' and 'iad' as he pronounces it.
- 'a" for 'an' for the definite article before l, n and r, unless it is markedly pronounced, as in a formal register.
- Negative irregular verbs starting with radical initial /t/ have been spelled with a 'd', reflecting the majority of the central dialects of Gaelic, including that of Skye.

On a few occasions I have elided two renditions of a particular story; I have indicated this in the Tape Citations where appropriate.

In some cases, where a speaker has tailed off or been interrupted, I have not put a full stop at the end of the phrase. I have also tried to indicate some of MacNeacail's emphases in speech through spelling, e.g. "No-o-o" or "Oh-h", when he draws out those words. Proper names and place names are spelled in English or in Gaelic, as appropriate to the pronunciation. The word 'Gaelic' is spelled 'Gàidhlig' when Iain uses a conspicuously long 'à' sound, otherwise the standard English spelling is used.

Citations of all types refer to all the quotes between them and the previous citation. In other words, only the last of a series of quotes from the same source concludes with a reference.

TRANSLATIONS

The translations are my own and are in bracketed italics following each extract; they include the speakers' initials where appropriate. I have tried to be fairly literal, without being slavish; I hope they read smoothly and reflect the register, range and flavour of the Gaelic.

In a few cases, where MacNeacail translates a phrase himself, or at least gives the meaning of it, I have not put in my own translation. English loan-words within Gaelic extracts are highlighted by putting them in italics.

EDITORIAL CONVENTIONS

The use of ellipses includes removal of some hesitation words and repetitive speech, such as 'you know', though some of these phrases have been left in to show the flavour of MacNeacail's speech. They are added either in the middle of a sentence, or at the end after its regular punctuation, e.g. !... or ....

Square brackets [ ] are used in the following ways: (i) [xxxx] or [i.e. xxxx] Word(s) added for clarity or explanation; (ii) [xxxx] Translation from the Gaelic; (iii) [xxxx] or [xxxx] 'Stage directions' that describe Iain's movements or emotions not expressed by his words alone; (iv) [?xxxx] or [?] Uncertain transcription or that an unintelligible word has been left out.

Italics indicate an emphasis or, in square brackets, a translation from Gaelic.

Short quotes are within double quotation marks (" "). I have used single quotation marks (' ') for highlighted phrases or words. Long extracts are indented and if the extract is from a tape transcription, the initials of the speaker are along the left margin.

METHODOLOGY SPECIFIC TO THE SONGS

The process of recording Iain's songs has taken place over several years. Our interviews have ranged over a wide variety of subjects and conversation has always been interspersed with singing. After building up a body of songs – sometimes in multiple renditions – we read through them together, recording further reminiscences about each one's genesis, Iain's corrections of mis-transcriptions or places where he had slipped in singing, his own interpretations for certain phrases, and alternative versions.

With Iain's help, I have tried to create texts that are correct in his eyes. His performances are, on the whole, very consistent, but many texts are composites to a degree, having been compared with and supplemented by verses recalled or corrected lines during our later recording sessions. A number of the songs, therefore, do not fully accord with any single taped version. I leave the making of more phonetically and dialectally exhaustive transcriptions of *particular* performances to others.

Dating the songs has been a challenge and I have relied primarily upon internal evidence. Often, if he made a song on a specific occasion, I have been able to date it from the event. Nevertheless, the order is somewhat conjectural and may be modified in the coming years if more songs come to light. All song titles are in italics.

Each song has its own line numbers; choral refrains are numbered only the first time they appear. The translations are indented and numbered like the Gaelic originals to make line-by-line reference easier. For further detail on individual versions, see Appendix Two.

Appendix Two

NOTES ON THE SONGS

These notes explain significant variations between versions of the songs and sometimes elaborate on translations or Iain's dialect. They are laid out as follows:

- Song number and title.
- Recorded and published versions of the songs. These are abbreviated thus: (i) Tape reference of the recording used in the initial transcription; (ii) Tape reference for the correction session with Mac-Neacail; (iii) References for different renditions of the song and other general remarks.
- Line-by-line notes, using the numbers above to refer to particular renditions, e.g.: (iii) gives "xxxx". Where MacNeacail provides a translation or an alternate version of a word, phrase or line, the source is likewise listed, to avoid repetition of long reference numbers. Literary usages or formal language are indicated by the abbreviation, "lit."

The 'RL' recordings referred to here were made in the early days of the School of Scottish Studies by fieldworkers and technicians who transported direct-to-disk machines with them all over Scotland. The four recordings of Iain were made in 1950 by Derick Thomson, on a collecting tour financed to measure the feasibility of establishing the School. The RL number indicates the original disk accession number and the copy number that of the back-up recording made shortly after the original. 'T' numbers refer to a tape in the School of Scottish Studies place-name archive. This one was made by David Clement in 1981.

See the Introduction for a list of standard abbreviations used.

1. Ho-ró tha mi fo smalan dheth

(i) SA1988.64.A7. (ii) SA1990.106.B1 and B3. (iii) a) SA1992.63.4, b) SA1992.65.3, c) TM1994.6.A6 and d) FW2.7.96. There are several pauses for thought on that first recording, but Iain recalled most of it. Six years later he recalled verse three when talking about beginning to compose.
Line 1: "Ho-ró" is simply a singable series of meaningless syllables, usually called 'vocables'. They are often found in Gaelic song, especially in the choral refrains of those used for waulking the tweed (see Campbell and Collinson 1969:227–238, 1981:318–323 and MacInnes 1971).
Line 3: "Chàich" on (ii).
Line 4: This is from (ii); it replaces the "'S chaidh mi ta..." of (i) which MacNeacail was unable to complete in the original rendition. On (iii:a) he supplies "sense" as a translation for "ciall".
Line 6: The Christian name is from (iii:a).
Lines 10–13: This verse is from (iii:c & d).

Line 12: This translation is based on (iii:d), where Iain glosses "faobhar" as "edge, the blade of a scythe", it is really the sharpness itself.

Line 14: The surname name is from (iii:a & b).

Line 16: (ii) has "gun d'dh'innis..." instead, meaning "she told...".

Lines 20–21: MacNeacail gave me an alternative for these two last lines: "'S ann thuirt i rium, 'chan fhaigh thu unns';/ cha [or nach] b'àist dhut bhith déiligeadh'," ["*She said to me, 'you won't get an ounce; you didn't used to be dealing',*"] i.e., as he puts it himself, "seeing I wasn't a regular customer, I won't get an ounce". He also does not make a great distinction between "chan àist mi" ["*I am not*"] and "cha b'àist mi" ["*I was not*"] both of which he offers in this line. The meanings of all these alternatives are roughly the same.

Line 22: Iain runs this line straight into a phrase: "that's Màiri's seanair [*grandfather*]" to explain that the man referred to here is his wife's grandfather. Because of his rapid speech it was difficult for me, in the early days of this project, even to recognise the transition between languages. Mrs. Costello draws attention to the frequent habit Irish traditional singers have of stopping to explain a textual or contextual detail such as this (1990:iv).

Line 23: "féin" (ii).

Line 24: "mur fhaigh..." (ii).

Line 25: This line is from (ii), on (i) he speaks the line, "gu bràth cha bhi mo chiall agam", "I will never have my sense", i.e. be sensible. The translations are essentially the same.

Line 28: The Gaelic for this line was unclear in (i); MacNeacail sorted it out on (iii:a & b).

2. Ho ho-ró air gach cailleach (Oran a' cheàird)

(i) a) NicGumaraid 1980b:B6 and b) 1980a:36–37. (ii) SA1990.107.B4. (iii) a) SA1992.64.3, b) TM1994.2.A8.

Line 1: (i:a and b) both have "Hiù ri bhi...".

Line 2: "'s air gach..." (i:a and b).

Line 5: MacNeacail sings this refrain after nearly every verse in several renditions of the song, but, for regularity, I have put it after all of them.

Line 9: (i:a) has "na làir bhàn".

Line 11: i.e. "he began to speak immediately".

Line 13: "domh", lit. Sometimes, MacNeacail leaves out "dhomh": "'S math as aithne thu, a shàir", making the meaning closer to "You are well known, my good man".

Line 17: Literally, "or Alasdair will be in your antlers".

Line 19: "Ploc", translated here as "sod", refers to any clod of earth.

Line 20: A "caoran" is really a small, dry fragment of a peat, usually used for starting fires.

Line 21: "Because it...wasn't cheap for him to get, you know." And she was not going to give it away for nothing.

Line 24: I put a grave accent on "e" as MacNeacail lengthens it to fit the rhythm.

Line 37: "Well,...I could have the Gaelic in there. I could say 'Chan fhàilnig e 'n aon nì' instead of 'guaranteed', but ach you can leave the 'guarantee' there,...just the same, but it's an English word instead of Gaelic.... It's the same as you would give a horse a guarantee."

Line 39: The Gaelic is from (ii). i:a and b have "chuir mi i far ghleus on sguaib", meaning that he put her out of the rhythm of sweeping, as in out of tune, 'a' gleusadh' being a verb often used for 'tuning' instruments.

Line 43: The sack referred to here is the one he took with him when he set out with the blacksmith to beg for goods. See the conversation before the song.

Line 45: "[To] make plenty of blankets. Aye 'gun taing'." "Gun taing" is literally "in spite of", here it has a meaning closer to "anyway".

Lines 46–49: (iii:b).

3. An t-each iarainn

(i) NicGumaraid 1980a:38 (where it is incorrectly printed in four-line verses). (ii) SA1990.107.A4–B1. (iii) SA1992.65.4. This is the only complete audio recording of this song.

Line 16: i.e. "protecting crops for their food". "[Putting protection] about what they were eating, you know" (ii).

Line 10: e.g. long tail hair.

Line 22: This line is a reference to the commonly held belief that horses and other animals had a special ability to perceive otherworldly beings and spirits. They are also said to become uneasy when passing a place where a tragedy has occurred, no matter how long ago. This explanation is often cited when a horse shies, seemingly at nothing.

Line 26: More usually "stràc", but Iain's dialect calls for this.

Line 28: In other words, it will not stop and try to graze when he is riding, a common enough occurrence with horses.

Line 29: "braonadh" in (i).

Line 32: i.e. "anything that makes trouble for it".

4. Tarbh Bhràigh Uige

(i) TM1994.5.A3–4. (ii) a) TM1994.5.A3 and b) FW2.7.96. There are no other recordings of the song. This song has been very difficult to recover and the version presented here is a reconstruction. A verse or two may still be missing; from line 29 onwards, the order is conjectural, based on several different interviews with Iain as he tried to recall the end of the song.

There is a similar tradition of songs about berserk animals to be found in Prince Edward Island, for example Lawrence Doyle's Bear at Grand River (Ives 1971:47–59), although the bear is far more anthropomorphised than MacNeacail's bull (or the deer and bull in songs 9 and 10).

Line 8: This line could be, "Thug e 'n gaiseadh as a' bhuntàta", meaning "He knocked the blight out of the potatoes".

Line 10: Alternatively, this could read, "shàilibh", the dative form of "heels", meaning they were on his heels.

Line 12: (ii:b).

Line 15: (ii:b); (i) offers "...san arbhar" here, meaning "...in the grain crop".

Line 16: (ii:b); (i) begins with "mìle"

Line 17: (ii:a) has "'S bu thogarrach..."; the meaning is essentially the same. (ii:b) has "gu h-eagalach...", "fearfully...".

Line 22: This line is probably not supposed to duplicate line 10.

Lines 23–4: (i) was missing a couplet, this was supplied from (ii:b). (ii:a) has "an dùil gum prannadh...", "hoping to pound...".

Lines 29–32: This quatrain is from (ii:b).

Lines 35–6: (i) offers the alternative of "thug gach fear dhiubh ris a' mhonadh/ mus toireadh e an t-anam beò dhiubh", "every one of them took to the hills/ lest he deprive them of their living souls".

Line 37: (i) has "'S gun do theich Sagart...".

Lines 39–40: this couplet is from (ii:b).

Line 39: (ii:b) offers the alternate line, "rinn e suas gu h-allamh/ air na sparran a's a' chlòsaid", "he made off nimbly/ into the rafters of the back room".

Lines 43–4: this couplet is from (ii:b).

5. Ho-ró chan eil an smal orm

(i) a) NicGumaraid 1980b:A9 and b) 1980a:40–41. (ii) SA1990.107.B7 and SA1990.108.A1. (iii) SA1992.63.4.

Lines 1–2: MacNeacail sings "Ho-ró tha mi fo smalan dheth/ on thug an òigh...", "Ho-ró I am downcast because of it/ since the young maiden [cheated]..." on (iii) and (i:a), but corrected the lines while recording. He did not sing the modified lines on (iii), even with my prompt sheet, as my writing was not readily decipherable and he was having trouble recalling the song. I offer "an smal" as a way of filling out the metre, as MacNeacail would surely want (see Chapter Four). While either couplet will fit, Iain is clearly not happy with the song as it was. He may also, over the years, have changed his mind regarding the situation described in the song.

Line 11: Iain himself supplies "a' còmhradh rithe" here, "conversing with her", but in (i:a) "a' stòraidh rithe" (literally, storying her or chatting with her) is what he actually sings.

Line 13: Or, "that we would reach an understanding".

Line 21: "She was feared of the bogeymans, you know, at night, coming home on her own." "Spectre", "apparition" or more colloquially "bogeys" will do as well.

Line 30: "Starran" is a platform and sometimes a stone causeway. In this instance, it refers to several stepping stones across a stream below the house where the encounter took place.

Lines 34–7: MacNeacail supplied this verse in (ii). It is not in (i:a) or (i:b).

Line 40: (iii) has "'s gad a rinn..." ["and though..."] making this line part of the previous couplet. The full stop would then be at the end of this line.

Line 45: i.e. "no one will convince me otherwise".

6. A Mhàiri bhàn, tha thu lurach

(i) NicGumaraid 1980a:30 (ii) SA1990.108.A2. (iii) SA1993.15.B14. This song is laden with beautifully phrased traditional Gaelic imagery for a woman's beauty (especially lines 9–12). Many other Sgiobair songs, e.g. A Mhàiri, a Mhàiri (17), use such representations as well.

There is no complete recorded version of this song. Montgomery 1980 has much of it and I recorded two verses and two choruses that Iain sang to give me the tune, which he did not remember on previous occasions (iii).

Lines 1–4: This verse is sung as a refrain after every verse.

Line 11: (i) has "do chas-dheud" here, but its meaning is not clear. The present version was supplied in (ii).

Line 13: i.e. "...that I would want in a person".

Line 16: i.e. the Isle of Skye.

7. Tha mi fo thùrs air bheagan sunnd

(i) NicGumaraid 1980a:31. (ii) SA1990.107.A2. There are no other renditions.

Line 2: (i) has "gur sgeul..." which does not fit very well.

Line 4: "Refusing me." (i) has "dùrachdainn" in this line, which is a different form of the same word.

Line 13: Professor Gillies suggests "...ruiginn thu", "...I would meet you" in this line, but it did not come up in (ii). See *An cuala sibh an car* (11, l. 45), for another use of this idiom.

Line 21: "'S ged...air seòl na dhà.... Aye well, it'll do like that, [or] 'dòigh na dhà', that'll do."

Line 24: "'If you didn't like it you'll never hear it out of me,' aye. Oh [*laughs*] you have the translation here!" (ii).

8. Nuair a thòisich iad ri bùidsearachd

(i) SA1989.26.A1 with the addition of verse five and occasional words from (iii:b). (ii) SA1990.105.B5. (iii) a) SA1992.64.2, b) NicGumaraid 1980b:A5, c) *An Sgiobair is Mórag*:1 and d) TM1994.8.8.

This song is sung to the tune of Màiri Mhór nan Oran's *Nuair chaidh na ceithir ùr oirre* (my thanks to Prof. Donald Meek for pointing this out). The first 'verse' is sung to a slightly different melody from the rest and its first line is later used as a refrain.

Line 9: (iii) has "'S ann fhuair na balaich ann an òrdugh", but the meaning is essentially the same.

Line 10: "Man a chasan", "about his legs" is an alternative.

Line 15: This line reads "a leithid feadh nan crìoch", "throughout the borders" in (i), but was changed by Iain in (ii).

Line 16: "He had a nice horn turning, you know" [*laughs*] (ii). MacNeacail says that the curves of a ram's horn and the tightness of those curves are measures of his value.

Line 18: The "Bòrd" referred to is the Board of Agriculture which assesses the value of animals for sale and breeding purposes.

Line 22: An Sgiobair supplies, "gu bheil cumadh air tha sònraicht'" in (iii:a) meaning "he has an exceptional form".

Line 24: This is from (iii).(i) has "eadar an t-sròn...", which would not make as good grammatical sense with the rest of the line.

Line 28: "The juice of him would be good, you know" (ii).

Line 29: "Màileid" usually means a bag or a wallet.

Line 31: "He would cook the liver in, with the fat...on the belly, you know" (ii).

9. An cuala sibh mun fhiadh

(i) a) NicGumaraid 1980b:B9 and b) 1980a:39. (ii) SA1990.107.B5. (iii) a) SA1992.64.4, b) TM1994.8.14.

The song is printed here in eight-line verses for reasons of space. It should really be in four-line verses. (iii:b) has an extra verse I did not have time to include, see track 10 of the CD.

Line 14: MacNeacail spelled "creachail" for me himself in (ii), translating it as "hillocky". It may be a dialect form of "creachainn" meaning "bare, exposed mountainous or upland ground". The problem there is that it would be at odds with the moistness associated with "lòn". (i:b) has the place-name "Lòin [sic] Mhic Neachdail" meaning "Nicolson's meadow", but Iain corrected that (ii).

Line 29: Iain sometimes sings "'nan crùbadh", "crouching" here.

Line 33: Iain offers "Ach nuair thig iad...", "But when they come...", as an alternative to this line (ii).

Lines 45–6: These lines literally mean that the lads would go to seed (as in a garden going wild), but taken with the next two lines implies that they would "go wild" in a different way.

10. An cuala sibh mun ùpraid (Tarbh Eighre)

(i) NicGumaraid 1980a:34–35. (ii) SA1990.107.A3 (iii) SA1992.65.5.

Line 4: "Cracte" is the past participle of the English "cracked". Words like "mixed" and "cracked" are often used in this way.

Line 9: "They couldn't control him you know" (ii).

Line 11: Literally "the Shaw". This is a form of reference found with many adjectival surnames, e.g. "An Dòmhnallach, Am Frisealach", "the MacDonald, the Fraser".

Line 13: (i) has "Gach fear làidir...", "Every strong man".

Lines 16–18: "He was trying to get a rope over his head if he could. [He tried to] throw them on, throwed it on like a lasso. But that failed" (ii).

Line 23: "The dykes are made of the soil,...aye they were made of soil, you know, the walls, you were building about [the crofts]" (ii).

Lines 26–7: "They went home, you know, with great hurry, when they couldn't subdue him" (ii).

Line 28: "Well he was a doctor to the animals, you know. 'Thàinig lighiche nam brùidean.'... That's what you would call the vet...aye, just a doctor for animals, a 'lighiche', that's a doctor" (ii). (i) has "Thàinig a rithist a' bhrùid ud", "The beast came there again".

Line 30: (ii) has "'S gun do ghabh e m'a chùl", "and he went round behind him".

Line 35: Or "ill-treated".

Line 37: "He would trap him, you know" (ii).

Line 38: "Nothing but their own eyes!" [laughs] (ii).

Line 42: "Gum biodh feum" or "Gu bheil feum a bhith cheannach" (iii), "It would be" or "It is necessary to sell him".

Line 59: "Bhiodh e 'ga reic...", "He would be selling it..." (i).

Line 61: "Bhiodh e...", "It would be..." (i).

Line 63: In (ii) MacNeacail suggests "go fàgail brass", as a different possibility for the last phrase, meaning it would be good for the local boys to leave a little cash in exchange for meat.

11. An cuala sibh an car a bha sa bhaile seo mun dannsa

(i) TM1994.5.B2. (ii) FW2.7.96. (iii) TM1994.5.B3.

This song should really be in four-line verses; it is in eight-line ones for reasons of space.

Line 6: (ii); "taing dheth" in (i).

Line 8: (ii) has "bha dùil ris...", meaning the dance was hoped for and anticipated.

Line 12: (ii); (i) has "na h-òighean ac' air làimh orra", meaning "with their young ladies at their sides".

Line 18: This line should perhaps read, "...gur cinnteach nach bitheadh maill' ann", meaning there would be no delay expected.

Line 20: (ii). Or, "...pipers, in spite of them". (i) has "Gun cuireadh tusa...", "You would send", and ends with "gun taing dhaibh", "for them".

Line 24: or "foreign songs".

Lines 33–34: This is from Iain's correction. (i) has "...bhon smeòrach us a' féasan. (ii) has "Bidh pairt gu leòr an tairbh ann, bidh uiseag agus smeòrach...", meaning "There'll be plenty of portions of the bull, there'll be lark and thrush". This would duplicate too much in the following lines. 'Sitheann' initially meant 'venison' or 'game', but Iain uses it here to mean any choice meat.

Line 35: "Taobh a dhamh" is dialectal for "taobh de dhamh". See *An cuala sibh mun fhiadh* (9) and *An cuala sibh mu'n ùpraid* (10) for the stories of the deer and the bull.

Line 39: (ii); (i) has "fiamh leotha", the meaning is essentially the same.

Line 44: (iii); alternatives are "Màrtainn fhéin air a' cheann sin", "Martin himself will be at the head of it" (i), or "...air a' cheann dhiubh", which does not make much sense (ii).

12. A Bheileag 's mór a chaidh do mhealladh
(i) TM1994.1.B12. (ii) FW2.7.96 and TM1996.2.

Line 1: Beileag is the diminutive form of the Gaelic name Iseabail [Isabel].

Line 6: This line refers to Beileag's mother or grandmother.

Line 8: (ii); "gu robh thusa..." in (i).

Line 19: "anns a' starsaich chaidh do chàradh" in (ii).

Line 27: (ii) provides several alternate readings here. One merely alters the tense, where the other uses different words. The meanings are essentially the same: "B'iongnadh liom nach do mhill a' fuachd e", "It was a wonder to me that the cold didn't ruin him" and "B'iongnadh liom nach lathadh a' fuachd e", "It's a wonder to me that the cold didn't numb him".

13. Thoir an t-soraidh seo bhuam
(i) a) NicGumaraid 1980b and b) 1980a:43. (ii) SA1990.107.B3. (iii) SA1992.65.6.

Line 9: i.e. "torturing me".

Line 15: This is from (iii). (i:b) has "tha thu gun fhoill..." here.

Line 19: i.e. "from the true Gillies lineage".

Line 20: "From whom you got...".

Line 24: i.e. "courting you".

Line 27: "Not having won you...".

Line 29: i.e. "beguile you" with implications of deception. Perhaps meaning that her family would take her aside and counsel her against him, or simply take her out of his reach.

Line 32: i.e. "win you".

14. A's a' mhadainn 's mi 'g éirigh
(i) SA1988.64.A12. (ii) SA1990.106.A3. (iii) No other renditions.

Lines 1–8: "Gleann" in line 4 refers to Gleann Hìonasdail, where he worked for the twelve years immediately preceding his forestry work. This verse bears a remarkable similarity to the first four lines of William Ross' *Oran a rinn am bàrd ann an Dùn-eideann* [*A song the bard made in Edinburgh*]. MacNeacail must have unconsciously used them as a model:

> 'Sa' mhadainn 's mi 'g éirigh, 's neo-éibhinn atà mi,
> > Cha b'ionann a's m' àbhaist, air àiridh nan gleann;
> O'n thàinig mi 'n taobh-s', chuir mi cùl ris gach mànran,
> > 'S cha bheag a' chùis-ghràine leam cànran nan Gall. (Calder 1937:74)

> [*In the morning I rise, it's unhappy I am*
> > *It's not thus that* [it] *used to be in the sheiling of the glens;*
> *Since I came over here, I turned* [my] *back on every entertainment,*
> > *And I do not think much of the chattering of the Lowlanders.*]

Lines 9–20: I have laid out the second and third verses differently according to their metrical form. They are also sung to a slightly different melody.

Line 29: Though one would expect "dachaidh" to be lenited, this is more variable in songs. Such delenition can also be found in Iain's everyday speech.

Line 30: "e" may also be the impersonal, as in "it's wet to the skin I am". "Dom'" is a dialect contraction of "do mo", but one would expect "gom'" here from "go mo".

Line 36: "Anns na chleachd..." in (ii). "Na" is a dialect version of the past tense marker "an do".

Line 39: There were, of course, no air services to the Islands in those days, but that did not stop MacNeacail from wishing.

15. Bidh mi cuimhneachadh 's ag ionndrainn

(i) SA1990.104.A3. (ii) SA1990.107.B6. (iii) a) SA1992.63.3, b) SA1988.64.A12, c) NicGumaraid 1980a:42, d) 1980b:A7, e) *An Sgiobair is Mórag*:2 and f) TM1994.8.7.

This tune is a modified version of the one used for *Nuair a thòisich iad ri bùidsearachd*. Like that song, the first 'verse' is sung to a slightly different melody from the rest and its first line is later used as a refrain.

Line 16: i.e. "I would not leave her out of my song".

Lines 20–21: i.e. "...and a wish that your affairs turn out for the best". "As feàrr", lit.

16. Nochd gur luaineach mo chadal

(i) RL 1681, copy 2466. (ii) SA1990.104.B5. (iii) a) SA1989.26.A12, b) SA1990.104.B5, c) T1182.B3, d) NicGumaraid 1980a:44–45, e) NicGumaraid 1980b:A11 and f) TM1994.8.1. It is interesting to compare more recent renditions of this song with the version recorded by Derick Thomson in 1951. They are almost identical although separated by thirty and forty years. Clearly the song and the events it recalls remain a very powerful experience. Iain used to sing this song at local céilidhs where it became quite well known. Perhaps by virtue of frequent performance it has been more firmly fixed in his mind than some other songs.

Line 4: "An Fhraing" in some versions.

Line 10: i.e. "envious of others' territory".

Line 11: i.e. "lest we forget".

Line 14: "de", lit.

Line 16: MacNeacail sometimes sings this as "chaidh a spealg as a chéil". The meaning is the same.

Line 17: "'S gun do thòisichear còmhraig" in (iii:d); (iii:e) sounds like "'s gun do thòisich ar còmhraig", "and our strife began".

Line 31: Literally "a pall from guns", guns being heavy artillery in this case.

Line 33: "'S e bròn..." in (iii:a), "It's the saddest...". "de", lit.

Line 41: "Bha móran..." in (iii:a), "It was many...".

Line 50: "do", lit.

Line 56: "do", lit.

17. Lìon a-mach go bàrr na cuachan

(i) SA1989.28.A15. (ii) SA1990.106.A4. (iii) TM1994.8.9. (iii) has an additional verse, about 'Dotair Charbost', which I unfortunately did not have time to include.

Line 4: More literally, "so many times that we cannot give tongue [to them]". This sounds rather like "...gabh ruinn cainn'" on (i), but Iain did not question this transcription and also provided the translation. As noted elsewhere, he also has a tendency towards indistinct palatal sounds. The dental at the end of "cainnt" is elided.

Lines 5–8: (i) MacNeacail remembered this verse after he had sung the rest of the song saying, "O dhìochuimhnich mi...fear as an toiseach". ["Oh, I forgot one at the beginning."] On the basis of this and from internal evidence, I place it here after the first reference to Mrs. Ferguson. After adding this verse, he repeated the first verse to re-close the song. I have only repeated it once, at the end.

Line 8: In other words, "no matter how [hard] they fought". This probably refers to the valiant record of the Clan Cameron in general, rather than to any particular event.

Line 11: i.e. "sporting and dancing...".

Line 13: i.e. "whisky".

Line 14: i.e. "it was bottled in Skye".

18. Spògan circeadh

(i) TM1994.3.A3. (ii) FW2.7.96. This short song of retribution is largely made up of lines from Màiri Mhór's Oran sàrachaidh [Song of oppression] (Meek 1977:43–4).

Lines 1–2: These lines are borrowed from Oran sàrachaidh (l. 1).

Lines 3–4: (ii); these lines are also in Oran sàrachaidh (l. 5); (i) has "...gach nì rinn uile dhiubh", "...every thing you did of them".

Line 6: (ii); (i) has "tuigeadh tu".

Lines 7–8: (ii); (i) has "'s e thug na spògan far h-eòin na Cuidirich", "and who took the feet off the Cuidreach fowls".

Lines 9–10: (ii); (i) has "duan seo...tuigeadh tu", this rhyme...you would understand".

Line 15: (i); (ii) "tha mi...".

Lines 9–16: This is the last verse of Oran sàrachaidh which fits Iain's purpose very well. Màiri Mhór's version runs:

> 'S ged rinn mi 'n duan duibh chan fhuath leam idir sibh,
> Bho'n dh'fhalbh am fuachd agus cruas mo thrioblaide;
> 'S gun thìll an samhradh gun chall 'san fhreasdal domh,
> Tha mi taingeil – thug ainneart leasan domh. (Meek 1977:44:ll. 61–4)

19. A Mhàiri, a Mhàiri

(i) RL 1680, copy 2465. (ii) SA1990.108.A4. (iii) a) SA1989.26.A2, b) T1182.B4, c) NicGumaraid 1980b:B4, d) NicGumaraid 1980a:33 and e) TM1994.8.6. Peter Stewart maintains that Iain may have originally made this song for a young man in Staffin to sing to another Mary. Iain's son Stanley reports occasional knowing looks being exchanged at céilidhs when this song was sung, but that is neither here nor there.

Line 5: Sgiobair usually retains the 'n' in "fàilnig" in song; the normal Skye form in speech is "fàillig" or "fàiling".

Line 7: "Gum bi t' ìomhaigh..." (i).

Line 17: "do", lit.

Line 24: "As feàrr", lit.

Iain often sings a schwa vowel sound at the end of a verse in order to release a consonant sound that would otherwise end the line. Many other traditional singers, in numerous cultures, do the same thing. I leave this feature out to preserve the metrics of the written line, even in this case when the word's pronunciation and spelling could justify it.

Line 26: i.e. "I would win your hand". "Féin", lit.

Line 31: MacNeacail always sings "blas na mil", though the everyday speech form would be "blas na meala". According to Dr. John MacInnes, "blas na mil" often occurs in songs, even in dialects where it would never be found in speech. MacNeacail often draws "mil" out so much that I was tempted to lengthen the vowel in this transcription.

Line 32: "Na deagh sgéil" in (iii:a), "sgeul" is sometimes feminine in Skye. The meaning here is "the young mouth of the kind modest words", or "the young mouth of the good reputation".

Line 34: See the first note for line 24.

Line 40: This line is actually more elided than the spelling shows; it is more like "téile 'nad...".

20. Chaoidh cha phòs mi, tha mi 'n dùil

(i) TM1994.2.A2. (ii) FW2.7.96.

Line 4: Iain sometimes sings, "...'s chan annasach", "and no wonder".

Line 15: (i) has "a bheireadh...", the meaning is essentially the same.

Line 16: Or, more colloquially, "a truer word was never spoke."

Lines 21–2: This couplet refers to the proverbs, "Is fheàrr a bhith a dhìth a' chinn na bhith a dhìth as an fhasan" ["It is better to be without a head than to be out of fashion"] and, "Is fheàrr a bhith a dhìth a' chinn na bhith dhìth an fhasain" ["It is better to be short of a head than to be short of style"].

21. Nach bòidheach Uige

(i) RL 1680, copy 2465. (ii) SA1992.63.1. (iii) a) SA1992.63.1, b) Bennett 1950, c) NicGumaraid 1980a:29, d) NicGumaraid 1980b:A1, e) An Sgiobair at Uig School:B1 and f) TM1994.8.2.

This song is printed in eight-line verses for reasons of space. Again, I have tried to break the lines sensibly and keep the translations alongside them.

Line 2: Iain usually does not sing the expected aspiration ("gur h-e"), but in this case he clearly does, indicating a more formal register.

Line 6: i.e. "sweetly". (iii:c) has "tùchaid" here, the meaning is the same.

Line 16: "Blàs" is the more historically correct spelling of "blàths" (Dr. J. MacInnes).

Line 22: "Ta'm biolair..." in (i) and (iii:a), lit.

Line 28: i.e. "adding its own beauty to it".

Line 32: (iii:b) has "a' tighinn 'na chéile" here, meaning "coming together".

Line 38: More literally "denial cannot be seen".

Line 41: "Tha sluagh..." (iii:a).

Line 44: "da", lit.

Line 46: "atà", lit.

22. 'Illean, na biodh oirbhse smalan!

(i) SA1989.28.B4. (ii) SA1990.105.B4. (iii) No other renditions.

Lines 1–4: This quatrain is used as a chorus after each verse.

Lines 3–4: i.e. "if the problem is that we drink, it's not as if we do it often".

Line 14: i.e. "our inspiration".

Line 27: What the Sgiobair actually sings here is "...air gach balaich," a slip between "gach balach" and "na balaich". In (ii), he corrected the line to read as it stands.

Line 28: This sounds like "their" on the tape, but is probably just elided in pronunciation.

23. Tha sluagh òg air dhol gu aimbeirt (Òran a' veto)

(i) a) SA1990.104.A6 and b) NicGumaraid 1980a:32. (ii) SA1990.108.A3. (iii) a) SA1992.64.1 and b) NicGumaraid 1980b:A3.

Line 5: The chorus is sung after every verse.

Line 10: One would expect "a lùib ris".

Line 19: This line may also imply "when judgement day comes", the time for moving to our final resting place.

Lines 22–5: This verse comes from (ii) and is only in one of the recordings (iii:a). "Anns na...", lit.

Lines 26–9: "de" in l. 26, lit. This verse reflects the fact that "uisge beatha" is literally "the water of life". As such it has become central to numerous rituals in the cycle of life (see Bennett 1992:throughout). The Sgiobair does not disapprove of its use in these rituals, nor as an essential part of proper hospitality.

Line 30: "do", lit.

24. Tha mealladh mór am measg an t-sluaigh

(i) SA1986.85.A5. (ii) SA1990.106.B9 and SA1990.107.A1. (iii) a) SA1992.65.1, b) SA1989.28.A14 and c) TM1994.8.3. Thanks to Dr. John MacInnes, and Professors Donald Meek and William Gillies for their help with the Biblical language of this and the next song. (iii:c) has an extra verse before the last one. I did not have time to include it in the text.

Line 4: "Eucoir" has connotations of sinful behaviour as well.

Line 5: "Le beachdan..." in (ii). The translation is the same, but without the possessive. "Gun bhuaidh", i.e. "without the spiritual power to convert" a person.

Lines 5–8: Without regard to Gaelic syntax or the lining of the original, this would read: "With their corrupted ineffectual opinions [they are] bringing people with pitiful souls (who will succumb to them) out of Egypt to drown in the Red Sea".

Line 9: "No strength, as you would say. They're weak...to go to the pulpit, you're weak going there in some way.... They were deficient in that, you know,...that's 'gun lùths', that's without strength or energy."

Line 10: As Dr. John MacInnes points out, 'concern' is a Puritan technical term (and older: *cura pastoralis*), referring to a Christian's care for another's soul as well as his own.

Line 12: i.e. the course untouched by divine guidance.

Line 13: "'S ad féin..." (ii).

Line 20: i.e. "by misinterpreting the commandment". "Bho'n àithnte" in (iii:a), "...from the commandment". I spell "àithnte" as MacNeacail's pronunciation requires.

Lines 23–4: These false Christians preach that "they can save you if you believe what they say", (ii) whereas Presbyterian salvation comes only from above.

Lines 25–8: This quatrain draws on the Tiomnadh Nuadh, Mata [*New Testament, Matthew*] XXV:1–13 in which the foolish virgins were deceived by the brightness of the sun into thinking that they would not need their lamps. They shaded their eyes from the sun with their coats during the day, but were caught unprepared when their husband arrived in darkness. Here Iain likens those who take a short term view of salvation to the foolishness of those who had not prepared themselves for a long wait.

Line 31: This line is from (ii). (i) has "càil a thròcair".

Line 34: See line 10n.

Line 36: "tà", lit.

Lines 37–8: i.e. "They will say for themselves, since their consciences are suppressed, that they are saved."

Line 42: This line sounds like "gu bheil an cridh' gun eòlas" in (i), meaning "their heart is without knowledge", but version (ii) works rather well, provided that the downbeat in singing is placed firmly on the first syllable of "iad".

Line 45: "...ann an tràth" in (iii:a), meaning "...in time".

Line 47: i.e. "They'll be closed up out" of eternal bliss and happiness.

Line 48: i.e. "contentment".

Lines 51–2: "People without grace will not understand it, you know, though it's knocking at the door, see?"

Line 53: 'The Elect' in the biblical sense.

Line 56: "The blood will give salvation, aye. Aye, that's it."

25. O anma, feuch an dùisg thu

(i) TM1994.8.4. (ii) FW2.7.96. (iii) TM1994.6.A1. This song is printed in eight-line verses for reasons of space. I have tried to break the lines and their translations in logical places.

Line 13: Meaning "made reparation for". (iii) has "'S e saorsainn...", "It is freedom".

Line 17: "Feuch nach cuir thu..." in (iii).

Line 24: "'S nach dig Sàtan air do..." in (ii). "...'s na dig nàmhaid...", "...nor enemy..." (iii).

Line 39: "It" refers to the unfailingness of His mercies. This could also be translated as "happy from Him is the number...", i.e. "he makes them happy".

Lines 41–8: This verse is from (iii). Line 42 is from (ii); (i) has "'s e Rìgh nan Glòir dol ann", the meaning is essentially the same. Line 46: (i) has "an còmhnaidh", which is slightly weaker.

Line 50: 'Sàraichean' is an elided form of 'sàraichidhean'.

Line 52: (ii) has "a bheir dhut gràs gu leòr", "that will give sufficient grace to you".

26. An Eaglais Shaor an Steòrnabhagh

(i) NicGumaraid 1980a:46–47. (ii) SA1990.106.A4 & 6. (iii) a) SA1988.64.B2 and b) NicGumaraid 1980b:B2.

Line 10: "That's a one that would direct you on the way,...'iùil' is a way" (ii).

Line 12: i.e. "...out of hand".

Line 17–20: i.e. Macrae was industrious.

Line 24: "Iarmaid" is a biblical word meaning a "little remnant". "An Glòir" is "in Heaven".

Line 26: i.e. "after your passing".

Line 30: "Gabh ris", "acknowledge": again a biblical usage with its basis in the words of Jesus.

Line 41: Literally "the true [Christian]", meaning 'the new man', i.e. a converted person. MacNeacail translates it as "a true Christian" (ii).

Line 43: Sometimes the Sgiobair uses an older syntax here: "gum b'Israileach dà-rìreabh thu...".

Line 46: "The best of the interpretation".

27. The news we've heard from Waternish (A song for Johannes Hellinga)

(i) SA1986.85.A2. (ii) SA1990.105.B2. (iii) a) SA1992.64.5 and b) Shapiro 1985. More background information is on SA1989.26.A8–9.

Line 3: Sometimes, Iain sings "that the noble Dutchman, Hellinga" thus filling out the metre. Otherwise, he truncates the tune slightly to accommodate the shorter line.

Line 5: (iii:a) has "Johnny".

Line 9: "Amsterdam" in (iii:b), but in (ii) Iain changed it to "Holland" which agrees with (iii:a). It would have to be elongated like the Gaelic "Olaind" in the next song to fit the rhythm.

Line 15: (iii:a) runs "gave them land to their desire". The line is a reference to Hellinga's sale of large portions of land for five pounds per acre; see the interview with the song.

Line 23: (iii:a) "to market", (ii) "and when they go to fair...".

Line 25: (iii:b) reads "Faisach" here, which doesn't agree with pronunciation or spelling rules.

Line 30: Pronounced "Gàidhlig", naturally, for the assonance with "Geàrraidh".

Line 31: According to (ii), this can either be "one foot high" or "three feet high" as in (iii:a) and (i) respectively.

Line 32: "...dry in Hàllain" in (iii:a).

Line 36: MacNeacail also supplied me with an off-the-cuff alternative line entirely in English: "'And though the drams would be three feet high,'...three or one! 'Ceud mìle fàilt' we'll send him,' 'a thousand welcomes send him,' you know". (iii:a) reads "...we send him".

28. 'S e seo a' sgeul tha taitneach leinn (Oran do Johnny Hellinga)

(i) SA1989.26.B1. (ii) SA1990.105.B3. (iii) SA1992.65.2.

Line 7: Godfrey, the present Lord Macdonald, at that time the owner of the Waternish Estates.

Line 9: Iain pronounces the name more like "John-es" rather than with the full three syllables of "Johannes".

Line 10: Iain sings "mhùirneach", "precious" or "beloved", but corrected it to "chliùteach" (ii).

Line 12: "That was to his backbone, you know, he was a kind man to his backbone."

Line 14: "Sùghmhor" literally means "juicy", or in this context "rich and fertile".

Lines 19–20: Or alternatively "Gun òr a bhith sa chùmhnant", "There's no conditions for gold being in the contract...he's giving them the land to their desire without gold being in the...contract". See the interview before *The news we've heard from Waternish* (27).

Line 23: "Leinn" is supplied in (ii) in place of "ann", meaning "there", which also works well.

29. 'S thoir mo bheannachd do dh'Eilean Iarmain

(i) SA1989.26.A4. (ii) SA1990.106.A5b. (iii) a) SA1989.26.A4 and b) T1185. The School of Scottish Studies' archive has a another song about a céilidh at the hotel in Eilean Iarmain, *Oran Taigh Osda Eilean Iarmain*, by Donald Nicolson, Camuscross, Sleat, Skye (SA1973.115.A3).

Line 1: Noble's estate offices and hotel, Tigh Òsda Eilean Iarmain, are located at Eilean Iarmain on the Sleat peninsula in the south of Skye.

Line 4: The Gaelic business college Sabhal Mòr Ostaig in Sleat, Isle of Skye.

Line 8: Possibly from "stòr", "to hoard" making the phrase mean "without hoarding", i.e. "generous". It may also be affected by "sòradh", "sparing" or "hesitating"; this word is now usually confined to verse.

Line 9: (ii) has "féin" here, lit. (iii) has "B'e siod...".

Line 10: (ii) has "nas feàrr" here.

Line 14: "Oilein" seems to be a formation with the same element as "oilthigh" and "oileanach", possibly from "àl", which ultimately has the same root. The word here may actually be "fhòghlam".

Lines 17–20: Added from (iii:b).

Line 24: Obscure.

Lines 25–8: Added from (ii).

Line 28: A reference to Noble's high regard for the islanders and his tenants. MacNeacail finds Noble a rare exception to the usual type of landlord. See *A time will come, a time will go* (30) for his perceptions of the old-style landlord.

30. A time will come, a time will go

(i) SA1988.64.A4. (ii) SA1990.105.B1. (iii) a) SA1989.25.B10, b) SA1986.85.A1, c) SA1992.65.5 and d) *An Sgiobair at Uig School*:B2.

Lines 21–4: This verse is from (iii:d). It is not in any other versions.

Lines 25–8: (iii:b) repeats this verse with a different first couplet: "The Cheviot sheep, the stag, the hind/ must quickly be disposed of/ and the land...".

31. Should I have time available (A song to Mr. Ball)

(i) SA1990.104.A1. (ii) SA1990.104.A1. (iii) No other renditions. More background may be found on SA1990.106.B4.

Lines 9–16: Iain stayed in Swansea for a number of months during the Second World War before being sent overseas; see Chapter Two for more details.

Line 18: (ii) "that ever came to...".

Line 23: "Commemorated" loses its last syllable to fit the metre.

Appendix Three

GILLEASBAIG AOTROM

IM: Gilleasbaig Aotrom, oh aye aye, he was a half-wit too,...but he knew how to live. Och he was quite familiar with people, my father and all these people at that time. [Iain must mean his grandfather as Gilleasbaig is supposed to have been on the go in the 1840s.]

TM: Where was he from?

IM: He was from Glen Hìniosdail up there, mhm and there wasn't a man about, that would know a better beast than him. They would take him down [and ask],..."What cow has the best calf here, the best?"

"Well that sir,...is the best cow," he says, [of a cow that the] milkmaid curses in his backside (she wasn't good to him you know). [*laughs*] ...The cow, wasn't good you know, but he was [born] of the best cow in the field. He would know that, you know. He had an eye for things like that, but he was witty,...and knew how to live on people.... Gilleasbaig Aotrom, you know, 'simple', 'aotrom', he was simple.... Gilleasbaig that would be Archibald, Simple Archibald,...you would call him in English. (SA1989.25.A9–10)

[He was of the] MacPhersons of Glen Hìniosdail. He was their grand-uncle, Dòmhnull Dhughail a bh'ann an Gleann Hìniosdail [*Donald (son of) Dougal who was in Glen Hinnisdale*]. Oh well your grandfather [and] your mother would know him [i.e. his grand-nephew] too, she would know the old man anyhow. Well he was their grandfather. Och...but...although he was what he was, you know [i.e. a "fool"], he was all there. (SA88.63.B24)

Sgeul Ghilleasbaig Aotruim	The Story of Simple Gillespie
Bha Gilleasbuig Aotrom, 's e duine a bh'ann a bhiodh a' falbh thall 's a-bhos as gach àite; sin 'n dòigh a bh'aige air a bhith beò. 'S ann a Ghleann Hìniosdail shuas a bhoineadh e. Ach ged a bha e leigeil air gu robh e rud nach robh e, bha e glic gu leòr air a shon fhéin. Ach dh'fhalbh e suas latha gu ruige Port Righeadh agus chunnaic e bàta iasgaich ann a' shin agus dh'iarr e trosg orra. Cha dugadh na trosg dha, ach dh'fhalbh e staigh a' bhàta 's thug e leis fear e fhéin. 'S ghabh e timcheall am baile am Port Righeadh, a' reic an trosg,	Light[*headed, i.e. simple*] Gillespie, he was a man who used to be going everywhere, hither and yon; that was how he made a living. It's up in Glen Hinnisdale he belonged. But though he let on that he was something that he wasn't [i.e. a fool], he was smart enough on his own behalf. But he went up to Portree one day and he saw a fishing boat there and he sought a cod from them. He didn't get anything at all, but he went inside the boat and he took one himself. And he took off around the township of Portree selling the cod,
"Dé tha thu ag iarraidh air?"	"What do you want for it?"
"Tasdan agus glainne uisge bheatha." O gheibheadh e sin!	"A shilling and a glass of whisky." Oh he would get that!
"O théid mi fhìn 'ga nighe gu ruige lón dhuibh." Dh'fhalbhadh Gilleasbaig gu ruige lóin 's cha tilleadh e fhéin na throsg;	"Oh I will go to the stream myself to wash it for you."

205

bha e cumail an trosg aige! Na dhéidh sin, rinn e air móran
thaighean agus nuair a thàinig e air ais, thug e leis an trosg agus
thilg e sa bhàta e.

"Tapadh leibhse, dhaoine còire," ars esan, "ma phàigheas e
cho math dhuibhse,...'s a phàigh e dhomhsa,...bidh sibh glé
thoilichte leis."
Cha dug e 'n trosg do dhuine bh'ann ach bha e ga ghlanadh
a's a' lón dhaibh, dhan a h-uile duine bh'ann, 's cha robh e
tilleadh leis. Seo an dòigh a bh'aige.
Dh'fhalbh e sin turas suas 's bhiodh e dol suas a dh'amharc air
Sutar, 's e ministear...shuas ann a Sléite bh'ann.... Ràinig e aig
meadhin-oidhche 's chuir e am ministear air a chois.
"O," ars esan, "dé chuir...aig an àm seo dh'oidhche thu?"

"O," ars esan, "Bha mi airson gu faighinn àite as a
fuirichinn."
"O uel, gheibh thu sin," thubhairt...Sutar ris. Seo mar a bha:
ghabh e staigh, 's fhuair e greim bìdhe co-dhiubh 's,
"O ma tha," arsa Sutar ris, am ministear, "chan eil àit' agamsa
dhuit ach air a' lobht shuas ann a' shin 's [?fuirichidh] tu ann.
Tha leabaidh ann a' shin agad, leabaidh mhath."
"O glé mhath ma-tha."
"Faigh an t-fhàradh 's cuiridh sinn an t-fhàradh ris a' rud 's
gheibh thu suas air."
"A uel," arsa Gilleasbaig, "tha mi smaoineachadh, o'n a tha
thu ràdh gu bheil a' leabhaidh cho math sin, bu chòrr dhuit a
dhol suas romhamsa an toiseach agus a shealltainn dhomh dé
cho math 's a tha i." Och dh'fhalbh am ministear suas 's nuair a
chaidh e suas, thug Gilleasbaig air falbh an t-fhàradh. "Ma tha i
cho math sin," arsa Gilleasbaig ris a' mhinistear, "gabh do leòr
go madainn dhith." Ghabh esan a' leabaidh aig a' mhinistear
a-staigh a's an taigh! [laughs] Tha sin cho ceart 's a ghabhas e!...
Och bha e, air a shon fhéin a h-uile h-uair a bha e; cha robh càil
ach sin aige.
O chaidh e Phort Righeadh, 's chaidh e, thug e drama dhan a
h-uile duine bha sa Royal. Thubhairt Fear a' Royal, Lachlann Ros
a bh'ann an uair sin,
"A uel, sìbh tha fortanach," ars [e], "an duine uasal a thachair
ribh a-nochd!"
"O," arsa Gilleasbuig, "cha dàinig a dheireadh ort!" 'S nuair a
sheall iad bhuapa, 's ann a bha Gilleasbaig muigh anns a' stàbull
's e suaineadh sùganan 's rudan timcheall air a chasan 's air a
làmhan 's cha robh e responsible for his actions ann. Cha robh e
cunntach airson càil a rinn e; sin an dòigh a bh'aige a' dol
timcheall....

Gillespie would go to the stream and neither he himself,
nor his cod, would return; he was keeping his cod! After
that, he went round many houses and when he came back,
he took the cod with him and he threw it in the boat.
"Thank you, good people," he said, "if it pays you as
well as it paid me, you will be very happy with it."

He did not give the cod to anyone there, but he was
cleaning it in the stream for them, for every one that was
there, and he wasn't returning with it. This was his way.
He went up on a trip and he used to be going to see
Sutar, he was a minister there up in Sleat. He arrived at
midnight and he got the minister up.
"Oh," he said, "what brings you here at this time of
night?"
"Oh," said he, "I was wanting to find a place where I
could stay [for the night]."
"Oh well, you'll get that," said Sutar to him. This is
how it was: he went inside, got a bite of food anyway and,
"Oh well," Sutar, the minister, said to him, "I haven't
any place for you but on the loft up there and you can stay
there. There's a bed there for you, a good bed."
"Oh very good then."
"Get the ladder and we will put the ladder against the
thing and you can get up there."
"Ah well," said Gillespie, "I think, since you say that
yon bed is so good, you ought to go up before me first and
check how good it is for me." Och the minister went up and
when he went up, Gillespie took the ladder away. "If it's so
good there," said Gillespie to the minister, "take your fill of
it till morning." He took the minister's bed inside the
house! That's as true as can be! He was [looking out] for
himself all the time he was [about]; he had nothing but
that [i.e. his wits].

Oh he went to Portree, he did [and] he bought a dram
for every person who was in the Royal [Hotel]. The Landlord of the Royal, Lachlann Ross it was then, said, "Ah
well, it's you that's fortunate," said he, "[because of] the
gentry that came across you tonight!"
"Oh," said Gillespie, "you haven't seen the last of it!"
And when they looked around, there was Gillespie outside
in the stable and he [was] twining coils and things around
his legs and his own hands and he was not responsible for
his actions there [so he didn't have to pay]. He wasn't
accountable for anything that he did; that was his way,
going around [like that].

Chaidh e turus eile, bha e ann an Uige 's bha searmon comanachaidh ann. Chaidh Gilleasbaig 's shuidh e shuas aig a' chùbaid.

"Dé thug ort fuireach shuas a sin?" fhios agad.

"A bha fhios a'm," ars esan, "gu robh móran shionnaich nar measg," ars esan. " 'S b'fheàirrd' iad brocair." [laughs] Agus sin mar a chaidh e, fhios agad, suas chun na cùbaid.

Agus nuair a chaidh iad a-mach,...chan eil fhios am gu dé 'n eaglais a bha siod gu dearbh, ach bha làir bhàn a-muigh a' feurach le cuideigin. ('S dòcha gur ann aig a' mhinistear fhéin a bha làir, chan eil fhios agamsa an ann go nach ann.) 'S ann a dh'fhalbh e 's fhuair e ròp agus cheangail e ri earball na làradh e agus cheangail e ris a' ròp a bh'air a' bhell...aig an eaglais. Nuair a ghluaiseadh a' làir, bha 'gliong-gliong' aig a' bhell, fhios agaibh – am bell a bh'aca. (B'àbhaist bell a bhith aca air an eaglais. Bha e air eaglais Uige uaireigin cuideachd, chan eil guth an-diugh air. Bha e ann a' Snitheasort cuideachd.) (SA1988.64.A1)

He went on another trip, he was in Uig and there was a communion sermon there. Gillespie went and he sat up at the pulpit.

"What made you stay up there?" you know.

"Because I knew that there were many foxes in our midst [i.e. the Church Elders]," he said. "They would be the better of a foxhunter!" [laughs] And that's why he went, you know, up to the pulpit.

And when they went out, I don't know which church it was at all, but a white mare was outside grazing with some others. (Perhaps the mare was the minister's, I don't know if it was or not.) So he went and he got a rope and he tied it to the tail of the mare and tied it to the rope that was on the bell of the church. When the mare moved, the bell went 'gling-gling', you know – the bell they had. (They used to have a bell on the church. There was one on the Uig church at one time too, there's no sign of it today. There was one on the Snizort [church] too.)

As the Gaelic poet Niall MacLeòid said, when retelling tales of Gilleasbaig Aotrom in his book Clàrsach an Doire,

Am measg amadain an Eilein air fad, dleasaidh "Gilleasbuig Aotram" an t-ionad is àirde.... Cha robh cuirm no fleadh, féill no banais, a b'fhiach ainmeachadh, a thachradh eadar dà cheann an Eilein, nach feumadh Gilleasbuig a bhi 'n sin. (MacLeòid 1893:229)

Amongst the fools of the whole Isle [of Skye], Gilleasbaig Aotrom must have the highest place. There wasn't a feast or festival, fair or wedding that happened from end to end of the Island worth mentioning, but Gillespie would have to be there.

MacLeòid says of Sutar, the new minister in Isle Ornsay, that he was "fòghlumaichte ann an iomadh cànain, ach duine aig nach robh ach fìor dhroch Ghàidhlig" ["educated in many languages, but a person who had truly bad Gaelic"] (MacLeòid 1924:230–1).

MacLeòid dates Gilleasbaig to the first quarter of the nineteenth century, rather at odds with Peter Stewart's comment regarding the stories: "Aye that's true, [he's] sixty years dead." Gilleasbaig is still a well-known figure in Skye and there are many stories told about him and a number of other 'wise fools' collectively referred to by the writer-schoolmaster William MacKenzie as "the originals".

Some of the exploits attributed to this "wandering fraternity of semi-lunatics" (MacKenzie 1930:60) are archetypal, like Gilleasbaig and the Cod, and others just accounts of witty or impertinent responses to questions.

For printed versions of some of these in English, see MacKenzie's Iochdar-Trotternish (1930:60–6) and in Gaelic, see MacLeòid's Clàrsach an Doire (1893:229–39), both of which also contain a satirical verse attributed to Gilleasbaig. Another written version is in Tocher 5:152–5. Other oral anecdotes and versions are on SA1955.138.12, SA1976.170.A5, SA1977.211.A1 and SA1986.79. (See also CD track 35.)

(The transcription of this tale was done by Peigi Bennett and me, with translation by me. I am grateful to the late Dr. Alan Bruford for his helpful cross-referencing suggestions.)

Appendix Four

CD TRACK LISTING

These track numbers are *not* the same as the song numbers, as I have included two extra songs, and some prose material, on the CD.

Most of the recordings were made in Iain's home over the last twenty years. The earliest were made by Derick Thomson in 1951, the latest by me in 1994. Iain's voice, therefore, ranges from that of a 48-year-old to that of a 91-year-old. Sometimes, there is some background noise from the wall clock, or especially from the nearby fire (often with the added excitement of sparking larch logs). In some cases, the songs' words will differ from those in the book, because the latter are composite texts. Two of the songs, tracks 10 and 18, have extra verses that I have not been able to include in the book; see the notes on songs 9 and 17 in Appendix Two for more information. Tracks 7 and 8 were only partially remembered. All of the songs are Iain's except Aonghas Fleidsear's *Òran a' Veto* (track 26), and the traditional *'S mór tha mi smaoineachadh* (track 23).

Tracks 17, 20 and 23 were recorded by Derick Thomson, tracks 6, 9, 22 and 26 by Catrìona NicGumaraid at the University of Dundee (1980), and tracks 10 and 28 by Uisdean MacCoinnich. My thanks to Professor Thomson, Catrìona Fleidsear and Catrìona NicGumaraid, and Fleòraidh NicCoinnich for their kind permission to use these recordings. Equipment used ranges from direct-to-disk behemoths, to Nagra and Uher open reel machines and DAT recorders. See Appendices One and Two for more information on individual recordings not detailed here.

Track	Title (and song number)	Source
1.	Ach 's e siod an aon dòigh a bh'againn...	SA1992.63.1
2.	Ho-ró tha mi fo smalan dheth (Òran an tombaca) (1)	SA1988.64.A7
3.	Ho ho-ró air gach cailleach (Òran a' cheàird) (2)	SA1992.64.3
4.	An t-each iarainn (3)	SA1992.65.4
5.	Tarbh Bhràigh Uige (4)	SA1993.15.1
6.	Ho-ró chan eil an smal orm (5)	NicGumaraid 1980b:A9
7.	A Mhàiri bhàn, tha thu lurach (6)	SA1993.15.B14
8.	Tha mi fo thurs air bheagan sunnd (7)	SA1990.107.A2
9.	Nuair a thòisich iad ri bùidsearachd (8)	NicGumaraid 1980b:A5
10.	An cuala sibh mun fhiadh (9)	TM1994.8.14
11.	An cuala sibh mun ùpraid (Tarbh Eighre) (10)	SA1992.65.7
12.	An cuala sibh an car a bha sa bhaile seo mun dannsa (11)	TM1994.5.B2
13.	A Bheileag, 's mór a chaidh do mhealladh (12)	TM1994.1.B12

14.	Thoir an t-soraidh seo bhuam (13)	SA1992.65.6
15.	A's a' mhadainn 's mi 'g éirigh (14)	SA1988.64.A12
16.	Bidh mi cuimhneachadh 's ag ionndrainn (15)	SA1992.63.3
17.	Nochd gur luaineach mo chadal (16)	RL1681, copy 2466
18.	Lìon a-mach go bàrr na cuachan (17)	SA1989.28.A15
19.	Spògan circeadh (18)	TM1994.3.A3
20.	A Mhàiri, a Mhàiri (19)	RL1680, copy 2465
21.	Chaoidh cha phòs mi, tha mi 'n dùil (20)	TM1994.2.A2
22.	Nach bòidheach Uige (21)	TM1994.8.2
23.	'S mór tha mi smaoineachadh (traditional)	RL1681, copy 2466
24.	'Illean, na biodh oirbhse smalan! (22)	SA1989.28.B4
25.	Tha sluagh òg air dhol gu aimbeirt (Òran a' veto) (23)	SA1992.64.1
26.	Oran a' Veto (Aonghas Fleidsear)	NicGumaraid 1980b:A3
27.	Tha mealladh mór am measg an t-sluaigh (24)	SA1992.65.1
28.	O anma, feuch an dùisg thu (25)	TM1994.8.4
29.	An Eaglais Shaor an Steòrnabhagh (26)	SA1988.64.B2
30.	The news we've heard from Waternish (27)	SA1992.64.5
31.	'S e seo a' sgeul tha taitneach leinn (28)	SA1989.26.B1
32.	'S thoir mo bheannachd do dh'Eilean Iarmain (29)	SA1989.26.A4
33.	A time will come, a time will go (30)	SA1988.64.A4
34.	Should I have time available (A song to Mr. Ball) (31)	SA1990.104.A1
35.	Sgeul Ghilleasbaig Aotruim	SA1988.64.A1
36.	Cha dùineadh tu beul bàrd...	SA1989.27.B3

ENDNOTES

[1] For example, see David Buchan's *The Ballad and the Folk* (1972), Nettl's *Folk and Traditional Music of the Western Continents* (1965) and McCarthy's *The Ballad Matrix* (1990).

[2] Many Scottish collections were said to be saving the 'last leaves' of tradition for posterity, but are now of limited use since the context in which the traditions lived and breathed are missing. I align myself with Scotland's two greatest collectors of folklore, Calum Maclean and Hamish Henderson who, "unlike their predecessors...did not view the songs as museum pieces,...rather they wished songs to live, as an important part of Scots culture" (Miller 1981:180). The term 'last leaves' was coined by William Walker and used by Alexander Keith for his *Last Leaves of Traditional Ballad Airs*, based on the collections of Gavin Greig in the North East of Scotland (Greig and Keith 1925).

[3] Her description, in the same passage, of those "in whom Imagination takes the place of acquired knowledge," applies to the Sgiobair very well, for he is a creator within his tradition.

[4] The veracity of oral tradition, even over centuries in many cases, has been proven by archaeological tests in the South-western U.S. and Greenland among other places (Montell 1970:xv–xvi).

[5] She feels most of his songs are fine, but is less certain of his deep interest in historical traditions and debates on the antiquity of Gaelic.

[6] See McKean 1992b and Bennett 1992:40, 98, 155, 180–2, 221–4 for just a few of the dozens of items that did not fit within the bounds of this book.

[7] Expressed in his plenary speech at the American Folklore Society's 1991 annual meeting in St. John's, Newfoundland, see also Halpert 1992.

[8] See Chapter Three for descriptions of céilidhs and of MacNeacail on his mettle at one.

[9] Curiously, Iain, Ciorstaidh, Dòmhnall and Mairead, all named after Mór's side of the family, were all left-handed, as was Mór herself. (FW13.3.93)

[10] Due to the limited number of surnames, a patronymic system is used throughout the *Gàidhealtachd*. A person is identified by a sequence of names, usually their own, plus that of their father and grandfather. Sometimes a nickname is substituted for the parent's name, e.g. Iain's son Uilleam, who would be Uilleam Sgiobair, William (son of the) Sgiobair. For an early eighteenth-century observer's view of Highland patronymics and how they function, see Capt. Burt's *Letters* (1974:2:122).

[11] A flauchter spade is a wide, flat-bladed spade usually used to remove the top layer of turf to allow the cutting of the peat below for fuel.

[12] For a more detailed description of a blackhouse, see Mitchell 1880:48–54, MacKenzie 1921:85–6, Bennett 1994:40–2 and Fenton 1978. Bennett also has an interesting comment on Mitchell's upper-class perspective (40, f/n 94).

[13] There are also a number of Nicolsons buried in the Uigg [sic] Cemetery in Prince Edward Island.

[14] Mike Kennedy points out that in many cases, in other parts of the Highlands, emigration was voluntary and that the real, long-term casualty of the Clearances was not people – they were, for the most part, better off – but Gaelic culture itself (1995:488 and the whole of Chapter Six).

[15] Whisky was an important feature in the customs of birth, christening, and indeed the whole cycle of life, see Bennett 1993:34, 60, 68 and throughout.

[16] Niall na Drochaid was so called because he lived next to the bridge over the Conon.

[17] Rack-renting is the practice of charging an excessive rent for houses and land, often equal or close to the full value of the property.

[18] A round tower high on the southern slope above Uig Bay, built by the landlord to house a gasworks. Its main role these days is as a subject for photographers.

¹⁹ Gladstone is sometimes so-called due to his involvement in 'the Irish Question', the vociferous campaign by Irish crofters in the nineteenth century for more land.

²⁰ Màiri Mhór nan Oran [Great Mary of the Songs], or Mary MacPherson, was a Skyewoman renowned for her songs about Skye and the crofters' struggle for land. She will feature prominently throughout the rest of this book.

²¹ Murdo also remembered an incident in his youth which gave him a real understanding of the dynamics of the 1877 flood:

> *I remember I went out in June – I had to mark all the lambs, you see. It started to rain, O Dhia [Oh Lord], it was heavy. I sheltered below a rock and I heard this noise. I didn't know on earth where it was coming from. (FW20.11.93)

The water had nowhere to go and the peat became sodden.

> Then I saw this hill flying out. I got the fright of my life then. O Dhia, it wasn't as bad as the one that was up there [in 1877, but] it's the heaviest rain I saw in my life, I think. And there wasn't a drop in Kilmuir! (FW20.11.93)

²² The Highlander 3.11.1877, quoted in Meek 1977:132.

²³ Or, "You got a miserly, insignificant fifty pounds and they made at least that much ridicule of you." Here is part of this verse from Màiri Mhór's poem as it appears in Meek 1977:

> 'S an àite nan deich ceud,/ A dhèanadh pàirt de'n chall a lìonadh,/ Cha robh ach leth-cheud spìocach,/ 'S gun d'rinneadh fhiach de dh'fhanaid air (p. 76, ll. 49–52).
> [In place of the one thousand,/ which would partly compensate for the loss [from the flood],/ there was only an insignificant fifty pounds,/ and at least that much ridicule (or scorn) was made of him.]

²⁴ This Stewart was a grandfather of Iain Stiùbhart of Glenconon on whose boat MacNeacail worked in his youth. He was born ca. 1820 and was a tacksman in Cuidreach later cleared to Cùil.

²⁵ "Deforce" is a Scottish legal term meaning to use force to prevent a police officer from fulfilling his duty. In the context of the land agitation, it usually refers to the obstruction of eviction orders, which are supposed to be delivered to the named recipient.

²⁶ According to Hunter the number was actually three hundred. One thousand, however, is the number quoted to me by many Skye people, indicating the impact the deployment had on the islanders' folk memory. Hunter also says that at the time the Marines' arrival was announced, innkeepers refused to put them up as they did not want to be identified as sympathisers with the government's position (1976:150).

²⁷ The Times 19.11.1884, quoted in Hunter 1976:150–1.

²⁸ I am grateful to Morag Henriksen, Headmistress of Uig School, for drawing this article to my attention.

²⁹ Urquhart was also, coincidentally, the grandfather of Iain's future wife Màiri Munro.

³⁰ A 'white-house' is immediately recognisable as a typical Highland house. They were stone-built to standard plans, available from the government during the reapportionment of crofts. There are usually two main rooms on each floor, leading to another common epithet for them, the 'two-up, two-down'.

³¹ Aonghas is a distant cousin of the Sgiobair, born and raised in Idrigill, the township that makes up the North side of Uig proper. To avoid confusion with the surname, he will be referred to hereafter as Aonghas Dubh [Black(-haired) Angus], as he is known locally.

³² The universality of nicknaming in Highland tradition may arise from the fairly rigid conventions for the naming of children after immediate ancestors as well as the geographic concentrations of a limited number of surnames. See Dorian 1981 for a good discussion of Scottish Gaelic far-ainm traditions.

³³ In April of 1908, Iain's father William was appointed to the school board at a wage of six pounds per year (USR1908:329). He served for several years as Compulsory Officer, in charge of investigating absentee students. (FW18.12.90:9) This must surely have given Iain extra incentive to keep up his attendance.

³⁴ Iain often says "learning" in place of "teaching" as the Gaelic is the same for both: "ag ionnsachadh".

³⁵ The history of Gaelic in education is largely one of missed opportunities. According to John Smith (1981), there was ample provision for Gaelic teaching in the 1872 Act, and in the addendum of 1873 which recommended that students be allowed to summarise, in Gaelic, a passage of English prose they had just read (p. 37). Later, the Napier Commission recommended a three-fold approach for the Gaelic speaking areas: (i) literacy in Gaelic should be taught first; (ii) teachers should be Gaelic speakers; and (iii) instruction in Gaelic should be encouraged (p. 46).

It is a great pity that none of these initiatives were followed up, largely because of the culturally genocidal policies of the establishment and the sense of inferiority that had been literally and figuratively beaten into the Gaels by the nineteenth century. Smith's article contains a comprehensive survey of Scottish education legislation relating to Gaelic.

[36] Reading and writing skills are of course two separate issues of literacy; mastering the former does not imply having the latter.

[37] See Chapter Three for a description of the céilidh scene in the Uig area.

[38] See Chapter Six for some of these anecdotes.

[39] One can only hope that the examiner was referring to his own lack of fluency, or at least to the infants' difficulty with scriptural language. Smith 1948 is a report on Gaelic speakers' (in)ability to understand the cultural content of standard school texts aimed at English and English-speaking children.

[40] Iain, like many other people, often finishes sentences with "'s", literally meaning "and", but not actually carrying any lexical weight.

[41] This is a pronunciation of 'agamsa' common in Trotternish and Duirinish. It elides the 'g' and introduces the epenthetic vowel.

[42] This would have been a large trip hammer.

[43] This nickname, Creag Ard, illustrates the tradition of referring to a person by a place name, usually a farm or related physical land feature.

[44] From Margaret Bennett (12.11.89).

[45] At the time the newspapers were full of the "Camilla-gate" story: the publication of the recording of a telephone conversation said to be between Prince Charles and the woman alleged to be his lover.

[46] Ross had to make a song in praise of a certain young woman, "she being in a great temper at the Bard because he had not praised her in a previously written song." (Calder 1937:132–5) The exchange continued when the woman commissioned another poet to make a satire on Ross and he responded with Òran eile do'n chailin cheudna [*Another song to the same girl*] (Calder 1937:136–41). Cf. Ives 1964:41.

[47] Angus Fletcher was another Uig composer whose work will be touched upon in Part II.

[48] What Iain means by this last comment is unclear. Perhaps he feels that the irregular pattern of verses two and three, or maybe the use of language in the whole song, does not reach the standard set by Dunnchadh Bàn, his poetic archetype (see Chapters Three, Four and Six). In my opinion – based on a half-completed comment several minutes later during the same interview – he feels that it needs further polishing to reach the standard, say, of *Nochd gur luaineach mo chadal* (16). As it stands, it is perhaps too much a collection of vignettes for this stage of his composing life.

A similar anecdote is told of Màiri nighean Alasdair Ruaidh. She was criticised by her chief for composing a song without his permission, to which she replied, "It is not a song; it is only a crònan [*a croon*]" (MacKenzie 1907:24).

[49] This may imply that the song was recomposed in the 1960s, based on a fragment he remembered making during his time in Corrour. If so, it is an interesting window on a composer at work, reshaping and polishing one of his creations. I believe that much of this song dates from the period in question, but that is only a conjecture based on the following data: (a) twenty years is his generic number for 'quite some time ago'; he uses it fairly often when dating songs; (b) it describes a period before his service in World War II, an experience which would have ameliorated some of the unpleasantness of life in Corrour; and (c) the late Thirties was a very productive period of composition, judging from the number of other songs from those years. Very possibly it was completed or reconstructed in later years, but in the end, I have judged it on the basis of its content.

[50] This phrasing shows the extent to which singing a song is, to some extent, recomposing it.

[51] A brand name of adhesive.

[52] i.e. taking her for piggy-back rides.

[53] Mrs. Ferguson was, incidentally, a niece of Jessie of Balranald (MacKenzie 1930:77, 1934:101). For details and several versions of the famous elopement of Jessie and Donald MacDonald of Mogastad, see MacKenzie 1930:101–4 and MacDonald 1992.

[54] See Chapters Four and Five for more discussion on what makes a 'good subject' and how a bard was expected to treat it.

[55] The Rev. Angus Smith was the Snizort minister at the time of the veto and naturally campaigned against licensing. He also protested against Sunday ferries to Skye. He now lives and works in Lewis (MacDonald 1992:63–70).

[56] A common reduction of "a bh'agamsa" with an added intrusive vowel.

[57] i.e. "as they were before" or possibly "as the pilgrims themselves".

[58] The "they" Iain refers to here are not the same evangelists castigated in *Tha mealladh mór am measg an t-sluaigh* (24). He has a much higher opinion of Macrae and his followers than of the 'pilgrims'.

[59] Interview with Peigi Bennett and Peter Stewart 3.3.90.

[60] Thirty-three years actually, see dates above.

[61] I overheard these words as I was leaving church with Iain one Sunday.

[62] The General Practitioner for the north of Skye for thirty-four years. At the end of 1992, Iain and Màiri attended Dr. Macrae's retirement party in Staffin, where Iain made the presentation of a plaque to him for his years of dedicated service.

[63] Song was also essential to nearly every aspect of working life, from rowing to reaping, from spinning to waulking, from milking to churning. This is true for many cultures, e.g. the Sia Indians of New Mexico: "My friend, without songs you cannot do anything." (White 1962:115 quoted in Merriam 1964:225)

[64] Bergin points out that many of the holders of bardic office in mediæval Ireland were highly trained writers and composers, but not necessarily inspired composers (1970:4).

[65] See Martin Martin's *Description of the Western Isles* (1884:116) for more details about the technique of composition and Bergin's *Irish Bardic Poetry* (1970:5–8) for a lengthy extract on the Irish bardic schools. The schools were mostly destroyed in the Cromwellian period (Gillies 1989b:245).

[66] Their poems are available in collected editions, see Watson 1934, Craig 1949 and Ó Baoill 1972.

[67] "At the proper moment she saw her poems running along the green turves that formed the intersection of wall and roof. The phrase used by the *seanchaidh* [tradition-bearer], who supplied...this information was: A' feitheamh na bardachd a' ruith air na glasfhadan." (MacInnes 1968:41)

[68] MacInnes notes that these two poets never married and that this was unusual for their time. He also says that they were accompanied on their travels by female companions whose role was to create choral refrains for their songs. (1968:41) These two points may hint at some doubt in tradition-bearers' minds regarding the two women's sexuality; perhaps this was the real reason for their being buried face down.

[69] The types of courtier were the *filidh* [the poet], the *seanchaidh* [the historian or tradition-bearer], and the *reacaire* [the reciter] (Thomson 1983:292). See Gillies 1989b and Thomson 1968 for thorough discussions of the court poets and their role.

[70] This may sound far-fetched to modern ears, but consider the now generally accepted connection between stress and psychosomatic physical illness. It is also implied that Màiri nighean Alasdair Ruaidh's satires were so powerful that, when a boat was sent to bring her back from exile, the crew was instructed not to take her on board unless she promised to make no more songs (MacKenzie 1907:24). Martin Martin states that the ruling classes would grant the bards anything they asked, "sometimes out of respect, and sometimes for fear of being exclaimed against by a satire, which in those days was reckoned to be a great dishonour". (1884:116)

[71] One of the last of the professional song-makers was John MacCodrum, an expert satirist whose songs were collected, edited and translated by William Matheson (1938). The volume also contains interesting biographical material including some of the financial details of being a professional (pp. xxiv–xxv). The poetry of other professional poets of this era is also well represented in collections such as *Eachann Bacach and other MacLean Poets* (Ó Baoill 1979), *Bàrdachd Shìlis na Ceapaich, c.1660–c.1729* (Ó Baoill 1972), *Orain Iain Luim* (MacKenzie 1964) and *Bàrdachd Ghàidhlig* (Watson 1959) to name just a few.

[72] The Statute actually says parents must send the eldest son or daughter to school in the Lowlands and "bring thame up thair quhill thay may be found able sufficientlie to speik, reid, and wryte Inglishe". [sic] (Donaldson 1970:174)

[73] See Hunter 1976 for an exhaustive and moving study of the people's transition from clansmen to crofters. Hunter also has a valuable and extensive bibliography. For a brief introduction to the Clearances and summaries of many of the major turning points of the 150 year crisis, see Thomson 1983.

[74] The clansmen in the past had entrusted much of the responsibility for their welfare to the chief, who was in most cases a relative. While a blood relationship, however distant, was the norm, it was not universal. In some cases, a tenant willing to declare loyalty to a particular chief was free to do so. He was then able to assume the clan name if he so wished.

[75] This propensity towards deeply felt religious beliefs was even remarked on by Julius Caesar: "The whole Celtic people is greatly addicted to religion." (quoted in Henderson 1992:250)

[76] MacGill-Eain is known to most European and world audiences as an award-winning literary poet, but he is also a tradition-bearer with a great first-hand knowledge of Gaelic song and its related lore. This background suffuses almost all of his own poetry.

[77] For a broad picture of the poetry relating to the land agitations, see Donald Meek's *Tuath is Tighearna* (1995).

[78] William Matheson echoes this appreciation in his edition of the songs of John MacCodrum where he says that one

person "might know thousands of lines of poetry, together with a large number of prose tales". (1938:xix)

[79] The Act improved the rights of the tenantry vis à vis the landlords by granting security of tenure, and the right of inheritance and by establishing a Land Court for the fixing of fair rents. Unfortunately, however, it did not provide a solution to the crofters' main grievance: land shortage that had been brought on by the landlords' re-enclosure of the common-grazings. No attempt was made, at that point, to re-apportion them. The Land League and other crofters' resistance organizations, therefore, did not see the legislation as the great landmark that we often consider it today. See Hunter 1986 for comprehensive detail.

[80] Dòmhnall Ruadh Phàislig [Red(-haired) Donald of Paisley], who made many songs on local issues in the new Gaelic community in Glasgow, is a perfect example of a poet in this new urban role. See Mac an t-Saoir 1968 and Byrne 1988.

[81] For example, Dòmhnall Ruadh Chorùna: òrain is dain le Dòmhnall Dòmhnallach a Uibhist a Tuath (1969), Sporan Dhòmhnaill (Mac an t-Saoir 1968), Sguaban Eòrna: Bàrdachd is Dàin Dòmhnall le Iain MacDhòmhnuill (1973), Na Bàird Thirisdeach (Camshron 1932). A further selection appears in the bibliography and in McKean 1993, though these are not intended as comprehensive lists.

[82] These poets' songs may be found in these books: MacChoinnich 1834; MacLeòid 1893; MacBheathain 1891 and Meek 1977 respectively.

[83] Poems and songs by Bàrd Ghrialain may be found in MacKenzie (1934:97–100); Calum Ruadh in Knudsen (1978) and MacNeacail (1975); and Fletcher in NicGumaraid (1980a and b). The Sgiobair and Calum Ruadh are not related; the surname MacNeacail/Nicolson is one of the most common in Skye.

[84] In the summer of 1992, I myself was part of an 'old-style' house-visit among the emigrant Scots of Quebec. It was full of stories of the old times, discussions of genealogy, jokes, news and local history – a genuine céilidh, though English is now the predominant language. See Bennett 1994:99–111 for descriptions of such céilidhs.

[85] See Bennett's The Last Stronghold (1989:55–8, 81, 118–9) and Hebridean Traditions of the Eastern Townships of Quebec (1994:99–111), MacNeill's Sgeul gu Latha (1987:22–37) and MacQueen's Skye Pioneers and "the Island" (1929:32).

[86] See Szwed's Private Cultures and Public Imagery (1966) for a further discussion of the need for catharsis in a community.

[87] See Chapter One for more information on An Sagart, who was not actually a priest at all, but a sharp and inquisitive questioner.

[88] Cameron was called after one of his farms in Lochaber following the custom of nicknaming discussed above; he died in 1856. Haldane's The Drove Roads of Scotland has some more biographical information (1968:66) and Reliquiae Celticae has a song composed by a mill-worker on the very farm after which the drover was called (Cameron 1894:340–1). Màiri Mhór's dialogue poem about Coire Chuinnlidh and her father may be found in MacBheathain 1891:130 and Meek 1977:54–6, 128.

Cameron was well known for his sharp eye at assessing the quality of stock (Màiri MacDonald 1977:195); similar talents are attributed to Gilleasbaig Aotrom, the wise fool.

Iain picked up a number of anecdotes about the drover when he was working in Coire Odhar [Corrour] (SA1988.65.B5, SA1991.93); I hope to publish these stories at a later date.

[89] A type of colic usually leading to haemorrhage and death (Scottish National Dictionary).

[90] It is worth noting that just a month before this recording, MacNeacail had made another song. I would be surprised if it proved to be the last.

[91] Usually a humorous or satirical sketch on a recent local or political event.

[92] This spelling reflects the Trotternish pronunciation of "mu dhéidhinn".

[93] Duncan Corbett was a postman and also Dr. Lamont's driver. After retiring, he moved to Capt. Fraser's tower above Uig Bay. Although most of his performing material was in Gaelic, one of his party pieces was MacAllister Dances Before the King and he would also sing songs such as The Garden Where the Praties Grow to the children at the Uig school year-end céilidh (from conversations with Iain MacLean (17.1.94) and Peigi Bennett (30.3.93)).

Katie Douglas, who lived in Kilmuir, used to write some of the sketches. Though English was her mother tongue, she was also fully fluent in Gaelic and became a great tradition-bearer and composer in her own right. Some of her poems and songs may be found in the booklet Sàr òrain le Catrìona Dhughlas (Budge 1971). Iain says that he would never leave her house without getting a song or two.

[94] This word seems to be based on "ùm(p)adalachd", which as a noun means "grossness" or "boorishness" (Dwelly).

[95] This remark about such 'short' verses implies that he doesn't value them as songs. The great poets Dunnchadh Bàn and Mac Mhaighstir Alasdair, however, both composed in the waulking song form, so the dismissal is a little surprising. In addition, plenty of other tradition-bearers of MacNeacail's generation (such as Calum Johnston of Barra (1981)) showed an interest in waulking songs and indeed many pupils learned them in school. MacNeacail's attitude perhaps demonstrates his intense focus on the descriptive songs of the eighteenth- and nineteenth-century poets.

[96] Màiri Mhór paints an idyllic picture of coming home from waulkings late at night, with nothing but a burning sod to light the way (Meek 1977:66, ll. 27–8). For a description of a Skye waulking in Màiri Mhór's day, see MacKellar 1888.

[97] Between the Napoleonic wars and 1937, the Isle of Skye contributed twenty-one Lieutenant- and Major-Generals, forty-eight Lieutenant-Colonels, 600 Majors, Captains and Subalterns, 120 pipers and 10,000 NCOs and men to the British Army (Henderson 1992:247).

[98] Some examples of this steadfast faith will be seen in discussions about his English songs and the Gaelic bardic tradition in Part II.

[99] 'Breac' means 'trout'. Perhaps MacNeacail is using it as a sort of generic word for 'fish'.

[100] These are six lines of an eight line verse from Duncan Bàn's *Oran Coire a' Cheathaich* [*The Song of Misty Corrie*], MacLeod 1952:168, ll. 2342–9. Here is the complete verse and translation as MacLeod has it:

> Tha bradan tarrgheal 'sa' choire gharbhlaich/ Tha tighinn o'n fhairge bu ghailbheach tonn,/ Le luinneis mheam-nach a' ceapadh mheanbhchuileag/ Gu neo-chearbach le chamghob crom,/ Air bhuinne borb is e leum gu foirmeil/ 'Na éideadh colgail bu ghormglas druim,/ Le shoillsean airgid gu h-iteach meanbhbhreac/ Gu lannach deargbhallach earrgheal slìom.
> [*In the rugged gully is a white-bellied salmon/ that cometh from the ocean of stormy wave,/ catching midges with lively vigour/ unerringly, in his arched, bent beak,/ as he leapeth grandly in raging torrent,/ in his martial garb of the blue-grey back,/ with his silvery flashes, with fins and speckles,/ scaly, red-spotted, white-tailed and sleek.*]

Iain pronounces 'slìom' more like 'slìum'. After reciting this verse to me on another occasion, MacNeacail translated it (including the two lines left out in both recitations). See Chapter Six for another rendition, MacNeacail's own translation and a fuller discussion.

[101] For a discussion of the only instance known to me when he did write one of his own songs, as a stage of composition, see *A song to Mr. Ball* (31) and the discussion of its composition later in this chapter.

[102] Christine Primrose's five-verse version may also be found on her LP *Aite mo ghaoil*. The first three are essentially the same as the Sgiobair's, but his verse four is not on her recording, so where he acquired it I do not know. A five-verse version of the song appears in *Eilean Fraoich* (1982:145–6). MacNeacail's first, second and fourth verses correspond very closely to the book's first, second and fifth verses. His third does not appear, and the book's third and fourth verses are not in his version. The same book offers the following information on the composer: "William MacKenzie (Uilleam Dho'ill 'ic Choinnich), crofter-fisherman of Shader, Point [in Lewis]. Born 1857. After the death of his wife, the family emigrated to Canada. He died at Fort William, Ontario, in 1907. A collection of his songs and poems was published in 'Cnoc Chùsbaig' in 1936." (146–7)

[103] In recent years, Iain's son Willie has been asking *me* to compose a song. He feels that having recorded so many of Iain's songs, I should be well able to make one myself. Experience of song, then, is judged to ease the actual creation of them. (FW20.11.93)

[104] This was common Scots usage as well.

[105] See Bassin's *The Old Songs of Skye* (1977) for more details.

[106] John MacDonald from Totescore, four months older than the Sgiobair, was actually engaged to Màiri Lamont, who was working as a cook at Uig Hospital where Isabel Gillies was a nurse. In 1993, I visited Johnny Alec in the Bughmore Home in Portree and told him about my project and about seeing Beileag. He remembered both her and Iain well and said, "O bha e math air na h-òrain." [*"Oh he was good at the songs."*] (FW20.11.93)

[107] Ives reports on a New Brunswick song-maker, Frank O'Hara, who, his informant said, "would make a piece of poetry, maybe six or seven verses. In that one night! Now that's wonderful, eh?" (Ives 1989:76)

[108] A term used to describe a song made for a particular event.

[109] This distinction is drawn by Bruno Nettl (1956:19) and quoted in Nash 1961:187.

[110] Alexander Carmichael mentions such spontaneous composition in *Carmina Gadelica* regarding a charm composed around the waulking boards (1928:385).

There is no reason why such spontaneous composition should not have taken place; I myself have, with three friends, kept a single song going for well over three-quarters of an hour without repetition of any but the choral lines. The structure of the verse was ABA'B, with a refrain of CB. We provided new lines for the A and A' parts, taking turns round the four of us and usually creating a 'set-up/tag-line' effect.

[111] This reminds one of the wealth of Gaelic songs which begin by telling the listener where the composer is, how she or he feels and how the song was inspired. A look through any of the collections (e.g. MacKenzie 1907, Watson 1959)

will reveal a generous number. There are also an infinite number of parallels in the English-language song traditions as well, e.g. "As I walked out one May morning...".

[112] Even in a tradition as removed as that of the Canadian Maritimes, walking and motion are found to be part of traditional composition. Frank O'Hara "might be haying, he could be doing anything.... But believe it or not, he would walk through that settlement, and he would make a piece of poetry, maybe six or seven verses." (Ives 1989:76) And Larry Gorman is described,

> pacing back and forth between the living room and the parlor, his hands behind his back and his head down, too absorbed in what he was doing to notice he was being watched. Every once and a while he would stop, walk over to a high desk in the living room, write busily for a moment and then go back to his pacing. (Ives 1964:42)

This image has several parallels with Iain. There is a difference in that a song often comes upon MacNeacail *while* he is walking as opposed to Gorman who, in this extract, walks in order to compose, but Sandy Ives tells me that Gorman is said to have done the same. (personal communication, July 1996)

In addition, Iain does not write his material down, even after completion, relying instead on a good memory and a solid grasp of the language, imagery and metres involved. (Gorman's role in his society as a maker of satires was not unlike that of the Sgiobair in his, though Iain is a far more likeable character.)

[113] In light of this comment, I was naturally particularly concerned that the transcriptions in Chapter One and Two be accurate in his, as well as others', eyes. He has patiently gone over every song text with me and made many helpful suggestions; I hope that they are now as he would wish them. In transcribing some of the songs, I was fortunate to have NicGumaraid's texts as a starting point. Her cassette and book were among the first publications to recognise the importance of recording and publishing bàrd baile song-poetry. As can be seen in Chapter Six (p. 166) the collection is still prized in the Uig area.

For this present book, he has gone over every song text, made many helpful suggestions and is quite satisfied with them.

Iain's son, John Angus:

> *I remember when him and Angus Fleidsear went down to Dundee to make that tape. It was about 1979.... Angus was well into his eighties and my father would have been about seventy-six. They drove all the way down to Dundee and Angus had thick, thick glasses and could hardly see. And he was well over eighty! (FW8.12.93)

[114] My thanks to Prof. William Gillies for pointing this out.

[115] This need is well-attested in song scholarship, for instance Mrs. Margaret Laidlaw's famous statement to Sir Walter Scott as he was collecting Scots ballads: "There was never ane o my sangs prentit till ye prentit them yoursel, and ye hae spoilt them awthegither. They were made for singing and no for readin: but ye hae broken the charm noo and they'll never be sung mair." (Henderson 1992:23) And cf. Christopher Maurer's statements about (and quoting) the Spanish poet García Lorca: "When his poems and plays were printed he considered them 'dead on the page', but when he read them to others he could make them live again and protect them – 'against incomprehension, dilettantism, and the benevolent smile'." (Henderson 1992:313) García Lorca's last point holds true for village song; take it out of its natural register and habitat and it is laid open to judgements under many criteria which it was not created to meet.

[116] Albert B. Lord in *The Singer of Tales* (1973) postulates a system of formulaic language which allows Yugoslav *guslars* to recreate their epic poems each time they sing them. See Buchan 1972 and McCarthy 1990 for applications of this theory to Scots ballad singing.

[117] Màiri Mhór's song, 'A' chlach' agus Màiri (first line, "Nuair a chaidh na ceithir ùr oirre") may be found in the older collection of her poetry, *Dàin is Òrain Ghàidhlig le Màiri Nic-a'-Phearsain* (MacBheathain 1891:62–4).

[118] The comparison with Uilleam Ros and Màiri Mhór, used by Shapiro for her evidence, is unconvincing for the following reasons. Firstly, both song-makers are well known in Skye and are admired by MacNeacail. Secondly, Màiri Mhór in particular holds a special place in his affections, not because he thinks of her as the best poet (he doesn't), but because of her Uig origins and her place in the history of Skye (see Chapter Six for more detail). Thirdly, no doubt songs by Màiri Mhór and other composers, such as Ros, would periodically gain popular currency, especially in the days of the taighean céilidh when the songs would be heard frequently. It therefore comes as no surprise that these song-makers would strongly influence Iain's own composition.

Of course, it may be argued that Màiri Mhór herself hewed to a "Skye contour" and that Iain, in adapting some of her melodies, does so as well. Perhaps his aesthetic has been conditioned by his tradition and therefore tunes which follow the contour are perceived as good. Even if all this is true, however, it does not go any further towards proving the existence of the contour. And while the idea of a regional breakdown of melodic shape is intriguing and perhaps even desirable, the data presented do not support the conclusion that it really exists in Skye, or anywhere else. In fact, the contour may well exist, but to prove it we need much more evidence than that provided by a handful of Skye's many song-makers, two of whom had such close ties.

In 1992, Dr. Shapiro told me she had considerably modified her position on this issue. The undoubted influence of the major printed collections (e.g. MacKenzie 1907) in creating a body of basic tunes from which others were made must also be taken into account. The question certainly needs further research.

[119] Expressed by Dr. John MacInnes in a discussion following a seminar I gave at the School of Scottish Studies, 15.5.90.

[120] Further research on this idea would undoubtedly yield interesting results. It would have the added attraction of being something in folk-song research that is actually measurable.

[121] Both Ó Madagáin (1985:178) and Eileen Costello (1990:iv) agree.

[122] Since the 1872 Education (Scotland) Act, virtually every member of settled society has been taught to read English at school. This has made the simple classifications of literacy and non-literacy outmoded, as they do not take into account the case of the bilingual who may be literate in one language and totally oral in the other or a combination of the two.

[123] See Matheson 1938:xix and MacKenzie 1907:155–6 for the story of a MacCodrum satire in reprisal for not being invited to a wedding.

[124] A viral disease that was introduced to Scotland following World War II to control rabbit populations. It has destroyed large numbers of animals and damaged many others.

[125] See Thomson 1968:73–4 for a description of the duties of the clan bard and the clan historian. The Sgiobair, when he acts as a commentator on local events, is actually functioning more like one of the court poets than the lyrical poets he so admires, such as Duncan Bàn.

[126] I am grateful to Sandy Ives for drawing this point to my attention. (personal communication, July 1996) A textual study of MacNeacail's songs along these lines would undoubtedly yield important results.

[127] Cf. Knud Rasmussen's Eskimo informant who says exactly this: "Songs are thoughts, sung out with the breath when people are moved by great forces and ordinary speech no longer suffices." (1931:321, quoted in Merriam 1964:175)

[128] He once sang to me some of *When I went to Glasgow first, a-mach gu tìr nan Gall*.

[129] Iain also recounts this story on SA1988.66.B4b and SA1989.25.A11. It is also to be found in Meek 1977:15–6, 19 and MacKenzie 1934:89–94.

[130] It is also important, when talking about satire, to remember the distinctions between the composer, the singer and the song:

> Of course what the author intended may be quite beside the point, while what the singer intends may be all important. A generalized satire about Baptists can be pretty pointed if it is sung when there is only one in the room. (Ives 1964:168)

From a listener's point of view, as well, the context in which satire and protest song are sung can be crucial.

[131] His style is far removed from that of one of Henry Glassie's informants, who said, "When it doesn't bother 'em, I get no kick out of it," (1970:14) although Iain does enjoy good-humoured reaction to his own songs.

[132] Iain has asked me not to include this song, due to its disrespectful nature.

[133] Folklorist Hamish Henderson has said, of some of the Gaelic waulking songs, that "one feels, at times, that all this emotion is only bearable because it is confined between the banks of traditional formulaic utterance." (1992:130)

[134] 'iadsan' and 'bòidheach' are pronounced 'àsan' and 'buaidheach' here, as is common in Skye.

[135] This is the first verse of Duncan Bàn's *Oran d'a Cheile Nuadh-Phòsda* [*Song to His Bride*] (MacLeod 1952:114, ll. 1628–35).

[136] For a discussion of this and Iain's opposing song, see case studies later in this chapter.

[137] The idea of personal vision crops up internationally, from proverbial phrases, such as "beauty is in the eye of the beholder" to modern songs, such as *If you could see her through my eyes*, from the musical *Cabaret*.

[138] See Ives 1978:406–7 for some reflections on the reshaping of reality inherent in any work of art.

[139] My thanks to Sandy Ives for this last point. (personal communication July, 1996)

[140] Portions of these case studies are taken from two papers that I presented at the American Folklore Society's annual meetings in Berkeley, California and St. John's, Newfoundland in 1990 (see McKean 1992a) and 1991.

[141] i.e. "the door will be bolted behind you." Alternatively, the Gaelic could read, "'S e 'n dealain...", though the 'n' does not sound palatalised. The line might then mean "it's the light of the door [that] is your way", i.e. "you'll be shown the door".

This text is taken in the main from NicGumaraid 1980a:13; I have amended the transcription in a few places, using NicGumaraid 1980b:A2, and the translation is my own.

[142] Though it is no paid position, An Sgiobair was appointed several years ago at the suggestion of Aonghas Dubh, who felt that he would never otherwise receive any honours for his poetry. See Chapter Six for more information on how this came about.

[143] He was born in 1857 and so would have been one hundred and thirty-six. (FW13.3.93)

[144] For a more thorough discussion of the linguistic aspects of this song, see McKean 1992a, though much of the description in that article may be side-stepped by listening to the CD that accompanies this book.

[145] As I noted in the introduction, this is one reason I have included the CD.

[146] Even a self-proclaimed saviour of tradition such as Kennedy-Fraser as much as says this: she claims to be aiding the "renascence" of traditional national song but, in fact, was plundering someone else's and forging it into her own (1926:147–8). Meanwhile, this ninety-three year old man in Cuidreach is still creating in a tradition she considered broken over seventy years ago.

[147] Several years ago, Margaret Bennett and I attended Iain's daughter Isobel's wedding in Uig, with the reception following in Portree. At the reception, Iain sang this song. His voice was full of raw emotion as he told the story of his people to the Scots-speaking groom's family. Perhaps he was making a deliberate point, perhaps not. At any rate, I was completely taken aback by the extra meaning that he packed into the song through the tremendous power of his performance.

[148] They play an important role in the lore of many Gaels of the older generation, e.g. Joe Neil MacNeill in Cape Breton, whose book *Sgeul gu Latha* has a whole section devoted to "Freagartan Amasach agus Daoine Beàrraidh", or as Dr. John Shaw translates it in the book, "Repartee and Ready Wit" (see MacNeill 1987:360–79).

[149] A mail-order catalogue delivered to practically every Highland household, from which many people did most of their clothes shopping.

[150] Stronaba, as it is spelled in English, is about two miles north of Spean Bridge, near Fort William. For those curious about the fabled Tòn an Eich, there are, in fact, three actual place names in the Ordnance Survey gazetteer which contain these elements: Allt Tòn an Eich [*Horse's Arse Burn*], which flows into the north side of Loch Ericht about ten miles southwest of Dalwhinnie, Meall Tòn Eich [*Horse's Arse Hill*], about four miles north of Killin, and Tòn Eich [*Horse's Arse*], just above Loch Turret Reservoir, two and a half miles northwest of Comrie (Ordnance Survey grid references: 279N5374, 334N5538 and 349N8029 respectively). There may be many more localised ones on the fieldwork tapes of the School of Scottish Studies place names survey.

[151] Cf. MacDhòmhnaill, "Bàird a' bhaile againn (An Dròbhair)" (1956:330), for an example of a quick exchange in verse between Iain MacCoinnich of Toscaig and the local bard, An Dròbhair.

[152] These are the first and last couplets of *Soraidh le Eilean a' Cheò* (Meek 1977:62–5, ll. 65–6, 71–2). Iain could not quite remember the second line and began, "'s caisteal" [*and a castle*].

[153] MacNeacail is referring to the legend that a Danish (i.e. Scandinavian) princess lies buried beneath the peak of Sròin-Bhaornaill, which is named after her (MacKenzie 1930:36). The full quatrain runs as follows:

Is nuair a thig an oiteag/ bho Lochlann òirnn a-nall,/ séideadh air Sròin-Bhaornaill,/ 's cùbhraidh gaoth do bheann. (Meek 1977:62–5, l. 31)

[*And when the breeze comes/ over from Norway upon us,/ blowing on Sròin-Bhaornaill,/ and the fragrant wind of the hill.*]

[154] This verse may be found in Meek 1977:62, ll. 1–8, where line 6 reads "grian nan speur...", "the sun of the heavens".

[155] This verse is from Duncan Bàn's *Rann do'n Ghàidhlig 's do'n Phìob-mhóir, 'sa' Bhliadhna 1781* [*Ode to Gaelic and the Great Pipe in the year 1781*] (MacLeod1952:270, ll. 3972–9). The verse in MacLeod and his translation run as follows:

'S i 'n labhairt bha 'sa' Ghàrradh,/ Dh'fhàg Adhamh i aig an t-sluagh;/ 'S i chainnt a bh'aig na fàidhean/ Thug fios Phàrrais dhuinn a-nuas;/ 'S i bhruidheann a bh'anns an fhàsach,/ 'N am tràghadh do'n Mhuir Ruaidh;/ 'S i nis a measg an àlaich/ Tha làthair anns an uair.

[*'Tis the speech used in the Garden – / Adam left it to mankind;/ 'tis the language spoken/ by the prophets/ who transmitted heavenly lore to us;/ 'tis the speech talked in the wilderness,/ at the time the Red Sea ebbed,/ and 'tis current in the generation/ existing at this hour.*]

[156] These lines are from MacIntyre's *Rann do'n Ghàidhlig 's do'n Phìob-Mhóir, 'sa' Bhliadhna 1782* [*Ode to Gaelic and the Great Pipe in the Year 1782*]. (MacLeod1952:276, ll. 4037–9. This is the complete quatrain and MacLeod's translation:

Tha gach duine 'g ìnnseadh dhuinn,/ cho cinnteach ris a' bhàs,/ gur i bu chainnt aig Noah/ 'n am seòladh anns an àirc.

[*Everyone declares to us/ that, as sure as death, it was/ the language Noah talked/ at the time of sailing in the Ark.*]

[157] There is an echo of this verse in English, in MacKenzie (1934:7): "When Adam first his Eve did meet,/ shimmering bright as morning dew,/ the first words he spoke to her,/ were 'Ciamar a tha thu 'n diugh'."

[158] Even Mac Mhaighstir Alasdair has lent his support to the argument in his poem *Moladh an Ughdair do'n t-Seann Chànain Ghàidhealaich* [*The Author's Praise for the Old Gaelic Language*] (A. and A. MacDonald 1924:4, ll. 57–60):

'S i labhair Adhamh/ ann am Pàrras féin,/ 's bu shiùbhlach Gàilig/ bho bheul àluinn Eubh!

[*It's [Gaelic] that Adam spoke/ in Paradise itself/ and it was fluent Gaelic [that came]/ from the lovely mouth of Eve.*]

[159] As noted before in the introduction to Part II, these are six lines of an eight-line verse from Donnchadh Bàn's *Òran Coire a' Cheathaich* [*The Song of Misty Corrie*]. See note 100 for full text and translation.

[160] Murdo Stewart of Glenconon tells me that "buidhean buirb" means some, or a few, spurts or spouts. He went on to say that he had has heard the word "buidhean" in Gairloch and Applecross.

[161] These two lines are from *Rann do'n Ghàidhlig 's do'n Phìob-mhóir, 'sa' Bhliadhna 1781* [*Ode to Gaelic and the Great Pipe in the year 1781*]. Here is how they appear in MacLeod (1952:272, ll. 3994–5):

'S i ceòl nam pìob 's nan clàrsach/ luchd-dàn' is dhèanamh dhuan.
[*'Tis the music of the pipes and harps,/ of minstrels and composers of songs.*]

[162] The finished songs were written down by the Rev. Donald MacNicol from the poet's dictation, further "revised and rewritten by [his] first editor, Dr. John Stuart, minister of Luss" and printed during his lifetime (MacLeod 1952:xxvii).

[163] In the Sgiobair's school days, the scholars may have been taught a few Duncan Bàn songs specially for the local Mòds. In later decades, however, they received regular and more frequent year-round tuition in Gaelic songs.

[164] As Ives notes, "irregularities in scansion disappear when sung". (1964:154)

[165] This is the first couplet of Ros's *Oran gaoil* (Calder 1937:58–65). MacNeacail has been recorded singing a number of Ros's songs, including the whole of this one, on T1185 (a tape in the School of Scottish Studies' place-names archive, recorded by David Clement).

[166] This is the first line of Duncan Ban's *Oran d'a Cheile Nuadh-Phòsda* [*Song to His Bride*] cited before (MacLeod 1952:114 ff). See Chapter Five for MacNeacail's complete version of the first verse.

[167] The late Aonghas Fleidsear told this to Aonghas Dubh who passed it along to me (SA1993.2.B1). It is usually said that Màiri Mhór was born in Skeabost (MacKenzie 1934:89, Meek 1977:14).

[168] This is verse two of MacLeòid's *Fàilte do'n Eilean Sgiathanach* [*Welcome to the Isle of Skye*] MacLeòid 1893:24–6. It is one of his most enduringly popular songs.

[169] Iain knows a number of Iain Dubh's poems, along with several interesting anecdotes about him, including stories that he had the *sgoil dhubh* [the black art] (TM1994.7.A3). One of Iain Dubh's songs may be found in William MacKenzie's *Old Skye Tales* (1934:87–8). Thomson 1974:233 echoes MacNeacail's claim of Iain's superiority. See Budge's "Bàird an Eilean Sgiathanaich" (1972) and John MacLeod's "Dòmhnull nan Òran, am Bàrd Sgitheanach" (1922) for more information on Niall's and Iain's father and his poetry.

[170] Calum Ruadh, incidentally, admires the same group of song-makers as the Sgiobair (Knudsen 1978:7).

[171] Such a close reading of Màiri Mhór's verse may reveal some weak language and, at times, a rather lax approach to the overall construction of her poems. Somhairle MacGill-Eain goes some way to excusing her for such weaknesses, usually on the grounds of "joie-de-vivre" or "big-heartedness" (1985:250–7). She is undoubtedly immensely popular with the folk, in name anyway, and, as any artist, for particular works.

[172] Additional fieldwork in Trotternish (using names of local poets that MacNeacail has given me to jog people's memories) would undoubtedly yield a number of these songs, but this work must be done soon.

[173] Hard work and tradition combine in another pipers' saying, which complements the Sgiobair's: "It takes seven years and seven generations to make a piper." An Irish version says: "It takes twenty-one years to make an Uillean piper: seven years learning, seven years practising and seven years playing."

[174] I have known that John Angus was interested since my early visits. On a recent trip, however, it became clear that Willie knows the first lines and many early verses for a number of his father's songs. In a conversation that night, he quizzed me on whether I had a particular song his father made and I would respond by reciting the first verse. This went on for quite some time; I think his opinion of me, the outsider and learner, has improved. (FW13.3.93:1) Cf. Margaret Bennett's experience with Frank MacArthur, a son of her main informant of *The Last Stronghold* (1989), who asked her for a text of one of his father's songs. He now sings the song himself. Bruno Nettl draws attention to the fact that the

scholar's presence may sometimes wreak havoc with a society's view of itself and of its music (1973:261). Changes in attitude like those described above surely reveal the positive side of such a presence.

[175] See Glassie 1970:42–52 for more discussion of the creator's relationship to society as a whole.

[176] A. M. Freeman has this to say: "However minutely a song may be discussed, only the vaguest references to the tune will be heard." (quoted in Ó Madagáin 1985:179) Edward Miller points out that melody and voice quality are of minor importance to bothy men in the North East of Scotland (1981:165). Mrs. Costello says the same thing of her turn of the century West of Ireland informants: "To him the air is only the medium of conveying pleasantly to the audience the story he has to tell." (1990:iv) Ó Madagáin discusses the point at greater length, emphasising that the singers' inability to articulate musical appreciation does not indicate the absence of a musical aesthetic. Language, he maintains, discusses language better than it does non-linguistic forms of communication. He goes on to say that people's appreciation of music is so instinctive that listeners could not necessarily say why they held certain opinions about a piece of music. Even so, they would travel some way to hear a singer that they considered "good" according to their aesthetic. (1985:179–81)

[177] The Gaelic word is 'domhainn' or 'doimhneachd' and is frequently used in discussions about bardic language and poetry. Martinengo-Cesaresco uses the word depth as well, though not just regarding language, but in relation to the skills and achievements of the "Keltic Bards" (1886:47); the metaphor is a well-established one.

[178] "*The more languages you understand, the better you understand humanity," Iain told me on my very first trip to Cuidreach. (FW9.12.88:4)

[179] Margaret Bennett tells of her main informant's wife's hesitation at recording the "reminiscences of an old man", but he replied that he was "only telling the truth" (1989:20).

[180] Dunnchadh 'Clachair', the famous storyteller from Peninerine, South Uist. See Craig n.d. for several of Dunnchadh's stories. Sadly, Anna Dhunnchaidh died early in 1993.

[181] I am grateful to Sandy Ives for flagging up this point. For some thoughts on creativity versus repetition in performing and song-making, see Glassie 1970:30–35.

[182] This could have been said by each generation of tradition-bearers and collectors for the last several centuries, and indeed has been.

[183] The ability to name objects and creatures has been an indicator of rank and power for millenia (for example, Adam's naming of things in the Book of Genesis).

[184] The appointment of Ailean Dall as bard to Glengarry at the end of the eighteenth century has some parallels with the Sgiobair's, though Ailean Dall was given a cottage and croft. Both men show some pride in their positions and in taking their places in Clan Gatherings and processions (MacKenzie 1907:324–5).

William Matheson recounts the story of John MacCodrum's appointment as bard to Sir James MacDonald in 1763. The latter was intrigued by MacCodrum's Aoir nan Tàillearan [Satire of the Tailors] and offered to give him a croft, money and meal if he would take up the position of bard. The poet held out for five stones of cheese per year as well and Sir James acceded (1938:269–72). According to Matheson, the Chief was "a keen upholder of traditions" (xxiv), as is 'Sgoire-breac' today to some extent, and used him to extend his knowledge of Gaelic (xxv). Incidentally, MacCodrum's predecessor, Duncan MacRuaraidh, held possession of a field near Cuidreach in Skye called Achadh nam Bàrd [the Field of the Bards] (MacKenzie 1930:79, Matheson 1938:xxiv).

MacNeacail's old-style fealty (as shown in his pride at being the Clan Nicolson bard and in his panegyric songs to Skye land-owners) has drawn criticism from some quarters. To my mind it is simply another indication of how firmly he is planted in the culture of another age. To condemn him for following the social order in which he believes would be as unwarranted as ridiculing a person born in 1800 for not knowing how to operate a motor-car. He follows the conventions appropriate to his own world-view.

[185] He has reiterated this sentiment on many other occasions, referring to various modern poets.

[186] Cf. the "Folk Song Festivals" in Latvia and Lithuania in which traditional songs are sung after fifty years of proscription. They were banned by the Soviet government under Stalin in an attempt to suppress nationalistic sentiments. They live on today, perhaps stronger than ever. (See Homeland, a film by Juris Podniez, Channel 4 Productions, 1991.) Cf. Professor F. J. Child's certainty that the Scots ballad The Twa Brothers no longer existed in British oral tradition. It surfaced very much alive when collecting began among the travelling people of Scotland after the Second World War (Henderson 1974:7).

[187] Bennett's Scottish Customs (1992) discusses dozens of examples of 'dying' traditions that have survived for centuries.

[188] This is rather different to the singer of 'pre-composed' songs, who is accountable directly to the approval or disapproval of his 'public'.

[189] William Ross is one poet whose public and private self merge in his love poems. I wonder, however, whether this would appear so clearly the case if we did not know as much about Ross' private life as we do. Perhaps some of the Sgiobair's songs of unrequited love fall into this category of merged identities of the poet and the protagonist, though he was undoubtedly never as desperate in matters of love as Ross was.

TAPE CITATIONS

These citations are listed by page number and consist of the first few words of each quote, followed by the tape and item number. Where a tape extract is made up of several items, citations are separated by semi-colons. Consecutive quotes taken from the same tape are listed under the first quote of the sequence. (Entries without ellipses refer to my points that rely on information from tape extracts.)

CHAPTER ONE

5 I never got... SA1990.105.A7.
5 Aye, my father... SA1988.63.B8.
5 Oh aye, she... SA1988.63.B14.
5 They would seem... SA1988.63.B8.
5 'S e balla cloicheadh... TM1995.3.A10f; Bha thu buain... TM1994.6.A6; ['S] dé bha... TM1995.3.A10a; Bha thu go math... TM1995.3.A10c.
6 Agus an uair sin lìon... TM1995.3.A10b; Dhèanadh e... TM1995.3.A10f; Agus bha an teine... TM1995.3.A10 e; 'S bha toll... TM1995.3.A10d; Bha ad [na... TM1994.6.A6b; Och cha robh... TM1994.6.A6b.
10 Och I remember... SA1988.63.B13–4.
10 [My mother's... SA1989.26.A5 and 6.
10 Tha an Clan... SA1989.28.A9.
10 Yes, I knew... SA1988.66.B14.
12 Well it was... SA1989.27.A4.
12 Well some of... SA1989.26.A7.
12 [His house] was... SA1989.26.B8 and 27.A1.
12 *I heard it was... FW20.11.93.
14 Ah, thuirt i... SA1989.27.A2.
14 They said the... SA1989.27.A3.
14 I heard the man... SA1989.27.A3.
14 Well you see... SA1989.63.B22.
15 Of course it's... SA1989.27.A5.
15 Och they couldn't... SA1988.63.B22.
15 Nothing at all... SA1989.27.A6.
15 *There was a... FW25.5.89:15.
15 That's what finished... SA1989.27.A5.
18 But...about... SA1988.63.B22.
19 a MacIntosh and... SA1988.63.B9.
19 Well, my parents... SA1989.26.A7.
19 The croft has SA1988.63.B11.
21 Cha robh taigh... TM1995.3.A10g.
21 Och, well what... SA1988.63.B13.

21 Och,...well it... SA1988.63.B21.
21 the rent was... SA1988.63.B21.
21 You would cut... SA1988.63.B10.
21 *I remember one... FW20.11.93.
22 Ach well, I... SA1989.28.A2.
22 because he wore SA1993.2.A3.
22 Oh yes, yes... SA1990.105.A3.
22 Aye, aye,...the... SA1990.105.A1.
22 You could learn... SA1988.63.B20.
22 very good at... SA1988.63.B20.
22 Oh yes, because... SA1990.105.A1.
23 a most backward... USR 1896:34; There is a... USR 1902:112.
23 didn't get the... SA1988.64.B9; [When the Education... SA1990.105.A1.
23 I just learned... SA1988.64.B9.
24 Oh, my father... SA1990.105.A1.
24 Ach at times... SA1988.66.B21.
24 Oh yes, we... SA1990.105.A3.
24 [You] could write... SA1989.27.A11–2.
25 Oh we hadn't... SA1990.105.A3.
25 His throat gave... SA1990.105.A2.
25 Angus MacDonald took USR 1913:222.
25 Oh, he was... SA1989.27.A10 and A3.
25 *Every scholar had... FW18.12.90:19.
25 A cup of... USR 1920:340.
25 There was one... SA1988.65.A1.
25 We were very... SA1989.27.A10.
26 Och, Dughal Ruadh... SA1988.65.A6.
26 Anna came down... SA1988.65.A5.
26 Well, it was... SA1988.65.A2.
26 You had the... SA1988.65.A3.
27 A hundred and... SA1990.105.A2; And he was... SA1988.65.A3.
27 School closed for... USR 1894:12.
27 they at least USR 1908:218.
27 All was well... USR 1908.

128 But I had... SA1990.104.A1.
128 So...you're still... SA1990.104.A5.
129 O, [laughs] tha... SA1989.26.A2.

CHAPTER FIVE

130 "Mairidh gaol is... SA1989.28.B6.
130 They were feared... SA1988.64.B6.
131 a good subject... SA1990.105.B4.
131 "Oh well," he... SA1989.25.B11.
132 I've only heard... SA1990.107.A3.
132 Well I didn't... SA1990.105.B2.
132 And why did... SA1990.105.B2.
133 Oh it was... SA1990.108.A4.
133 An t-òran... SA1993.4.A7.
133 Really?... SA1989.28.B11.
133 Iain Noble asked... SA1990.108.A12.
134 Well, you could... SA1990.107.A5.
134 "Ach no,"... SA1990.106.A5a.
134 Iain MacInnes... SA1988.64.B3.
135 Well,...she was... SA1988.66.B4b; 'S e na dh'fhu-
laing... SA1990.106.B6.
135 And that's what... SA1988.66.B4b.
136 Sin an aon... SA1990.108.A1.
136 No I don'... SA1990.108.A5.
136 And some people... SA1990.108.A4.
136 Oh they were... SA1990.107.B2.
137 If you were... SA1990.107.A1.
137 I know of... SA1993.3.A3.
137 And he might... SA1993.3.A8.
137 There was a fellow... SA1986.85.A5.
138 Oh I got... SA1989.25.B5.
138 Bha mi eòlach... SA1988.64.B2.
138 O fhuair mi... TM1994.6.A2.
138 Och cha bhithinn... SA1989.25.B7b.
138 Siod an aon... SA1988.64.A12.
138 Ach bha...rudeigin... SA1989.28.B4.
139 Oh well, how... SA1990.106.B2.
140 "Uel, chan eil... SA1989.27.B3; He had an...
SA1990.108.A14.
141 Oh well, that's... SA1990.108.A14.
141 I think Macrae's... SA1990.105.A6.
141 You would like... SA1990.108.A14.
141 [I would] take... SA1990.107.A2.
141 Just for the... SA1990.106.B2.
141 You would like... SA1990.108.A14.
143 There was a... SA1986.85.A5.
143 Would people expect... SA1990.108.A3.
144 Bha latha ann... NicGumaraid 1980b:A2.
145 *There's no better... Expressed on several occasions.
146 Well, there were... SA1986.85.A1.

CHAPTER SIX

149 Oh yes, he... SA1990.106.A2.
150 And that's when... SA1989.27.B1; He had the...
SA1990.106.A2; Oh he was very... SA1989.27.B1.
150 Agus bh'e tidseadh... SA1988.66.B5.
151 So there was... SA1988.66.B12; He met a...
SA1990.106.B6; But I mean... SA1988.66.B12.
151 Och well we... SA1988.66.A6–8.
152 While Willie was... FW20.11.93.
152 Aye, they told... SA1988.66.B1.
152 The best song she... SA1990.106.B6.
153 Is that right... SA1989.27.B3.
154 Thubhairt Dunnchadh... SA1988.63.B17.
155 But what is... SA1989.28.B14.
155 Ah, they say... SA1989.28.B13.
155 Well,...tell it to... SA1989.28.B13.
156 Well look at the... SA1989.28.B13.
158 *Oh Alasdair Mac... FW17.12.90:10; Alasdair Mac
Mhaighstir... FW18.12.90:11.
158 So where did... SA1988.64.B9.
158 Oh well, he... SA1990.106.B6.
158 I wouldn't say... SA1988.64.B10.
159 according to both Iain... FW13.3.93:2 and
SA1993.15.A15; often took lifts... SA1988.66.B1.
159 Ach cha robh ainm... SA1988.66.B1.
159 he has recounted SA1988.64.B12.
160 Ach cha dèanadh... SA1988.66.B2.
160 Oh-h Neil MacLeod... SA1990.108.A8.
160 *not one line... FW17.12.90:7.
160 It's not for... FW17.12.90:5.
161 No, I didn't... SA1990.108.A9.
161 Aye, he was... SA1990.106.B6.
162 Who can step... SA1990.108.A8.
162 Ah, but all... SA1988.66.B13b.
162 *You can make... FW18.12.90:3.
162 Iain says he... SA1988.64.A11.
163 Cha robh duine... TM1994.1.B13.
163 several of the... SA1988.64.A12 and FW12.1.90:1.
163 The impression... SA1993.2.A7.
164 He was always... SA1993.3.A6.
165 quite popular at... SA1990.105.A5.
165 *He had very... FW5.3.90:2.
165 *Now that's great... FW5.3.90:4.
165 *Oh yes, he... Interview 30.3.93.
165 *I thought there... Interview 29.1.93.
166 Seven bibles... FW27.12.92.
166 On one occasion... SA1993.4.B10.
166 You were saying... SA1993.4.B2.
166 She also notes... SA1993.4.B9.
167 Cha do choinnich... TM1994.1.A12.
167 O uel, gur... TM1994.1.A6.
167 An e fìor... TM1994.1.A12.
167 Cha bhiodh... TM1994.1.A14.

SELECT BIBLIOGRAPHY

This bibliography contains all the works cited within the text and a selection of others. It does not include much in the way of methodological material. For a complete list of works consulted, including many collections of *bàrdachd bhaile*, see my Ph.D. thesis (McKean 1993). 'Mac' and 'Mc' are alphabetised accordingly.

ABBREVIATIONS USED

de.	deasaichte [editor] for Gaelic books
diss.	dissertation
ed./eds.	editor/editors
edn.	edition
intro.	introduction
JAF	*Journal of American Folklore*
MS	manuscript
n.d.	no date of publication found
n.p.	no publisher found
SGS	*Scottish Gaelic Studies*
SGTS	*Scottish Gaelic Texts Society*
SND	*Scottish National Dictionary*
TGSI	*Transactions of the Gaelic Society of Inverness*
trans.	translator
unpub.	unpublished manuscript or typescript

BIBLIOGRAPHY

Aarne, Antti, and Stith Thompson. 1961. *The Types of the Folktale: A Classification and Bibliography.* FF Communications, No. 184. Helsinki: Academia Scientiarum Fennica.

Bassin, Ethel. 1977. *The Old Songs of Skye (Frances Tolmie and Her Circle).* London: Routledge and Kegan Paul.

Bennett, Margaret. 1980. "A Codroy Valley Milling Frolic." In *Folklore Studies in Honour of Herbert Halpert.* Kenneth S. Goldstein and Neil V. Rosenberg (eds.), pp. 99–110. St. John's: University of Newfoundland.

    1989. *The Last Stronghold.* Edinburgh: Canongate.

    1992. *Scottish Customs from the Cradle to the Grave.* Edinburgh: Polygon.

    1994. *Hebridean Traditions of the Eastern Townships of Quebec: A Study in Cultural Identity.* Unpub. Ph.D.: University of Edinburgh. Forthcoming in 1997 as *Oatmeal and the Catechism.* Edinburgh: John Donald.

Bennett, Peigi (née Stiùbhart). ca. 1950. MS collection of songs made for her own use by Peigi Bennett of Balquhidder, Perthshire, formerly of Glenconon, Isle of Skye.

Bergin, Osborn. 1970. *Irish Bardic Poetry.* David Greene and Fergus Kelly (eds.). Dublin: The Dublin Institute for Advanced Studies.

Bloomfield, Morton W. and Charles W. Dunn. 1989. *The Role of the Poet in Early Societies.* Cambridge and Wolfeboro: D. S. Brewer.

Bowra, C. Maurice. 1962. *Primitive Song.* London: Weidenfield and Nicolson.

Browne, Ray. B. (ed.). 1970. *Folksongs and Their Makers.* Bowling Green: Bowling Green University Popular Press.

Buchan, David. 1972. *The Ballad and the Folk*. London: Routledge and Kegan Paul.

    1992. Review of *The Ballad Matrix: Personality, Milieu, and the Oral Tradition*, by William B. McCarthy. In *Folklore* 1992/2:248–50.

Buchanan, John Lane. 1793. *Travels in the Western Hebrides: from 1782 to 1790*. London.

Budge, Dòmhnall (de.). 1971. *Sàr Òrain le Catrìona Dhughlas*. Leeds: John Blackburn.

    1972. "Bàird an Eilean Sgiathanaich." In *TGSI* 47:392–403.

Burne, Charlotte S. 1914. *The Handbook of Folklore*. London: Sidgwick and Jackson.

Burt, Capt. Edward. 1974. *Letters from a Gentleman in the North of Scotland to his Friend in London...begun in 1726*. 2 vols. Orig. 1754. Facsimile of 5th. edition (1818). Edinburgh: John Donald.

Byrne, Michel. 1988. "Dòmhnall Ruadh Chorùna and Dòmhnall Ruadh Phàislig." Unpub. honours diss.: University of Edinburgh.

Calder, George (ed.). 1937. *Songs of William Ross in Gaelic and in English*. Compiled by John MacKenzie. Edinburgh: Oliver and Boyd.

Cameron, Alexander. 1894. *Reliquiae Celticae: Texts, Papers and Studies in Gaelic Literature and Philology*. Vol. 2: *Poetry, History and Philology*. Alexander MacBain and John Kennedy (eds.). Inverness: Northern Counties Newspaper Printing and Publishing Co.

Campbell, John F. 1890. *Popular Tales of the West Highlands*. 2nd edn., four vols. Paisley and London: Alexander Gardner.

Campbell, Donald. 1862. *A Treatise on the Language, Poetry and Music of the Highland Clans: with Illustrative Traditions and Anecdotes and Numerous Ancient Highland Airs*. Edinburgh: Collie.

Campbell, John L. 1933. *Highland Songs of the Forty-five*. Edinburgh: John Grant. [Reprinted in 1986 as SGTS No. 7, Edinburgh: Scottish Academic Press.]

    1950. *Gaelic in Scottish Education and Life: Past, Present and Future*. Edinburgh: W. and A. K. Johnston.

    and Francis Collinson. 1969. *Hebridean Folksongs*. Vol. I. (*A Collection of Waulking Songs by Donald MacCormick*). Oxford: Clarendon Press.

    1977. *Hebridean Folksongs*. Vol. II. Oxford: Clarendon Press.

    1981. *Hebridean Folksongs*. Vol. III. Oxford: Clarendon Press.

Camshron, Urr. Eachainn [Rev. Hector Cameron]. 1932. *Na Bàird Thirisdeach*. [*The Tiree Bards*.] Stirling: Eneas MacKay.

Carmichael, Alexander. 1928. *Carmina Gadelica: Hymns and Incantations*. 2nd edn. Vol. I. Edinburgh and London: Oliver and Boyd.

Census 1981. 1983. *Census 1981: Gaelic Report (laid before Parliament pursuant to Section 4(1) Census Act 1920)/Registrar General Scotland*. Edinburgh: Her Majesty's Stationery Office.

Child, Francis James. 1965. *The English and Scottish Popular Ballads*. Reprint of 1882–98 1st edn. Dover: New York.

Coisir a' Mhòid: The Mòd Collection of Gaelic Part Songs. 1912, 1925, 1935, 1940, 1953. Vols 1–5. Glasgow: Alexander MacLaren.

Cooper, Derek. 1970. *Skye*. London: Routledge and Kegan Paul.

Costello, Eileen. 1990. *Amhráin Mhuighe Seóla: Traditional Folk-songs from Galway and Mayo*. Conamara: Cló Iar-Chonnachta [Connemara: West Connaught Press]. [Reprint of 1923 edition.]

Craig, K. C. (de.). 1949. *Òrain Luaidh Màiri Nighean Alasdair*. Glasgow: A. Matheson and Co.

    n.d. (ed.). *Sgialachdan Dhunnchaidh*. (After 1944.) Glasgow.

Creighton, Helen and Calum MacLeod. 1964. *Gaelic Songs in Nova Scotia*. National Museum of Canada Bulletin, No. 198. Ottawa: R. Duhamel.

Delargy, James H. 1945. "The Gaelic Story-teller, with some notes on Gaelic Folk-tales." In *Proceedings of the British Academy* 31:177–221. London: Geoffrey Cumberlege.

Devine, Thomas M. 1988. *The Great Highland Famine: Hunger, Emigration and the Scottish Highlands in the Nineteenth Century*. Edinburgh: John Donald.

Dòmhnallach, Dòmhnall [Donald MacDonald]. 1969. *Dòmhnall Ruadh Chorùna: Òrain is Dàin le Dòmhnall Dòmhnallach a Uibhist a Tuath*. Glaschu [Glasgow]: Gairm.

Donaldson, Gordon. 1970. *Scottish Historical Documents*. New York and Edinburgh: Barnes & Noble and Scottish Academic Press.

Dorian, Nancy. 1981. *Language Death*. Philadelphia: University of Pennsylvania Press.

Dundes, Alan. 1965. *The Study of Folklore*. Englewood Cliffs: Prentice Hall.

    1972. "Folk Ideas as Units of World View." In *Toward New Perspectives in Folklore*. Americo Paredes and Richard Bauman (eds.), pp. 93–103. Austin and London: American Folklore Society.

    1978. *Essays in Folkloristics*. New Delhi: Meerut Folklore Institute.

1980. *Interpreting Folklore*. Particularly the essay, "Texture, Text and Context," pp. 20–32. Bloomington: Indiana University Press.

1989. *Folklore Matters*. Knoxville: University of Tennessee Press.

Durkacz, Victor E. 1977. "Gaelic Education in the Nineteenth Century." In *Scottish Educational Studies* 9/1 (May):18–28.

1983. *The Decline of the Celtic Languages*. Edinburgh: John Donald.

Dwelly, Edward. 1949. *The Illustrated Gaelic-English dictionary*. 5th edn. Glasgow: Alexander MacLaren and Son.

Eilean Fraoich. 1982. *Eilean Fraoich, Lewis Gaelic Songs and Melodies*. Published by Comunn Gàidhealach Leòdhais, 2nd revised edn. Stornoway: Acair.

Fenton, Alexander. 1978. *The Island Blackhouse*. Edinburgh: Her Majesty's Stationery Office.

Fine, Elizabeth C. 1984. *The Folklore Text: From Performance to Print*. Bloomington: Indiana University Press.

Fleidsear, Aonghas. See NicGumaraid, Catrìona.

Forbes, Alexander R. 1923. *Place Names of Skye and Adjacent Islands: with Lore, Mythical, Traditional, and Historical*. Paisley: A. Gardner.

Freeman, Linton C. 1957. "The Changing Functions of a Folksong." *JAF* 70:215–20.

General Register Office (Scotland). 1983. *Census 1981: Gaelic Report (laid before Parliament pursuant to Section 4(1) Census Act 1920) / Registrar General Scotland*. Edinburgh: Her Majesty's Stationery Office.

Gillies, William (ed.). 1989a. *Gaelic and Scotland/Alba agus a' Ghàidhlig*. Edinburgh: Edinburgh University Press.

1989b. "Gaelic: the Classical Tradition." In *The History of Scottish Literature*. Vol. I (Origins to 1660). Aberdeen: Aberdeen University Press.

Glassie, Henry. 1970. "'Take That Night Train to Selma': An Excursion to the Outskirts of Scholarship." In *Folksongs and Their Makers*. Ed. Ray B. Browne, pp. 1–68. Bowling Green: Bowling Green University Popular Press.

Goldstein, Kenneth S. 1971. "On the Application of the Concepts of Active and Inactive Traditions to the Study of Repertoire." *JAF* 84:62–7.

Gordon, Seton. 1929. *The Charm of Skye: the Winged Isle*. Cassel and Company: London.

Grant, Isabel F. 1961. *Highland Folkways*. London: Routledge and Kegan Paul.

The Graphic, an Illustrated Weekly Newspaper. No. 784, Vol. 30, December 6, 1884:587 & 592.

Greig, Gavin and Alexander Keith. 1925. *Last Leaves of Traditional Ballads and Ballad Airs*. Aberdeen: The Buchan Field Club.

Grigor, Iain F. 1979. *Mightier Than A Lord: the Highland Crofters' Struggle for the Land*. Stornoway: Acair.

Haldane, A. R. B. 1968. *The Drove Roads of Scotland*. 2nd edn. Edinburgh: Edinburgh University Press.

Halpert, Herbert. 1951. "Vitality of Tradition and Local Songs." In *Journal of the International Folk Music Council* 3:35–40.

1992. *Coming Into Folklore More Than Fifty Years Ago*. In *JAF* 105/418:442–57.

Henderson, George (ed.). 1893. *Dàin Iain Ghobha: The poems of John Morison, the Songsmith of Harris*. Glasgow and Edinburgh: Archibald Sinclair and Norman MacLeod.

1910. "Aonghas nan Aoir." In *TGSI* 26:458–65.

Henderson, Hamish. 1971. *Bothy Ballads: Music from the North-East*. LP and booklet. No. 1 in the Scottish Tradition Series. London: Tangent Records for the School of Scottish Studies.

1974. *The Muckle Sangs: Classic Scots Ballads*. LP and booklet. No. 5 in the Scottish Tradition Series. London: Tangent Records for the School of Scottish Studies.

1992. *Alias MacAlias: Writings on Songs, Folk and Literature*. Edinburgh: Polygon.

Herskovits, Melville J. and Frances S. 1947. *Trinidad Village*. New York: Alfred A. Knopf.

Herzog, George. 1938. "The Study of Folksong in America." In *Southern Folklore Quarterly* 2:59–64.

1950. "Song: Folk Song and the Music of Folk Song." In *Funk and Wagnalls Standard Dictionary of Folklore, Mythology and Legend*. Vol. II. Maria Leach (ed.), pp. 1032–50. New York: Funk & Wagnalls.

Honko, Lauri. 1985. "Empty Texts, Full Meanings: On Transformal Meaning in Folklore." In *Journal of Folklore Research* 22:37–44.

1992. "The Unesco Perspective on Folklore." In *FF Network* No. 3 (January). The Folklore Fellows: Turku/Helsinki.

Hood, Mantle. 1971. *The Ethnomusicologist*. New York: McGraw Hill.

Humble, B. H. 1934. *The Songs of Skye*. Inverness: Eneas MacKay.

Hunter, James. 1976. *The Making of the Crofting Community*. Edinburgh: John Donald.

Ives, Edward. D. 1962. "Satirical Songs in Maine and the Maritime Provinces of Canada." In *Journal of the International Folk Music Council* 14:65–9.

1964. *Larry Gorman: the Man Who Made the Songs*. Bloomington: Indiana University Press.

1970. "A Man and His Song: Joe Scott and 'The Plain Golden Band'." In *Folksongs and Their Makers*. Ed. Ray B. Browne, pp. 71–146. Bowling Green: Bowling Green University Popular Press.

1971. *Lawrence Doyle: The Farmer-Poet of Prince Edward Island, a Study in Local Songmaking.* University of Maine Studies, No. 92. Orono: University of Maine Press.

Kennedy, Mike. 1995. *Is leis an Tighearna an talamh agus a làn (The earth and all that it contains belongs to God): The Scottish Gaelic settlement history of Prince Edward Island.* Unpub. Ph.D.: University of Edinburgh.

Kennedy-Fraser, Marjory. 1926. *A Life of Song.* London: Oxford University Press.

Knudsen, Torkild. 1978. *Calum Ruadh, Bard of Skye.* LP and booklet. No. 7 in the Scottish Tradition Series. London: Tangent Records for the School of Scottish Studies.

Lee, Laurie. 1984. *Cider with Rosie.* First published in 1959. London: Century Publishing.

Lomax, Alan. 1962. "Song Structure and Social Structure." In *Ethnology* 1:425–51.

1968. *Folk Song Style and Culture.* Washington: American Association for the Advancement of Science; reprinted New Brunswick: Transaction (1978).

and John. 1934. *American Ballads and Folk Songs.* New York: MacMillan and Co.

1941. *Our Singing Country.* New York: MacMillan and Co.

Lord, Albert B. 1973. *The Singer of Tales.* 5th edn. New York: Atheneum.

Lumley, Frederick. 1925. *Means of Social Control.* New York: Century.

Mac an t-Saoir, Dòmhnall Ruadh (Phàislig) [Red(-haired) Donald MacIntyre (of Paisley)]. 1968. *Sporan Dhòmhnaill.* Somerled MacMillan (ed.). Scottish Gaelic Texts Society, No. 10. Edinburgh: Scottish Academic Press.

Mac an t-Saoir, Donnchadh Bàn [Fair(-haired) Duncan MacIntyre]. 1908. *Òrain agus Dàna Gàidhealach. Songs and Poems in Gaelic.* Edinburgh: John Grant. See also MacLeod, Angus (ed. and trans.).

MacAoidh, Rob Donn. 1871. *Orain le Rob Donn, Bàrd Ainmeil Dhùthaich Mhic-Aoidh; Maille ri Eachdraidh a Bheatha, a Chliù, 's a Bhàrdachd, am Beurla.* Edinburgh: Collie and Son; and MacLachlan and Stewart. See also Rob Donn MacKay 1829.

MacBain, A. 1891. See MacBheathain, A.

MacBain, A. 1922. *Place-names in the Highlands and Islands.* Stirling: Eneas MacKay.

MacBheathain, Alasdair (ed.). 1891. *Dàin is Orain Ghàidhlig le Màiri Nic-a'-Phearsain.* [Poems and Songs of Mary MacPherson.] Inverness: A. and U. MacChoinnich.

MacChoinnich, Iain (ed.). 1834. *Orain Gàelach le Uilleam Ros.* [Gaelic Songs by William Ross.] 2nd edn. Glasgow: John Reid. [Re-edited in 1937 by George Calder.]

MacDhòmhnaill, Coinneach. 1956. "Bàird a' bhaile againn (An Dròbhair). [Our village bards (the Drover)]. " In *Gairm* 16:328–30.

MacDhunléibhe, Uilleam [William Livingston]. 1882. *Duain agus Orain.* [Lays and Songs.] Glasgow: n.p.

MacDonald, Rev. Archibald. 1894. *The Uist Collection, the Poems and Songs of John MacCodrum.* Glasgow: Archibald Sinclair.

MacDonald, Rev. Archibald and Rev. A. MacDonald. 1924. *The Poems of Alexander MacDonald.* Inverness: The Northern Counties Newspaper Printing and Publishing Company.

MacDonald, Donald A. 1978. "A Visual Memory." In *Scottish Studies* 22:1–26.

1992. "The Balranald Elopement." In *TGSI* 56:52–112.

MacDonald, Fiona. 1992. *Island Voices.* Irvine: Carrick Media.

MacDonald, Kenneth. 1968. "Unpublished Verse by Sìlis ni Mhic Raghnaill na Ceapaich." In *Celtic Studies: Essays in Memory of Angus Matheson 1912–1962.* James Carney and David Greene (eds.), pp. 76–87. London: Routledge and Kegan Paul.

MacDonald, Màiri. 1977. "Drovering." In *TGSI* 44:189–197.

MacGill-eain, Somhairle [Samuel/Sorley MacLean]. 1985. *Ris a' Bhruthaich: the Criticism and Prose Writings of Sorley MacLean.* William Gillies (ed.). Stornoway: Acair. (Contains reprints of articles that originally appeared in various periodicals. Page numbers are as in *Ris a' Bhruthaich*.)

MacInnes, Rev. D. 1890. *Folk and Hero Tales.* No. 2 in the Argyllshire Series. London: David Nutt.

MacInnes, Rev. John. 1951. *The Evangelical Movement in the Highlands of Scotland, 1688 to 1800.* Aberdeen: Aberdeen University Press.

MacInnes, John. 1966. "MacMhuirich and the Old Woman from Harris." In *Scottish Studies* 10/1:104–7.

1968. "The Oral Tradition in Scottish Gaelic Poetry." In *Scottish Studies* 12/1:29–44.

1971. "The Choral Tradition in Scottish Gaelic Waulking Songs." In *TGSI* 46:44–65.

1979. "The Panegyric Code in Gaelic Poetry and Its Historical Background." In *TGSI* 50:435–98.

1981. "Gaelic Poetry and Historical Tradition." In *The Middle Ages in the Highlands.* Loraine Maclean (ed.). Inverness: Inverness Field Club. 142–63.

1988. "Gaelic Poetry in the Nineteenth Century." In *The History of Scottish Literature*. Vol. 3. Douglas Gifford (ed.), pp. 377–96. Aberdeen: Aberdeen University Press.

MacKay, Rob Donn [Brown-haired]. 1829. *Songs and Poems in the Gaelic Language*. Inverness: Kenneth Douglas. Revised and re-edited by Hew Morrison in 1899.

MacKellar, Mary. 1888. "The Waulking Day." In *TGSI* 13:201–17.

1889. "The Sheiling: Its Traditions and Songs." In *TGSI* 14:135–52.

MacKenzie, Alexander. 1914. *The History of the Highland Clearances*. Inverness: Eneas MacKay.

MacKenzie, Annie M. 1964. *Orain Iain Luim*. Edinburgh: Scottish Gaelic Texts Society.

MacKenzie, J. (ed.). 1907. *Sàr-obair nam Bàrd Gaelach or the Beauties of Gaelic Poetry*. (1st edn. 1841.) Glasgow: MacGregor Polson and Co.

MacKenzie, Rev. Kenneth A. 1875. "Teaching Gaelic in Highland Schools." In *TGSI* 4:181–8.

MacKenzie, Osgood Hanbury. 1921. *A Hundred Years in the Highlands*. Many reprints. Revised edn. 1965. London.

MacKenzie, William. 1930. *Iochdar-Trotternish*. Glasgow: Alexander MacLaren.

1934. *Old Skye Tales: Further Traditions, Reflections and Memories of an Octogenarian Highlander*. Glasgow: Alexander MacLaren.

MacKinnon, Kenneth. 1972. "The School in Gaelic Scotland." In *TGSI* 47:374–91.

1977. *Language, Education and Social Processes in a Gaelic Community*. London: Routledge and Kegan Paul.

MacLeod, Angus (ed. and trans.). 1952. *The Songs of Duncan Ban MacIntyre*. SGTS, No. 4. Edinburgh: Oliver and Boyd.

MacLeod, John. 1922. "Dòmhnull nan Òran, am Bàrd Sgitheanach. [Donald of the Songs, the Skye Bard.]" In *TGSI* 29:119–33.

MacLeòid, Niall [Neil MacLeod]. 1893. *Clarsach an Doire: Dain, Orain, agus Sgialachdan* [*The Harp of the Grove: Gaelic Poems, Songs, and Readings.*] 2nd edn. Glaschu agus Dùn-Éideann: Gilleasbuig Mac-na-Ceardadh agus Tormad MacLeòid [Glasgow and Edinburgh: Archibald Sinclair and Norman MacLeod]. (Reprinted by Gairm in 1975.)

Mac Mhaighstir Alasdair, Alasdair. See A. and A. MacDonald 1924 and Derick Thomson 1996.

Mac na Ceàrdadh, Gilleasbuig. 1879. *The Gaelic Songster: An t-Oranaiche*. Glasgow: Archibald Sinclair.

MacNeacail, Calum. 1975. *Bàrdachd Chaluim Ruaidh.* [*The Poetry of Calum Ruadh.*] Leabhar 40 [Vol. 40]. Glaschu [Glasgow]: Gairm.

MacNeacail, Iain. See NicGumaraid, Catrìona.

MacNeill, Joe Neil. 1987. *Tales Until Dawn, Sgeul gu Latha*. John Shaw (ed. and trans.). Kingston and Montreal: McGill-Queen's University Press.

MacQueen, Malcolm. 1929. *Skye Pioneers and "the Island"*. Winnipeg: Stovel.

Martin, Martin. 1884. *A Description of the Western Isles of Scotland, ca. 1695*. 4th edn. Glasgow: Thomas D. Morison.

Martinengo-Cesaresco, Countess E. 1886. *Essays in the Study of Folk Songs*. London: Carrington.

Matheson, William (ed.). 1938. *The Songs of John MacCodrum, Bard to Sir James MacDonald of Sleat*. Edinburgh: Oliver and Boyd for the Scottish Gaelic Texts Society.

1970. *An Clarsair Dall: Òrain Ruaidhri Mhic Mhuirich agus a Chuid Ciùil*. [*The Blind Harper: The Songs of Roderick Morison and his Music.*] SGTS: Edinburgh.

McCarthy, William B. 1990. *The Ballad Matrix: Personality, Milieu and the Oral Tradition*. Bloomington: Indiana University Press.

McKean, Thomas. 1992a. "A Gaelic Song-maker's Response to an English-speaking Nation." In *Oral Tradition*.

1992b. "Bha Mi 'n Raoir an Coille Chaoil and Gilleasbaig Aotrom: the Wise Fool." In *Tocher* 45:160–9.

1993. *The life and songs of Iain 'an Sgiobair' MacNeacail and the function of song in a Hebridean community*. Ph.D.: University of Edinburgh.

Meek, Donald E. 1977. "The Gaelic Poets of the Land Agitation." In *TGSI* 49:309–76.

(de.). 1977. *Màiri Mhór nan Òran*. Glaschu [Glasgow]: Gairm.

1995. *Tuath is tighearna Tenants and landlords: an anthology of Gaelic poetry of social and political protest from the Clearances to the Land Agitation (1800–1890)*. SGTS No. 18. Edinburgh: Scottish Academic Press.

Merriam, Alan 1964. *The Anthropology of Music*. Evanston: Northwestern University Press.

Miller, Edward K. 1981. *An Ethnography of Singing: the Use and Meaning of Song Within a Scottish Family*. Unpub. Ph.D.: University of Texas at Austin.

Mitchell, Arthur. 1880. *The Past in the Present*. Edinburgh.

Montell, Lynwood. 1970. *The Saga of Coe Ridge: A Study in Oral History*. Intro. Knoxville: University of Tennessee Press.

Montgomery, Catrìona. See NicGumaraid, Catrìona.

Morrison, Hew. See MacKay, Rob Donn.

Murray, I. H. 1980. *Diary of Kenneth MacRae, a Record of Fifty Years in the Christian Ministry*. Edinburgh: Edinburgh Banner of Truth Trust.

Murray, Murdo. 1946. "Màiri Nighean Iain Bhàin." In *TGSI* 37:294–319.

Nash, Dennison. 1961. "The Role of the Composer." In *Ethnomusicology* 5:81–94, 187–201.

Necker de Saussure, Louis A. 1822. *A Voyage to the Hebrides, or Western Isles of Scotland; with Observations on the Manners and Customs of the Highlanders.* London: Phillips and Co. (Originally published in 1821 as *Voyage en Écosse et aux Iles Hébrides* in Geneva.)

Nettl, Bruno. 1964. *Theory and Method in Ethnomusicology.* New York: Free Press of Glencoe.

1965. *Folk and Traditional Music of the Western Continents.* Englewood Cliffs: Prentice Hall.

1983. *The Study of Ethnomusicology.* Urbana: University of Illinois Press.

NicGumaraid, Catrìona (de.). 1980a. *Orain Aonghais agus An Sgiobair.* Dundéagh [Dundee]: Catrìona NicGumaraid.

(de.). 1980b. *Orain Aonghais agus An Sgiobair.* Cassette release. Dundéagh [Dundee]: Catrìona NicGumaraid.

Nicolson, Alexander. 1881. *A Collection of Gaelic Proverbs and Familiar Phrases, Based on MacIntosh's Collection.* Edinburgh: MacLachlan and Stewart.

Nicolson, Alexander. 1930. *History of Skye: A Record of the Families, the Social Conditions, and the Literature of the Island.* Glasgow: Alexander MacLaren.

Ó Baoill, Colm (ed.). 1972. *Bàrdachd Shìlis na Ceapaich.* [*The Songs of Julia (MacDonald) of Keppoch.*]. Edinburgh: Scottish Gaelic Texts Society.

Ó hÓgáin, Daithi. 1982. *An File.* Baile Atha Cliath [Dublin].

Ó Madagáin, Breandán. 1985. "Functions of Irish Song in the Nineteenth Century." In *Béaloideas* 53:130–216.

1993. "Song for Emotional Release in the Gaelic Tradition." In *Irish Musical Studies 2: Music and the Church.* Gerard Gillen and Harry White (eds.). Dublin: Irish Academic Press.

Ó Suilleabháin, Seán [Sean O' Sullivan]. 1942. *A Handbook of Irish Folklore.* Dublin: Folklore Society of Ireland.

1973. *Storytelling in Irish Tradition.* Cork: Mercier Press.

Owen, Trefor M. 1958. *Fieldwork in North Uist.* Unpub. report of fieldwork undertaken for the School of Scottish Studies: University of Edinburgh.

Rasmussen, Knud. 1931. "The Netsilik Eskimos: Social Life and Spiritual Culture." In *Reprint of the Fifth Thule Expedition 1921–24.* Vol. 8.

Register of the Privy Council of Scotland. 1891. David Masson (ed.). Edinburgh: H.M. General Registry House.

Richards, Eric. 1973. *The Leviathan of Wealth.* London and Toronto: Routledge and Kegan Paul and University of Toronto Press.

1982. *A History of the Highland Clearances: Agrarian Transformation and the Evictions 1746–1886.* London and Canberra: Croom Helm.

1985. *A History of the Highland Clearances, Volume 2: Emigration, Protest, Reasons.* London, Sydney and Dover: Croom Helm.

Ros, Uilleam. See MacChoinnich 1834 and Calder 1937.

Ross, James. 1954–5. "The Sub-literary Tradition in Scottish Gaelic Song Poetry." In *Éigse* 7/3:217–39 and 8/1:1–17.

1955. "Further remarks on Gaelic Song Metres." In *Éigse* 8/4:350–8.

1957. "A Classification of Gaelic Folk Songs." In *Scottish Studies* 1:95–151.

1961. "Folk Song and Social Environment." In *Scottish Studies* 5:18–39.

Scottish National Dictionary. William Grant (ed.). Edinburgh: The Scottish National Dictionary Association.

Shapiro, Anne D. 1975. *The Tune-family Concept in British-American Folk-song Scholarship.* Unpub. diss: Harvard University.

1985. "Scottish Regional Song Styles." In *Music and Context: Essays for John M. Ward.* Anne Dhu Shapiro (ed.), pp. 404–17. Cambridge: Harvard University Press.

Shaw, John. See MacNeill 1987.

Sinclair, Archibald (de.). n.d. *Filidh nam Beann, the Mountain Songster.* Glasgow: A. Sinclair.

1876–9. (de.). *An t-Oranaiche.* Glasgow: Archibald Sinclair.

Sinclair, Rev. Archibald MacLean. 1881. *The MacLean Songster: Clarsach na Coille: A Collection of Gaelic Poetry.* Hector MacDougall (rev. and ed.). Glasgow: MacLaren.

1898. *Na Bàird Leathanach: the MacLean Bards.* Vol. I. Charlottetown: Haszard and Moore.

1900. *Na Bàird Leathanach: the MacLean Bards.* Vol. II. Charlottetown: Haszard and Moore.

1904. *The Gaelic Bards from 1825 to 1875.* Sydney (C.B.): MacTalla.

Smith, John A. 1968. "The Position of Gaelic and Gaelic Culture in Scottish Education." In *The Future of the Highlands.* D. S. Thomson and I. Grimble (eds.), pp. 57–92. London: Routledge and Kegan Paul.

1981. "The 1872 Education (Scotland) Act and Gaelic Education." In *TGSI* 51:1–67.

Smout, T. Christopher. 1986. *A Century of the Scottish People 1830–1950.* New Haven and London: Yale University Press and Collins.

Szwed, John. 1966. *Private Cultures and Public Imagery: Interpersonal Relations in a Newfoundland Society*. St. John's: Institute of Social and Economic Research.

    1970. "Paul E. Hall: A Newfoundland Song-Maker and Community of Song." In *Folksongs and Their Makers*. Ed. Ray B. Browne, pp. 149–169. Bowling Green: Bowling Green University Popular Press.

Thompson, Stith. 1955. *Motif-Index of Folk-Literature*. Copenhagen: Rosenkilde and Bagger.

Thomson, Derick S. 1954. "The Gaelic Oral Tradition." In *Proceedings of the Scottish Anthropological and Folklore Society* 5:1–17.

    1955. "Scottish Gaelic Folk-poetry Ante 1650." In *SGS* 8/1:1–17.

    1968. "Gaelic Learned Orders and Literati in Medieval Scotland." In *Scottish Studies* 12, i:57–78.

    1974. *An Introduction to Gaelic Poetry*. London: Gollancz.

    (ed.). 1983. *The Companion to Gaelic Scotland*. Oxford: Blackwell.

    1984. *Why Gaelic Matters*. Edinburgh: Saltire Society/An Comunn Gaidhealach.

    1985. "Tradition and Innovation in Gaelic Verse Since 1950." In *TGSI* 53:91–114.

    (ed.). 1996. *Alasdair Mac Mhaighstir Alasdair, Selected Poems*. SGTS. Edinburgh: Scottish Academic Press.

Tocher. 1970-present. Alan Bruford (ed.). Edinburgh: School of Scottish Studies.

Vallee, Frank G. 1954. *Social Structure and Organization in a Hebridean Community: A Study of Social Change*. Unpub. report of fieldwork undertaken for the School of Scottish Studies: University of Edinburgh.

Warner, Anne and Frank. 1984. *Traditional American Folk Songs from the Anne & Frank Warner Collection*. Anne Warner (ed.). Syracuse: Syracuse University Press.

Watson, J. Carmichael (ed.). 1934. *Gaelic Songs of Mary MacLeod*. Glasgow: Blackie and Son.

Watson, William J. 1922. "Classic Gaelic Poetry of Panegyric in Scotland." In *TGSI* 29:194–234.

    1946. "The History of Gaelic in Scotland." In *TGSI* 37:115–35.

    (de.). 1959. *Bàrdachd Ghàidhlig*. 3rd edn. Stirling: A. Learmouth.

Withers, Charles W.J. 1984. *Gaelic in Scotland, 1698–1981: the Geographical History of a Language*. Edinburgh: John Donald.

INDEX